ASTRAY

ASTRAY

A HISTORY OF

WANDERING

Eluned Summers-Bremner

REAKTION BOOKS

For Tom, who guided us

Published by
REAKTION BOOKS LTD
Unit 32, Waterside
44–48 Wharf Road
London N1 7UX, UK
www.reaktionbooks.co.uk

First published 2023
Copyright © Eluned Summers-Bremner 2023

Printed and bound in Great Britain by TJ Books Ltd, Padstow, Cornwall

A catalogue record for this book is available from the British Library
ISBN 978 1 78914 704 9

CONTENTS

INTRODUCTION

Before we existed, the materials that would mutate and later form us wandered. Before we lived in houses and planted crops and developed writing, we were nomadic. And before we become extinct or transform beyond recognition we will, at nature's bidding, traverse the warming world we have made, its increasing entropies propelling us to move to perhaps less threatened places. This book is a history of the role wandering has played in our genesis, our social being and the artefacts and means of communication and sustenance we make and use. Its title, *Astray*, suggests something off, out of order, mistaken. This is a common association humans make with wandering. To wander is to err; a straightforward way of doing things is best. And while there are plenty of occasions in life when straightforwardness is needed, our history shows that such methods are often arrived at through a process of trial and error, of free-form thinking, and equally often by means of chance encounters, happy adaptations, unforeseen acts. One of the reasons we may have come to value the linear and ostensibly straightforward is because it is the kind of formal procedure that seems to explain itself. Things going on step by step in an apparent series can have a lulling effect on our psyches. We imagine that habitual momentum means that things have always worked this way.

But most of human history has been experimental and chaotic. We now know that the varied conditions in which Bronze Age nomadic steppe tribes lived meant that some practices were probably adopted by a range of groups in different contexts while others remained more localized.[1] This makes it difficult to assume, as we used to, that homogeneous populations met other homogeneous populations as they moved through a landscape; that groups belong to regions and, as they encounter others, evolve into something resembling proto-modern states. To a human population, much that is going to happen in the future is unknown, because, as our situation with regard to climate change and not-so-distant financial crashes shows, when comfortable enough we tend to default to the improbable belief that whatever we are used to can continue with little cost. We moderns face unknowns as well because the complex systems that govern much of our lives are prone to lurches, their usefulness dependent on their incorporation of, and responses to, the intrinsically uncertain, the rogue. In the past, more of the future was unknown because fewer things *were* known. But it seems wise, given our unavoidably challenging future, not to foreclose too soon the idea that what holds across a place and time like the Bronze Age Eurasian steppe is less a sense of humanity defining itself than an ability to alter previous practice and to work with unlike others, strategizing around such realities as climatic alteration or the sudden availability of a given resource.

So the assumption that to wander is to depart from something – a path, a moral code, an ethos – may be a modern mistake, an industrial or proto-industrial valuing of product over process. This is not to say that wandering is not tensile, a dynamic in which reference points play important roles. But the roles they play may have less to do with departure from and recognition of things known than with alteration and adaptation of them, and also, paradoxically for those of a linear persuasion, with future life. Australian Aboriginal Dreaming practices, which form humanity's oldest continuous cultural history, centralize wandering and preserve the reality of cosmic continuity for all, a working abstraction – that is, a larger principle related to but independent of merely current circumstance – born of the sometimes near impossible challenges of the ancient desert world. Among this idea's many virtues is that it cannot be colonized, because it attaches to no particular group or being or even, necessarily, landscape, since water, food, cooperation and cultural maintenance are its enablers. In ancient Greece, a novel kind of social organization arose whose outlines are discernible in today's democracies. The trial of Socrates shows that wandering in the form of incessant questioning of the nature and purpose of human laws, such that when we do not know how something works it is best to face this unknown rather than mimic the postures of probably equally uncertain others, is at the heart of a society built less on allegiance to particular kinds of divinities than by humans, for humans, with our intrinsic fallibilities and our reason's self-reflective power. After all, to act from a place of unknowing is still what we do when we vote democratically, since the result will derive from the sum total, strategic voting notwithstanding, of everyone's desires.

To wander, then, I will argue, is often to productively encounter limit, not least the effects of the limits of human knowledge, but equally those tendencies towards false certainty and self-delusion I have outlined above as unfortunate characteristics of our species. In the book's first chapter, 'Errancy', and its brief final section, I suggest respectively that the Western historical association of wandering with error, and the difficulties we face – and sometimes make – around questions of what to believe and in whose current and future interests we should act, are potentially much richer and contain more practical, ethical and phenomenological possibility than we have assumed. For to wander is not only to encounter limit but to respond to it with the full acuity and inventiveness that can follow upon complete disorientation if we first disable, or ignore, the panic response, the belief that loss of pathway, habit or known marker makes us helpless or spells our end. If that were true, those pathways, habits and markers were unlikely ever to have been formed. In this way, too, to wander may be to overcome certain limits, especially those borne of attachment to the familiar, the ones we do not think of as limits until a crisis intervenes.

Medieval Christian Europe believed in human errancy as failing, for instance, but it also developed compelling methods by which the known and unknown might inform and interrupt each other. The period valued knowable pathways but also put them into question, made them into puzzles. To be lost in a dark forest, like Dante at the start of the *Inferno*, is to have left a path, but it is also to be amid a space of organized cosmic memory, alive with startling insights and potential knowledge. It is a form of full involvement in the world. Other kinds of errancy, too, are built into the Western world's self-understanding, and like the Christian kind they often all but undo the idea of teleological – end-focused – destination that they claim to serve.

In Virgil's *Aeneid* a group of refugees from the losing side of a war largely fails to fulfil its imagined destiny. But the poem does not give us a list of errors made and wrong paths taken so much as show, at the level of poetic line and mortal sinew, of affective impulse and moral constraint, how having a grand aim in someone else's country will bring you face to face with your own condition, your own alterity. It will show you what you *cannot* do directly, that your intention was unavoidably dreamlike, more a vagary built on old failures than an arrow seeking a mark. It will reveal that while you and your group thought you could do this thing, you forgot that the gods who helped begin it were, like you, imperfect, and that, like them, you would have to deal with recalcitrant others in and beyond your group with every step you took. That this story of human failure and unmet goals has come to be associated with its opposite, with the future founding of a powerful city-state, shows among other things that wandering in failed service to an ideal has a strong hold on our imaginations. And while the *Aeneid* is full of frustration, it is also full of drive, of clashes with obstacles. Equally clearly, drive itself is necessarily circuitous. We simply lack the ability to foresee the nature of entirely new conditions, so to encounter them often means changing course, even if subtly, or going around them in an unforeseen way.

Unknown prior conditions, too, mean matters are seldom as simple as yield or fight. Accordingly, Chapter Two explores the role played by wandering in our cosmic, human and socially democratic beginnings, including in ancient beliefs about how human lives are made. Characteristic is the macroscopic nature of such explanations, for to the ancients it made little sense to focus on the human in a world where the human is mercilessly subject to larger, and largely unfathomable, forces. Here, too, though, is a point of connection with our own time. A focus away from larger forces in the sense of failing to build in sufficient placeholders for unknown – and unknowable – future impacts on current advances brings us closer to those larger forces, in the form, for instance, of our difficulties with the planet's climate. When we learn or master something, some attention is diverted from our awareness of all we do not know. This is partly why Plato's *Timaeus*, in which a wandering cause represents the recalcitrant properties of matter but also the beginnings of change in any form, is structured so as to model our tendency to forget certain facts or necessities when engaged in world-building. Thus, we need models for how to collaborate on correcting prior oversights without endangering what we have already built.

'Others', the book's third chapter, treats nomadic histories, from Darfur in Sudan to the Eurasian steppe and the wanderings of Prester John, an Eastern king imagined into being by Christians on crusade. One of the strengths of nomadic empires – also found in Native American history, considered in Chapter Five – is a tendency towards decentralized organization, in which groups continually transition into one another. This is one of several ways in which nomadic practices may pass beneath the radar of the settled, who in the past have often assumed such social forms to be chaotic and disorganized, when they are in fact more mobile, more suited to mobility and perhaps more robust than those of settled groups. Equally unnoticed may be the contributions made by nomads to settled civilizations, especially in the region of southwest Asia sometimes called the Fertile Crescent, where agriculture first arose, and on the novelty of which we are apt to focus.

Here, the nomadic environment, Arabia and Eurasia's grasslands and deserts, forms by far the largest sector of the region, so settled groups both absorbed nomadic elements and had to trade with them. And it may be that the innovations of settled life – towns, writing, place-based governance – emerged as a way to manage friction between mobile and non-mobile elements. Written records may have helped establish fairness and stabilize relations in towns and nearby regions as they justified rates and kinds of resource distribution. Geographical challenges such as drought, meanwhile, when crops fail and pastoralist products are attractive, require negotiation with mobile pastoralists. The nomad/settler division may not have existed in the Neolithic period in the form it does today, for the term 'nomad' covers a variety of specific lifeways and a 'revolution' involving the planting of crops does not happen suddenly. At least one scholar thinks that nomadic and settled peoples were involved in a repeated 'diverging and merging' as they faced, together, the pressures and difficulties of their location.[2]

The matter of nomadic resource-sharing is important to our history. Because such customary practices tend to become prominent to the settled when there is a breakdown of some kind, as happened in the late 1980s and the 1990s in Darfur, this essential aspect of nomadic lifeways may go unnoticed. It matters because resource cooperation is not only cooperation. It is also a matter of correctly assessing how far one's current supplies will last and the likely impact of the number and range of events that might occur between now and one's next place of access to water, harvestable crop stalks and so on, as well as what to do if there is competition.

Other humans are one variable among others to be considered, but about which flexibility is possible, in part because other variables are also important. Cooperation with others is part of scaling resource requirements from the present into the future. Again, working out how to factor the needs of others into a range of possible events that might affect us while we move is a skill humanity will need to revive where it has been lost, for resource competition and scarcity are inevitable components of our coming lives, as they are for many in the present.

One of our most important nomadic groups, who frequently live as settled, is the Rom, who are unique in not tracing their identity to a particular homeland. They originally travelled before the European Middle Ages from India to the Middle East and thence to Europe and are likely descended from low-caste wandering tradespeople and musicians. Their endurance over centuries without myths of home or revered texts recording an ethical code is especially impressive (although they do practise ancestral Romani law). Instead, Roms are consummate border workers. As well as preserving a distinction between themselves and *gadje* (non-Roms) by maintaining a division between the clean upper and unclean lower body, they sometimes play to *gadjes'* mistaken views of them, for instance that they can foretell the future, making a mobile space for their being and world view to which *gadje* are not permitted access. Because they do not dream of a homeland, the Rom are also arguably our one remaining link to a time when our only homelands were mobile and made the way Roms earn their living: not only through trade but performative exchange, where the grounds of belonging – including the right to take food or water – can shift from moment to moment.

This ability to use language to reconfigure the terms of the world, as 1990s Hungarian horse traders did when engaging non-Roms in the performative challenges of the luck Roms typically live by, emphasizes language's ancient symbolic function.[3] It is telling that when despotic powers force removals of populations to other places or allow artificial famines to unmoor them from land, as Russia did to Ukraine in the 1930s and as Maoist China did to its peasants at the end of the 1950s (episodes treated in 'Sorrow', the fifth chapter of this book), they first destroy the symbols, nationalist or ancestral, by which the subject people understands itself. Sometimes the despotic power makes a new symbol, as Soviet Russia did in fabricating the kulak as someone for peasants to blame, instead of the government, for the theft of the people's livelihood.

This symbolic construction and/or destruction increases the chances of early despair and makes recovery harder, but it is significant that it needs doing at all. For it shows that our survival is connected not only to the needs of the body but to certain kinds of belief. If we flourish in the ever-shifting world where managing luck is our ancestral ability, if we believe we can have an identity distinct from that of our more powerful neighbour, if we have practised a communal method by which the wandering dead are appeased, then we may have a different view of what is being done to us from that of the despotic power. We know that we may lose the means to make sense of our changed reality – for starvation shrinks the world horribly – but perhaps not entirely. Sometimes a memory of the symbolic work of seeing the world as responding to us, and ourselves as having the means to negotiate with it, survives this destructive process.

This was certainly the case with the eighteenth-century version of one of the world's most useful inventions, narrative, which, in the modern novel, bears in its form the mobilization, often against their will, of millions of humans from their places of birth to new places of work from the seventeenth to the early twentieth centuries. Considered in Chapter Four, the novel encodes the means by which the industrializing world understood, perpetuated and sometimes checked itself as it set about the processes of resource extraction and incipient futures trading that imperil our lives today. Its creation of readers who identified with imagined strangers whose lives were governed by chance and accident as much as by birth or standing was unprecedented. And it owed as much to the forces of distant markets, long-term credit arrangements, and those unfree others whose labour made the markets and products and credit necessary and possible as to the desire of middle-class readers for something new.

Chapter Six, 'Chance', extends this treatment of a world in which wanderings from course in the form of accidental possibility inspire us to our own day, when such possibility is vexed by its opposite, the colonizing of human desire by technology companies promising new places to wander on- and offline. Almost all such initiatives bear hidden costs, and few, if any, make us intrinsically freer than previously. Nor, unless we are extremely rich and furtive (or simply have others manage our riches), do the kinds of financial machinations by which the wealthy keep their money wandering the world unseen, protected by shifty linguistic manoeuvres as much as by companies, bankers and banks. 'Hobo' life and the spaces of potential disaffection inhabited by the precariously employed also have things to tell us about the relation of liminality to community. For those who embrace the fleeting as a way of life – whether by choice or circumstance – increasingly *constitute* communities, just as the conventionally settled kinds are having to reckon with the fact that being in one place for life may be an idea whose time is past.

Or perhaps, in its historical anomalousness, this idea was always a kind of mirage born of denial of a longer view of human environmental relations. Every city, nation-state and government building, after all, is supported by a plethora of wanderers from elsewhere who, in addition to those in more public, legislative roles, perform the daily labour that keeps it running, whether in the form of imagined threats to its integrity or by the largely unseen sweat of their work. Of course, wanderers typically sustain nation-states and other agents of populational stability in both these ways, often simultaneously, as Plato knew when he placed wandering craftspeople beyond citizenship in his ideal republic. Yet we should be clear what this implies.

A wanderer present in both these forms to a person who (over-) identifies as settled has a definitional mobility by dint of the fact that at least one of the wanderer's sustaining functions goes unseen.

This mobility is real, for all that fear of wanderers is often mistaken, and for all that not all such workers identify as wanderers, especially if they have reached a long-sought goal. And yet returns and departures may be closely entwined in these kinds of lives, as they are in those of the more concertedly mobile, and as they are not to the same degree in those of people who have never had to wander. This process helps wanderers resist encapsulation and instantiate possibility, as the question of whether to stay or go is continually revalued. Good at change, in their enduring dexterity wanderers reinvigorate our history, reminding us that what we once were – able to invent and cooperate in the moment in adverse conditions – we will need to be again. If we allow ourselves to fear wandering, or, alternatively, romanticize and so divorce it from our lives, that day may seem to happen upon us all too soon.

1

ERRANCY

'Halfway through the journey of our life', as Dante's epic poem about this world and the next begins, Dante the pilgrim comes to in a dark wood, having 'wandered off the path, away from the light'. Trying, later, to put words to this experience, he faces a conundrum. To attempt to express how 'wild and rough and tortured' were the ways of this great forest is to re-encounter the way it made him feel: afraid to the death, mystified, alone. Errancy, a word meaning in English 'the condition of erring or being in error', in its original Latin form had a double meaning: to roam or wander and to be mistaken, while the ancient Indo-European root word, *er*, meant simply 'to move', 'to put in motion' or 'to go'. There is, thus, a historical tension at the heart of errancy between a freer, more general action of wandering without fixed direction and the later sense of the verb 'to err', indicating a 'specific aberration' from a path.[1]

To take the latter meaning first, human wandering, whether physical or mental, is often the result of not knowing we are in error or that there is a clearer pathway we might be traversing than the one we are on. At the same time, as Kathryn Schulz points out in her book *Being Wrong* (2010), to be in error is ultimately an enriching experience.[2] When we find we are wrong about something, our orientation to the world changes. Things become newly alien, and we must revisit the basis of our assumption that things are as we have previously found them, and sometimes the assumption that the world is a place in which we naturally belong. Consequently, to be on the right path can itself mean feeling lost, at least for as long as it takes to assent to a new way of proceeding. And right paths themselves might never be discovered were it not for our tendency to stray from previously found ones, to enjoy the relative freedom that wandering, including wandering in ignorance, brings.

Dante the pilgrim is not wandering in freedom at the beginning of the *Inferno*. But the fact that describing his state of lostness and terror entails revisiting it can be related to a feature common in Western medieval literature that may help us recover some of the complexity the idea of errancy as mere error hides from view. As a product of fourteenth-century Christian Europe, literary writing, including Dante's, frequently figures and encodes in its form the enigma of the Incarnation, through which God is believed to have entered history both as a man and as the divine Word, as indicated in the Gospel of John.[3] What Cristina Maria Cervone has called 'Incarnational thought experiments' with a 'circling or spiral feel' about them are common in European texts from this period, and we can also find traces of them earlier. This kind of writing reminds us both of the bodily origin of all words and of the tendency of figurative language to create or expand inference, to point beyond itself and depart from semantic norms. Incarnational language is mysterious because the Incarnation is mysterious, and by indirect means texts that explore this conundrum can reproduce, and explore, aspects not only of the phenomenon of God become man, but the feelings of confusion and perplexity that are part of the human experience of that event. To speak of his experience of being lost in a dark forest, Dante the narrator recreates the fear he felt as Dante the pilgrim, but he also says that he found much good as a result of it. Yet the good he finds is inseparable not only from the lostness that led to it but from the dark wood first encountered, which is associated with the Word as a source of salvation and (sometimes initially confusing) guidance. The way out of the forest, he will learn, is to recognize that a forest is a way to God in itself.[4]

Selva oscura

At the time of writing the *Commedia* (*c.* 1308–*c.* 1320), Dante had been exiled from his native city of Florence for at least five years on fabricated charges of extortion for which the punishment was death. As a prior (leading magistrate) of the city, he had opposed the efforts of Pope Boniface VIII to gain control of it by confirming a sentence against three of the pope's agents and, in June 1300, sentencing to exile some of the leaders of the two factions of the Guelf party, who had caused bloodshed and related strife. As a White Guelf, Dante and others were sentenced when the Black Guelfs, acting in the pope's interests, carried out a coup in November of the following year while Dante was in Rome as the pope's envoy. To Dante, Boniface represented corrupt Christian leadership, but he could have been under no illusions about the underlying causes of civic violence in Florence. The inheritance laws and practices of thirteenth- and fourteenth-century elite Florentine families were based on not ceding power to those outside those families, and they were accustomed to going to war with each other to defend them. This is why Dante's Hell contains leaders of both Guelf and Ghibelline parties, the larger grouping containing Black and White Guelfs.[5]

Nonetheless, while several scholars have taken the wood in which Dante the pilgrim is lost to represent sin, the darkness of ignorance and 'moral confusion', such error as exists can only reside in the mind and heart of the pilgrim (or in those of a pope, or the leaders of a city). The forest itself is a much richer image, and as Lawrence Warner shows, one of its most common references since the days of early Christianity was to the 'salvific obscurities of the holy scriptures'.[6] Fear in the face of the scriptures was itself not uncommon. This was in part because of the possibly eternal consequences of getting one's interpretation wrong, and also because by the thirteenth century the writings of the early Church Fathers and later glossators comprised so much material that, as the thirteenth-century Franciscan theologian St Bonaventure put it, beginning theological study felt exactly like entering a pathless, impenetrable forest.[7]

The *Commedia* is a simulacrum of the afterlife,[8] a place to which only God, the Devil, saints and angels can testify as having been, and so it follows that everything in the poem must undo human preconceptions about what this other world is like. Dante the writer does this by causing Dante the pilgrim to have experiences in which he is alerted by his intellect and senses to the fact that the events he encounters are altering the information his senses and intellect receive. Of the many features of the poem that have perhaps unnoticed bearing on the lives of twenty-first-century humans, this structural element, operating on micro- and macrocosmic levels within its architecture, is one of the most important. The *Commedia* undoes the current terms of human experience and prepares its pilgrim-traveller and its readers for realities to be experienced in the future that they will not necessarily have the resources to understand.

The poem does this, first, by means of the rhyme scheme Dante invented, *terza rima*, which performs and encodes a forward and backward motion in which 'identity' is repeatedly lost and replaced by a new element (aba, bcb, cdc and so on). Dante also invents words and turns language against itself to convey the acute intensity and disorientation of hellspace, Purgatory, and Paradise, or lightspace. On passing through the gates of Hell, the pilgrim is assailed by a plethora of contradictory elements: 'Words which were pain . . . hands clapped together . . . air without stars'.[9] Working synaesthetically, the poet has the pilgrim driven by acute affective pressure to make sense of his environment. The imagery is of simultaneous trenchancy and evanescence. Sounds 'turn about in the perpetually dark air like sand when the wind blows it' (*Inferno* III.28–30) and the pilgrim, as Steven Justice notes, craves the apparent sense-making comfort of sight. Further on, the traveller comes 'to a place where every light is silenced' (v.28), and the catachresis – a perversion of meaning, metaphor's displacing function further displaced – and the sounds it describes make the situation real because unseen but sensed.[10]

Although Dante does not emphasize the parallel, some elements of hellspace also belong to the medieval forest (*selva* in Italian). To medieval Europeans the word *silva* referred not only to wood and forests but to all matter in its originally chaotic form. It translates the Greek *hyle* (matter, or stuff), which was itself adapted by Aristotle from the word for 'wood', because Greek originally had no word for matter that was not type-specific. In the second half of the third century CE, Calcidius used *silva* to translate *hyle* in Plato's *Timaeus*, making part of that work available to the West. It became import-ant to thinkers and writers of the largely French twelfth-century 'renaissance' who sought to understand the world on scientific prin-ciples. Calcidius writes a long section of commentary on *silva*, using the word for the disorderly, mobile matter from which the *Timaeus'* craftsman-god creates the universe, as the next chapter will explore. *Silva* thus connotes the bringing of matter to form. It refers to wood and forests because these are places of elemental matter and poten-tial,[11] there needing to be some material substrate on which to base cosmological thinking, as Aristotle found. Uncultivated, forests are disorderly for humans, so are like the errant matter Plato's demiurge makes into various objects.

The medieval forest understood as *silva* – as *unformed* matter – was not experienced with the physical senses alone. For medieval Europeans there were few ways to physically overview a forest, which represented to them the Eastern wilderness of the early Christians who took to the deserts in the third and fourth centuries, possibly as refugees, and the contemporary dwelling place of fugitives and thieves.[12] It was frightening and alien. Medieval European methods of learning – reading and observing, memorizing and retrieving con-cepts, facts, large bodies of writing and terms – frequently used trees as memory storage models (also gardens, buildings and the feathered segments of angels' wings). In this way the infinity of knowledge could be rendered in finite form without sacrificing structural or cosmically regenerative principles. Living twigs store natural information necessary for forest renewal, information that comes from the universe as a whole, and human minds can store information in carefully designed arrangements of twigs and branches, this matter remaining alive for future transmission and dispersal when its base components are tended by the memory worker.[13] The method is a way to avoid making factual or unwise errors and to enable ruminative wandering in one's memory stores for creative and pedagogical purposes.

In this way *anima*, the world's active principle (or its soul, in some understandings), and *silva*, its materiality, conjoin so that even fleeting thoughts and insights can be lodged in a mentally (re)constructed tree or similar structure. This gives on to a larger, incompletely navigable forest or other landscape comprising unknown facts and unencountered things. And while forests can represent the pages of books because books and trees both have leaves, we should not ignore invisible components. This is particularly important given the modern human tendency to erroneously equate seeing with knowing. For medieval Europeans, by contrast, the sounds of words were perhaps the best representatives of *silva* and *anima* working together, because they are 'material, substantial, *and* unseen', as well as being easier to produce given the exigences of manuscript production. Unseeable matter and cosmic arrangements producing unforeseen changes, then as now, need quantifying, recording, recalling and responding to with new kinds of actions, new forms of life. In the *Commedia*, the impetus to change begins with an absence of certainty and a perilous sense of moral errancy. Fixity of conscience is problematized throughout.[14]

Matter and energy work together in hellspace such that Dante the pilgrim's attempts to understand what he encounters are repeatedly overtaken by new experiences, and as he proceeds through the afterlife his mind departs from itself (*Paradiso* XXIII.44), his senses are disturbed and his ability to remember things wanes. Near the end of the journey the poem itself 'jumps' ('And so, in presenting paradise,/ The sacred poem has to make a jump/ Like one who finds something in his way'), as does the narrator's pen (XXIII.62; XXIV.25), to show that mortal time is fragmenting further, linearity no longer holds, and the pilgrim is in divine (or cosmic) time, which is both unified and multitudinous. As time runs out, every element becomes equalized, including every element of language. Leaves return to trees in an eternal springtime (XXVIII.116). The poem's jump recalls the way mountains, seas and other land masses move or act errantly in images familiar to early and later Christians from the Psalms.[15] Diverse languages merge as the angels in Canto XXVIII sing '*perpetual[e]mente "Osanna" sberna*' (XXVIII.118), a hymn of praise conjoining Latin, Hebrew and an Occitanian commonplace (*sberna* indicating the twittering of birds) with Italian, the phrase meaning to 'ex-hibernate', from Latin *ex-hibernare*, to come out of winter or from Hell's icy rain (*Inferno* VI.7–9). But this is also a time of crisis, dispossession and world loss, as a forest can burn up into heat and light and make way for other kinds of living.[16] The pilgrim's former life fades, and the leaves of the book of the universe are shot through with an irradiating energy overwhelming in impact, interrupting and transforming his sense of what a world can be.

Lost paradise

Moving back in time, world loss of another kind is depicted in Christianity's story of the first humans' errancy. Christianity arose in the East, but the Eden narrative, the primal myth of the religion that provided Eastern and Western Europe with its world view for over a thousand years, is part of the reason errancy – wandering – has been so closely associated in the West with error. The environments in this chapter that would come to be considered 'Western' show a through-line of concern with the relation of freedom to constraint, of free-ranging movement and desire to error, renovation and redress. While later chapters will amend this European focus, oversights, many produced in and by the West, now enable chaotic forms that replicate their original conditions at scale and in other contexts. We are thus increasingly attuned to the involvement of errancy-as-freedom with error, which can limit freedom, including freedom of choice. Meanwhile, it is salutary to consider earlier versions of world-altering errors that produced undesired errancy, if only so we can recognize earlier humans dealing, like us, with a necessarily partial sense of the outcomes of choices.

The story of humanity's fall and departure from paradise origin-ates with the Hebrews, a word meaning 'wanderer' that appears in the historical record after the fourteenth or thirteenth centuries BCE to describe the descendants of Abraham who had settled in Canaan, in the ancient Near East, centuries before. Related in Genesis, the first of the five books of Hebrew scriptures that were held to be written by Moses and part of the Old Testament of the Christian Bible, the Eden narrative probably cohered in its current form in about the seventh or sixth century BCE. In 587–586 BCE Jerusalem was destroyed, the Kingdom of Judah fell to the Babylonian Empire and Judean elites were deported to Babylon. The story of the creation of the universe and the fall of humanity may have been written from exile, and exile in any case became newly central to Jewish history from the time of the captivity.[17]

An innovation of the Genesis story is the fact that humans are made in God's image. Unlike in the Babylonian creation epic *Enuma Elish*, creation in Genesis is not founded on the remains of the dead and humanity is free rather than enslaved. In the second book of Genesis, God creates the human being, *'adam*, to work the *'adama*, or the earth, places this human in the garden and creates woman to give strength to humanity. Within the garden – possibly a forest, as only trees are mentioned – are two significant trees: the tree of life and the tree of the knowledge of good and evil. The injunction to avoid eating the fruit of the latter seems to be an injunction to avoid attempts to become godlike and lose the conditionality of human being.[18] The tree is thus a marker of limit or arbitrary distinction.

When the serpent speaks to the woman in Genesis 3 it does not ask her questions, as many translations suggest. It speaks selectively and summons doubt instead. The Hebrew Bible scholar Everett Fox claims that the serpent uses *aposiopesis*, an 'uncompleted phrase' that invites the listener to complete it. It thus draws the woman into dialogue or participation. Then, it lies and tells her only part of what it knows, inviting her mind to wander. In some ancient commentary on the story, Adam does not relay God's prohibition to Eve in the same words God used, and the serpent exploits the ambiguity. Adam instead says to Eve: 'You shall not eat of the fruit of the tree . . . neither shall you touch it, lest you die.'[19] To disprove the truth of this claim, the serpent shakes the tree and, having proved that touching it does not cause death, causes Eve to doubt the other things Adam has told her. So she eats the fruit of the tree and shares it with Adam.

The snake's slyness or double-mindedness transfers itself to the humans once they eat from the tree, for it is then that they realize that they are naked: they experience their natural state and have a view of it that finds it wanting. This is the result of the earlier uncertainty, introduced by the snake, about what the divine command means. When God expels the humans from the garden, the story returns to where it began, with the human's loneliness and the creation of a companion. The combined human action leading to the Fall produces a new loneliness: separation from God for the first time. Thus the tree of life is barred to them. And it is from this point that humanity is made to wander: the human's 'stature was diminished, his light . . . dimmed, his food changed, he became a restless wanderer on the earth, and death was inflicted on him and on all generations'.[20]

Later, the wandering to which the first humans were consigned in the Hebrew scriptures was figured according to the model of a labyrinth, which while allowing for a reversal of one's pathway typically provides a single, undeviating path to a centre. Perseverance in following a labyrinth's winding path became a way to figure and achieve redemption, especially in medieval Europe. The earliest reference to a labyrinth is found on a Mycenaean clay tablet from Knossos dating from around 1400 BCE, while the earliest possible use of a labyrinth design is Neolithic, in which period the relation between death and reincarnation becomes important to humans.[21] Mazes, which offer the walker many choices as to pathway and which usually involve backtracking after choosing a wrong path, are depicted in manuscripts from about 1420 CE, although they appear in the written record in Greek antiquity. Virgil's *Aeneid* (*c*. 29–19 BCE) has Aeneas' son Ascanius devise a maze-like 'Trojan ride' to honour Aeneas' father, Anchises, a game in which young men on horseback trace a complicated pattern likened to the play of dolphins in waves that figures the Trojans' ocean-going journey. While the underworld is alluded to by such games – the occasion here is Anchises' funeral – so is victory over the monster at the Cretan labyrinth's heart. Theseus, who slays the beast in the original story, is likened to Aeneas in Virgil's poem, and Aeneas would later be figured as a precursor of Christ, who descends to hell at Eastertide to free souls bound by sin or unknowing.[22]

Refugees, wartime, Rome

Although it has often been read as a text in praise of imperial power and self definition, Virgil's *Aeneid* is also the story of a group of wanderers, refugees from a lost war who, on reaching their destination, become embroiled in conflicts that remain unresolved by the poem's end. The narrative begins with a storm at sea initiated by the goddess Juno and ends with its hero, Aeneas, killing Turnus, his rival for the hand of King Latinus' daughter. The fact that Turnus has admitted defeat and begs for mercy shows that the Trojans' progress 'wandering,/ Fate-driven, year on year around the world's seas' (1.31–2) has been circular. For the *'saevique dolores'* or 'wild grief' whence Aeneas acts in Book XII (945) is ultimately indistinguishable from that of Juno, who rejoices in Troy's fall and whose *'saevi . . . doloris'* or rage (1.25) helps to propel the Trojans on their journey.

The *Aeneid* repeatedly figures Rome as an undecidable entity, a zone of desire, a future home for the Trojans. It is 'compellingly adaptive' and is characterized by contrast with other identities: 'Trojan, Carthaginian, Italian, and Greek'. Aeneas, like the Italians, is 'part of the world of mythic Greece', and while Aeneas' ancestor Dardanus is the basis of his claim to settle in Italy, Italian Trojans, Italian Greeks and others make for overlapping histories and indivisible claims. The *Aeneid* brings the reliability of the words and actions of even Jupiter, the king of the gods, into question. In Book I he soothes Aeneas' mother Venus by saying that Aeneas will rule three years in Latium, his son thirty, and makes the task sound easy (1. 265–71).[23] But in Book X he claims that he had forbidden the Trojans and Italians to fight (X.8) and swears on the Styx, the river said in Book VI to force gods 'to keep their word, in terror' (VI.324), to confirm his neutrality. He does intervene in the war, however, on more than one occasion later on (X.622–5; XII.833–6).

The father of the gods' authority being thrown into question gives us a sense of the epistemological difficulties of Virgil's time and place of writing. When Virgil reached manhood, Rome was in anarchy, and by the time the young Octavian, who would later become Augustus, Emperor of Rome, began his reign in 44 BCE following the murder of his adoptive father Julius Caesar, the Republic had known civil war for a century. The *Aeneid*, whose story begins in flight from defeat and ends in civil conflict and on which Virgil would have worked before completion of his *Georgics* in 29 BCE, is written amid acute national uncertainty. When Jupiter fails to keep his word, having gained his own divine status by subduing the gods before him, we might see Octavian in 43 BCE providing troops to the Senate to counter Mark Antony's siege of Mutina in northern Italy. On victory the future emperor switched sides to align himself with Antony and Lepidus, an alliance that would not endure. Octavian's reign in his own name and then as Augustus, the title he received in 27 BCE, was not without abuses. Repeated conquests had transformed the agricultural economy, dispossessed farmers and brought the Senate and people into conflict. While Octavian's situation was strengthened by the naval victory against Antony at Actium in 31 BCE, portrayed as the defeat of an Eastern (Egyptian) power, he waited two years before returning with his armies to Italy. For 29 BCE marked not much more than a decade since he had declared his political opponents wanted men whose lands could fund further conflict.[24]

Aeneas, who both is and is not the allegorical ancestor of Augustus, represents in part what the latter might become. And the *Aeneid's* temporality is vexed by its task: to portray the struggle to found an empire that *will have been* long lived and glorious but which is not yet either of these things. The poem's structure, in which the Punic Wars with Carthage of the third and second centuries BCE are anticipated by the first four books while the last four figure the civil wars of the first century BCE,[25] makes Roman identity a question. The errancies the work depicts – both the errors the characters make and the Trojans' wayward course and short-lived Italian presence – foreground the unresolved. Characters are absent when they should be present, paternal advice is disregarded, by the close of the work several dead remain unburied, and cyclic violence compounds already muddled ancestral lines.

Also present throughout the *Aeneid* is an acute sense of primal enmity, as perhaps we might expect when the gods cannot be trusted. The active involvement of the natural world with human affairs is a standard feature of ancient literatures. Yet as the fury

of the conflict between Latins and Trojans increases, Virgil's sim-
iles themselves become transfused with military qualities. It is as
though the discontinuity effected by simile and the shared vision
that may result collapse into each other.[26] War is shared by not
only every human but every element. In Book X, packed troops
are like 'winds in the vast sky/ Battl[ing] with equal bravery . . ./
A stalemate of themselves' (x.356–8); a shepherd's fires 'a battle
line' of 'fierce, unbroken burning' in which flames 'conquer' land
(x.406–9). The Latins and their armies massing sweetly '[sing]
their king' like swans but are followed by 'a soaring, hoarse cloud/
Of birds' (VII.698–705) that are the only sign of the approaching
army. The contradiction of a sweet song and a hoarse cloud figures
the watcher's unknowing or distraction as a seeming throng hides
battle lines (VII.703). Soon the allies are 'as many as the glittering
Libyan waves' or 'wheat ears scorched by spring sun' and 'the earth
[is] stunned with tramping' (VII.718–22).

Landscape becomes battleground more obviously once Juno
uses the Fury Allecto to inflame Turnus with rage so he will fight
the Trojans unremittingly. As the Latins line up, their blades a
'blackly bristling crop' instead of the agricultural kind, sun on
armour is likened to the sea's surface before 'a tidal wave' makes 'its
lowest depths heave skyward' (VII.525–30).[27] A similar confusion
of reference between land and sea, featuring two Latins (Italians),
occurs in Book X as Turnus is drawn into the waves by the false
Aeneas Juno has made, leaving the Rutulian on the ship bewil-
dered, with the sea an unreachable 'wafting path' to the land of his
fathers (x.687). Mezentius, joining the fight on land, is 'like a rock
in desolate waters', bearing blows like 'wind and waves' (x.693–4;
also XII.365–9). Here the transpositions abroad in the landscape
put the Latins in the place of the Trojans, who have been alternately adrift and purposeful in the first half of the poem. As the
two Italians fighting for their country are figured in the place – the
sea – lately occupied by the refugees, we are reminded not only of

the interchangeability of both sides in the war but of those whom Octavian's confiscations made refugees in Italy.

It is in Book VI, however, that wandering is most clearly associated with an alteration of nature that might augur altered destiny. On the Trojans' arrival in Cumae the narrator tells the story of Daedalus and the Cretan labyrinth, itself told in images on Apollo's temple doors. The labyrinth was built to house the Minotaur, the half-beast, half-human offspring of Pasiphae, whose union with a bull was enabled by the inventor Daedalus. Minos then commanded Daedalus to design a labyrinth in which the beast could be kept beneath the palace where the inventor was also interred. The transition to the story is abrupt and so is the story's end as the Sibyl arrives to tell Aeneas that 'this is no time' for staring at images (VI.37). And although we assume Aeneas has been reading the narrative, we do not actually see him do so. The lack of direct connection between Aeneas and the story, as William Fitzgerald notes, invites the reader to consider what the relation between the two might be.[28] Abrupt transitions contrast with the labyrinth's circuitous path to a goal in which the end cannot be seen, the latter the Trojans' situation. The cutting short of the story also presages the *Aeneid*'s ending, as we will see, where staring at images spells the untimely death of Turnus.

The mode by which the labyrinth narrative is conveyed, *ekphrasis*, emphasizes contrasts, as its task is to prove that a poet's verbal art can create pictures in the minds of listeners that are richer than those in other, visual forms. The craftsperson or artist is by convention defective in some way, to convey the contrast between his diminished bodily state and his works' increase of beauty. Thus Hephaestus, the Greek progenitor of Vulcan who in Book VIII makes Aeneas' shield, is traditionally a blacksmith whose defect is lame feet, to signal his enhancing the fleet feet of horses. The poet's traditional defect is blindness, his experiential darkness contrasting with the luminescent pictures he makes appear in listeners' minds. But Virgil does something potentially new here. The artwork described is one in which the artist's own story is portrayed,[29] and in this rendition the defect of the artist consists not in a mark he bears on his person but in an inability to create (twice) because of an internal impediment (grief, guilt or both). For the scenes on the frieze that Daedalus cannot create are those in which his creative abilities may have led to the death of his son, Icarus.

On their journey out of the labyrinth Icarus ignored his father's advice to take a middle course through the heavens lest the sun melt the wax that held his wings' feathers on, and so fell to his death in the waves. As Daedalus 'sw[ims] into the ... North,/.../ His wings like oars' (VI.16, 19), his journey is likened to that of the Trojans from peril in Troy to Italy, and Aeneas, too, is about to go underground to tread strange pathways and receive paternal counsel. Daedalus' hands fall from the artwork he is making, as Icarus fell, and, as Fitzgerald notes, the transition from the unfinished artwork to Aeneas' unfinished journey occurs within a single hexameter.[30] As Aeneas enters the land of the dead he is thus hurried away from the chance to contemplate an absence, an absence that expresses an inability borne of grief and the risks involved in artistic and political invention.

These concerns return later when, near the end of the battle for Italy – a battle portrayed as labyrinthine (XII.481, 742–3, 753, 763–4) – Turnus, defeated, begs for mercy before his countrymen or that his father receive his dead body home. At this Aeneas hesitates, in a moment Michael Putnam identifies as the setting up of an ethical quandary hitherto unknown in epic poetry, provoked by Virgil's giving voice to the vanquished.[31] In the place of the *Iliad*'s Achilles to Turnus' Hector, Aeneas is given the opportunity to choose how to respond, and he makes the choice, or feels compelled, to act and speak in the person of Pallas (XII.948), a young man who had been in a quasi-paternal relation to him. As Aeneas disobeys, not for the first time, his father's underworld injunction to 'spare the conquered' and 'subdue the proud' (VI.853–4), a similar guilt to that Daedalus would have experienced over the death of his son may also affect Aeneas. For Aeneas had been unaccountably missing from the fighting in Book X at the point when Pallas entered the fray, leaving him alone on his first day of battle (X.508).[32]

Perhaps fuelled by this conflicted knowledge, what arrests Aeneas' 'halting change of heart' and possible movement towards mercy (XII.940) is the sight of Pallas' baldric (sword belt) shining on Turnus' shoulder, which returns Aeneas emotionally to the moment he learned of his young friend's death, the baldric commemorating the 'wild grief' he felt then and igniting the 'hideous rage' he feels now (XII.941–6). Turnus' plea for mercy, for extra time, is disallowed because Aeneas reads the wearing of the belt as an extra insult to his friend's memory.[33] The belt itself records an act of excess because it is murder out of place, the slaying of the sons of Aegyptus by 49 of King Danaus' fifty daughters on their wedding night, a time of hopeful beginnings not murderous ends. As Turnus dies, his body's cold is described in the same words used to describe Aeneas' cold in Book I of the poem (XII.951; I.92), confirming the loop made by Aeneas expressing, as on previous occasions, the equivalent of Juno's anger. As Aeneas uses his sword to kill Turnus he completes the function of the belt (a loop that holds a missing sword, that of Pallas), but causes an extra death that he could have forgone without forgoing victory.

While in response to this artwork Aeneas, unlike Daedalus, fails to act out of pity, which emotion led Daedalus to enable others (Icarus, Theseus, Ariadne) to escape the labyrinth, the poem allows its readers and hearers to consider the possibility. But at this point, too, the *Aeneid* shows that temporal and sensory contradiction can be unavoidable in battle, and so perhaps Aeneas' and Daedalus' situations cannot easily be compared. The sight of the baldric ends a halt or 'time out' for Aeneas, returning him to the imagined scene of Pallas' death (a death he did not directly experience), and Virgil complicates this moment by his earlier addition to the baldric of the name of its maker, a detail not found in the description of Hercules' baldric in the *Odyssey* (XI.699–705), the prior reference. It is instead derived from the word the *Iliad* uses to describe 'battle din', Clonus (X.499).[34]

Yet the scene the belt depicts is one the shock of which – frozen in time and emphasized by serial action, each link referring to the same act repeated – suggests a moment's silence or a dead span of time, as when one or more of the senses cuts out amid the overload of combat, the din of slaughter. Or as when the wedding night husbands meet their ends, for silent coordination was the method of the Danaids' murders, not a loud rush into fighting. The switch of implication, while potentially confusing for the reader or hearer who picks up the Homeric echo, itself suggests the disorientations of battle, the noise, in the war-systems sense, that has to be parsed or navigated at speed before action. As we know, Aeneas resumes violent motion at sight of this frozen moment, allowing himself to be propelled by shock into an act that is equally violent. But the poem requires the reader or hearer to work through the contradictions of his so doing.

Virgil's final simile in Book XII shows Turnus, tiring in battle, as though in a dream in which one's limbs and voice are paralysed (XII.908–14). This contributes to the strange dislocation of the poem's final scene, which is so overloaded with intertextual references, especially to Homer, that it seems a place of imagination, of dizzied retrospection more than current event. The sword belt, however, has a real referent: the memory of the Danaids' slaughter of their husbands, rendered in the form of statues of the women in a portico framing the temple to Apollo Augustus dedicated in 28 BCE. The import of the figures is ambiguous, like Aeneas' final act. They may reflect Roman guilt and repentance or the city's pride in its ability to defeat its foes, with Antony and the Egyptian Cleopatra suggested by the murder of the sons of Aegyptus the work records.[35] As Turnus wearies and Aeneas halts, the sight of the baldric causes

Anchises' words to his son about Rome's future to be forgotten. In those words, sparing the defeated and establishing a custom of peace are to be the new arts to replace the old of sculpting in marble or charting the skies (VI.847–53). Yet Aeneas fails to break with the past, opting instead for the familiarity of a feeling – loss – from which he fled at the outset of the story.

Designs on creation

Errancies are built into the ethos and design of a set of texts produced by the descendants of those the Greeks and Romans called *keltoi* (Celts), who lived in considerable numbers north of the Alps and beyond the Mediterranean littoral in the Iron Age in semi-mobile groups. Following the migrations dated between about 375 and 568 CE, in which many moved to new parts of Europe as Roman imperial power waned,[36] the Irish and Anglo-Saxons of the sixth and seventh centuries developed traditions that, in concert with those from the Christian Mediterranean, led them to produce a labyrinthine visual language with which to express complex cosmological ideas. Before considering this language, it is worth turning for a moment to the imperial world that post-dated Virgil, whence the shape of the change in world view that helped bring these texts about began to form. Under pressure from Christianity, which brought to Roman state religion such logical and rhetorical paradoxes as the Word made flesh and God made man, poetry from the empire's latter days focused on contiguity rather than continuity, placing fragments of the work of earlier poets in new combinations, 'exploiting . . . contrast' on multiple levels so that the miniature and episodic rather than the reach of an extended journey were to the fore. Words achieved a new kind of physical presence and were often treated talismanically. What has been called an 'aesthetic of discontinuity' begun as early as Ovid is seen to contrast with the epic continuities to which Virgil strove.[37]

Virgil was to become 'the common property of pagans and Christians', and the *Aeneid* was itself broken up and recast by both kinds of authors, while the ancient interest in inversion and temporal complication was to become a mainstay of Christian art and writing. Christianity enabled access to a structural errancy, an internal dislocation related but not reducible to worldly events, even if it did so in part by strengthening the imagined power of evil to a much greater extent than had pagan religious traditions. The fourth-century fathers who left their Egyptian villages to meditate on the divine in the desert, for example, realized a disengagement they had sought and found difficult to achieve in their villages, where physical and verbal violence in the face of crippling taxes and in defence of the right to the Nile's water were well known.[38] Renunciation made for an existence no less fraught with physical and spiritual dangers, but it placed the challenges of village life in a larger context. Where in a village one was vexed by proximity to one's neighbours, the incoherence of one's own character was heightened by remote desert life.

When the sixth- and seventh-century Irish took up the idea of unbelonging as belonging they called not only inhospitable pieces of land 'deserts' but also the uninhabited ocean, on which they set forth in a *peregrinatio* that would make each new home a place of exile. Human errancy was divine opportunity, for God directed the wind and waves. The Insular gospel-books made by the Irish and Anglo-Saxons ('Insular' referring to their combined islands) extended, in images and letters, the late antique rejection of linearity. In Virgil, violation of norms at the level of line and phrase was, among other things, a way to keep in listeners' and readers' minds the unforeseen costs of fulfilling a hoped-for destiny. The long *catenae* or 'chains' of paradoxical images of a fourth- and fifth-century writer like Paulinus of Nola went further, paralysing the 'discursive and referential forms' of language so as to throw the reader 'against the possibility' of something beyond it.[39] For these later writers, the contradictions of letters and symbols were signs of the greater mystery of God's decision to clothe his Word in mortal flesh.

We can see the pictorial treatment of the letter as an image in itself, begun by authors such as Paulinus, Ambrose and Augustine, taken up in the Incipit (beginning) page of the Gospel of Matthew in the Lindisfarne Gospels, a sumptuous text probably made from about 715 to 720 at Lindisfarne, also known as Holy Island, off the Northumbrian coast of Britain. Stylistic elements of the worlds of the ancient Celts, Picts, and German and Scandinavian peoples can be seen in many of the pages of such books, in which the runic forms letters take meet the Greek letterforms of Christianity.[40] The combination may have contributed to the historiated initial, a letter containing an image or images relating to the text, which seems to have been invented by Insular artists. On the Lindisfarne Matthew incipit page, the large letters reading *Liber generationis ih[es]u [christi] filii david filii abraham* ('A record [or "the book"] of the genealogy of Jesus Christ, son of David, son of Abraham') resemble the raised golden filigree or enamelling found in Iron Age Celtic La Tène metalwork, while the fact that relatively few letters expand to fill most of the page emphasizes the Word's iconic status.[41]

In Eastern Christian traditions the prevalence of icons – images indicating the divine by means of symbolism rather than direct representation – meant that Christ was seen as 'mystically embodied and concealed' in scripture. This tendency may contribute to the 'carpet' pages that embed Cross motifs in a multitude of repeated, interlaced figures so that to locate the Cross is to complete a visual puzzle, as figure and ground are given equal value. Byzantine, Syriac, Armenian and Coptic (Egyptian) traditions inform the books, and there are references to Coptic and Armenian monks in Irish litanies, to Western pilgrims visiting the East, and guides to visiting Egyptian monasteries. The knotwork displayed in red and blue in the 'bow' of the 'L' and body of the 'i' in the Matthew incipit image is another well-known figure for the cross, since '[a] knot was a crossing' of one line or thread behind another, 'a "crux"' which, like the scriptures, required undoing or 'unfolding' by interpreters. A knot or tangle also figured Christ's Incarnation, in which the divine and human were inextricably mixed, human waywardness wrapped in the greater conundrum.[42]

The idea informing Irish *peregrinatio*, that of the body as a 'temporary tent' wandering through existence, belonged to a view of the world in which spiritual time and space were paramount. The Gospels were seen, through Christ, to break the hold of Judaic law on the Hebrews, who carried the Ark of God's Covenant with his people shrouded in a tent or veil on their desert wanderings. The Latin word for book, *liber*, also refers to freedom. This may be the reason that in all of the incipit pages in the Lindisfarne Gospels, the text breaks the interlaced frame in two places, at bottom right and at top left of each page, and in all but the Luke incipit page at bottom left as well, symbolizing the escape from the old law bought by the Crucifixion. An errancy or uncontainment denotes a more direct way to the holy through Christ's body, as indicated by St Paul's Letter to the Hebrews.[43]

Relatedly, the quadrupeds contained in the panel to the left of the letter 'L', the single beast head with which the panel terminates, the small bird in the triangularly shaped lower part of the panel below the orange and blue intertwined beasts, and the beast and bird forms elsewhere on the page refer to the Eucharist, in which Christ's body and blood are consumed. Inhabited vine scrolls, first appearing in classical tradition and later symbolizing the partaking of Creation in the tree of life, figure Christ in the form of the 'living vine' who through the Mass feeds and sustains his people. Additionally, as the sense of abundant life in these pages indicates, the fact that extracts from the Gospels were placed at various points in the liturgical cycle of the year meant that the images and letters in gospel-books were never seen as static. The change and continuity of the liturgical cycle showed the way past, present and future were believed to coexist, while the individual elements of such pages could shift according to context and 'the preoccupations of the reader' or viewer.[44]

The visual ambiguities of the recombinant plant and animal forms we find in the gospel-books had earlier been used in dress accessories by fifth- to seventh-century Germanic elites to signal a desire for the social advancement of their families. The impact of Christian approaches to the world on these people's worlds was significant and long-standing. For pagan Scandinavian and Germanic cultures, those things that governed the course of a life or lives were thought to reside outside it: in fate, in the gods, in arcana. So while a cross such as the one that jests for primacy with apotropaic yoked beast heads as a protective charm in the well-known seventh-century Sutton Hoo helmet shows the Anglo-Saxons' love of riddles and other conundra, there the cross is merely a symbol like others. In the Anglo-Saxon poem 'The Dream of the Rood', by contrast, a tree becomes both cross and man, a retainer, whose task of bearing Christ is heroically passive.

Heroic passivity is itself a new contradiction. In the poem essential elements, not all of them visible, work in different ways at the same time, and there is a sustained emphasis on the value of the unseeable and on thought about the unseeable, or contemplation as a form of engagement.[45] In submitting to death by crucifixion, Christ rendered fate 'a servant force' of the Christian God, who could thus be moved by entreaty. Once the formerly external element of fate was put into circulation by means of Christ's death and resurrection, fate became fluid and transmissible and able to be changed. For the Saxons, written words (runes) already had invisible power. On conversion, their understanding of the Eucharist was that to consume the Word was to consume God's power of making.[46] So while mobility was key to the value of the incarnate Word for such transitional communities, equally important was the melding of two world systems in which the second put to work the eternal 'outside' of the first. Now the invisible had an incorporative power,

Amors, economy, romance

A further turn on the transition to this symbolic economy occurred in the twelfth century when the elites desiring familial advancement were the aristocrats and townspeople of northeastern France. In the new form of romance, written for performative narration of which there were variously 'secular' and 'sacred' versions, the art of inter-lace we have observed in Celtic gospel-books is used to express, in narrative terms, a new understanding of time. As a term, 'interlace' derives from textile weaving, in which threads hold a work together by disappearing, as one thread or strand moves temporarily behind another before re-emerging. Romance, in which there are multiple narrative threads, is traditionally distinguished from its epic pre-decessor, the *chanson de geste* ('song of heroic deeds'), on the basis that narrative line stands for lineage and that epic songs of deeds trace relatively simple genealogical lines. Common to interlace in romance are 'multiple characters, temporal imbrication, and spatial displacement'.[47] One character's story will be abandoned in favour of another and returned to later, conveying the impression that dif-ferent trajectories, to varying degrees related to each other, occupy the same or a similar span of time.

The understanding of time developed in romance is that of a mercantile economy in which time needs to be measured to enable complex exchange transactions. Yet credit, increasingly used in this period, requires belief and implies change, and the invisible power of capital promises something in excess of mere equivalence, a genera-tive conflict in which the dissimilarity of things might be proposed and then combined. What is promised in terms of love is similar and is demonstrated in Chrétien de Troyes' *Yvain, the Knight of the Lion* (*c.* 1177) when we see Yvain experiencing, by inference, love and hate together when he does battle near the end of the poem. This is a form of complex interiority we take for granted today but which was new at time and place of writing.[48] It is related to the need to maintain honour in love relations, itself a dynamic of the visible and invisible because while honour, or suiting one's action to one's own and another's station, is a matter of public agreement, erotic desire depends in part on the as yet unseen.

In romance, famously, desire does not follow the path agreed upon for its expression. A typical plot involves a knight who fights an adversary and falls in love with a woman, so that love (*amor*) and war, or love and the prospect of death by combat, are both involved.[49] An obstacle is also typical, and must be overcome before ongoing love can be achieved. In *Yvain*, the protagonist leaves King Arthur's court in order to avenge his cousin, who has been bested in a fight with a lord whose lands he has ruined by magically summoning a violent storm. Yvain mortally wounds this knight and falls in love with his widow, Laudine. Lunete, Laudine's maid, intervenes and Yvain and Laudine marry, but wandering resumes when Yvain leaves the court with his fellow knight Gawain, having promised to return within a year or forfeit the love of his wife. When Yvain misses the deadline, shame and guilt drive him mad and he wanders the forest, naked, surviving by killing animals and eating their uncooked flesh.

Yvain's journey back to sanity begins when he meets a hermit whose inferior bread he eats, then the meat the hermit cooks from the animals Yvain kills, then the better bread the hermit buys by selling the animals' skins. With the help of a magic ointment, sanity is restored and numerous adventures follow, including rescuing a lion, saving Lunete from burning (the indirect result of Yvain not returning in time to Laudine) and freeing by combat a castle full of enslaved female silk workers. The final part of the romance consists of an extended fight between Yvain and Gawain, neither of whom knows the other's identity, in respective defence of two sisters' claims on their father's estate, only one of which is valid. Lunete intervenes a final time, and Yvain and Laudine's love is resumed.

Twelfth-century French romance has been read as a form in which the earlier reliance on military action as a demarcator of social privileges by a warrior aristocracy yields to those of a fiscal kind. Warfare no longer belonged to a single class as increasing numbers of non-nobles in the pay of counts and lords bore arms. Jousting in tournaments became tamer, displays of wealth more than prowess. In this understanding, chivalric (knightly aristocratic) honour is reformulated according to a system of new ethical priorities having to do with commerce.[50] And undoubtedly, the burgeoning commercial economy is at work in these texts. Chrétien's patron, Marie, Countess of Champagne (*r.* 1164–98), was the wife of Henry the Liberal, Count of Champagne (*r.* 1152–81), and daughter of King Louis VII of France and Eleanor of Aquitaine. Henry ruled over a large feudal complex to the east and west of Paris that included the town of Troyes, this being the town Henry took for himself, assigning others to his brothers. The region's poor soil was one reason for the twelfth-century revival of Champagne's fairs, which thrived under their respective counts' protection.[51]

The six fairs held in the county of Champagne at staggered intervals throughout the year joined the western Mediterranean economies of Italy and France with the cloth-producing Low Countries and enabled trade in textiles, spices, dyestuffs, metals, animal skins and other wares. The fairs performed the function of non-existent towns between Flanders and Italy, not only 'feeding, sheltering, and entertaining well-travelled merchants' but serving as the '"clearing house" of international commerce'. Letters of exchange enabled merchants to trade at a distance by means of proxies or partnerships and extensive credit systems were developed. The fairs were used as banks in which promises themselves could be sold at discounts, with the arrangements agreed to by parties recorded in 'Letters of the Fair'. This made it possible to avoid moneychangers and carrying large sums of cash around.[52]

We can see parallels to these practices in the way that so much of what happens in *Yvain*, including speech, involves the complex play of seen and unseen things that act simultaneously according to working principles that are obscure. An example is when Lunete, who has the role of middleperson representing Yvain's value to her mistress, appears in the space between the grate of the castle door and the door through which Laudine's dying husband has fled and offers her services to Yvain on credit. It emerges that Yvain spoke kindly to Lunete once when she was sent to Arthur's court with a message, and her 'exchange' for this 'honor' is the 'reward' of future help. Lunete conjures rich food, wine and cloth from nowhere (1046–54) and offers Yvain, as security, a magical ring that makes him invisible (1022–37). While such rings had many sources in the Celtic folklore that informs Chrétien's romances, as Eugene Vance observes, they can also be connected to coinage, as well as to the currency of speech. Lunete and her ring not only distract Yvain by rewarding him with a supply of current luxuries. They also, less obviously, hide the murder of Laudine's husband and make Yvain appear as his natural replacement, feasting on the equivalent of the murdered lord's goods.[53]

There was considerable interest in this period in Europe in the nature of money as a sign in a system conveying meaning, and thus with money as analogous to words. Coinage had grown at a fast rate since the tenth century but the debasement and manipulation of currency helped produce the entirely new phenomenon of 'unstinting credit'. Key to its operation was the fact that 'a small investment of hard cash' could be put to markedly different uses simultaneously. Relatedly, the twelfth- and thirteenth-century theologians and philosophers who were the precursors of the *modistae* or speculative grammarians were less interested in the inherent truth of a part of speech or grammar than the mode – or conditions – in which it operated, how the distribution of its value worked. Monetary exchange and the dialectical processes by which medieval European thinkers worked out the principles of language's conveyances were close kin.[54]

There were, however, limits to these speculations. Likelihood of return on investment and likelihood of language working to the greater human good still tended to come down to the value of the word of a given human (which included for medieval Europeans the word of God). From the twelfth century, aristocratic properties in France were gradually converted into earners of money rents to free up capital, so that an inherited 'good name' accrued profit. Inheritance structures themselves had begun to lateralize given the proliferation of urban households and the challenges of preserving the fortunes of noble families from the ravages of disaffected sons. Aristocratic marriage partners had begun to desire the mutual consent that the lower classes more or less already practised, and the Church moved to support this and curtail the rights of powerful aristocratic families who might threaten its own model of succession.[55]

In *Yvain*, Chrétien is acutely wise to these challenges of advancing lateralization and to the fact that increasing the number of pathways to a desired end can increase the desire, and need, for final resolution. Yvain has given his word to Laudine to return to his responsibilities by a certain time. When he fails to do so, his honour, or the value of his word underwritten by deeds, must undergo renovation. Once this has occurred, the number of adventures in which his martial prowess is required increases. The narrative threads diversify at pace with his fame as a fighter. Yet the only time in which Yvain is self-consciously 'watching the clock' as he fights a foe is when he knows he has to kill a giant who is tormenting townspeople in time to also free Lunete from burning. This is because Lunete is his only way back to Laudine. Only Lunete, like the moon, can make change to order,[56] or increase by unseen means the value of Yvain in the eyes of his abandoned wife, and she needs to be kept alive to do it.

Visibility and invisibility are important here. Yvain, invisible, fell further in love with Laudine as, replacing her dead husband who could look on her at will, his attraction to her grew in proportion to her outward signs of grief (1146–76, 1285–6, 1416–539). The grief she might feel for Yvain if he were killed was a useful unconscious 'plus' with which to temporarily stay the 'minus' of logical guilt, which assumption also involves an unconscious leap in time. Frank Brandsma has noticed that in *Yvain*, interlace is used to increase stress on characters' relations to time while obviating space. Surroundings are not described as indicators of characters drawing closer to each other towards resolution, as we might expect. Instead, a sense of development is conveyed by, for example, the young woman who has taken the role of the (wronged) younger sister in the romance's final dispute meeting the same people Yvain has in series as she approaches him.[57] This, along with the sense that 'beginnings' recur repeatedly (Lunete is only properly introduced to the reader some time after she has shown her usefulness to Yvain, for example), means that time, not space, and time's new strangeness, not wandering in forests or wastelands, are the pressing realities with which the narrative is most concerned.

And time is not visible. In *Yvain* its only near relation, or true representation, is the approaching duel between Yvain and Gawain, in which the two close friends fight unknowingly to kill each other on behalf of two sisters and then, upon learning each other's identity, try to outdo each other in declaring themselves defeated (Laudine does not know that Yvain, or the masked 'knight of the lion', is her husband either). Chrétien makes the final fight the occasion for a bravura theological commentary on the paradoxical equivalence of love and hate (6021–81) that accompanies the knights' own realization of (near) equivalence.[58] But the payment, and the prize, were paid and won already when Yvain promised to return to Laudine, having promised something similar earlier by dint of marriage. At the time of the first event, however, Yvain had allowed Lunete as mediator to enable Laudine to quickly overcome her grief, which in turn enabled Laudine and Yvain, who was in love with her because of it, to marry. Laudine's quick change of heart was 'bought' on Lunete's estimation of Yvain's future worth, and Yvain was the customer who preferred not to dwell on how the grieving goods were got or how the means of their getting increased their lustre.

With no time for grief and no thought, on Yvain's part, of his experiencing a grief like Laudine's, he had still to experience it upon the breaking of a promise. Lunete puts her mistress' marriage oath in play at the romance's end by asking her to take another oath to help the anonymous knight of the lion achieve his lady's love again (which Laudine rightly calls 'a fine bit of business' (6764)). The way this is done is markedly similar to the peace-making recorded by many twelfth-century French legal documents in which disputes are settled, whether by promise of exchange or agreement to ignore or cease unwanted actions. Such contracts are legal stand-ins for a given party's word, which represents their honour. The agreements halt the potential infinity of threats by neighbours or relatives to one another's honour that is the working currency of aristocrats and others. And the word of 'pes', when given as the fleeting representative of a person or part of a community, is an agreement to speak no more and perform no more deeds in pursuit of a matter. It is key that when agreement is reached, or when a moment of agreement can become a record – there are typically 'Lunetes' involved as well as officials – everyone completes their business quickly.[59] So Laudine pardons the kneeling Yvain, her 'pes' now given in deed as it was earlier in word, and Yvain too is now bound to silence as to his guilt or increase of valour.

THIS CHAPTER BEGAN with a man halfway through the journey of his life coming to in a dark forest. We are not entirely done with the twelfth-century French, whose international ambitions, and their music, will appear in Chapter Three, the former as part of the phenomenon known to historians of Europe as the Crusades. I have slightly underplayed 'errantry' as popularly imagined in *Yvain* and like texts in order to explore the medieval interest in errancy itself because this interest was thoroughgoing and a precursor of our own difficulties with economic and symbolic wishfulness. But I have also done so because the rich figures of thought used by Chrétien, Dante, Virgil, the Celtic gospel-book artists and by labyrinth- and later maze-makers have one note of caution in common. All – as witness Chrétien's *amors*, Virgil's 'battle din', the Celts' play with figure and ground, the labyrinth's journey and end and the light that in Dante is surprisingly silenced – allow the play of likeness and difference to occur in such a way that we are reminded that pairs of things are always falsifications, and that a further turn of events is as likely to introduce new problems as resolve the old.

Unremarked costs and attachments to deferral are things that, on balance, our human ancestors were better placed to deal with than we are, if only because they were closer in time to the trials and errors of our beginnings. Dante's journey in the *Commedia* ends with a 'flash' in which what his mind had 'desired came to it', but it comes, importantly, at the point of failure, not achievement, of imagination, even while imagination, experience, learning and other resources have helped make the poem (*Paradiso* XXXIII.139–42). Desire and will are 'turned like a wheel' but not a wheel that can be pictured. And because Dante has left a poetic record that consents to its own undoing on this score, when we read of desire and will turning 'all at one speed,/ By the love which moves the sun and the other stars' (XXXIII.144–5), we should recall not only the darkness with which the journey began but the reason the flash of fulfilment is momentary. It is because darkness to ourselves, like space–time, is our condition, and because errancy may mean that these are the only places to which we will ultimately prove to have belonged.

2

ORIGIN

There is a strong tension between knowledge and conjecture, or law and happenstance, built into our understanding of our cosmic origins. Today, most people know that the universe we are part of was probably formed, about 13.8 billion years ago, by an instance of singular combustion that created what we now know as 'space, time, energy and the laws of nature', or the logic of observed events occurring in our universe. The more we learn about the hows and therefores of this process, the less we know about the whys and wherefores. Physicists know that the Big Bang, as our originating event has come to be called, was probably kick-started by a fluctuation in the quantum vacuum that led to the process known as inflation, a remarkable expansion of space, since which time the universe has been cooling. The difficulty of ascertaining why this occurred derives from the inherent uncertainty built into all quantum operations. There is no such thing as empty space, just as there is no such thing as matter that is not in some form of recalcitrant motion. While it is possible to calculate the probability distribution for physical events, the events that gave rise to us are – perhaps peculiarly – resistant to full explication.[1]

This difficulty is at least partly due to the fact that we cannot get outside our universe, but can only observe, measure and falsify by experiment what we find within its workings. Its early period has been reconstructed as that in which inflation was followed by a process known as primordial nucleosynthesis. This produced atomic nuclei, or protons and neutrons bound at the centres of atoms by strong nuclear force. Of the four fundamental forces of physics – electromagnetic, gravitational, and strong and weak nuclear – the latter is especially interesting for our purposes. Strong nuclear force produces atomic nuclei by stopping like-charged protons from flying apart from each other. Weak nuclear force initially determined the relative number of protons and neutrons to be bound. It also uncoupled from one another smaller elementary particles without electric charge known as neutrinos that travel at close to the speed of light.[2]

Because they are without electrical charge, neutrinos, like ghosts, wander effectively ('ghost particles' is in fact one of their names). They are very hard to detect, but are produced, for instance, at the heart of the Sun as hydrogen fuses into helium. Because weak nuclear force has a shorter range than that of electromagnetism and gravity, neutrinos pass through physical obstacles easily.[3] Indeed, trillions of them pass through our bodies each second. There is a congruence between the way in which neutrinos were discovered and what they do, insofar as they were lit upon haphazardly by a means not officially condoned by science. Before 1956, when they were first detected, neutrinos were dreamed up in one of those ad hoc hypotheses that often pre-date important scientific discoveries, in this case to save the known laws of the conservation of energy and momentum from being falsified.

In 1914 James Chadwick, who would discover the neutron in 1932, was studying the discharging of electrons from radioactive nuclei, or beta decay, whereby nuclei with too many neutrons transform a neutron into a proton to improve stability. The proton's positive charge must, however, be balanced by a corresponding negative charge, and to his surprise Chadwick found that the beta decay electrons sent out as a result of the transformation of neutrons into protons did not have a fixed amount of energy. The 'conservation of energy dictates that the emitted electron's energy *must* equal the difference in masses of the two nuclei (times the square of the speed of light)' if all relevant variables are considered. In 1930 Wolfgang Pauli proposed what he called a 'desperate remedy' to this conundrum – which was, happily, correct. He invented a particle that could not as yet be detected. This particle would exist in the atomic nuclei and consist of variable energy such that, when this energy was added to that of the emitted electron, 'the total would match the mass difference between the two nuclei' that provide the energy quotient of the beta-decay electrons. The law of energy conservation would thus be saved.[4]

Neutrinos, driven by weak nuclear force, are fast, mobile and abundant. They are also asymmetric under parity, which means they only interact with matter in one of two directional ways. Owing to the other three forces governing things in our universe's early stages – gravity, electromagnetism and strong nuclear force – the moment when the first atoms formed is preserved as a snapshot indicating the point at which matter and radiation first uncoupled. Neutrinos, the intrinsically misbehaving element needed to explain how certain observable deviations from proven laws of energy and momentum hold, continued at this time to wander around the universe. Their temperature was close to that of the 'photons of the cosmic background radiation', photons being the elementary quanta of light plus all other forms of electromagnetic radiation. Observing this cosmic background radiation, specifically its directional dependencies, shows that the expansion of the universe amplified small initial quantum fluctuations as matter was spread about. Matter's waywardness grew, or mattered more, even as gravity was pulling these vagrant materials into objects in which the first stars, which would in turn give rise to us, were duly born.[5]

Nor should we forget the role of the oceans in our genesis. It is thought that life on earth may have originated in the deep volcanic vents of the sea floor, where conditions favouring microbial extremeophiles – infinitesimally small microbes that shape the chemistry of the sea and the earth's atmosphere – thrive. A curious unmooring of the term 'life' from the organisms it once described can be seen in our relations with these microbes, as it can in our relations with other essential components of living beings such as DNA. Microbial extremophiles have been described as 'long-lost relatives, environmental stewards, and biotech workers', given the roles they can play in helping manage the planet's oceans: digesting oil spills, providing enzymes that enable the copying of DNA in laboratories or bacterial matter for pharmaceuticals. Marine microbes, like DNA, have contributed to an expansion of the category of life beyond the once dominant forms of the natural and biological, such as the reconstruction of the history of planetary life on the model of a tree. 'Life' is now more conceptually diffuse than previously, 'spilling across scales and substrates', alien to itself.[6]

Contemporary disasters and pandemics and the complexities evinced by non-human networks show a world not oriented towards us, even while our interactions with it have produced and exacerbated some of these events and conditions. It is we who are now alien to future life, as seen in the population migrations caused by climate changes we have produced as well as by our ability to create systems whose logics we cannot fully control. Yet in this, we are more like our ancestors than we might think. As Eugene Thacker notes, every study of the nature of life thinks of life in terms of 'something-other-than-life', such as time and temporality, or form and causality, abstractions that enable us to diverge from ourselves sufficiently to contemplate the larger meaning of existence. The flipside of this procedure is an often unnoticed anthropomorphism, seen for example in the idea of oceanic microbes as relatives and workers (or the idea of genetic material as selfish, to use another well-known example).[7] Both abstraction, a rigorous mental movement away from habitual modes of thinking, and a stabilizing concrete image or other temporary locator seem to be needed to enable life as it is lived to unfold in an experiential stream. The chief difference between our human ancestors and ourselves is that they did not so often create abstract systems, or images, songs and stories, that centralized them.

Dreaming and invention

In Australian Aboriginal cosmology, constituting the longest continual cultural history in existence, we can see why this is so. The forerunners of *Homo sapiens* arose in Africa some 200 million years before the present, whence they began to migrate to Asia, Europe and Australia, reaching the latter continent some 50,000 years ago.[8] Most of Australia in the years in which its early inhabitants were learning to sustain life there was acutely inhospitable to humans. The physical environment was unpredictable, resources were scarce, and without the ingenuity that enables maximum mobility, survival could not have been achieved. Our human forebears in this and other places were nomadic. They hunted and foraged for food and water of necessity, and their mobility produced deliberate innovation, not only in methods for procuring food and water but in social and symbolic terms as well. Increased physical movement crossing oceans and adapting to environments low in resources, as in Australia, meant social groups were no longer always supported by daily interactions. The separation and reconvening of groups meant those absent had to be imagined, effecting a mental departure, performed communally but also individually, from the present. As Josephine Flood observes, traditional Aboriginal society included 'sophisticated religion, art and social organization, an egalitarian system of justice and decision-making, [and] complex far-flung trading networks'.[9] Survival in one of the world's harshest environments was supported and partly effected, however, by Aboriginal systems for symbolizing and recording how their world began.

Australia itself is the product of drift, having existed, until about 120 million years ago, as part of Gondwana, a southern supercontinent comprising 'Antarctica, southern India, most of Africa, Madagascar, much of South America and the nucleus of New Zealand'. Humans first crossed to Australia from southeast Asia when the last ice age locked water elsewhere and sea levels fell, creating more dry areas between the two regions. Some Aboriginal people, such as the Rirratjingu people of Arnhem Land in northern Australia, trace their history to an ancestor who crossed the sea, but all trace their ancestry to spirit beings who once wandered the land, creating and naming the rocks, mountains and other natural features of the landscape. Central Australian Aboriginal people speak of a creation period (the Dreamtime) when the land was flat and featureless, until giant beings in the form of animals and insects who lived as humans emerged from the earth's surface. The fact that the animals' life spirit or creative power remained behind them in the places where they camped or had adventures shows that early Australians needed to grasp the principles by which such animals, and the real forebears on which they may be based, survived in the challenging environment.[10] The animals live human lives because human lives were necessarily lives of continuity and coexistence with those of animals, as well as with the seasonal and atmospheric forces with which some form of reckoning was needed, but which were ultimately beyond human control.

One of the most significant figures of the Dreaming is the Rainbow Serpent, associated with clouds, making lightning, rain and floods, and creating rivers and gorges. This ancestor is also linked to the Wandjina, giant creator beings in human form that control the wet season's life-giving rains, and which are featured in rock paintings in the Kimberley region of Western Australia. Together, the Rainbow Serpent and the Wandjina symbolize the interaction of the human being with the land's resources. The paintings indicate the place at which each Wandjina ended life on earth. Their haloes represent hair but also monsoon rain clouds, the latter shown by the predominance of white in the paintings. The heads are mouthless because if they had mouths, endless rain would fall from them, this belief indicating that Wandjina both make and are their images (the mouthless heads also bring to mind the need to preserve one's internal water system in the desert). Yet the Wandjina cannot cause rain to fall if the custodians of the shelters fail to renew their power through ritual touching of the paintings into life before the onset of each wet season. The Wandjinas' function as part-human, part-spirit beings is indicated by the red ochre sometimes used to represent their head haloes. As Deborah Bird Rose puts it, the 'earth is the repository of blood from Dreaming deaths and births, sexual excretions from Dreaming activities, charcoal and ashes from their fires'. And as humans consist of blood and water and will die from an injudicious loss of either, so the Wandjina, too, are seen as containers for these things.[11]

We can see an example of human invention in the face of threats to human life preserved in memory at Uluru, in central Australia. Uluru is believed by the Anangu, the collective name for the Pitjantjatjara and Yankunytjatjara people who are the custodians of this site in the Dreaming, to have changed into its present form – a rock containing many waterholes – in the creation (Tjukurpa or Tjukurrpa) period, or the time 'before time could be counted'. At the top of the Tjukiki Gorge, which is part of Uluru, a tall rock slab represents the *piti* or wooden seed-carrying dish of the Kuniya women, who once camped at a large flat sandhill around a waterhole in this part of the country. The sandhill is Uluru itself, and the waterhole is one of many that, as a result of rain run-off from the top of the rock pooling naturally inside it, makes the ground at its base fertile for plants, animals and humans and explains the rock's great importance to the people.[12]

The more inhospitable the environment, the more the ability to move is paramount, requiring invention at fundamental levels. The people of ancient central Australia were arguably the most nomadic Aboriginal Australians, and they extended self-sustenance in ways attested by the archaeological record. The seeds carried in the dish now represented by the *piti* rock near Uluru would have been harvested from grasses on the nearby plain. A rockhole near the top of the gorge represents the campfire on which the Kuniya women cooked the seeds, while small grasses and bushes growing in the gorge represent the women's hairs. Seeds were dependable sources of food, and seed grinding, performed in the region about 4,000 years ago, was costly of time and labour. It is likely that without the people diminishing this labour by using sandstone millstones to grind seeds into a paste after winnowing and husking, the populations in this region would have perished at greater rates than they did. At the least, this decision would have improved people's quality of life.[13]

The records of the creative acts performed by animal and human forebears preserved by Australian Aboriginal people in song, art, story and ritual performance also refer to significant geological events. Archaeological evidence confirms the transformation of Uluru from what was once a sandhill into its present form, which is said to have occurred miraculously in the creation period. About 600 million years before the present, the fracturing of the nearby Lake Amadeus Basin caused rocks made of sediments layered onto granite, lava and other substances some 600 million years before that to overflow the basin's edge and fold into each other.[14] This eventually produced the mountain range known as Kata Tjuta, meaning 'many heads' (or the Mount Olga group, as it is known in non-Aboriginal mapping systems), and Uluru itself. Uluru is thus made of sandstone – it is, in other words, a 'sandhill' – with its many caves and bays formed by weathering and erosion some 70 million years before the present.

In the story of the Kuniya, who in the creation period are non-venomous carpet snakes, a record of all the elements necessary to sustain human life is preserved in miniature. There is a naturally generated water source and a naturally generated food source, the latter extended by timely invention. But there is something more, too. The record itself instantiates the creativity that surviving major climatic changes, such as the sea level rise that drove increased numbers inland some 12,000 years ago, and the need to find new food and water sources, entailed. And the early humans who first recorded these events in transmissible song and story are believed to have *become* the landscape: in the Kuniya's case, the rocks, caves, bays and waterholes that feature in the narrative. The rock and its natural features thus symbolize the desert's extreme inhospitability to humans, an inhospitability that earlier humans found a way to manage and survive. The caves and bays that the fracturing, folding and recombining of the physical substance of Uluru caused contain many rock paintings and became sites for the generation of many further stories, all of which explain one or more components of the land's formation.

In this world view, the caves' value does not lie in the shelter they provide. To a people who can survive life in the comfortless interior of the continent, it is more important to preserve in these sites something that will remain for other humans yet to come. It is the endless passing back and forth and recombining of the many elements in a given Tjukurpa narrative that is the most important aspect of human survival in this instance, re-enacting as it does the geological fracturing and recombining of elemental components. The stories are valuable because they record very precisely how the formation of a landscape causes the formation of a people when both are in a state of adaptational change. The caves provide shelter, we might say, for continuity itself, of which no one person can be the symbol or the owner.

This means, however, that every regional people has a responsibility to maintain contact with its ancestral beings, a process that is both unitary and interactive. There are no demarcation lines between people as such, but points in space where Dreaming tracks, ancient and contemporary, form webs of complementary meanings. Both content and process are important. When a Dreaming track marking an ancestral being's passage, or part thereof, is sung by one person or group of people, it can be recognized by others who bear responsibility for adjacent tracks. To sing part of a Dreaming track is to maintain law and practise neighbourliness, both essential in ancient Australia's pitiless desert world. Negotiation occurs, then as now, as Dreamings are danced and sung and as a sung path calls forth the memory and sometimes the alteration of another.[15]

Songs, like Dreaming tracks performed in painting and other forms, are sacred, and to perform them is to 'carry' or keep safe the country. A painted design can instantiate both an ancestral being, such as a honey ant or plains wallaby, as well as the events that produced the being or that they once discharged. Paintings often represent a view from above and collapse time zones together, perhaps partly as a result of the necessary ability to decode tracks and likely movement within a landscape. Coming upon a deserted campsite, an Aboriginal person early in the country's human history could 'tell from looking at the earth how many men, women and children had left their marks behind, where they had slept, what they had eaten, [and] when they had last been there'. They could also tell from tracks what kinds of birds and animals were nearby, 'what they had been doing before his [or her] arrival and what they were likely to be doing' now.[16]

Although paintings encode meanings and activities of long-standing, they are also manifestations of transience or the uncontainable power of a cosmically creative moment. Paintings created by the Yolngu of Arnhem Land, which may have taken hours or days to finish, are often covered or destroyed within hours of completion. Sometimes only the artist will see the painting. For the Yolngu a correct design must be achieved, for instance by using subdivisions and 'geometric background patterns', but this is a preliminary component of the process. As a painting approaches its final stages, important transformations occur by means of outlining and other patterning, and these activities take up most of the time spent making the painting. 'Before cross-hatching the painting looks dull,' but after cross-hatching it attains a 'shimmering brilliance', known as *bir'yun*, which represents phenomena such as the play of sunlight on water or the iridescence of the wings of a moving dragonfly, moments of joy or dread or wonder in nature. Such moments belong to *wangarr*, the Yolngu ancestral beings, and the emotions they cause, as well as the transformation of a painting from bright to dull again when a painter returns to the main camp or ceremonial ground, are forms of ancestral interaction.[17]

As Howard Morphy notes, the transition from 'dark and dull to light and brilliant' effected in painting can also be discerned in songs and song cycles believed to have been sung by ancestors. Although ceremonial painting has been carried out by men more than by women, ancestral tales are regularly told by women in the more everyday form of sand story, which involves narrating aloud while gesturing with fingers and drawing on sand. Most of the graphic forms used in sand story can refer to many components: a circle, for instance, could be the hole of an animal's lair, 'a water hole, a hill', a 'particular variety of wild fruit' and so on.[18] Understanding sand story thus depends upon a knowledgeable audience and the storyteller's skill. Among the Walbiri of the Northern Territory, a space cleared in sand creates a stage or screen, while erasure normally effects division between scenes. Graphic elements such as half-circles, circles and meandering lines indicate the spatial relations of human and other actors while the narrative moves cyclically through time.

In observing sand storytelling practice among Walbiri women, Nancy Munn found that erasure within scenes did not occur. A single actor's activities would be figured by marks laid on top of each other designating sitting, eating, sleeping and so on. As well as expressing the continuous present of ancestral time within which human activities are made meaningful, sand story is also characterized by 'rapid fading'. No story forms a whole on its own, and no story is repeated in the exact same way twice. The 'finale' of a story is often shown by a person or ancestral figure going into the ground, marked by making a hole in the ground signifying a person's death or an ancestral figure's returning to the earth after adventures. Munn found that a formulaic ending often involves all of the characters in a story coming together and going into the ground or into a significant object such as a fighting stick or hill. The verbal expression common to this development, *lawa-djari-dja-lgu*, means 'they became nothing then'. The figures, ancestral or human, return to their point of origin and the tale is ended.[19]

The cyclical form of sand story provides scope for inventions and is readily used by children. The emphasis is less on particular actors than on the *way* ancestors lived, which is also the way Walbiri live in the present. A rather different kind of narrative process is involved when a woman first feels the quickening that indicates she will bear a child. Each child conceived is understood to be a living expression of the Tjukurpa being who dwells at the site where the child is first felt or 'found' by its mother. Among the Martu of the Western Desert, it is believed that ancestors left behind places where 'spirit-children' live. Often clever and quick-witted, spirit-children wander in search of food and drink and may enter the body of a mother in the form of a particular animal, plant or mineral she encounters. To an extent spirit-children are autonomous, but the father of a child may participate in its finding by seeing it in a dream or encountering it when hunting.[20]

In her work with the Yagga Yagga people at Balgo, the anthropologist Sylvie Poirier found a dream to be an essential component of a spirit-child's passing from the ancestral to the human realm, partly because a dream requires telling and listening and the creation of a cooperative environment. A mediatory form the mother encounters, such as a yam she ingests, becomes the agent of conception (biological conception is not denied but does not have the significance of cosmological explanation). This agent, *tjarriny*, a local element, is incidentally important: it enables the tracing back in time of a story about a child's conception to be agreed upon by the mother- and father-to-be and other relatives.[21] At conception, thus, a mother- and father-to-be are tasked with remembering recent events together – a hunted animal may have behaved unusually, or a particular kind of food may have made the woman ill. Dreams are also recalled at this time.

In this way, preparation for the birth of a human being means revisiting the conditions of early human life on land. The conception object or agent involves a 'complex interplay of the random and the preordained'. Conception is a contingent event but is linked to the enduring ancestral realm by means of the establishing of a communal story. A common motif in Western Desert conception narratives is a spirit-child who appears suddenly, then disappears and is not seen again. Recognizing the sudden appearance and disappearance of a harbinger of conception requires cooperative mental alertness, as does, during pregnancy, the spirit-child's ability to change and adopt different forms. The spirit-child's relative autonomy as well as the agreed-upon anomalous element(s) surrounding its first appearance indicate that human life is not a 'given' of existence: the spirit-child does not fully belong to the human realm until it is born.[22]

Spirit-children are often to be found near water – unsurprisingly, as in the desert water and the remembering of its locations are indispensable to future life.[23] The anomalies built into accounts of conception involve imagining a surplus of meaning in the natural environment. This surplus is a way of symbolically prefiguring while also including in a current world view the emergent child. When a birth story and ancestral node and pathway back to origin have been established, an emergent life cannot be taken lightly. The surplus of life attains the created meaning in which humans can never cease engaging, and which is essential to human continuity in any form.

Love, strife and learning

It is notable that, as humans take more responsibility for explaining how our world – the planet and the cosmos – began, we become at once more central and more irrelevant to it. The question of our role and place in the cosmos also energized the first thinkers we call philosophers, from the Greek city of Miletus on the Aegean coast of Asia Minor in the sixth century BCE. This aristocratic, secular society, a city-state or *polis* like the city-state of Athens to emerge later, was relatively free to govern itself and its inhabitants spoke a common language. It was open to influence from its colonies in the Black Sea, southern Italy and other Mediterranean ports and from earlier centres of civilization such as Mesopotamia and Egypt.[24] Three of the first thinkers in Western history to speculate concertedly about the physical nature of the universe came from this area. We call these thinkers 'Presocratic', in part to indicate that their conjectural efforts made it possible for Plato, Aristotle and later thinkers to formulate bases on which arguments about the nature of the material world could be built.

While none of our, nor the Presocratics', explanations use models that can 'close' the question of why the conditions of life on earth came about, thus retaining scope for further divagations, Empedocles (*c.* 490–*c.* 430 BCE) and Plato (*c.* 427–*c.* 347 BCE) make wandering central to their accounts of cosmic origins, with specific reference to the materiality we embody and encounter on a daily basis. Plato's teacher Socrates (*c.* 469–399 BCE), while not generating origin stories of his own, nonetheless plays a key role in Platonic thinking, as in the political life of fifth-century BCE Athens, by insisting on embodying *aporia* in relation to the lives and views of others. We might gloss this quality as the affective disquiet – and the provocation – of the genuinely homeless, or the genuinely human and creative, mind.[25]

As a doctor from Acragas, an important Greek city in Sicily, Empedocles founded a medical tradition that rivalled the Hippocratic by developing an integrative approach to healing based on observation. He was also a politician, and while his idiosyncratic views may seem far removed from the cooperative ethos of Australian Aboriginal accounts of cosmic origin, there are, nonetheless, commonalities. Human lives are terminal, but vital life forces – in Empedocles, souls – are not. Humans living now are the result of ancestral decisions and actions. Empedocles also goes further than other Presocratic philosophers in his attempt to develop a comprehensive account of world formation in the systematic terms made available by earlier Presocratics.[26] A key part of his cosmology is an ethical practice based on the belief that humans are integrative components of their environments. Empedocles' understanding of world formation involves the influence of two cosmic forces – Love, Harmony or Friendship (*Philia*) and Enmity or Strife (*Neikos*) – which operate in phases, and four elements: fire, air, water and earth. When Love dominates, elements are eventually bonded to form a sphere, and when Strife dominates the elements are separated from one another to an equivalent degree. Both Love and Strife function in between these states of extremity, with the transition from the domain of the one to the other occurring gradually. Elemental compounds, including living beings, are formed in the transition periods, where they also die and undergo intermediate transformations.[27]

More fragments of Empedocles' writings survive than for any other Presocratic philosopher (the companion source to extant pieces of his works is the testimony of other authors). The fragments pose many challenges to interpretation. The discovery in the early 1990s of over seventy further fragments, however, known as the Strasbourg papyrus, offers important clues to Empedocles' thinking. The first person plural is used to refer to occasions when nature's finitude, shared by humans, operates under the sway of Love, which joins elements together, but the third person is also used in close proximity to the first to describe this kind of union. The phrases 'we come together into one *kosmos*' and 'we were coming together in the mid-most places' (14.58, 36; 14.58, 56), which have an identificatory or participatory cast, might imply that Love has a beneficent influence on humans. But an adjacent shift to the third person ('all these things come together into one', 14:58, 58–9) indicates that such beneficence only applies to the cosmos as a whole in its constitutive elements or compounds and not to humans in particular. And as we consist, fundamentally, of 'a mixture of elementary ingredients' that continue to exist after 'the temporary compound we are has ceased to be', we must revise our understanding of birth and death accordingly. Only our makings may be immortal or infinite, and we only 'temporarily assume mortal forms'.[28]

While human origin occurs under the influence of Love and Strife, Empedocles identifies himself as a long-lived daimon or being, 'a fugitive from the gods and a wanderer' (14.9 (115), 13), because he has 'pollute[d] his . . . limbs with [the] bloodshed' of an animal or human and sworn a false oath (14.9 (115), 3–4). He must now, like any living being that has 'introduce[d] Strife into its composition', become other living beings until he is purified of Strife, a complex task given that sexual reproduction increases Strife and actions causing Strife can be performed unwittingly (14.25). Although Strife is dominant in the fifth-century BCE Greek-Sicilian present, there is almost no time at which it is not possible for Love or Friendship's 'local concentration' to be increased.[29]

The cure for the kind of wandering Empedocles is undergoing is a kind of 'right living' and 'right knowing' enabling the best actions. People, in Empedocles' view, are made to wander in ignorance when they fail to pursue causal explanations for things and rely instead on popular perceptions (14.42 (4), 1; 14.43 (2), 1–6). They should train the body and mind together, the former through breathing practices and the latter through daily reflective memory work. Jean-Pierre Vernant, following the sociologist Louis Gernet, notes that the ancient term *prapides*, which meant 'diaphragm' originally and which pertains to learning to control breathing in meditation, can be connected with intelligence, such that for Empedocles, to train the body is by definition to train the mind.[30] And like all educated ancient Greeks, Empedocles believes that 'the blood around the heart in humans' – that which is closest to the vital centre of the human as encountered on any fifth-century BCE battlefield or place where a medic like himself might be needed – 'is thought' (14.148 (105), 3).

As a citizen trained in the transformative properties of words, Empedocles must also preserve orally transmitted memory through poetry, a task inseparable from exploring the operational principles of the physical world. The second-century CE explorer Pausanias describes the first of the Boeotian muses as Melete, or Practice, the other two being Mneme, or Memory, and Aoede, Song. A significant component of the work of the earliest bardic Greek brotherhoods, or groups of inspired poets, was memory training for practical purposes. Without it, given that 'recitation', or return to the known, and 'improvisation', or departure for the unknown, were the twin means by which oral compositions were crafted,[31] they could not have identified invention or expressive changes in world view, in their own work or that of others. Nor could they have profited from such innovations either directly or in terms of the symbolic capital gathered from audience response. Both memory work and the ability to manage sudden insight are necessary to an effective song.

A practice followed by the sixth-century BCE Pythagoreans, who developed the understanding of a *kosmos* as a functioning world system consisting of musical and mathematical as well as living elements, was to remember all the events of a given day before turning to the act of sleeping. This memory training, a way to avoid wandering in ignorance with regard to the causes of events in life, was also the way to attain immortality, or what we might call a better understanding of our relevance or irrelevance to cosmic processes, an understanding always subject to mortal qualification. This training is probably related to a scene at the close of Plato's *Republic* when human souls, having been allotted the term of their next lives, come before the Throne or Spindle of Necessity and move, together, to the well-known 'plain of *Lethe* through a terrible and stifling heat' in 'a land without trees or . . . vegetation'. As Vernant notes, there is ambiguity about the next event mortals at the end of life encounter. They drink from the river Ameles, a term that has not been used, so far as we know, to describe the world of the dead until this point in Greek history.[32]

Translated as 'freedom from care', the river's function accords with a common reading of Plato whereby an afterlife of ease is the just reward of a life well spent. Yet the connection between the plain of Lethe (suffering) and the river Ameles (relinquishment) in Plato may be darker and more complex than it appears. In the earlier, mythical understanding of world composition that pre-dated that of the Presocratics, wandering in error is caused by *até* (ruin) and *lethe* ('oblivion', or suffering without understanding) hiding 'the straight way of truth and justice from the human soul'. In Empedocles the *daimones* fall from Aletheia (unconcealedness) to Até, and in Plato the plains of Aletheia and of Lethe are similarly opposed. Additionally, when Plato's mortals pass through the barren plain of Lethe and drink from the river Ameles they are not only forgetting their past lives but encountering what in mythological terms was once the powerful river Styx,[33] the site, in the earlier Hesiodic world view, of the confluence of the immortals' power and the force of time and dissolution to destroy it.

In Hesiod's eighth-century BCE *Theogony*, the river Styx is the form taken by the god Horkos ('oath'), to which the other gods resort when they find themselves in unresolvable discord. When the water of the Styx is sought for this purpose, the god who has false intentions when the water is sprinkled on the ground becomes breathless and voiceless and endures long years of mortal exile.[34] Empedocles' 'false oath', which leads to wandering in barrenness through a fall from unconcealedness, and Plato's river Ameles, which follows upon a journey through barrenness and transmutes Horkos' power to resolve and exile into a relinquishing of memory, form a continuity around the question of the basis on which a mortal or immortal can gain self-knowledge. If even the immortal gods require a figure (Horkos/Oath) against which to measure purity of intention, a figure they fear and before which some will waver, then the mortal of the post-mythological age will not discover what has driven him – for a day, a year, a lifetime – without a practice embodying the earlier marker of immortal limit. Nightly recall, involving resolution, followed by yielding to sleep's oblivion, are practical consequences of being human following the discovery that cosmic operations can no longer be solely attributed to gods.

If 'right knowing' is difficult of attainment, 'right living' is no less so, and depends upon Empedocles' disciple Pausanias grasping what Empedocles has to teach him. Because 'Philia binds' and 'Neikos releases', a healer must also understand how bodies are crafted or fastened together and how they re-form themselves so as to be able to 'bind and release at the right moment'. In fifth-century BCE Greek understandings of human generation, including Hippocratic accounts, the seed of human life comes from all parts of the body and is present within male and female bodies. The rubbing and other movement involved in heterosexual activity causes seed from, for example, the spinal marrow and the kidneys to be transmitted between bodies, and in the female body the blended seed forms 'the embryonic kernel' of an emergent human. But sexual activity is also Strife, or releasing, as a later fragment from Democritus reveals: 'Sexual intercourse is a mild apoplexy; for man issues from man and is torn away, separated by a sort of blow.' On the macrocosmic level subterranean fire is the cause of the differentiation of elements beneath the earth, whence plants and rocks and the first men and women emerge, the belief in an earlier race of godlike humans being a ubiquitous component of ancient Greek cosmology. Strife '"frees" the . . . strength of fire' that causes cosmic germination, and Aphrodite, another of the names Empedocles gives to Love, draws seed from the parents and mixes and fastens it in the centre of the female body as she also mixes it in the earth.[35]

The slightly later Hippocratic text *On the Nature of the Child* details how parental seed is blended and condensed by heat in the womb so that 'a warm "breath"' develops within it, making a channel that becomes the umbilical cord. Similar elements move towards similar elements until bones 'become resistant' and 'branch off like a tree'. Analogously, in the cosmogony presented in the fourth-century BCE Hippocratic text *On Flesh*, initial agitation occurs when three elements are separated. Heat rises to form heaven while earth, retaining heat, remains below, and thick, wet air spreads around earth. 'While everything spins', heat retained in the earth causes putrefaction, which forms bones, while gluey materials form 'sinews and veins' as body parts re-form themselves. Empedoclean cosmic cycles function comparably, and it is important to note that Love or *Philia*, which binds, also has a deadly dimension. Aphrodite sucks elements and parts into the centre of the cosmos, 'nail[ing] them in bodies she then destroys . . . suffocating everything in a deadly embrace in which there are no more distinctions'. Strife gradually regains mastery by causing elements to move so that 'all the limbs of the god [tremble], each in turn', before the limbs move to find each other (14.82 (31), 1–3).[36]

While Love and Strife have distinctive phases in cosmic generation, then, their activities are imbricated, as are processes of human and cosmic generation. During each transition period the *kosmos* perishes to give rise to other *kosmoi*, and we read that as animals, including humans, are formed in the phase of increasing Love, while Strife retreats:

> . . . many neckless faces sprouted,
> and arms were wandering naked, bereft of shoulders,
> and eyes were roaming alone, in need of foreheads.
>
> (14.130 (57), 1–3)

A related passage presents a strange geographical image that does not occur elsewhere in Empedocles or in other ancient Greek authors. It describes how 'mortal limbs' come together 'through Love into one', while at other times the limbs are 'split apart through evil Quarrels' and 'wander each kind separately on the furthest shore of life' (14.59 (20 and Strasbourg papyrus ensemble c)). This evocative phrase, suggestive of exile but also extremity, indicates that in this world view every human action has consequences for others. Heterosexual acts cause reincarnation as wandering limbs are redistributed, and it is because of this that Empedocles forgoes and forbids Pausanias the eating of flesh. To do so is to keep 'wandering limbs imprisoned' so they cannot dissolve and take new form.[37]

In a sense, Empedocles teaches Pausanias how to avoid the life or lives he has himself lived. When he tells his disciple that he will 'learn all the drugs there are as a safeguard against evils and old age' and 'stop the force of the tireless winds that rush/ over the earth and devastate ... plowed fields' (14.40 (111), 1, 3–4), he indicates the possibility, but also the cost, of knowledge about the causes of events cosmic and human. For in order to 'change black rain into seasonal dryness/ for people, and summer-drought' into 'tree-nourishing waters' (6–8), Pausanius must 'cover up' (*stegein*) or contain Empedocles' teachings in his 'voiceless heart' (14.41 (5), 1–2). Recall that for the ancient Greeks the heart is the organ of thought and the seat of the mind's deliberations, and that Empedocles' swearing of a 'false oath' may have caused him to wander through lifetimes as a mortal. Pausanius is instructed here not only to retain knowledge but also to learn when to speak and when to maintain silence in terms of allegiances to existing codes of honour.

The opacity of human motivation effectively underwrites the emergence of democracy in Athens, a political form in itself unexpected and one that arose 'at first almost unobserved'. After the Mycenaean collapse at the end of the thirteenth century BCE, people began to move across Attika so that those who owned land had to interact with newcomers. In 594–593 BCE Solon, Archon of Athens, began to create boundaries in the region to resolve the problem of too many people working too little productive land, the collapse of agrarian networks and debtors being exiled or enslaved. Numerous public and private debts were abolished, and Athenians working lands became entitled to 'own' the lands they worked, provided they did not infringe on those of others. A new sense of civic belonging emerged. Laws were publicly displayed, and at the end of Solon's reign a civic centre (*agora*) had been established in which it was forbidden to build residences so that it could serve as a place of public assembly.[38]

It was the reforms of Kleisthenes in 508–507 BCE, however, that made Solonian efforts a formal reality. Civic status became inseparable from involvement in the *polis*, so that without participating in the assembly or justice systems a citizen could not secure life or land. Yet the Greeks 'saw religion as the cohesive force in every kind of social grouping', and for them, thus, an oath was 'a form of self-consecration' that could conflict with civic duties. 'The humblest citizen was . . . constantly forced to choose between "respecting" and "defiling" the gods' of a given region or community. Perjury, impugning the gods by committing oneself to an action or state of mind and intention falsely, along with breaking an oath, caused intergenerational punishments. At the same time, oaths could not be easily forgone, as even the 'clubs that existed to provide mutual aid in court cases' were founded on them.[39]

Under Kleisthenes Athens was organized into *demes*, administrative centres for local inhabitants constituted across the region and thereafter by lot, so that all ten tribes had members from 'city, coast, and inland' areas. Citizens became known by *deme* rather than by family, and rural and urban areas were united. As *demes* were largely self-organizing and functioned as the active link between people and *polis*, pre-existing religious confraternities played a significant part in them. Robert Connor argues that sixth-century worship of Dionysos was itself an instantiation of a new kind of community. Unlike the Pythian god Apollo at Delphi, Dionysos was accessible to all and, having himself 'come from abroad', appealed especially to wanderers and exiles, those without inherited rights and excluded from cults associated with established families. Dionysos, 'the god of liquid elements – wine, milk and honey', makes boundaries fluid, but he also represents the fact that those who came to Athens from elsewhere were essential to the experiment that Athenian citizenship became.[40]

By the mid-fifth century BCE all adult males whose families owned land could take part in the Athenian assembly and participate in the election of 'major administrative officers'. There was payment for jury service, and, after the crushing defeat of the Peloponnesian War (431–404 BCE), payment for attendance at assembly. Magistrates were selected by lot, which diminished aristocratic influence. While inherited privilege could be suspect, so was expertise however, as the fate of Socrates shows. Athenian leaders were the first politicians to '[seek] power by persuasion', and, given the high value placed on oratory, courts were more concerned with 'questions of motive, standing, and substance' than with juridical precedent, even though the former could be hard to ascertain. Socrates, though, claims to be on the side of civic obligation and established moral law. He insists, in a wager made with his person, that the continually examined life, and not merely the outwardly appealing or readily explicable life, should be available to all.[41]

Homeless mind

Socrates' own origins are unclear. Born in about 469 BCE, he was indicted in Athens in 399 BCE, found guilty and executed in prison by poison. Both Plato's and Xenophon's accounts of his trial treat Socrates as the subject of an oracular pronouncement by Apollo at Delphi. While the charge brought was, in both versions, corrupting the young and failing to recognize the gods of the city, the force of the former charge depended on the latter, and Athenian law did not have a detailed definition of piety. Both Xenophon and Plato indicate that the charge was related to Socrates following an interpretation of the Oracle at Delphi that was seen by others to conflict with his duty, as a citizen of Athens, to the city. But the specific charge Socrates disobeyed, in Plato's account at least, was a magistrate's order conveyed to him during the reign of the Thirty Tyrants (404–403 BCE) to travel to arrest Leon of Salamis and bring him to Athens, knowing that he would be taking him to his execution (*Apology* 32c–d). While neither Plato's *Crito* nor his *Apology* indicate clearly what Socrates' duty to the non-democratic legal regime would have been, the *Apology* makes clear that Socrates did not regard this order to have supplanted the existing laws of Athens. The Thirty erased but did not repeal laws, and a tyranny does not necessarily alter the power of established law by other means.[42]

It is the nature and manner of Socrates' defence that is interesting for our purposes, for it clearly shows that Socrates derived his mandate for action in support of Athenian law from the requirement to respond interpretatively to oracular pronouncement. In Plato's account Socrates' disciple Chaerephon asks the Pythia whether anyone is wiser than Socrates and is told that no one is, a fact to which Chaerephon's brother testifies at Socrates' trial. Xenophon has the Oracle say that no one is more 'liberal-minded or just or upright' than Socrates,[43] but Socrates clearly derives his mandate for conversing about wisdom from the negative form of the pronouncement. While Socrates never claims to know that he knows nothing, his daily conversations with the citizens of Athens, 'these wanderings of mine', as he describes them (22a), show him that those who think they know things seldom do, the inference being that Socrates, at least, does not fall prey to this positivization of the Oracle's answer.

The Pythia's function was 'to tell the divine purpose in relation to coming events', and the most common type of question was whether a given course of action was better than another. An indication of 'divine purpose' certainly requires further human interpretation given the gods know more than humans about likely outcomes, and a negative answer may open more questions than it resolves. It is this quality of inscrutability that Socrates responds to with his unusual mode of life, a kind of civics of unsettlement that is equally inscrutable (33). He remains in Athens to 'perform something like labours' – insistently questioning all who claim to know things about their beliefs – so that the Oracle's negative response to a question about wisdom attains some meaning (22a). It is in this sense that Socrates responds to the originary conditions of Athenian democracy, which were to find and debate ways to manage diversity and conflict on human and larger generational or cosmic levels. The Delphic Oracle was thought to be at the exact centre of the Hellenic world, that is, the world that those who came to live in Athens took to be theirs by identification with the city more than by accident of birth or heritage. Socrates resists the charge that he is a Sophist (33a)[44] on the basis that Sophists, experts in the art of rhetoric, wander from place to place receiving payment for imparting novel ways of thinking. To do this is to make wisdom the product of techniques taught by others, rather than using one's own lack of certainty to participate in the democratic form.

And unlike the Sophists, Socrates remains in Athens, despite the view that other places are more effectively governed. For Plato's Socrates, Sophists do not displace citizens from assumptions supporting the belief that they are living good or just lives, assumptions on which they may rely unthinkingly. As if in teasing answer to the charge that Socrates offers superficial, roving wisdom for personal gain, Socrates' defence in Plato's *Apology* is formally or structurally digressive. The digression occurs, moreover, at the mid-point of the text of Socrates' words at trial, just as the Oracle, a check on human motivation, is at the sacred centre of the life of Athens, and as resolution is practised, altered and revised by talking in the city's central civic places. Here Socrates posits two hypothetical objections to his claim to serve the interests of the city: first, the question whether he is ashamed to have put his life in danger, and second, why he has not formally involved himself in politics, given his concern with other people's beliefs (28b, 31a).[45]

To the first objection, Socrates claims that fear of death should have nothing to do with moral judgement. If he were 'posted by the god ... to live as a philosopher examining [himself] and others' and deserted this post through fear of death, he would indeed be claiming wisdom he could not have. To 'fear death ... is to think one knows things one does not know', for no one knows what death is like and only the belief that one does could make a person fear it (29a–c). To the second objection, why he has not entered politics, Socrates defers to the 'divine and superhuman' thing that has vexed him since childhood, which drives him to be at home nowhere and to trouble the views of others (31c). This disables him from being a popular leader of fellow citizens. In this defence, however, Socrates does not rely on a second-order authority named 'the gods', for it is made clear elsewhere in Plato that Socrates does not believe the Oracle's pronouncement about him is true because it is an oracular pronouncement. For Socrates an action is not worth doing because the gods love it. If a thing is worth doing it is for reasons humans must discover. In this way, as Francisco Gonzalez puts it, 'questioning the divine is Socratic piety.'[46]

While Xenophon maintains that Socrates believes that 'the royal art' of democratic governance resides in static instrumentalities – 'to make the citizens rich, free' or 'undisturbed by faction' – Plato's Socrates makes a different claim. He seeks the moral reasoning according to which such actions should be pursued. Correspondingly, Plato's Socrates supports thought mobilized in the form of just or useful actions rather than envisaged outcomes: the exercise of 'fiscal prudence, of military science, of shrewd diplomacy'. While these actions are likely to benefit more people than will a preconceived understanding of the good, Socrates' view of 'the royal art' is yet more radical than this in Plato. While no one citizen is master of 'the royal art', every person in a democracy, including, in Athens, the unfree such as slaves and women, is obliged to seek it. Everyone should be ruled by his or her or their knowledge of the good in the performance of his or her or their duties, a knowledge only attainable by free-ranging thinking, and everyone is a master of some part of state craft achieved through the rational operation of mind and body.[47]

Socrates' wager with his life and his refusal to escape from prison indicates, at the least, that he was himself governed by a conception of the good that exceeded an account of his physical well-being. 'The function of Socratic *aporia*', a disquiet of the mind, the embarrassment of hearing that no one than yourself is wiser, 'is to create new movement'. Socrates the gadfly disables others from 'walking . . . in a straight line' (*Apology* 30e).[48] But he also enables them to form reasons for their actions that do not falsely substantiate democracy's promise that the law safeguards citizens' freedom, as does, for instance, the idea that democracy involves copying other citizens' actions. Instead, people can and must use their freedom to interpret, debate and, when necessary, trouble the law as to its reason for being, since the law is created by humans for humans.

Disaster and rebuilding

Socrates' provocative influence is arguably one of the reasons Plato wrote dialogues, or conversations. And Plato's own account of the origin of the cosmos is given, from the mouth of one Timaeus, in answer to a question from Socrates about the city's constitution or 'political structure' described on the previous day (*Timaeus* 17c). Socrates wants to know specifically how the others (Critias, Timaeus, Hermocrates and an unnamed fourth) think the city would conduct itself at war, including how it would 'go about negotiating with other cities' (19c).[49] The *Timaeus*' mapping of cosmos planning and making correspondingly performs a task that is challenging and unavoidably imperfect. The cosmos is apparently unique and self-sufficient, like Athens in its idealized form. But the cosmos is necessarily maintained – and repaired – by humans, who cannot understand all its workings completely. The absences and false starts Plato builds into the story should be seen in light of these realities, as should the radical decision to make the creator of the cosmos a *demiourgos* or 'craftsman', a person whose roles in war- and peacetime were as essential to the city-state as they were undistinguished and largely unremembered. There is ambiguity about the term *demiourgos*, which Plato exploits. In fifth- and fourth-century BCE Athens, the *demiourgos*, potentially the most mobile of city dwellers, is subjugated. What brings people together as citizens is opposed to the specialization required of trades. This does not obviate the dependence of the city upon its artisans, however. Plato seems alive to the contradiction whereby, while the soldier and the farmer still depend on the gods for some aspect of the fulfilment of their labours, the artisan depends only on his trade, which no citizen can do without. It is in this sense that, as Pierre Vidal-Naquet has claimed, the artisan is the 'hidden hero' of Greek civilization.[50]

The *Timaeus* begins with a question from Socrates about the whereabouts of the fourth person present at the preceding day's discussion of the city's structure, and a request that the current day's talk provide something that was missing the day before. Socrates had been asked for his views on 'matters of government' (20b), and as the *Timaeus* begins he reiterates the point previously reached up to the characteristically Socratic point of narrative disruption. In asking for a war story, Socrates has counterposed to a narrative rendition of ideal governance both the founding condition of Athenian democracy – antagonism and resolution – and its most ubiquitous test. He begins by expressing dissatisfaction with the way the preceding day's discussion rendered the city static, like living animals in a painting one desires to see 'engaged in some struggle or conflict' (19b). In referring to the ideal city as set out in the *Republic*, Socrates indicates another significant instance of something missing. In that text, the only means of 'realizing the ideal city' is the rulership of the philosopher kings.[51] On the day the *Timaeus* conversation begins, then, the three interlocutors, covering for an unexpectedly missing fourth, must do what the philosopher kings, who only think and rule, cannot. They must respond to Socrates' challenge by modelling the social challenge made by the provisionality and wilful animality of war.

The speakers have previously agreed upon their speeches' order. Timaeus will speak about the world's creation up to the point of the creation of human beings. Once humans are made, Critias will, reprising Socrates, 'receive' the best educated ones from him and establish them as Athenians fit to participate in the story (27a–b). In this way the other remaining speakers will have moved to fill the gaps surrounding Socrates' summary. Critias responds to Socrates and presents an opening for Timaeus, whence Timaeus will describe the planetary beginnings that precede Socrates' earlier account of an ideal state and Critias will describe the citizens' exploits in wartime from there. In reality, however, this is not what happens. When Timaeus ends his creation narrative Critias' story about Athens and Atlantis begins, only to break off unfinished.[52]

Critias, then Timaeus, then Critias thus provide three provisional responses to Socrates, and, as scholars have noted, the role of contingency in world creation and good governance is underlined. The reader is given a 'careful disorder' that will recur in Timaeus' account of world-making. In an illuminating discussion of the structure of the *Timaeus*, Verity Harte shows how its account of world creation is a 'pretence of sequence' that is actually a performance of repeatedly retraced beginnings, three in all. In the first beginning, the craftsman god makes the body of the living creature that is the cosmos (31b), then its soul (34b), the other planets (38c–d), and then the 'rational part' or soul of the human being (41d–e).[53] He then begins the story again by describing how the *demiourgos* would first have had to form, from pre-cosmic vestiges of fire, air, water and earth, the elements of which the cosmos' body was made (53b). Since the third beginning, at 69a8, proceeds from the two earlier accounts of world and elemental creation to detail the construction of the human soul and body but does not revisit originary wandering, it need not concern us further.

Before Timaeus' narrative begins, Critias explains that in the inherited story he plans to tell, the city of Atlantis, which can be seen as contemporary Athens given a mythical cast, will achieve good governance and excellence in battle, at which point it will suddenly be extinguished by disaster from the sea. Before his second beginning, Timaeus has provided an explanation of 'intelligent craftsmanship', the first or macrocosmic part of world-making (47e). Now, he must provide an account of microcosmic things that have to be made by necessity (47e), where necessity means chance or disorder, and also potential calamity, either because a physical process has what we would now call chaotic principles or because its nature resists good design.[54] Here Timaeus introduces 'the wandering cause', the nature of which is to 'cause movement and change' (48a), and the narrative, in turn, returns to the first act of making to perform its second beginning. This suggests that the wandering cause, a first principle whose nature is mobile and erratic, nonetheless plays a formative role in good world-making and good war negotiations.

Structurally, the wandering cause 'causes' the first repetition in the narrative, which shows the nature of the first creative act to have been one of 'intellect'. The wandering cause must now, of necessity, be included in world-making, hence the creation of the four interactive and non-static elements. As Harte notes, each of the three demi-urgic accounts of creation varies as to which activity the craftsman god enacted first, and all involve imposing order on things found 'moving in a disorderly fashion' (30a5; 69b3).[55] Fittingly, the mobile, 'wandering' cause is in the medial position of the dialogue in at least two threefold performative schemas. It is introduced by the middle speaker – and in the second of that speaker's three beginnings – in the consecutive series Socrates, Timaeus, Critias that substantially begins, sustains and ends the dialogue as we have it (with Critias' account uncompleted). And it occurs second in the series Critias, Timaeus, Critias, which respectively foretells disaster to Athens, shows how to make and remake its components (in Timaeus' narrative) and then how to build it again (in Critias' account of Athens as Atlantis). The wandering cause thus necessitates, in the case of the first series, the mediatory acts of negotiating competing narratives, as Socrates', Timaeus' and Critias' speeches are consecutive attempts to reach a more satisfying account of world-making proper as well as war negotiation and world rebuilding. And in the second series, the wandering cause necessitates the discovery and enactment of solutions to cosmic disasters, with a focus on the local level of making elemental forms.

The narrative's second beginning entails an account of the pre-cosmos before the *demiourgos* begins his labours. In the first act of macrocosmic world-making, only an unchanging model and material copy were needed. To form elements, there will need to be an account of space, a matter Timaeus calls 'difficult and obscure' (48a) and 'the *receptacle* of all becoming' (48a). The term used to describe the receptacle, *khôra*, first appears in Homer to describe 'land', 'ground' or 'region'.[56] In the *Timaeus* it refers to both that in which and that out of which the elements of the cosmos are made. While it is both space and matter, it never changes its character so as to alter the things made within it, although it may appear differently at different times (50a, c–e).

Plato uses several analogies for the receptacle, one being that of the 'neutral base' artisans make to which they add the makings of perfumes (20e), another being the mouldable material used to shape gold. Of this material, we cannot readily say in what component resides the 'goldness', because gold can take different shapes and because metallurgy is extraction, smelting, refining – all processes involving change (50a–b). Donald Zeyl suggests we see the receptacle as a wave of the sea, which 'needs a material substratum throughout its journey' if it is to be itself, for 'no wave is at any time waterless.' Yet it is not only the matter in question – water – that makes a wave a wave, but rather the 'continuity' of a 'contiguous series of "places"' that it occupies while it exists, not unlike the way the wandering cause both links and interacts with the evolving demiurgic abilities of the human. David Sedley similarly suggests 'a gap in traffic' as an example of an integral, ultimately characterless space without which there could be no progression or meaningful movement within a system of transport.[57]

Lastly, we come to the receptacle's shaking, in which it 'sways irregularly in every direction as it is shaken' by the things it contains, 'and being set in motion it in turn shakes them' (52e). This shaking separates the elements so that, as in a sieve, heavy, dense material congregates together while lighter and more unlike material moves further apart. So the elements take their respective places in the cosmos. The sieve in question is a 'hand-held [basket] . . . used in agriculture for sorting grain, oats, barley'. And the places to which the elements go are like the unformed regions of the pre-sixth-century BCE Greek Aegean in which people gradually separate, move and come together to achieve social form. Note that Plato's analogies for world-making are, like Empedocles', artisanal. Luc Brisson finds 'iron working and welding' in addition to smelting, carpentry, potting, painting and weaving in the dialogue. In Empedocles, Aphrodite's *crafty hands* or devices make 'bolts' or 'pegs of love' (14.137, 8) that she uses to 'rivet', 'solidify' and glue or bind elements together at the centre of the cosmos.[58] But Aphrodite's labour must yield to Strife, which makes the world's limbs or mortal components shake and come apart so the world can change as it interacts with human beings.

We could say that the Greek city-state, in peace and war, materializes the models of world-making presented by Empedocles and Plato, which would not, in itself, be surprising. 'From the time of the Dark Ages', a Greek city was 'a fortified settlement' that controlled a fertile valley or central plain. If border posts were overrun, the hoplite or landed citizen army phalanx would fight in the plain from a position chosen for advantage. Since phalanx combat makes three sides (flanks and rear) weaker, defeat in the plain would cause a retreat to the outskirts and an eventual inward besieging of the enemy. 'In a last extremity', refuge could be taken in the acropolis, from which it would still be possible to strike back at looters once they came. While this pattern shows similarities with the sequential or continual phasing of Harmony into Strife and War in Empedocles, it is also relevant to the *Timaeus*, in which the craftsman must persuade his heterogeneous materials into workable form, but can only persuade them so far. Plato calls the cosmos the 'result of necessity being conquered by intelligent persuasion' (48a),[59] but the dialogue as a whole suggests that this 'conquering' in the form of 'persuasion' needed to be done, in the world from which the 'likely story' comes (30b), repeatedly.

Why? By the time Plato wrote his late dialogues, to which the *Timaeus* and *Critias* belong, the previously accepted rules of war in Athens had changed. From the early to mid-fifth century BCE, the hoplites' role in stabilizing the city was undertaken by the navy. And as Athens became an empire, its fleet was increasingly made up of poorer, unlanded citizens and slaves. Athenian hoplites also became marines and engaged in scavenging and plundering. The fleet drew *metics* – 'resident alien businessmen, bankers, and traders, an entire shadow city of outsiders' without 'formal rights in the polis'. During the Peloponnesian War, Athens' landless population was comprehensively slaughtered. The time of seasonal battles in defence of land in which non-combatants were largely untargeted and surrendered opponents not unduly pursued was over. In the fourth century BCE, when the *Timaeus* and *Critias* were most likely written, mercenaries replaced citizen-soldiers, conflicts between rich and poor escalated, and the city faced repeated civil wars.[60]

One of the greatest threats to amity in the Greek city-state was *'stasis'*, the taking of positions that became parties and later factions. Vidal-Naquet argues that in Atlantis, the city Plato invents in the *Critias* to stand for Athens, the Greek city-state 'meets and vanquishes herself'. But who is the victor? While the 'structure of Athens is fixed once and for all' – as fourth- and third-century BCE Athens was forced to focus its military energies on defensiveness – that of the imagined city, Atlantis, 'is a continuous creation'. Critias presages his inherited tale with a digression he says is Solon's, about the tale of Atlantis Solon heard having come from the Egyptian tongue, and says this is to avoid '[surprise] if you should . . . hear Hellenic names given to foreigners'. As Critias is speaking Greek, the digression is unnecessary unless the point is to indicate the inevitable intermingling of populations. In other ways as well, Plato's Atlantis as Athens is structurally built by 'the play of *apeiron*', of mixedness or 'non-identity'.[61]

In the *Statesman*, Plato has the Eleatic Stranger tell a story about the cosmos' movement in which it is also made clear that human creatures, the 'parts' of the cosmos no longer able to be grown 'within the earth', must now be self-reliant in the sense that they, like the gods, can reverse established orders. And when change is necessary in a society such that it must help repair its world, persons with knowledge of *kairos* – of how the indeterminacies of time enable us to thrive in indeterminate conditions – will be needed. Thus, the true statesman will be one who knows not only what the best course of action in a given situation might be, but what might be the right moment in which to perform it.[62] Of necessity, such knowledge is often second nature to the one – like the refugee – for whom work gives home its meaning, and which work allows the settled the less examined meaning of theirs. In collaborating, as in the Greek city-state of Plato's time, on the question of what is lost and gained both by established habits of self-protection and greater change in service of the world we live in, humans may yet find ways to foster forms of life that neither disregard the past nor halt invention. In the next chapter we will consider some challenges to the formation of habits early humans faced as they met wanderers whose worlds' *raison d'être* altered their own *raison d'être* in turn.

3

OTHERS

I n January 2019 citizens of Sudan, Africa's largest country, chanted 'We are all Darfur' while calling for the ousting of its thirty-year president, Omar al-Bashir. The move was in part a response to the president blaming rebels from Darfur for destabilizing the country. The claim was unlikely to stick as the Sudanese Professionals Association, a group of trade unions representing doctors, lawyers and journalists, joined with other protesters in identifying with the country's most under-resourced and under-represented region. Protests were triggered by the government's late 2017 plan to end wheat subsidies. While the decision was partly reversed in response to protests in early 2018 as the price of bread doubled, Sudan's economy contracted substantially that year, producing an inflation rate at around 70 per cent – second only to Venezuela's – and a populace that, in 2019, clearly felt it had nothing more to lose. Identification with Darfur at least partly disables the way in which, accelerating in the 1980s and continuing until at least 2006, a series of misleading binary oppositions has been used by successive Sudanese governments and Western media to imply that conflict in Sudan is inevitable and unresolvable.[1] One among these, nomad/settler, makes Darfur's history relevant to this study. This binary, along with others including Arab/African and light-skinned/dark-skinned, has not only caused people with a long history of managing conflicts over natural resources to see those on the other side of the construct as an existential threat to their livelihoods, or as 'others' to themselves. It has also been used to make aspects of this (mis)perception factual, as governments sought to increase discord in the populace by arming particular groups.

Devils on horseback

Darfur, in the west and southwest of Sudan, has a sustained history of continuous state formation. The sultanate that was formed in 1650 at Al-Fashir, having adopted Islam as state religion in 1800, remained autonomous until 1916. The British, who took formal control of Sudan in 1914, set up the Native Administration system by which chiefs administered 'tribes' for the government, with a *dar* (homeland) accompanying each chieftaincy. This was a colonizer's version of tribal hierarchies, based on ethnicity rather than citizenship and privileging settled groups. It was undertaken in part to weaken the power of southern tribes of cattle herders, and education and advancement favoured those at the top. Sudanese people in the centre of the country watered by the Nile have tended to regard Darfurians as low-status labourers. With Sudan's independence in 1956, Khartoum continued the Nilocentric trend. The questions were whether Sudan should unite with Egypt to the north, and what status should be given to the south. This debate lent itself to an Arab/African division because non-Muslim Sudanese have historically been more prevalent in the south.[2]

While Darfur has always been ethnically mixed, Native Administration cemented the idea and practice of tribal land rights. In the 1970s President Ja'afar Nimeiri dismantled the system specifically to cut across tribal *dars*, leaving a power vacuum. Sahelian drought in 1973 and 1983–4 pushed northerners south from the Darfur savannah, which is normally without rainfall for eight to eleven months annually. The displaced, attempting to settle in the south and west, met demands from settled Fur for homeland rights due to pastureland being overtaxed by nomadic herders. Yet Darfur has traditions of reconciliation, and relations between farmers and cattle nomads accessing post-harvest pastures have historically been good. While Native Administration impoverished the landless Arab tribes of north Darfur most of all, identity in Darfur has historically been fluid, with tribes sometimes transitioning from herder to farmer and changing their self-description from Arab to African, or the reverse.[3] When land failed more irretrievably in the 1970s and '80s and more herders tried to access the richly watered region of the Jebel Marra mountain range of the former Fur Sultanate, identity categories hardened too. A terrible irony was that as Cold War superpower military investment waned, illegal arms markets reopened, and refugees from Libya's 1978–87 wars with Chad fled across Darfur's borders with captured weapons, so that '*dar*less camel nomads' and other wanderers moved not in the old way of neighbourly accommodations to herds but by arms trafficking. While an obvious means to livelihood, these arms destroyed the nomadic honour code. Ancient lifeways requiring 'loyalty, hospitality, and strenuous self-discipline' while camel herding included 'communal responsibility for homicide'. But ready availability of AK-47s (Kalashnikov rifles) changed this. Payment for a single massacre could exceed the camel wealth of an entire ancestral line.[4]

The Nimeiri government ignored the 1980s drought, which led to famine in 1986–7. Continuing disinterest in Darfur produced, however, something arguably more consequential: lost reference points enabling near parodies of nomadic lifestyles at scale. As Arab Chadian rebels sought Jebel Marra they were pursued into Sudan where paramilitary forces rustled weapons along with camel herds, while Khartoum did nothing to stop Muammar Gaddafi's Islamic Legionnaires following deep into the interior, historic – now motorized – caravan routes. Libya also provided weapons for Sudan's war in the south. The government then armed groups of Arab militants with land grievances – the Murahaleen (nomads), or *fursan* (horsemen), the precursors of the Janjawiid (perhaps from *jinn*, devil, and *jawad*, horse) – which it then blamed for acting as armed units, using the language of criminality and banditry. While criminal elements certainly existed, the government's initial arming of tribal militias was opportunistic and in time they also provided cover. 'Tribal conflict' between nomads and farmers enabled the denial that a war was going on at all.[5]

Drought – absence of water, of usable land – coupled with absence of governance made for increased polarization and stasis once a neighbouring war and arms flow were added in. This stasis was readily disguised as age-old movement, as a cycle (nomads versus settlers) that always returns. But it was a cycle that increased in vehemence as its terms were unhooked from the customary reference points that had enabled accommodations. From the 1980s to the 2000s, first small arms, then militia, then war gave the binary Arab/African (or Arab supremacist/Fur nativist) false trenchancy, and this in turn supported ethnic cleansing. In 1994 Omar al-Bashir's government divided Darfur into three states, with the aim of diminishing Fur power. In the 2000s government air force helicopter gunships, often foreign mercenary-flown, bombed Fur villages with Janjawiid on horseback or armoured vehicles following, killing potential rebels, raping women, burning villages and poisoning wells. Tribes that supported the Fur rebellion were also targeted, and about 1.8 million people were displaced.[6]

The government's continued mobilization of *dar*less camel nomads, *dar*less smaller tribes and Chadians in addition to the army against the 2003 Fur rebellion of non-Arab sedentary and nomadic groups was thought by some to serve the purpose of keeping the army from rising against the government, given a high proportion of its soldiers are from the west. Some refused to attack their home villages, so more Janjawiid were recruited. The Janjawiid are the precursors of today's Rapid Support Forces (RSF), who in June of 2019 brutally targeted civilians in reprisal for the April protests. Their current leader, Mohamed 'Hemeti' Dagolo, owns gold mines and a trading company and most likely controls migration across the Sahara to Libya under the Khartoum process, whereby the EU funds Sudan to deal with trafficking and people smuggling from the Horn of Africa to Europe. The RSF is now effectively the Sudanese infantry, and Hemeti's mercenary endeavours proceed without oversight. Alex de Waal calls him not so much a nineteenth-century freebooter as 'a twenty first-century phenomenon: a military-political entrepreneur whose paramilitary business empire transgresses territorial and legal boundaries'.[7]

Futures

Nomadic elements being used for government enforcement is nothing new. But it is worth considering the international conditions of Hemeti's rise. Since 2001, U.S. concern with Africa has focused on its oil reserves and its role in countering terrorism. The second Bush administration seemed to believe that terrorists hide in secret, foreign lairs that are always 'elsewhere', while yet battle could be taken directly to them. However the history of guerrilla operations shows that not only does the successful terrorist routinely pass among the general population, but a given percentage of a population will assist a terrorist either passively or actively in the interests of something it fears losing or something it hopes to gain.[8] America, a wealthy, settled nation that is largely untroubled by sustained, outright conflict, is inclined to fear Middle Eastern or African others who would attack its grand buildings and cherished institutions. It wants cheap African oil, to continue selling its arms to African nations for hefty sums and for Africa to reduce terrorist threats to America.

The problem comes with how such goals are to be achieved. De Waal characterizes African political markets as rentier operations because African leaders at all levels are skilled at deriving maximum circulatory value from the perception of opportunity accompanying access to tangibles whose benefits are intangible and may thus be increased. Power is consolidated not, as in Cold War times, by means of 'geostrategic rents'[9] – that is, not on the basis of a given region's likely value to one or another superpower and thus to others – but in the much more fluid, self-propagating manner with which we have become familiar since the 1990s. The decentralizing practices of globalization provide increasing opportunities to do more things for more people, or to promise to, while the outcomes of increased opportunities to game systems and graft earlier sharp practices into more network nodes are less seldom foreseen, or are foreseen and disavowed, by Western powers.

Renting a plot of land out as a military base is a way to maximize the number of international players who owe the renter loyalty that can in turn be used to garner and offer favour to others. European and U.S. arms manufacturers want to keep export income up, yet the latest weaponry is not necessarily needed to wage wars. Arms manufacturers compete not on the basis of specifications and high-end conventional weapons systems but on an array of side benefits: 'an elaborate apparatus of offsets, kickbacks and commodity barter (especially oil) that comes with being a major arms purchaser'. Such a person brokers imagined and real opportunities for the advancement of others' self interests, opportunities that destroy and enable people along with the capability of land. While in Africa oil income is not readily spread to the wider economy, artisanal minerals like gold and coltan (used in the making of electronic devices) can be mined and transported by smaller-scale investors dealing with 'provincial elites, such as army officers, rebel commanders' or the chiefs of local tribes.[10] Khartoum's historical neglect of the west – inhabited by poor farmers, landless herders and the (former) national army's lowest ranked – meant that maximizing ways of extending favour to others would likely reach saturation in someone of Hemeti's kind.

Hemeti's forebears are from the Rizeigat tribe of Chadian camel herders who sought refuge in Darfur in the 1980s. Darfuri farmers looking to prosper at this time harvested and sold crop stalks rather than allowing pastoralists to feed on them. Animals were let loose into their farms. Farmland blocked migration routes and pastoralists looting livestock worsened their conditions, having more animals to feed from waterless reserves.[11] As mentioned earlier, identity in Darfur has historically been fluid. The terms 'nomad' and 'sedentary' were transmorphic well before Native Administration divided some of the country's people into likely sounding tribes. Why the situation in Chad, Darfur and Sudan since the 1970s is so important is because in this region the terms 'nomad' and 'sedentary' have all but changed places, each becoming fixed to the other's historical field of reference. The working inversion of a distinction of such longevity and significance for humanity's thinking about its past social forms, a distinction formerly occupied more interchangeably in Darfur, shows the fractal impact of first colonization and then globalization in the continent.

In the modern language of rights settled groups in the region with *hakura*, or rights by ancestral charter and long practice, claimed theirs as 'customary' and 'tribal'. Those 'with diminished or no homeland (*dar*) rights claimed access to productive natural resources' as citizens, as the moderns of modernity who are national subjects and residents of towns. Racism and ethnic wars developed as each side saw itself losing control. Khartoum and Gaddafi's Arab Gathering (nomads or funders of nomads) countered Darfur's sedentaries, aligned with the Chadian non-Arab forces of Hissène Habré. The term Janjawiid was revived at this time, having been used in the 1960s pejoratively to describe poor nomads. The Janjawiid became part of a larger, ongoing crisis of nomadism across the Sahelian belt which the glamour of the 'war on terror' only increased, with teen and pre-teen recruits flocking to mobile militias from Sierra Leone and Liberia to eastern Congo and from northern Uganda to Mozambique.[12]

Hemeti became the political CEO of a transnational empire, or the government's chief nomad warlord, in part because Khartoum relied overlong on being able to keep the distant west of Sudan, with its complex of border loyalties, *at* a distance, despite it being recruiting grounds for the army. Perception of distance was compromised by the government's need to seem to have favours to give, something that translates to power in many African cultures. And by dint of the way the capital of land or arms (or oil or gold or diamonds), along with reputation, can broker a future ever less subject to the colonial fiction of separable nations, Hemeti bided his time in Sudan's hard-won Sovereignty Council before playing key roles in the October 2021 coup, forestalling the scrutiny of business interests promised by the democratic process.[13]

But there is something else in play here. Nomadic histories provide nomadic peoples with advanced skills of symbolic distance perception and scaling. What was once a matter of calculating how long it might take to manage one's household until the next remembered watering place and what to do when encountering others in similar straits became a matter, for some in this region, of bypassing such exigencies altogether. Yet when this occurs the exigency itself, in the form of the memory of the need for not only physical but human – that is, meaningful and cooperational – survival, is still present. It is otherwise shorn of content and available for continual reinvestment.[14] One no longer herds camels but providers of money for guns and, in time, things yet more untrackable. In bypassing something like historical arrangements around water, urgency itself can be magnified, which is a recipe not only for further wars but for further capricious severings of ancient affects – the progenitors of feelings about places and resources – from customary management. Because that process is already in play in wars – by definition occasions when each side believes affect or feeling about resources or pride and honour is unrecognized by the other and to convey it force is needed – it can produce further wars we may not recognize as such in time to comprehend or intervene in them. We may also fail to grasp the impacts of these not-quite-wars on living places.

Nonlinearity

I suggest above that the destruction of nomadic lifeways costs *everyone* in a given region, including sedentaries. This is because nomadic groups preserve the ability to function at the interstices not only of regions but of world views and to scale the complexity of their production and survival up or down around a range of more and less predictable conditions. A growing body of scholarship now recognizes the extent to which our understanding of civilization privileges sedentary agricultural societies, thus obscuring the way all political arrangements develop, which is by way of trade-offs made with others in order to support beneficial relationships over time. Because nomads must sustain such relationships over spatial distances while managing transport and other kinds of logistics, their cultural practices are often syncretic and adoptive rather than separatist and divisive. And efficacious political systems can be generated in nomadic polities by 'activating the political impact' of itinerant or fleeting groupings of power and ideas, since a mobile or semi-mobile population cannot take the stability of climatic, political or socio-economic conditions for granted.[15] But nor, increasingly, can settled populations.

Why was it that humans, who for most of our history have been nomadic, chose to settle and domesticate? While the ultimate reasons may continue to elude us, the intensification of resource use involved in growing crops and keeping animals, thought to have started between 15,000 and 5,000 years ago, was perpetuated once it began to support larger populations, since more food was needed to sustain them. Permanent agricultural settlements first emerged in Iran, Iraq, Syria and Turkey in the region sometimes called the Fertile Crescent, with domesticated plants appearing around 8500 BCE. Good levels of energy relative to output were provided by wild cereals with large edible seeds in collectible quantities, enabling a relatively easy transition to cultivation. The Mediterranean climate, a diversity of plants and animals, and possibly minimal competition from hunter-gatherers combined to make this part of southwest Asia dependent on crops and domesticated animals by about 6,000 BCE. While hunters and cultivators have historically lived side by side in several of the world's areas, because people in the Fertile Crescent supported themselves so effectively, features we associate with civilization – cities, writing, government, law – came into recognizable being there for the first time.[16]

These developments affect how we see the mobile pastoralists in and near the Crescent, pastoralists being those who move herds for pasture, and arguably how we see nomads in general, long thought of as existing outside civilization. While I focus below primarily on the horse-riding nomads of the Eurasian Steppe, other nomads with long histories include the yak herders of the Tibetan Plateau, the sheep and goat pastoralists of southwest and central Asia, the Bedouin – camel-herding nomads inhabiting the Sahara and Arabian deserts – and the cattle nomads of the sub-Saharan African savannah. There is overlap in types of livelihood: some mobile pastoralists also farm and fish. And unlike foragers, pastoral nomads have often proved to be equal or superior to their settled counterparts in organization and influence. Nomads do not need written records, and while these have historically made it easier to study the achievements of settled, literate polities than to study nomads, a further reason is that the records of settled polities are readily simplified. We can track the development of law and government in the southwest Asian Neolithic (the Fertile Cresent) because a relatively stable, localized population pertains and because, since the 1648 Treaty of Westphalia that ended the European Thirty Years War, the territorial sovereign state system, which contains similar elements, has been the default mode for understanding human habitation.[17]

Yet tying historical developments to fixity of place skews records. Nomad–settler interaction is important because the nomad-inhabited deserts and grasslands of Arabia and Eurasia, often described as peripheral to the Crescent, form 'the dominant landscape of the region'. Settled civilizations often gain or become more established by absorbing nomadic elements. Some consider that the adoption of elements of steppe (mobile, horse-mounted) warfare by the Chinese may have helped create a unified Chinese state in the late third century BCE. And Anne Porter finds that, looking for the causes of settled socio-political organization in the Crescent, some of the period's key attributes – urbanism, residence-based governance, writing – likely resulted from tensions within society *between* its mobile and non-mobile components, rather than from the intrinsic advantages of settled life.[18]

A focus on the state has meant that, until at least the 1970s, nomads were seen to inhabit relatively unorganized kinship groups. In fact, nomadic polities transmitted less their ethnic culture than an organizational or imperial formation, originally made up of several different cultural elements and with a strong emphasis on warrior loyalty, or belonging through praxis. Earlier scholarship also tended to assume routinely hostile nomad–settler relations. But while raiding was a significant part of nomadic lifeways, ancient pastoralists needed outlets for their products, outlets indiscriminate raiding would destroy. Mesopotamian towns needed regular access to such goods as wool for weaving, which must have been acquired from local pastoralists. Drought, which sometimes renders nomad–settler relations hostile, might also be a time when 'economic interdependence' is greatest (just as the Darfur region was not always ridden with conflict). Diminished crop production might make farmers more dependent on the milk and meat of pastoralists, while pastoralists might sell off herds in response to demand and temporarily perform settled work.[19]

The association of social complexity with settled cultures is especially problematic in relation to steppe nomads. The Eurasian Steppe is a large mass of grass flatlands stretching from Mongolia to Hungary and covering about one-seventh of the world's land, with the planet's greatest variation in temperatures from summer to winter. Its far north lies under permafrost, beneath which is forest and beneath that desert, bounded in the south by Central Asia's mountains, the Caspian and Black Seas and the Caucasus Mountains between. Trees occur only on riverbanks and the uninterrupted expanse of the steppe is often likened to that of the sea. The domestication of the horse, so important to steppe life, may have occurred as early as 4800 BCE, and horses were ridden perhaps before 3700 BCE.[20] Mobility in the steppe increases late in the second or early in the first millennium BCE, with south Siberia and central or eastern Kazakhstan a potential epicentre. Possible explanations include the drier climate of the first millennium and increased population in Central Asia producing resource competition, as well as the technologies the Scythians pioneered.

The Scythians, who spoke Iranian and flourished between 900 and 200 BCE, revolutionized steppe warfare, terrifying settled Greeks. A short, compound bow made of wood, sinew and animal horn enabled shooting from horseback, including twisting and firing backwards when pursued. Scythians left rich burial mounds (*kurgans*) containing horses and other valuables, and wore and treasured intricately worked metal jewellery in the distinctive 'animal style' depicting, among others, stags, bears, wolves and mythical beasts. Greeks like Herodotus marvelled at their habits of drinking undiluted wine (the Greeks added water) from their vanquished enemies' skulls and sharing fighting duties with their women. Darius, ruler of the Persian Empire from 522 to 486 BCE, whose deeds Herodotus recounts in Book IV of his *Histories*, is initially puzzled by their methods. Taking withdrawal to be a sign of weakness, he asks the Scythian king Idanthyrsus why his fighters engage in 'aimless wandering', or repeated withdrawals. The king says that without fixed lands to defend, nomads are free to choose when and where to engage an enemy. Herodotus provides a classic description of nomadic fighting method, involving retreating while destroying vegetation and filling in wells, and dividing forces so one can fight while others ride ahead for reinforcements. On this occasion the Persians exhaust themselves pursuing a smaller Scythian party leading them to the larger, at which point the Persians are themselves pursued. Darius survives only by abandoning most of his army, making for Thrace.[21]

The model according to which the genesis and diffusion of nomadic cultures on the steppes has been understood can be problematic, positing as it does a single place of origin north of the Black Sea, from there spreading westwards to eventually form statelike nomadic polities. The account smuggles in assumptions that pertain to settled societies that may foreclose interpretations of the archaeological record. Among these is the idea that Eurasian nomadic societies formed cohesive groups, derived from the 'Andronovo cultural community', a name for similar archaeological findings (burials, ceramics, seeds) of Bronze Age remains from the Central Asian and western Siberian steppes. These groups then become 'regional entities' on their way to something approaching statehood, replacing others as they go, forming an 'ethnogenetic stage' for evolution. However, the western, central and eastern steppe zones featured different kinds of herds and land use patterns as nomads responded to the distinct ecology and seasonal variations of their surroundings. To enable a focus away from sedentary, statelike entities in which material practices and objects equate to types of people and towards the variegated conditions in which nomads lived and made survival and trading choices, Michael D. Frachetti has developed a paradigm originating in economics that he calls 'nonuniform complexity'. In this understanding, some practices are 'homogenized' among diverse groups or are mutually reshaped while others 'remain locally or specifically defined'. The discovery of an uneven distribution of, or mixture with, unusual elements or things may signal not so much populational movement – different peoples bringing their own kinds of pots or other items to a place

– than 'strategic and coincidental' interactions across a network necessarily defined by flexibility, resulting in varied access to goods. A short chronological distribution of objects might indicate less a sudden influx of newcomers followed by assimilation than a 'pulse of material distribution' deriving from interactions between seasonally mobile peoples who valued procuring a limited quantity of exotic materials and who extended or altered their 'pastoral orbits' to this end.[22]

This way of thinking is arguably closer to how pastoral nomads lived their lives, developing histories of habitation defined by unpredictable climatic changes, uncertain political negotiations and exploitation of available supplies. Such histories are also non-linear, defined not in terms of progression but by the unforeseen nature of necessary interactions and responses to them. Further, when conflict produced new formations in the steppe it was the defeated who passed their influence to new masters, which complicates the idea of victorious westward migrants subsuming others. Because nomads could move on or assimilate, defeat was often voluntary, meaning that victors could be equally changed by the process. All nomadic polities consisted of several groups who had joined a victorious confederation, the name of which did not designate ethnicity. In a reversal of the historical record with regard to settled life, steppe history is 'a sequence of conquering minorities'.[23]

That said, steppe life made everyone more or less constantly ready to do battle, since enduring the climatic extremes on horseback ensured that only the strong survived. Toughness and mobility were helped by cooperative organization. The Xiongnu (also known as the Huns) organized their army in units of 10, 100, 1,000 and 10,000, a form common in the Central Asian nomadic world. This was an institution of transition, demonstrated at its greatest strength by the thirteenth-century empire of the brilliant Temüjin, or Chinggis Khan. The Mongolian nomadic leader of Chinggis' time ensured that family loyalties were kept from being too influential by means of the *keshik*, the group of non-tribal companions who formed a war leader's household, selected on the basis of loyalty and talent and bonded by common dramatic and dangerous experiences that were frequently celebrated and recalled. While fighters becoming 'soft' by association with settled life was a problem, the 'spirit of the steppes' was retained by ensuring that groups transitioned into each other constantly. This is why the term for these groups in Mongol sources, rather than 'tribe', is *irgen*, meaning 'a community of common "shape, form, vocabulary, dialect, customs and manners"'.[24]

Nomads routinely traded with settled societies, and as raiding was a source of nomadic prestige, tribute was often paid to avoid it. As much as or more than monetary cost, settled states such as Byzantium and China resented paying tribute to those they saw as inferiors and often tried to disguise the nature of the relationship by naming payments imperial gifts. The Chinese paid the third-century BCE Xiongnu more if the Xiongnu would express their relationship to the Chinese in Chinese terms, while nomads typically expressed the requisite form of submission but ignored the content. Vagabondage, or the glamour gained from the nomadic way of life, is a kind of buffer against the settled, the motor of a cycle of re-adventure perennially possible among those who select themselves for potentially harsher conditions.[25] For the settled, by contrast, definition seems to increase in importance as knowledge of the rigours of the human–landscape relation fades. Status and office themselves mostly command the respect of those lower on the social scale because such respect is no longer routinely proved through battle with one's surroundings. But if nomads cannot be made to pretend that settled societies have an extra (symbolic) function making them superior to nomadic polities, beyond the advantages of settled life such as greater leisure time and more material goods, then it is harder for the settled to maintain the fiction that sedentaries are intrinsically better – more developed, more able – than nomads.

Otherworlds

Nomads protected the network of shifting, often dangerous cara-van routes connecting Eurasian cities that came to be known as the Silk Roads, 'the largest single network of exchanges on earth before the sixteenth century'. These routes brought Chinese goods, espe-cially silk, westward into Iran, to be sold at profit throughout the Mediterranean, while China imported goods from Central Asia and western lands (peaches from Samarkand, lions from Iran). Nomads were also part of the genesis of the First Crusade (1095–9). The understanding of the Crusades as a holy war for souls is something of a back-formation. The terms designating crusading in 1095 were *peregrinatio* (pilgrimage), *iter* (path or way) and *expeditio* (exped-ition), and crusading was, especially early on, more amorphous than the precise numbering from First to Eighth or Ninth implies. The event later called the First Crusade was initially understood as a pilgrimage to the Holy Land to assist Eastern Christians and gain remission of sins. Leaving home comforts to go on crusade was an extension of the medieval Christian's duty to be a stranger to worldly desires, even while, contrarily, many crusaders expected to receive captured lands.[26]

Because of the significance that recapture of the Holy Land, chiefly Jerusalem, came to have for the crusading movement, it is often forgotten that the impetus was provided by the Byzantine emperor Alexios 1 Komnenos (*r.* 1081–118), whose lands were threatened not only by the Turks but by nomadic Pechenegs and by Norman victories in Italy (and the Normans who first departed France on crusade were, as Steven Runciman reminds us, them-selves 'only a few generations removed from nomadic free-booters'). The collapse of Byzantine control in Asia Minor led to a loss of faith in the emperor and a renewal of nomadic (Pecheneg) and Turkish attacks. Alexios' anxious requests for European help in the early 1090s, cannily focused on the precariousness of Jerusalem, energized Pope Urban II, himself threatened by a rival, to reconcile with Constantinople, the Eastern and Western churches having dramatically parted in 1054.[27]

While the response to Urban's call to crusade at Clermont in November 1095 was spectacular, the 'precise military objectives' of the First Crusade and the question of leadership remained obscure. This was in part because Alexios was to be the commander once Byzantium was reached. Armies of crusading knights were preceded by a more disorganized group including women, elderly people and children that came to be known as the People's Crusade and which lacked clerical approval. Inspired by the wandering preaching of Peter the Hermit, this group first murdered Jews in the Rhineland, then the Hungarian army's leader before destroying the livelihoods of Belgrade's citizens. On arrival in Asia Minor they were swiftly dispatched (except for Peter the Hermit, who survived them). Jerusalem, recaptured for Christendom, fell to Saladin in 1187. The nadir of crusading efforts was the famous diversion from the Holy Land of the Fourth Crusade (1202–4), when knights from the West, indebted to Venice, fought in Italy before attacking Constantinople and destroying the heart of imperial Christendom.[28]

An arguably more significant consequence of the Crusades was the setting up of regular trading channels enabling northern Europe, through Italian intermediaries, to connect to the commercial circuits already joining the Middle East to India and China. For centuries before, as Janet Abu-Lughod points out, northern Europe was largely cut off from more effective world economies, an 'upstart peripheral' to a continuous operation. Thirteenth-century Afro-Eurasia saw not only Western incursions but nomadic assaults from the East. The Mongols ravaged northern China, Iraq and Persia (Iran), assimilating Turkic peoples into their ranks. By the late thirteenth century their realm extended from Ukraine and Russia to China, Manchuria and Korea and formed the largest contiguous land empire in history. Once conquest was achieved, trading routes from the Sea of Japan to the Black Sea were protected and it became easier for merchants to calculate risk and profit.[29]

The Mongols were so terrifying that Europeans called them 'Tatars' or 'Tartars', beings from Tartarus, a medieval name for hell. But Europe sent visitors to find out more about them, including John of Plano Carpini, who delivered letters from Pope Innocent IV in 1246, and Friar William of Rubruck, who went to Mongolia in 1253. We owe to a Mongol defeat a highly nomadic story concerning one Prester John, a Christian priest and ruler over a wondrous Eastern empire. Prester John did not exist, and belief in him most likely arose from the defeat of Sanjar, a Seljuk Turkic ruler of Iran, by a Buddhist Khitan warrior in 1141. While the first crusaders had driven the Seljuks from the Holy Land, the Persian (Iranian) Seljuk realm had prospered in the early twelfth century under Sanjar. They fought the Khitan of northern China, a nomadic pastoral people who called themselves the Liao dynasty. As this empire collapsed a breakaway group led by a member of the imperial family, Yelü Dashi, established a new steppe empire which defeated the Muslims at the Battle of Qatwan (1141), the Muslims losing some 30,000 men.[30] For Western Christians, the idea that a 'barbarian' nomadic tribe could defeat a powerful Islamic ruler was shocking, and news of the defeat spread to the crusader states and thence to Europe. Along the way, the victor became a Christian priest and king of impeccable descent. After the Turk Zengi took Edessa, the capital of the northernmost crusader state, on Christmas Eve in 1144, belief in the powers of Prester John could have severely imperilled crusaders. What need to fight the Turks if a descendant of the Magi was at hand to rescue Christians? Prester John's hybridity as a Christian king of India would not have seemed so strange to those who had left on crusade as Westerners and found themselves, in the words of Fulcher of Chartres, become 'Orientals' in victory.[31]

How Yelü Dashi became Prester John is a strange and convoluted story. Before Qatwan, a tale circulated about a 'Patriarch John' who had left India for Rome in 1122 to be recognized as Patriarch of the Indies. The tale appears in two unrelated sources that testify to a common historical kernel, although the visitor may not have come from India, and was later grafted onto the nomadic victory. There *were* Nestorian Christians (those who separate the divine and human components of Christ) in India, and the story of the Indian Christians is told in the third-century CE *Acts of Thomas*, which source this visitor may have known. But what ensured the longevity of the legend, and Prester John's later appearances, was a letter (*c.* 1165–70) claiming to have been written by him, giving a detailed description of his kingdom. Arrived at by way of a desert that takes the visitor past Babylon and the Tower of Babel, it contains many precious gems and exotic beasts. There are healing waters and beautiful women who appear four times a year and breed no daughters. There is no poverty, dishonesty or greed.[32]

As Keagan Brewer argues, this likely Latin forgery, which 'functioned almost as a genre . . . rather than as a single piece of writing', was so wildly popular that, while testifying to probable belief in Prester John, it does not necessarily imply that people believed he was as the letter presents him. Rather, the tradition's inventiveness shows that Prester John was the means by which Western Christians understood that there were Christians beyond Europe, like and unlike themselves. After the Mongol conquests opened Asia to Europeans in the thirteenth century, Prester John appeared in other non-Christian places as the representative of Christians. One version of the story presents the deeds of Chinggis Khan as those of 'King David', a Christian king and Prester John's great-grandson. Prester John's journey to Rome for papal recognition partly sanctifies the wandering permutations of his story, while his kingdom provides a template for interpreting the tales of returning Eastern travellers. Back home in twelfth- and thirteenth-century Europe, the sublimating of violent impulses into cultural products was also effected by the poets and composers of Occitania in southern France known as the troubadours.[33] Their output's enigma and oscillatory impulses are key to their longevity in history.

Violence at home

Western European courts were, like those of India, highly peripatetic when placed in a world historical context. Power was distributed in relatively small 'court-centred polities' whose relation to one another was often unsure, so kings and courts were often on the move, including on military campaigns. This made for changing gatherings of officials, followers and allies and a corresponding emphasis on gaining personal favour for advancement. Gerald of Wales (c. 1146–c. 1223), who spent time at the English court of Henry II and Eleanor of Aquitaine, described court life as hellish with tumult, lies, malice and routinely fluctuating feelings and expectations. Walter Map (c. 1140–c. 1210), in *Courtiers' Trifles*, agreed. The court is 'constant only in inconstancy', and, if not hell, then 'a place of punishment' where hopes are perpetually raised but never redeemed.[34] These are commonplaces, so the focus on shifting favours runs through the work of troubadour lyricists too. Their music first developed in west-central France and then further south in Languedoc and Provence in the second part of the twelfth century, the main period of activity. Many troubadours were relatively wealthy, some were minor nobles, while the poorer sought patronage where they could find it, including in Aragon in Iberia (Spain). Several went on crusade. Some 450 are known, including a few *trobairitz* (women composers). We know about them from archival sources, references to each other's work in the songs, and the *vidas* and *razos* (lives and circumstantial anecdotes) that accompany the lyrics. Our records of troubadour song begin at least a hundred years after the time of first performance, and it is common for songs to lament the lost past. Over three hundred musical settings for 246 poems survive.[35]

Troubadour song is characterized by an extremely creative mixing of themes, styles and structures, the musical as unpredictable as the poetic, and this hallmark variability was probably even greater in performance. Instability, especially oscillation, and contradiction are signs of virtuosic form. 'I keep silence', sings Bernart de Ventadorn (*fl.* 1147–80), a silence he is, in singing, breaking, and 'joy overcomes and conquers', it is something to be endured. 'May the love you deny me hate me always', sings Guilhem de Cabestanh (1162–1212), 'If my heart ever turns.'[36] Feeling is constrained by regulation, producing a paradoxical alterity: the strongest emotion cannot be expressed. It is conveyed through opposites, which mask it. Discerning the impassioned cause of feeling is part of the poetic game. Peire Vidal (*fl.* 1183–205) sings: 'Such love cuts the heart/ For I have seen none more lovely or soft.' And Raimbaut d'Aurenga (*c.* 1147–1173): 'Now is resplendent the inverted flower along the cutting crags and in the hills. What flower? Snow, ice and frost which stings and hurts and cuts . . . but joy keeps me green and jovial now'. Melodies may exaggerate tension or end inconclusively before the *tornada* (a lyric's final lines, usually a fragment that brings the song into the maker's present) to emphasize the singer's incomprehension of love's power.[37]

And yet it would be a mistake to see in these songs something primarily private and inward, for in this time and place the public realm of law and property and the private realm of 'anger, love . . . and healing' are one. The mobility of aristocratic and royal courts in twelfth-century southern France meant that nobles and royals had to work continually to ensure that the bonds of fidelity tying commoners to nobles, and nobles to each other, so important in a world of unstable liaisons, were effected, believed in and recalled. The 'genius of the courts of Occitania', thinks Fredric Cheyette, 'was to discover the way to cultivate that belief, to teach the virtues of fidelity as a spirited game and make mastery of its refinements the definition of who belonged, the *way to fidelity itself* into a passion. The secret was music and poetry.' The lyrics' violent contrasts make the tensions of the journey to fidelity memorable and learnable. They are indirect, involving otherness or the unexpected, which requires attention, and they enact a sublimation of what, in a noble household by this time, cannot always be an outright brawl.[38]

Displacement is also effected by the lyrics' dialogic properties, for the strophic *canso*, the first type of troubadour song, which has turning or alternation in its form (Greek *strophe*, turning, from *strephein*, to turn, bend or twist) and which contains variegated sequences of repetition and variation, had a counter-form, the *sirventes*, a satirical treatment of someone else's song. Similar debate forms include the *tenso*, the *joc-partit*, which canvasses question and answer, and the *descort*, or 'discordant' song, which may contain deliberately muddled rhymes, stanzaic disagreement and multiple languages, representing love's unconveyability and confusion. As Judith Peraino puts it, paraphrasing Jofre de Foixà (d. *c.* 1300): 'the melodies of *descorts* should violate the rules of good behavior; they should be delinquent.'[39] But they can only do and be so when the rules for good behaviour are known. These forms make the way to perform 'courtly' or faithful behaviour complex, problematical, transfixing. Love expressed in lyric builds difficulty into court relations, a difficulty that, once enjoyed in personal and social contest, is hard to disown.

The exigency considered earlier around access to water in nomad and settler custom, which can transmute away from custom in times of conflict, becoming difficult to contain, is present here in the form of perceived threats to honour and reputation. 'Injury and deception' were most feared in castellan (castle or noble house) communities, since interests, especially around inheritances, were often opposed. The *lauzengiers* – rivals, slander-bearing spies, *others* – who frequently appear in troubadour lyric show courtly life to be full of competing allegiances. Most nobles (and many commoners) owed service to more than one (other) noble. The combative *sirventes* were more numerous at times of political tension. Courtly lyric is also seen as a continuation of *chanson de geste*'s epic combat, the *lauzengiers* embodying the less readily identifiable enemies resulting from the shift from trial by physical testing to trial by verbal inquest. When words, rather than deeds, become the currency of interpersonal relations the lyric masks violence but also ensures that it continues by maintaining it within set terms. This is also in part why the attentions of the courtly lady (*domna*) seem unavailable. She anchors competition between rivals, and that struggle never ends. Someone else will take her attention if one does not win it oneself by creative or other prowess. The lady's imagined power, making her sometimes a threat, a beloved enemy who can cause death, represents not only a potentially infinite field of rivals but also other realities. Women, like Ermengard of Narbonne (1127/9–1197), were sometimes rulers, but of course this did not always make them men's equals. They were both active and passive, adored and decried, and their representation in courtly lyric may show the contradictions of their position in this time of changing inheritance structures, as Chapter One explored.[40]

A formal representative of the instability built into medieval European lyric is the refrain, an isolated phrase that is repeated within and often between compositions and which became increasingly common in the thirteenth century. Inherently paradoxical, a refrain, once seen – in a now discredited view – as a fragment of an earlier lost whole, is an independent element within a song, but it is also dependent on the genres within which it appears. Refrains can circulate anonymously and have a 'wandering existence' between forms. 'Neither . . . internal nor external to a work in which they appear', they open onto the element of otherness associated in the West with wanderers because it is not clear exactly where they come from, or whether these imports from another context disrupt a work or draw it together, as identity can be strengthened by a stranger. Referring to an unknown site of lyric origin that is simultaneously a common world of public speech (which may in turn be a way to mask a private statement), refrains may also enable change management.[41]

Every citation sets up new connections, and the interaction of the refrain, accompanied by its missing origin, with the rest of the song can represent either the alteration of something traditional (the refrain as common speech) by a new context or the alteration of the context by the unlocatable phrase.

Medieval song was a profoundly social practice, and the circulation of refrains reminds us not only of the creative role played in it by contradiction but of encounters with the unmasterable that can shape social endeavour. We have been tracking strategies for managing this element that result in potentially new polities, some real, some imagined: in Sudanese professionals taking on the neglected region's name, making centre into periphery; in nomads choosing to pass their expertise to new masters in the steppe, making conquering cooperation; and in the Prester John legend's syncretizing otherness for home consumption, reminding Europeans of the larger world. A figure for the unmasterable we have not yet considered is related to medieval lyric and is, like the refrain, officially unassimilable while everywhere to be found. This is the singer, the player, the entertainer (*joglar* or *jongleur*), a class of person rhetorically placed outside the social world yet continually appearing at the centre of a variety of domestic and official scenes.

The outside: players, peasants, fools

The medieval *jongleur* was a performer, often a singer and often itinerant. The term also referred to actors, mimes, musicians, buffoons, jugglers and acrobats, and was connected with other professions for which the primary instrument was the body, such as prostitution. Jongleurs were thus deemed close to the fleshly appetites the Church condemned, while a link with bodily contortion suggested not only sexual acts but mocking God-given form. Like prostitutes, jongleurs could not 'sue in church courts, enter holy orders, or receive the eucharist'. They were thus bound to live as outsiders to the norm. Yet kings and clerics hired them. Churches and monasteries sometimes needed outside musicians for particular ceremonies.[42] Minstrels (musicians) were employed by city governments for civic and religious events. While some appointments were regular, most jongleurs were probably relatively mobile, earning their living from a combination of skills and trades. As well as travelling for civic or Church work or at weddings, bathhouses and inns, minstrels travelled to minstrel schools in northern French, Flemish and German cities to share skills and material. Some troubadour lyricists, especially those dependent on patrons, probably performed their compositions, while singing would be a choice for nobles, who could have others perform their songs.[43]

The iconography of the jongleur and the fool are frequently conflated, and the wild, naked state in which fools were sometimes shown can also recall jongleurs. French city rules frequently specified that jongleurs from elsewhere could not play at private events until eight days had passed (probably to reduce conflicts and competition). If a townsperson broke this rule, sergeants and judges could take the jongleur's clothes. Jongleurs were often paid with clothes, and their taking and giving associates jongleurs with homeless beggars, for whom clothing was a traditional form of charity. It was to act in concert for their livelihoods against such risks that jongleurs formed guilds analogous to those supporting other crafts and trades. Numerous confraternities (brotherhoods), charitable organizations dedicated to a patron saint or miraculous event, also helped, saying prayers for them after death and employing them in annual celebrations.[44]

While the jongleur's duplicity is chosen, his reality feigned, the fool's folly is involuntary. In the European Middle Ages the fool is also the unbeliever. In the words of Psalm 53:1: 'The fool says in his heart, "There is no God."' V. A. Kolve has noticed something about this figure that helps us understand the threat felt by the Church from secular performers: 'Better than any other image during the medieval centuries, [the God-denying fool] kept the possibility of nonmeaning open, the questions too confidently answered by religious faith alive.' He notes that 'pictures of a fool alone, or looked on only by God, or rebuked by a king frustrate a symbolic transfer to others more mentally competent. Their specification is stubbornly literal, their hidden logic unacknowledged anxiety and fear.' The non-meaning figured by the fool registers the fact that something is missing, for which absence there is, although the fool cannot access it, a cure. For the lostness of the fool is so extreme that it almost meets the lostness Christ endured for sinners. Christ, the holy fool, also went to the outside, experiencing abandonment by God while his disciples fled in terror. Yet jongleurs' performances rivalled those of clerical preachers, especially on holidays.[45] And the Church's most theatrical event, the Eucharist, celebrates a double reality (death and life, man and God) in one act, the sacrifice in which God's son experienced abandonment to perform redemption. The jongleur as fool, by contrast, expands rather than reduces possibilities. Specialist in double acts and free from theological rules, he puts non-meaning – in the form of *any* chosen element – into circulation. He facilitates rather than blocks symbolic transfer.

The secular performer had always had the ability to 'twist and turn' words and actions for dramatic purpose. But by the mid-thirteenth century in the schools (universities) in which clerically approved ideas were tested, some radically new concepts about value in human exchanges were taking form. It was beginning to be seen that the free exchange of the 'self-equalizing marketplace', with the addition of some allowed fluctuations, was a more reliable way to ensure social equality and good order than reference to received static values and 'order ... by decree'. Individuals were less responsible for the outcomes of their acts than previously, since even attempts to cheat one's opponent at market could be regularized by mechanisms derived from an improved understanding of quantification and measurement, especially with respect to change and motion. These conditions ought to have made it harder to see the jongleur, whose traditional crimes are free movement, changeful acts and persuasively meeting demands, as the enemy of good social functioning. And if they did not, jongleurs developed impressive strategies to counter such allegations, as Carol Symes's work on the confraternity of the jongleurs of Arras shows.[46]

The twelfth-century growth of credit in urban European centres, increased lay literacy and Church moves to improve the standard of clerical education produced, by the thirteenth century, large mobile populations of students and masters, especially in Bologna, Paris and Oxford. These caused the Church concern. It wanted a monopoly on education and had long seen free movement as wandering, a social and theological evil. Freedom of physical movement was matched in the universities by speculative scholastic methods, especially disputation as verbal debate.[47] Greater literacy among laypeople and urban affluence also produced persistent heresies, all of which allowed lay preaching and to some degree rejected wealth, recommending the early Christian or apostolic life. While itinerant preaching hermits were a problem for orthodoxy, dissident communities were the greater threat, potentially rendering the Church's cumbersome organization redundant. For these groups, it was the Church and not they that had wandered from gospel precepts.

In the mid-twelfth century the Humiliati (Humble Ones), who shared a common life, helped the poor and preached the gospel, were papally sanctioned. Others were not so lucky. In Lyon, Waldes, a prosperous cloth merchant, began to preach and dispense his wealth. A regional famine in 1176 made this welcome but showed up wealthy clerics, and the Waldensians, or 'Poor Men of Lyon', were condemned in 1178. The theology of the Cathars, or 'Good Christians', was more extreme, deriving from an early heresy, Manichaeism, which held that everything material was evil. Right living meant abstaining from sexual activity and food obtained from procreating animals. The Cathars, primarily active in southern France, were viciously persecuted, first as objects of the Albigensian Crusade of 1209–29 and then by a Church Inquisition established in 1234. Unsurprisingly, this made them more mobile, and while our understanding of them is coloured by the only sources being Orthodox, Cathars were clearly able to travel to each other's houses and to communal worship sites despite persecution. Eventually, their identity as wanted fugitives itself became a form of Christian imitation, proof that they were living an apostolic life.[48]

The order founded by Francis of Assisi in 1208–9, a brotherhood of more dedicated wanderers seeking to live simply, preaching the gospel on foot, did achieve orthodoxy but fell prey to contradictions. After Francis's death in 1226, the obligation to own nothing was circumvented to enable training, first by setting up trustees and then by the Holy See owning Franciscan books, lands and buildings. Wandering Franciscan women, initially free to accompany the brothers, connoted unprotected chastity and were forced to become an enclosed order (the Poor Clares) in 1219. Friars, including the Black Friars or Dominicans, whose mission was to combat Catharism, were especially active recruiters in university towns. By the fourteenth century England was vexed by begging friars, many of them university-trained elites whose begging seemed a sham. They were also seen to devalue a sacrament like confession, which was exchanged for money (thus approaching the sin of simony). Unlike the parish priest, the friar had no obligation to ensure reformation in the sinful – fewer confessions, after all, meant lower earnings – and other rights, such as burial rights, were seen as encroachments upon legitimate priestly income.[49]

Wandering is also central to fourteenth-century England's most innovative and puzzling poem, William Langland's *Piers Plowman*. The usual suspects, minstrels and friars, are present for censure. And the protagonist Will, who embarks on a quest to learn how to 'Dowel' (do well), 'Dobet' (do better) and 'Dobest' at living a Christian life, frequently wanders from purpose. So do other characters and elements. *Piers* exists in more than fifty manuscript copies and was highly influential, as shown by later poems featuring Piers (Peter) the Plowman and by his appearance in the letters of the English rebels of 1381. There are three main versions, now agreed to have been written chronologically, the A text (1360s) being less developed than B (1370s), and C (1380s) having elements that show it to be a response to Piers's co-opting by the rebels, a usage Langland would not have condoned.[50]

Piers is rightly described less as a poem than as a participatory event, a form of mortal combat and attempted moral revolution, and less as a narrative than a taking apart and reconstituting of 'ways of perceiving and evaluating the world'. Although it is organized, after a prologue, as a series of twenty journey-like 'steps' or *passuses* (21 in the C version), nothing in it is linear or what we initially take it for. Its dream vision form, in which medieval European poets could express personal views by claiming they arrived in dreams,[51] makes for several disruptions as Will falls asleep and wakes again, with two dreams occurring inside others. The poem is an allegory, or representative version, of the spiritual life, in which Will meets animated aspects of fourteenth-century English society (such as Meed, or Money), its church and the Church's teachings (such as the seven deadly sins). Although we see Christ harrow Hell, defeat Satan and free sinners near the end, by the final passus the Church, figured as the Barn of Unity after harvest, is undone by greedy friars while Conscience, an erstwhile guardian, departs in search of Piers or Christ.

An especially fruitful line of recent enquiry into the poem's unruly escape from all known categories concerns its animated allegorical figures, or personifications. Figures such as Lady Meed and Conscience (awareness and ethical integrity) are intrinsically ambiguous because the quality for which the individual is named can mutate further in the individual. Such forms of 'other-speaking' were common in late medieval Europe, when the paradoxes inherent in Christian theology were pressured by the question of how to tell which kinds of otherness might be God speaking to humanity and which humans justifying behaviours as godly to themselves. With the wealthy and powerful Church in crisis, itinerancy and poverty rising, friars betraying gospel hope and 'Lollards' – followers of John Wyclif's teachings – accessing it in forbidden vernacular versions, personifications are sites where Langland stages one large, participatory 'shape-shifting identity' representing Christendom's imperilled soul.[52]

Change, the poem's constant, is disjunction, alienation, but can also be subtle. A self is always becoming another, a thing impossible to know. Meed, representing financial corruption, seems less damaging when appearing as a courtly lady who may marry Conscience, but this transition whereby money's taint is masked by words and deeds is itself the kind that money effects, its commutability the source of its power. Langland uses paradiastole, a rhetorical technique by which a virtue or vice is redescribed as something similar, to represent hypocrisy, showing 'the manipulability . . . of moral categories.'[53] Throughout, the speech and action of personifications shade into something more or less virtuous, as when Patience, telling Haukyn the Active Man (representing life in the world) about the virtues of poverty, veers towards self-satisfaction: poverty becomes something that need not be relieved (XIV.191–273). Or when Peace, who at first denies Friar Flatterer entrance to Unity's barn, is persuaded to do so by Courtesy, the name for a sum of money given by grace as a favour (XX.339–55). Grace or right action becomes massaged speech, as though the adjacent Friar's tendency to flatter is catching.[54] So Peace ushers in a source of conflict.

Langland's genius is to model Incarnation in terms of what Mark Miller calls 'structural antagonisms', making it less a way out of something than an impossibility with which humankind must contend. Irresolution builds as the people 'working and wandering'[55] at the poem's beginning yield to scenes that, once problems of discernment and right living arise, are themselves disrupted by further scenes, the problematic nature of which conveys Incarnation as a search for equivalence, for at least one virtue, practice or authority that can prevail over at least one previously elaborated harm. But this equivalent is never found. The fact that Christ took human form increases rather than decreases the sinful subject's questions, for now a solution to the problem of corruption should be possible. It is as though God's gift to humans is to magnify their unbelonging, to show them the brokenness of the world. Yet it is significant that Langland uses the word *auntred*, meaning 'ventured', a medieval romance term, to depict the Incarnation and not the more standard *exinanivit*, which means 'brought to nothing, voided'. 'Auntred', connoting hazarding one's life, depicts Christ's decision to '[venture] himself and [take] Adam's nature' (C xx.31) as a moment of risk and fragility,[56] a radical self-emptying that is yet involved at every point with the dilemmas of fleshly existence. This version of a Christ potentially in peril, as though God's relation to his creation *is* to be involved in its peril, counters the poem's rendition of wandering as labour avoidance. This latter, a common late medieval English trope, makes extreme economic precariousness into something feigned. Christ, however, inhabits real precariousness, and not to gain from others but to redeem.

In the famous ploughing of the half-acre scene a wandering figure called Waster, among others, refuses to work until Hunger arrives (C viii.122–3, 128–35, 325–40). As Robert Epstein notes, Hunger is not simply famine, which would affect all equally. Instead, Piers summons Hunger the personification to distinguish between the workers and the lazy, who have previously depended on the workers. The contexts for this episode are crop failures and the Plague which had ravaged England in 1348, almost halving the workforce and inflating peasant wages. Between 1338 and 1344, because of drought or frost, only two harvest years were good, and between 1353 and 1370 eight were bad, several approaching famine. There had also been a famine in 1316–17. The response to growing post-pandemic worker power was a series of labour statutes, the first in 1351, tying agricultural wages to pre-pandemic levels and forcing peasants to remain in the manors of their birth to stop them moving in search of higher earnings.[57] Prison sentences could be awarded for giving alms to 'able-bodied' beggars.

Simultaneously, the statutes increased the labour supply by requiring everyone to work, including those formerly supported by alms from working others. Thus 'the lazy' include the blind and lame (C VIII.188) whom Hunger drives, implying that they had previously been faking. In fact they had not, but as lords and upwardly mobile peasants responded to famine by cutting staff, and mercantile piecework paid some only in part, the poor appeared increasingly in cities.[58] There, they were seen by existing city dwellers as criminals or 'false men' (C VIII.229) *because* they were visible, and could be mentally grouped with actual criminals there already. Vagabondage – fleeing the statutes – prostitution and other crimes were undoubtedly practised by some incomers, but it was their suddenly increased numbers, overwhelming as they did existing social provisions, that produced an arbitrary visual limit whereby those with sufficient goods feared those with none, and to avoid supporting them called all pretenders.

In C version V.1–104 Will wakes and, finding Conscience and Reason 'in a hot harvest' (7), responds to Reason's questions about his fitness to work in Langland's voice, defending the work of a man in minor clerical orders. As Anne Middleton shows, this is a clear response to the 1388 Statute of Labourers, an obsessively retributive document that adds to earlier statutes the requirement that those in 'unnecessary' trade or crafts perform field work at harvest, that those labouring since the age of twelve remain labourers for life, and that beggars be forced to work, while those who cannot remain in their locations. For the lower classes all uncircumscribed wandering, understood as mobility of body and aspiration, is now outlawed. The statute envisions a system of 'internal passports' for all categories of person moving to and from work or on pilgrimage, except lords and their servants. Vagrancy's 'performative indeterminacy', formerly a secondary aspect of worker mobility, is now a major ailment, fixity of identity the cure. The result is the production of 'the figure of the alms-seeking able-bodied vagrant', a largely fictitious being understood to peddle fiction. The statute rhetorically creates the object it fears, for post-1381, vagrancy is associated with violent sedition, although the 1381 rebels were not mostly vagrants. Yet criminal vagrants become a class who may rise against the nation or support foreign invasion.[59] Fraud and force are their weapons: they must be disarmed.

In response to Reason's quizzing, Will as Langland provides his own 'internal passport', explaining what he does and why he travels. His responses are truly vagrant, their sources and registers of many kinds. His first defence is weak: he is 'too weak' and 'too tall' to bend to field work (23–5). His next is stronger. As a cleric he should be exempt – the Church had its own methods for dealing with 'irregular' vocations – and until the age of twelve he was no peasant, so by implication cannot continue as one now (35–41, 54). Yet, riskily, he says he lives alternately in country and town (44), a dangerous refutation of the statute's call for all to belong to a single dwelling. But he is on the statute makers' side: 'since serfs' kids have been made bishops', love and holy living are extinct (70, 80). The best work is prayer and penance, for 'not from the soil' does man live alone and God's will provides. Will is certainly a holy fool who jests and wagers faith, and his way of life is modelled, here, on the gospel's call to participate in God's soul-harvest. The passage's scriptural references are enigmatic and include reference to behaviours good in God's sight but illegible to others, which is close to feigning.[60] And while enigma is typical of the poem, Will is also responding to the statute's enormous reach. Reason and Conscience, defending a document that would fix every non-noble lifestyle and every non-noble person, are faced with a performance of the mobility the statute aims to stop, delivered aslant – which it also aims to stop – escaping the law's letter, continually shifting from lower to higher ground and changing the referential premise.

The subtly alienating, transmorphic processes we saw personifications engage in earlier are relevant here, for William Rhodes has identified Langland's personifications, by nature part-person and part-abstraction, as potential renditions of economic agency, since to be an economic agent is to act according to one's will while subject to invisible forces. The poem gives form to material pressures increasingly distributed across a power network and not readily pictured, to convey to people the complex causes of their conditions and show why economic realities are hard to change (because they are embedded in social relations but are now being rescripted as supply and demand elements, for instance). In the half-acre scene, Hunger partly represents the landowners and prosperous merchants who, having sought to artificially repress the labour market in post-plague conditions favourable to peasants, and with the class mobility-increasing properties of credit anathema in the hands of the likes of the rebels, (re)invent the feigning vagrant as the thief of workers' profits. But the vagrant more accurately represents the capital mobility from which even peasants benefit in certain conditions.[61] For elements that move through a system changing shape and form and reference are the very stuff of business. Money and the processes it spawns can equalize themselves at market, but if vagrant transformations of canny kinds are taken out, little will move there either. The vagrant's hyperbolically fixed form thus partly represents the attempt by the wealthy in post-pandemic England to fix or artificially control the labour market.

Like the desperate wanderer, *Piers* is pressured by the 'empty' moment of longing – no home, no food, no shelter, or, on another level, no clear guide to each right action – that is not empty because the body's demands, or scripture's commands, overflow it, and because humankind's sinful condition cannot, on earth, be overcome.

Christ perilously took on humanity's limits in the Incarnation, while *Piers* reaches its repeatedly, and finally in a quotidian apocalypse that suggests that doom is already abroad, passing notice. But while I have emphasized the poem's rivenness, the work can also be read as a rendition of the multiple forms participation in a godly life can take. Christ is Piers the Plowman, plowing is God's work, and the poem continually stretches understanding of difficult theological concepts such as the Trinity and natural ('kynde') knowledge such that life is a form of loving God and one's fellow humans once its contradictory richness is understood.[62] Humanness is riven in *Piers*, but also cumulative: problems increase, but so do possibilities for redemptive participation. And there is a lesson for our relation to our planet in the poem. Alterity or unbelonging can be used to model systems in which exceedings of limit are countered by invention so attuned to our self-regard that we must yield false certainties and imagined safeguards – like the idea that one owns rather than stewards land or that economies are salvific – to gain necessities. Yielding self-deceptions enables better questions. Focusing on necessities for all requires solutions. We are already this world's others or antagonists, but we can (re)learn its ways, itself a necessity given the way apocalypse has morphed and spread, its imagined closure neither final nor far off but now, and rising.

Extremity and misrule

Early modern England continued to pass strict labour laws and to demonize the displaced. Famine, increased population and inflation, enclosure of arable common fields – especially for sheep for the lucrative European wool market – and Henry VIII's appropriation of monastic lands, including hospitals, expanded the numbers of landless poor in the sixteenth century. From 1563 leaving employment without testimonial incurred a vagrancy charge with whipping and imprisonment. From 1572 beggars' children could be forced to work.

Labour was enforced in bridewells (correctional houses). Such measures increased the unrest authorities feared, but fear of vagrants was out of all proportion to their power and number. As earlier, aspirational mobility was curbed, but sixteenth- and seventeenth-century England also became obsessed with popular pleasures, outlawing maypoles as well as impugning drinkers in alehouses. The poor had to prove sobriety to deserve relief.[63]

Wages having almost halved between the 1560s and the 1590s, the poor once again flocked to cities. There, mistaken beliefs about vagrants thrived: that they wandered aimlessly by choice, feigning poverty and injury, and that they belonged to well-organized, thieving brotherhoods with a secret language designed to dupe citizens.[64] Rogue literature featuring 'valiant beggars' – feigning vagrants – flourished throughout sixteenth-century Europe but especially in England, and especially in famine years. Vagrants' powers of dissimulation, including forging documents, crippling their children and impersonating the middle class, were imagined to be so extensive that they likely represent a generalized anxiety about reading social placement in the period. Those departing the social margins for the centre feared counterfeiters, perhaps in fear that such a reading might be made of them. Belief in vagrant hierarchies was probably due to belief that all social activity required hierarchy, although disbanded soldiers, who were often owed pay and kept their weapons, were one group whom the wealthy might more reasonably fear.[65]

William Shakespeare's play *King Lear*, first performed in London in 1606, is a dramatic laboratory for these concerns. Featuring a king who gives his lands to his daughters with the intention of living, homeless, with each in turn, and a subplot echoing filial rebellion in which an aristocrat feigns beggary, it is also a play in which the king, unhoused in mind and body, jeopardizes the realm. First performed at court for King James I, who had sought to unify Scotland and England in 1603, the play shows the dangers of geopolitical division and explores the role played by civil unrest in a universe without divine providence, foreshadowing England's later Civil War. Enabled by the pagan setting and influenced by Shakespeare's reading of Machiavelli and the morally sceptical Michel de Montaigne, this absence of divine law is variously canvassed. Lear's decision to divide his kingdom proves unwise, even unkingly, but his youngest daughter, Cordelia, is the play's first openly insubordinate character and the first to voice what Michael Neill calls its 'principle of frustrated expectation and evacuated meaning'. While her sisters flatter their father in return for lands, Cordelia, when asked what she can better say for better lands, says, 'Nothing',[66] for love is enacted rather than spoken. For this she is disowned.

When the bastard Edmund convinces his father, Gloucester, that his brother Edgar is plotting treason, Edgar too is disinherited, while Gloucester is then betrayed for treason and, in punishment, though innocent, loses his eyes. Again, something is added – Edmund's manufactured letter, and seeming evidence of blows from Edgar, like the sisters' exorbitant words – and something lost, dramatically and unfairly, by the innocent. This quality of excess up close to absence also informs the play's concern with homelessness. As Linda Woodbridge notes, no interiors are provided at Goneril's and Regan's houses, where ambition is all. Regan refuses hospitality to her father (2.4.234–5), and Gloucester is blinded while a guest in Cornwall's home. The word 'home' is used twice in its emergent meaning suggesting the unwelcome penetration of a body when Gloucester and Lear, respectively, are shut out of houses (Gloucester: 'These injuries the king now bears will be revenged home' (3.3.11–12), and Lear: 'But I will punish home' (3.4.16)). Households fail, and Goneril and Regan, seeing Lear's knights as 'rufflers', the rogue literature term for demobilized, vagrant soldiers, cut their numbers, turning them outdoors.[67]

It is on the storm-swept heath at the play's centre, however, that nature's excess meets the homeless human's absence of comforts and importance. These scenes teem with strange connections between life forms even while human life is threatened, suggesting that it is subject to laws beyond human grasp. Lear goes mad and commands the winds to 'strike flat the world' (3.2.7) while he discovers what 'poor, naked wretches' feel when a body's clothes, 'looped', 'windowed', 'ragged', are its only housing (3.4.28, 31). Familial ties severed, the characters speak past each other in broken phrases, Lear mad, Edgar feigning as the rogue 'Poor Tom of Bedlam', but this increases creaturely connections. Poor Tom has been a hog, fox, wolf, dog and lion (3.4.91–2) and he eats the 'frog, the toad, the tadpole', the lizard and newt, which eat cow-dung and worse (3.4.125–9), while to Gloucester his unknown son is man as worm, and men are to the gods as flies to boys: mere targets (4.1.35, 38). When Gloucester, led by Tom, believes he is at Dover, crows and jackdaws appear as beetles, fishermen as mice, as Tom imagines Gloucester's fall (4.6.13–14, 17–18). Beings feed on others, not unlike Lear's elder daughters and Edmund, or Lear himself before his madness, hungry for praise. Humanity is dispersed across a forcefield, and even while, to Lear, Tom is 'the thing itself', 'a poor, bare, forked animal' of which he has taken 'too little care' (3.4.104–6, 32–3), these life forms that coexist with humans or which humans become provide no graspable field of reference. Too many links destroy meaning in the press and welter of existence and creaturely collocation that make up houseless life.[68]

Everyone important in the play leaves home, Lear leaves his senses and Cordelia and Lear, among others, leave life altogether by the end. Viewers, too, leave a relatively comfortable space for one less so at certain moments. Chris Fitter has observed 'deictic swerve[s]' in the play, whereby the audience is unexpectedly made conscious of its own presence. In Act 3, Scene 4 the storm-wracked 'houseless heads' of the 'poor naked wretches' referred to by the kneeling Lear, about to enter a hovel (3.4.28, 30), are also 'the *groundlings*' heads',[69] groundlings being the poorer attendees at the Globe Theatre not seated in roofed galleries but standing in the open centre (often getting wet, this being England). The homeless king is at their level.

Then, when Gloucester, mistakenly believing he is at Dover cliffs, falls onto the flat stage – technically a pratfall – and does not move, Edgar, failing to awaken him, wonders whether he may in fact have died. Edgar-as-Tom has played the scene comedically just prior, for only the sightless Gloucester does not know the flat ground is all there is when Edgar says, 'How fearful/ And dizzy 'tis to cast one's eyes so low' (4.6.11–12).

Gloucester's stillness produces audience uncertainty, and Fitter reads Edgar, who soon after tells his father to 'bear free and patient thoughts' (4.6.80), as a type of the parish officer. For this is the kind of injunction on which parish relief for being poor, homeless, old and disabled depended. Without self-humbling postures such as occupying seats labelled 'for the poor' in church there was no assistance.[70] Gloucester, neither certainly alive nor certainly dead, forces viewers away from siding with Edgar against the laughable other towards the space of that other, occupying uncertain ground. As the moment in which the appropriate response to the prone Gloucester is far from clear expands, fear passes to the son from the father, who has had to ask for help to end his life. And this is where Shakespeare leaves the human in *King Lear*, in the space without clear definition and reception experienced by the homeless. On the heath one is part of a field of mutating life forms pursuing others, with little claim. A joke at one's expense might spell one's accidental end instead of the final act one planned. In the last part of this chapter we will consider a people whose way of life, because it turns accident into a medium of exchange, has much to offer a world in which exchanges around unforeseen events will determine humanity's future purpose.

No homeland: the Romani link

This chapter ends as it began, with nomads, the others we all once were. Sometimes regarded as the ultimate others because they have no homeland, the Rom are wanderers with a clear identity and impressive adaptational powers. Their language, which has no written tradition, is related to modern Indo-Aryan and earlier Sanskrit. While its first written traces, said to be Egyptian (hence 'gypsy'), appear in England in 1547, the Romani term for men, *rom*, like Armenian *lom* and Syrian and Persian *dom*, provides a better clue to ethnic origin. These terms correspond with Sanskrit *domba* and modern Indian *dom* or *dum*, signifying a group of various tribes. In Sanskrit, *domba* came to mean a '"man of low caste living by singing and music"', and modern Indian preserves a '"caste of wandering musicians" (Sindhi)' and '"low-caste black-skinned fellow" (West Pahari)'. Doms, possibly of Dravidian origin, exist today as vagrant Indian groups, their professions including basket-making, scavenging, blacksmithing, metalworking, storytelling and music-making.[71]

We do not know why the Rom left India more than 1,000 years ago, migrating westwards in specialist trade service groups. Linguistic evidence shows they spent considerable time in the Greek-speaking part of the Byzantine Empire. 'Egiptians', meaning 'Gypsies', are referred to in thirteenth-century Byzantine tax law, and 'Gupti' or 'Tsigani', a term of Greek origin, in the fourteenth-century Balkans, while many Roms in fourteenth-century Wallachia and Moldavia and fifteenth- and sixteenth-century Romania were enslaved. In Modon, a Venetian seaport, we find a community of Roms said to be from 'Gyppe' or 'Little Egypt' who, while later driven out by the Ottomans, carry letters of recommendation and safe passage from the pope to European princes. In Deventer in the Netherlands the arrival of 'Lord Andreas, Duke of Little Egypt', accompanied by one hundred 'Gypsies' and about forty horses is recorded in 1420, and dark-skinned, colourfully clothed Roms, telling fortunes and travelling with extended family, carry such letters throughout the fifteenth century across Europe.[72]

Most often the letter-bearers claim to be on penitential pilgrimage. Referred to in Spanish Romani as '"*o xanxanó baró*", "the great trick"', the extravagant adoption by Roms of concerted penitential movement, supported by papal letters, was a brilliant strategy that, for a time, provided safety. Giving to pilgrims enabled non-pilgrims to share in the spiritual value of pilgrimage, and a story held that the inhabitants of Little Egypt, long Christian, wandered in penance for backsliding. Princes also supplied letters that were promptly copied. Eventually the game was up, and, first from Germany and then elsewhere, Roms were expelled on charges of performing sorcery, thieving and spying. Criminalization increased after the Thirty Years War, in which many Roms served, when travelling gangs of robbers, often former soldiers and those the war had impoverished or displaced, stole from sedentaries to stay alive. Roms, increasingly associated with these wanderers, were arrested and tortured into providing information about crimes.[73]

The tenacity with which Roms have endured over centuries with 'no priestly caste', no recognized linguistic standard, 'no texts enshrining a corpus of beliefs and code of morality, no appointed custodian of ethnic traditions', is remarkable. One way they have done this, even while absorbing numerous cultural influences, is to preserve a clear distinction between themselves and *gadje* (or *gadze*), the Romani word for non-Roms. Most Romani travel is seasonal and many do not travel, although there are always meetings of larger *kumpania* (clans) on particular occasions, and it is not primarily their mobility that distinguishes them from *gadje*. *Gadje* are regarded as unclean, for Roms observe a clear distinction between the (clean) upper and (unclean) lower body, and secrecy about Romani ways is enabled by *gadje* gullibility. In the past especially, many Roms will have been inconsistent and 'incomprehensible about any matter they do not want to discuss', throwing stereotypical ideas about them back upon *gadje*.[74]

This is not simply mirroring. Because Roms' only homeland is the Romani way of life, historically consisting of service work for *gadje*, we can say that Roms are the one people we have whose only home is human exchange, or language. A scrambling of stereotypes shows that *gadje* terms do not necessarily apply to Roms, but also that there is another, undisclosed reality that Roms can choose whether or not to share.[75] And although we could not say that historically no Roms are involved in conflicts over resources (for thieving to survive is arguably that), the space-making border work of a scrambled performance – turning *gadje* perceptions back upon *gadje*, suggesting that there is something else beneath – preserves an important human function. It reminds us that all landed belonging must at some point yield to engagements with those from elsewhere. On such occasions the rhythm of performative challenge, of agreement or disagreement, of exchange enabling common understanding or of managed dispute must often serve as makeshift ground if war over resources is not to follow.

The space of exchanges Roms live by, without a dream of homeland, can become charged with an energy in which the terms of belonging are continually remade. Everything is to be played for, and, as Michael Stewart's observation of Romani horse traders in 1990s Hungary shows, the space of unknown future action in which a buyer's or seller's position can be changed in relation to another's is all important. While breeding horses might make more money, buying and selling creates opportunity, and Roms, at the bottom of the heap in an economic system understood to work rationally, have minimal investment in its laws of loss and gain. Instead the market becomes a heroic arena in which prices are the result of bargaining. The terms of trade can alter, a hunch can be backed, someone, seeing a future possibility, might coerce another into seeing the world as he sees it. Dressing like wealthy landowners, Roms adopt the role of those who have historically managed peasants as Roms now do at markets. Speech and performance are means by which Roms 'make money turn around . . . and come to us'. The luck that is an attribute of Romani being must be lived up to and extended to others.[76] Exchange interactions are home ground.

While it might be claimed that such Roms are simply fantasizing, as when a horse is kept for future trade at the price of a family going hungry, further functions are at work. To maintain the ongoing rhythm of interaction is to maintain the memory that borders sustain meaning. Most important among these may be the invisible border central to our being, the one we passed on our way to becoming humans – those who create meaning in and by means of each other's wagers and surmises about ourselves, our world and others, rather than taking these as given. When no homeland supports a people's livelihood or wealth creation, that people, who have not lost anything, embodies a relation to the future we will all increasingly embody, that of responsive adjustment to planetary conditions. The border work Roms do testifies to a point of historical change we are likely to face again, and the space of 'no homeland' but the ones we make turns unbelonging itself into a link, and exchanges into potential futures. If *gadje* cannot be, like the 2019 Sudanese in relation to Darfur, 'all Rom', let us consider the possibility – one the next chapter will test – that what we call peripheries become central to human movements over time because they preserve in their sometime exclusion by others not only knowledge of what we were but ways to manage what we become.

4

STORY

In the 25th chapter of *The Lost Books of the Odyssey* (2007), Zachary Mason's sharp-eyed telling of ancient tales about Odysseus, we find the Greek epic hero alone in a cabin in snowy woods, with no idea how he came there. His curiosity eventually uncovers a hidden book, which tells the story of Odysseus, 'soldier and diplomat', and on rereading it to the end where the hero walks inland 'with an oar over his shoulder until someone mistakes it for a winnowing fan' he experiences a 'shock of revelation'. It is, of course, his story. The 'essential insight is that the text is corrupt, or . . . incomplete, or of a calculated obscurity' because this man, Odysseus as was, has done what 'the cleverest of the Greeks' would have had to do to escape the wrath of Poseidon. He has travelled far from gods and men and used his considerable mental powers and force of will to rid himself of memory and thus 'been himself no more'.[1] The text is partly dark to him because his life story is attached to him now by the slenderest of threads. The obscurity derives from concerted forgetting.

Odysseus had earned Poseidon's anger by slaying the sea god's one-eyed giant son Polyphemus, as relayed in Book IX of Homer's *Odyssey*. Having told the man-eating giant his name is 'No one', Odysseus and his men escape as Polyphemus calls to his friends that 'No one' is killing him.[2] In the underworld Odysseus learns that after reaching home and slaying the suitors vying for his wife Penelope's hand he must make a further journey, taking his oar to a place where, the sea being unknown, it is mistaken for a tool for winnowing grain (XI.138–50). He must plant it in the earth and sacrifice to Poseidon. Only then may he return home. In Mason's story Odysseus is troubled by questions about who he is and who built the cabin. But having recognized himself in the tale while having forgotten so much else, and knowing how unwilling the past Odysseus would have been to yield up knowledge of his identity, the present Odysseus is able to do it. He burns the book, 'the last link to who [he] was', cancelling debts and enabling a new beginning.[3] The man who was once Odysseus is now no one.

Departing

It is loss that gives the Odysseus of 'The Book of Winter' a sense of who he can become. Being 'no one' is liberating, enabling action. He will have to kill a wolf for clothing, a bird for food when the cabin's biscuit supply ends. Returning to Ithaca is unlikely. He would not know the way and has forgotten friends and family. But, having found the courage to let all attachments go, he may yet have these things again in an unknown future. Self-recognition has gone, but as the act that made its going possible shows, he remains strong-willed and ingenious. Odysseus' story has endured because its many turns on his search for home after war are occasioned by and met with his trademark inventiveness. The hero fits the story, and the story of homeward trials can figure the shape of many lives, wartorn or more outwardly stable. This chapter will consider wanderers similarly fated to lose touch with who they were: those with the 'wrong' ethnicity cast out of early modern Spain; Africans taken by the Atlantic slave trade, forced to endure the traumatic Middle Passage; Europeans driven from villages by land enclosures and from land to sea by naval impressment.

But equally it will consider how these wanderers were not reduced to these changes. Many retained or found in themselves the courage and resourcefulness to make of their dramatically altered lives a story. Tracking the stories occasioned by forced wanderers, I also have in mind a larger question: whether the experience of mass displacement and unbelonging, collective events not typically known as such in the undergoing, fuels the creation of and creates an audience for tales about one man or woman who, in surviving the odds, represents the larger group humanity, stories such as we find in modern novels. I do not want to claim this recent form has a single cause so much as give the sense of individual alienation that industrial modernity wrought in so many its due as the part-cause of a new kind of story. Building up over time, especially in the West, confusion borne of the pace of change may have made the tale of a protagonist's wanderings a tool for living, a resource playing out the self-reflection and forward drive those with the capability to do so were already enacting, as shown by some who have left accounts of their life's journeys.

The *Odyssey*, dating from around the eighth century BCE, may be the first story in which duality is present from the first, the tale's form enacting key attributes of the protagonist. Unlike the *Iliad*, which opens with a reference to its wrathful hero, Achilles, Odysseus is introduced for the first time in the epic unnamed, an absent presence:[4] 'Sing to me of the man, Muse, the man of twists and turns/ driven time and again off course . . ./ . . . heartsick on the open sea' (1.1–2, 5). It is not until the 24th line that we learn the hero's name. In hiding his identity from us, the poem's opening performs Odysseus' central quality: his cunning or inventiveness and ability to deceive and hide himself. His mind falls easily to twists and turns, as does his homegoing journey and as does the sea, the story's primary element. Its god-sent twists and turns keep him from reaching home for around ten years, sometimes as a result of his wilful actions.

Odysseus continues to elude us until Book V. We learn first of how his absence is experienced by others: his son Telemachus and his wife Penelope. The gods depart for two places in books I and V,

Athene to Ithaca to press Telemachus to search for his father, and Hermes to Ogygia to tell Calypso to send Odysseus home. Although there is Iliadic precedent for their dual journeys,[5] their presence at the start of an epic is new and fits a tale with a complicated structure, more than one focus of attention, and a protagonist who is always potentially of at least two minds. Once Odysseus reaches Scheria at the end of Book V, we learn of what he has previously endured in flashback as, in Books IX to XII, he tells the Phaeacians who live there of his travels. Books XIII to XXIV detail the hero's return to Ithaca disguised as a beggar who gradually reveals more of himself to those who know him, his revenge on the suitors besieging his house and his reunion with Penelope, Telemachus and his father Laertes.

Before the *Odyssey* ends Odysseus tells Penelope about Tiresias' prophecy that a final journey yet awaits him. It is no lightweight matter. Ancient Greeks used the sea/land border to orient them-selves, travelling and settling close to it. Colonizers seldom ventured far inland. To lose sight of the coast from any point threatened water and food supply. And while it was clear to the Greeks that the seas they did not reach were fearsome and destructive, Alex Purves suggests that, as terrible as the ocean wastes were, their conceiv-ability made them less unsettling than another realm. Deep inland where no border marked the limits of the known, everything – civil-ization, certainty, sanity – could come undone. Tiresias' prophecy thus creates in the *Odyssey* a strange future space that can never be known in epic terms, because to go there is not to conquer but, if one survives, to be remade. And while Tiresias says that Odysseus will return to Ithaca to die 'a gentle . . . death' with his people around him, that death will come 'far from the sea' (XI.153–6), the phrase lending intriguing weight to Mason's suggestion of another end: the people of Odysseus' second life inland, those he has yet to meet in a new beginning.[6]

Odysseus tells Penelope that this journey will be an 'unmeasured' labour,[7] and the context in which he reveals it is the couple's first new night together. To give them more time, Athena '[holds] back the night' at 'the edge of the earth' and Dawn 'at Ocean's banks' (XXIII.276–8). The altered temporal boundary is the occasion for Odysseus revealing a borderless future space where the work to be done cannot be measured. Occluded from the poem and the measured beats of Homer's verse, the future journey also involves a dismantling of metaphor,[8] that means by which we domesticate the foreign, making shock thinkable by transposing one thing into another. Metaphor is undone when Odysseus takes the oar into the new country, since Aristotle defined metaphor as carrying over a name 'that belongs to something else' to a new object. Here, the name changes as the object endures, and with the loss of the facility of extending name, the ability to harmonize the foreign with the known falters. Odysseus will lose his bearings and, significantly for one whose chief quality is quickness of mind and speech, words may fail him.[9]

Purves calls this a 'near impasse' that dislocates epic from its role once heroes have died or returned from their journeys. One can discern here a space signifying the possibility of later, as yet unthought forms, perhaps even the space in which will germinate the seed of the ancient and modern novel. Unlike other heroes Odysseus lives easily in suspension, as his return home disguised as a homeless beggar shows. He 'embraces . . . obscurity' for what it can show him about his old yet new situation.[10] It is unlikely that his talent for dissembling will be much needed back in Ithaca. But the inland journey will meet the very darkness his mind has been to others. He will not know others' thoughts as they will not know his, and so his departure from home will not only be an act of faith in our ability to adapt, but in experiencing our selves as others do by losing our sense of who we are completely. We seldom quantify as a basis of decisive action the unknowing that is as essential to our being and civility as reason. Perhaps because of this, the unknown often takes our plans off track. Yet a wanderer's willed yielding of past connections can make possible new pathways on the basis of a loss shared, even if unknowingly, with others. Capability may survive loss of memory, and the choice to live as no one always makes possible a story.

Hinterland

We have Spain to thank for the beginnings of the modern novel, in works centred around inventive, peripatetic 'no ones' whose actions and demeanour respond to the empire's emphasis on blood purity and noble lifestyles. The anonymously published *Lazarillo de Tormes* (1554) instigates the picaresque, its popularity increased by that of Mateo Aleman's *Guzmán de Alfarache* (1599, 1604), with Miguel de Cervantes's *Don Quixote* (1605, 1615) the best known instance of the form. The *pícaro* is a vagabond of humble origins who lives on society's margins by his or her wits, showing honour (*honra*) to be a hollow, fraudulent convenience. Inverting the terms of Golden Age chivalric romances, which resonated with the Spanish *Reconquista* – the attempt to reclaim Iberia (Spain) from Islamic rule through the thirteenth to fifteenth centuries – and with Christopher Columbus's and Hernán Cortés's fifteenth- and sixteenth-century voyages to discover New World treasure, the picaresque novel showcases the chaos of the era.[11]

In the eighth century around three-quarters of the Iberian peninsula came under Muslim rule and until the reconquests Muslims, Jews and Christians lived in relative harmony. The conquest of Muslim Granada and Christian aggression towards Jews made for a less cohesive society than previously. Many of Spain's later problems begin here when, as the kingdom's interior begins to fracture, it is propelled into three largely disastrous ventures: joining with other kingdoms in a 'new, united Spain', military conflict in the peninsula and elsewhere, and expansion into a recently discovered New World as an imperial and colonial power. Anti-Jewish massacres occurred in several major cities in 1391 and thousands of Jews were forced to receive Christian baptism. So, in the early sixteenth century, were Muslim Moors, henceforth Moriscos.[12] Both *conversos* (Jewish Christian converts) and Moriscos were persecuted and suspected of insincerity. After the fall of the last Muslim stronghold, Granada, in 1492, Spain expelled unconverted Jews, while the Moriscos were expelled in 1609.

It was not only on matters of religion and ethnicity that the emergent nation was divided. Further contradictions between appearance and reality negatively impacted national wealth. Ferdinand and Isabella married in 1469, ostensibly uniting Castile and Aragon, establishing law and order on the peninsula and pacifying powerful nobles. The war against Granada partly achieved the latter, but fifteenth-century Spain was poor, with royal debts met by means of *juros*, annuities repaid from ordinary revenues which effectively mortgaged state income, of which 68 per cent went towards debt repayment by 1556. The crown offered patronage, including tax-exempt land grants in conquered areas, to nobles in return for personal and military service, thus forgoing land as well as tax revenue. Hoping for riches, especially gold, and needing a route to foreign wealth that cut out the Muslim middlemen it distrusted, Spain supported the voyages of Columbus, resulting in the 'discovery' of Hispaniola in 1492 and, by the mid-sixteenth century, considerable wealth from American silver mines.[13]

However, seeking wealth from abroad while ignoring the successful artisanal enclaves and business acumen of Muslim and Jewish groups at home meant sacrificing a useful multiplicity for an improbably linear story, that of Christian New World dominance led by Spain. Ferdinand's successor Charles I became Charles V, Holy Roman Emperor, partly on the strength of large loans from the Fuggers, a prominent family of Augsburg bankers, and committed Spain to war with Protestant German princes and their allies for more than a century. General taxation and international borrowing were needed to fund these wars, but as nobles were largely tax exempt, the burden fell on the rest of the population. Loans raised against Peruvian silver benefited foreign lenders and venture capitalists, while news of colonial exploitation weakened the nation's standing.[14] By the turn of the seventeenth century debt, contempt for commerce and obsession with internal aliens were rife. The aristocracy had embraced debt as a lifestyle. Tax-free nobility patents and crown lands given to loyal individuals denied commoners access, locking large estates in private ownership.[15] The poor were disproportionately affected by the influx of American bullion, the liquidity of which caused inflation, and by the increasingly high taxation needed to fund foreign wars. Monetary inflation was one reason early seventeenth-century Spain exported raw materials and imported finished goods. The economy of the nation proud of ridding itself of aliens was thus subject to foreign interests at every turn.[16]

Rural Castilians, unable to pay taxes, fled to cities, while peasants borrowed money through *censos*: loans issued by individuals or civic institutions to be repaid in annual percentage payments. Defaults meant more land passed into the urban possession of money-lenders. Anyone with money to spare could lend it, so land, already mortgaged, became an investment vehicle more than a productive resource. Owners and labourers had no incentive to work it, which increased food shortages and thence prices.[17] The abandonment of land and the extension to all of a mentality whereby living on rents showed one's superior social status was also the logical outcome of the fixation on blood purity. In the 1540s statutes of *limpieza de sangre* (purity of blood) were issued in Toledo to keep *conversos* out of a range of clerical and civic positions, a practice ratified by Philip II in 1556. Since even a humble peasant of 'old Christian' stock might be considered more honourable than a recent convert, peasants with spare cash, in addition to merchants and clerics, might purchase the non-labouring status they felt was rightfully theirs by lending money. Yet to buy the status one supposes oneself to already possess through blood purity is clearly contradictory, further confusing a social order 'already … rendered fluid by money'. 'No one', observes B. W. Ife, 'could be certain which was the true indicator of status: inherited wealth, new money, or Christian blood'.[18]

The picaresque novel responds to these contradictions, exposing, in method and form, the facade whereby supposed social 'reality' consists of performative masking. Its apparent realism was innovatory. In contrast to the idyllic, labour-free settings in mid-sixteenth-century pastoral stories and chivalric romances, the picaro must work, or trick or rob others to eat. *Lazarillo de Tormes* shows an anti-mercantile world in which nobility is all, but so, correlatively, is masquerade. Penniless, young Lazarillo is given away as guide to a blind man who, while outwardly godly, gains money by trickery and from whom the anti-hero quickly learns to steal. He then serves a priest, who starves him, and a noble master concerned only with appearance whom Lazarillo has to provide with food. He works for other masters as a water carrier and town crier before marrying the local arch-priest's mistress in a successful 'profit-sharing agreement'.[19]

An indictment against Lazarillo regarding his mode of life leads him to write his story, a narrative that arraigns the system that produced him, forcing him to leave the countryside for the city and live as someone he is not (he is likely a *converso*), using guile to advance himself. Because the story is written in response to a specific charge, there is tension between scenes which are undeniably true to life and the purpose of the narrative. We witness in the narrative construction, including the defensive prologue, the same persuasive strategies by which Lazarillo convinces those he meets to do him favours, the story foregrounding the unstable basis of decisions about what to believe.[20] Lazarillo's defence fails – he is too clearly the rogue – but authorially introduced contradictions in the form of upstanding, abusive characters, deceptive priests, manufactured miracles and ironic language mesh with the dissembling of early modern Spain. Obliquity is unavoidable for so-called *conversos*, regarded as duplicitous even when they were not, but nobles and the nation were equally living lies. Spain's disavowal of its Jewish and Moorish expertise and its grandiloquent attempts to attain it in other ways led it to end as it began, crippled by debt to the powers whose like it had destroyed at home. Partly because of this, the realism that is the picaresque's gift to the novel's future – low-life characters, a window on a formerly hidden world – is from the first in tension with the satirical intent that invites distrust.[21] Realism is the production of reality's appearance, and this appearance could always be otherwise. Fictional worlds might be recognizable, but they are not self-contained. Just as in the world that gives birth to them, someone is always pulling strings.

Guzmán de Alfarache (1599, 1604) is a much more unwieldy, digressive narrative containing many interpolated forms. Guzmán too is a *converso*, whose wanderings, involving ever greater criminality, produce despair. There is a subplot allegorizing the theft of the narrative itself, a reference to a 1602 continuation by another writer. Finally sentenced to a term in the galley of a ship for his crimes, Guzmán helps quash a revolt, allying himself with the establishment. And yet his narrative authority and defence of his behaviour is everywhere undone by incongruity, not least the apparent anger displayed by Aleman at another's having attempted to co-opt his story. The counterfeit character of the rogue and the fact of the counterfeit story become entwined.[22] And yet again, the ultimate targets are the paradoxes of sixteenth-century Spanish life, in which redemption, if possible, is never final. Thus Guzmán's story ends inconclusively, at sea, the most unstable place and that by means of which the nation sought a new future, one that brought new problems to accompany the old.

Delusions about freedom and new beginnings are famously to the fore in *Don Quixote*, the story of a squire who sells his lands to buy books whose outdated world view of chivalric romance causes him to reinvent himself as the knight Don Quixote of La Mancha.

Taking to the road, eventually accompanied by his own squire, Sancho Panza, he seeks adventures in which numerous representatives of rural and urban industry, from windmills to fulling mills to flocks of sheep, galley slaves and silk-selling merchants, are all mistaken for timeless instances of nefarious wrongs the hero must right with his – usually combative – actions. Naturally, he fails, but with each new failure grows more committed to the madness, born of romantic fiction, that others see but which he does not, while these others deceive him further when they are not extricating him from unnecessary problems. Clearly, this is a story about Spain's imperial fantasies, rendered as a profound mistaking of the nature of an increasingly globalizing world. Like Don Quixote's adventures, Spain's New World money sustained a facade of enrichment in certain times and places, as when the bourgeoisie moved to Madrid and Seville in the later sixteenth century when Castile failed, but as money still went into unproductive lending or trade in foreign hands, nothing changed. The 'adventures' were forms of adherence to unsustainable ideals.[23]

With the chivalric romances that afflict Don Quixote indicted as sources and exemplars of the nation's imperialist fantasies, the novel takes aim at their means of self-authorization. Following the earliest romances, sixteenth-century Spanish versions often claimed to be true histories. A romance's preface typically described a chanced-upon manuscript written in another language and translated into Spanish, the adventures witnessed by a historian.[24] Cervantes parodies this, claiming that Part One's first eight chapters belong to an author whose work is based on unnamed Spanish sources. A second author has edited them – Cervantes himself. However, the narrative suddenly ends when Don Quixote and an opponent are about to clash swords in Chapter Eight, and we are then told of Cervantes's discovery of some old books in a Toledo street market which, when translated, reveal a different story from the one we have read.[25] The chronicler of this version, the Arab Cide Hamete Benengeli, is, according to Cervantes, untrustworthy, thus reversing the traditional arrangement whereby a revered source grounds the tale. With the Arab author unreliable, Cervantes needs to intervene in the story.

While all of this emphasizes the artificiality of the original form and the falsity of the means and content of the national mythos it supports, Cervantes too faced a false continuator who published a sequel to Part One in 1614 while he was at work on Part Two, and Part Two discredits the spurious version. *Don Quixote* is helped in this by the extraordinary number of kinds of literary forms it incorporates or refers to, not only romances but sonnets, ballads, proverbs, plays, political commentaries and explorative tales. Allied to the dialectical tension caused by the mad knight's having to engage in dialogue with the down-to-earth Sancho, by which his madness is somewhat tempered (although not on the subject of chivalry), this depth of engagement with the literary past and present gives the novel a wider purview than the continuation, in which Don Quixote forsakes his beloved Dulcinea and retires to a madhouse, his madness the story's beginning and end.[26] In *Don Quixote*, by contrast, the hero's madness is a means to bring all of the influences of Spanish society to bear on the question of how a nation can persist in an unsustainable fiction about itself to the detriment of its people and resources. The arguments between Sancho Panza and Don Quixote about the nature of reality and how it can be known strike at the heart of the nation's international condition.

Perhaps no episode has more to say about this than the Cave of Montesinos section in Part Two, which incorporates reference to the enchantment of Dulcinea, one of Sancho's key tricks on his master. Earlier, charged with speaking to Dulcinea on Don Quixote's behalf, Sancho decides to call the first peasant girl he meets Dulcinea, since his master, having never seen the supposed original, will not know the difference (II.10, pp. 515–21). When Sancho and Don Quixote next see three peasant girls approaching, Sancho convinces Don Quixote that one of them is Dulcinea, under an enchantment from which the knight may rescue her with his deeds of valour. Don Quixote's visit to the Cave of Montesinos, a version of the descent to hell or the underworld experienced by Odysseus and Aeneas, has many contemporary overtones. Dulcinea and two maids are there, one of whom asks Don Quixote for the loan of six *reales* for her mistress, to which Don Quixote says he can only offer four. He expresses the desire 'to be a Fúcar', Spanish for Fugger, the German banking family that had taken on most of the Spanish crown's debt, so that he might offer more (II.23, pp. 612–13).

As Ning Ma notes, Dulcinea is a parody of Spain, its extensive debts and the late sixteenth-century bankruptcies they produced. Charles V had leased the nation's largest mercury mines at Almadén in the Sierra Morena mountains to the Fuggers in 1525, which gave the family a significant stake in the world silver trade, as mercury was the basis of a new refining technique that increased productivity tenfold. The mine employed convict labour in 1566, in what observers found to be 'hellish scenes of backbreaking labour'.[27] Contact with mercury caused physical harm and high mortality among miners, news of which Cervantes's work as a government clerk would likely have brought him word. Conditions in American silver mines, where indigenous and African slave labourers worked, were even worse. The basic rope ladders by which such workers went to and from the mines with heavy loads of ore are alluded to by the rope with which Sancho and a companion let Don Quixote down to the cave and up again.

Dulcinea's degradation to the status of a peasant girl offering a petticoat as loan security and the sleeping knight in the cave show the nation's enchantment by mineral wealth and that wealth's failure to amend its crises to be continuous. Through its protagonist and the nation his wanderings represent, *Don Quixote* showcases the material, economic and ideological processes by which an emerging modernity buys freedoms, and the delusions to which those freedoms give rise. From the seventeenth to eighteenth centuries, many of the world's workers were forced to move in service of an increasingly powerful transatlantic economy promising liberties that those workers and other displaced peoples did not receive. While ignoring the cost of what is promised has a long way to run, the bringing of once peripheral stories into the highway of an emergent literary form that is canny about its productive circumstances informs the eighteenth-century novel. Excluded peripheries, the profit-bearing drivers of industrial modernity, are apt to return to prominence in other forms, posing questions about the sustainability of a given world view. The early modern picaresque bequeaths to the later novel the potential to stage reality effects that, while fictional, are true to history. The idea of normative, linear progress will be challenged by the novel, and the picaresque will prove key to that end.

'Unconquerable mind': people on the move

By the early seventeenth century increased numbers of English people were on the move as a result of inflation, famine and enclosure of common lands.[28] Two forms of punishment for vagabonds helped bring vagrants together. Impressment of vagabonds for naval campaigns and to avoid a felony trial increased in the later sixteenth century, and vagrants constituted a significant share of armies. Transportation for vagrancy to colonies in the Caribbean, Europe and America began in earnest in the early seventeenth century. Many sent were young and poor, including children. From the late fifteenth and early sixteenth centuries common lands in villages were increasingly enclosed for commercial farming. Enclosure in England had several phases and differed between regions, but overall resulted in the loss of arable fields and meadows, common, permanent pasture land, and 'waste' land at margins.[29]

The pre-enclosure open-field system divided arable fields into strips worked by individuals, available for villagers to gather leftover grain from after harvest. In some places animals were also grazed in open fields post-harvest and at fallow times, while village common and waste land supported animals, provided fuel, food, building and repair materials and supplies for artisanal labour such as gathering rushes and sticks to make baskets and brooms. While not all areas had common lands, those that did lost more and more of them. The former peasantry became split between aspirational tenant-farmers and the increasing landless poor.[30] Wage labour did not replace these benefits, because subsistence losses were several in kind and because enclosure costs were passed on to tenants and rents often increased. Some landowners fixed rents regardless of harvest fluctuations. Between 1700 and 1850 estates were consolidated and many tenants lost life leases and customary tenure. Just as significant was ideological change. The idea that people had a right to gain a living from land in common was replaced by the idea of land as possession from which maximum profit was to be gained.[31]

But the idea of land as common to the life right of all was an old story not readily yielded. It had biblical origins, and when first the Levellers and later the Diggers withdrew from the labour wage process in the mid-seventeenth century, levelling fences and digging and planting in unwanted common ground, this was a key basis on which they did so. They were helped by the democratization of print and by wartime chaos.[32] When Gerrard Winstanley and his fellow Diggers planted vegetable seeds in the dirt of St George's Hill near Cobham in Surrey on Sunday 1 April 1649, they were raising a new race of 'Adams' made from dust by founding a new form of community. About thirty members arrived within a week, followed by further settlements in south-central England in later months, the movement enduring for just over a year. 'Poor harvests, trade disruption, disease, bad weather . . . [and] heavy taxation' in 1647–9 and the demand to quarter the army in the 1640s contributed to the Diggers' sense that the common people were owed help by parliament, and that parliament's victory over Charles I should free them from some of this pain. A way to abolish the tyranny of private property by building self-sustaining community, digging was also symbolic: an uprooting of harsh practices to spread freedom and a seeking after truth.[33]

Radicalism as a form of public culture was assisted by the absence of monarchical or parliamentary authority between 1646 and 1648. But even earlier, during Kett's Rebellion in 1549 and the Midlands Rising of 1607, what was objected to was not only small-scale enclosure but what we might call an annexing of imagination as well as opportunity,[34] a curtailment countered by such rich figures of hope and allegiance as the 'Oke [Oak] of Reformation' of the people's court, presided over by yeoman farmer Robert Kett and his band on Mousehold Heath near Norwich. Land owned but not shared limited the freedom and pleasure in life formerly to be found by the poor in relatively meagre circumstances, as though the ability to mobilize these experiences was a threat rather than a resource for all. Yet this earlier way of living represented, albeit at times unconsciously and though born of hard conditions, a valuable alternative to the world reduction of subjecting everything to profit. Recall that the Diggers dug only for sustenance, and despite enduring violence did not raid enclosed land. They simply withdrew their labour from the private land market. And they were not the last to claim that the right to subsist belongs to everyone. Later in the eighteenth century and in our own age of ecological devastation, these claims were and are equally strong.[35]

While the dispossessed were being brought together in the army, navy and in the colonies, arguably the first international factory labour force was being formed at sea. As Marcus Rediker notes, 'during the early modern period, merchant capitalists were organizing themselves, markets, and a working class in increasingly transatlantic and international ways.' As capital concentrated in merchant shipping, so did workers, and this large mobile workforce, possessing no craft skills or tools, was the forerunner of the industrial worker with nothing but labour to sell.[36] A strong working identity was formed among seamen, whose task was to cooperate in an enclosed, supervised setting with up-to-date machinery in the movement of cargo. Yet desertion was common. The work was dangerous, the food poor, ship discipline harsh and potentially disabling, and disease often rampant. Wages were often held over for years at a time. A deserting English seaman could hope to escape a brutal captain or dangerous port and sell his labour for the trip home to London.[37]

There was not much shipowners or captains could do about the autonomous mobility of the sea worker, nor about the bonds formed amid the harshness of seaboard life. While three-quarters of an English ship's workforce were supposed to be English this was seldom adhered to, and African, Portugese, Dutch, West Indian, Irish and American sailors worked English ships, while sailors were frequently multilingual, a further aid to mobility. Sailors' struggles with oppressive conditions informed radical seventeenth-century movements, but one of the most dramatic and effective protests was to turn pirate, which Anglo-American sailors did increasingly between 1716 and 1726, after a trade slump in 1715.[38] The years 1650 to 1730 are typically called the Golden Age of Piracy, although the lines between piracy and privateering were often fluid. The first generation, the Elizabethan buccaneers of 1550–80, who attacked the ships of Catholic Spain, also destroyed and ransomed cities, like today's state-sponsored terrorists. Sir Francis Drake and Walter Raleigh were knighted for their efforts. The Netherlands followed similar policies.[39] The Indian Ocean and Madagascar pirates followed in the 1690s, while the eighteenth-century pirates, from whom the outlines of the most dramatic and often romanticized stories come, were the most numerous and successful.

These wandering 'multiethnic freebooters' numbered around 4,000 in their decade of operation. They captured and plundered hundreds of merchant ships, disrupting trade in strategic capital areas: the West Indies, North America, West Africa. Their lives were short – one or two years as pirate was common – and their ends often brutal, with a campaign of gallows terror leading to their demise. In contrast to their experiences in merchant shipping, pirates practised an egalitarian social order. Officers and captains were normally elected, and the latter had unchallenged authority only in pursuit or escape. The highest authority was expressed in a common council, which met regularly and included every man on board. Food and booty were distributed equally, along with chances to be first to board prize vessels. And significantly, given their programmes of equality, pirate captains were not always men. Anne Bonny (1697–1782?) and Mary Read (1685–1721) are the two best-known female pirate captains, but there were others, including, in the early nineteenth century, Zheng Yi Sao (1775–1844), a former prostitute who as an esteemed military commander led a pirate confederation that became a commercial empire in the South China Sea.[40]

Some early buccaneers, many of whom had escaped the savageries of the nascent Caribbean slave system, formed runaway or maroon communities, especially in the mountains, where they hunted and gathered food. Later, similar communities formed in the Americas. These multiethnic groups included indigenous peoples as well as escaped slaves, indentured servants, demobilized soldiers and the unemployed.[41] Life in southern maroon communities, such as in the Great Dismal Swamp between North Carolina and Virginia, where several thousand lived – including initially English radicals as well as Indigenous Americans and escaped indentured servants and slaves – was hard and appealed mostly to young men without families. Maroons also traded successfully. In Jamaica they kept in touch with plantations, trading in ammunition and provisions, and in Jamaica and Saint-Domingue (today's Dominican Republic and Haiti) controlled the movement of foodstuffs and other consumer goods between cities and countryside. 'Wandering higglers', enslaved and free women brokers in goods for sale by slaves, who were often allowed to raise their own fruit and vegetables, were also important sources of news about uprisings and related opportunities, a form of physical and mental mobility impossible for authorities to fully control.[42]

The horrors of Atlantic colonial slavery, the most significant mobilization of capital, people, ships, material resources, manufactures, finance and news of the modern period, are well documented. Around 12 million people were captured on the African coast between 1500 and 1870, more than 1.5 million of whom died during the Middle Passage, the traumatic voyage from Africa to the New World, a further unknown number before embarkation, while on arrival between 'a tenth and a fifth ... died within a year'. The degree of organized human trafficking and dehumanizing labour coordination was harrowing and unprecedented. Before late seventeenth- and eighteenth-century plantation slavery, or what Ira Berlin calls 'slave societies', some enslaved people and other Africans had relative mobility and freedom to conduct their own affairs. Many Atlantic Creoles, people of African descent with connections to the larger Atlantic world, served as intermediaries between Africans and Europeans at the outset of the trade, using their linguistic and diplomatic skills and knowledge of commercial practices to transcend a single locale and occupy the interstices of African and European worlds.[43]

Cosmopolitan Creole communities in America provided many opportunities. Before the sugar revolution slaves in America often socialized with and worked alongside those sent from England, Ireland and elsewhere as indentured servants, convicts and political refugees, whose lot, especially in the north, could be comparable to theirs. Slaves in the Chesapeake (Virginia) were often able to hire out their free time, sell handicrafts they made and form partnerships with their owners by exchanging their produce for the right to work independently. While slaveowners were not always happy with such arrangements, slaves who were free to trade cost less to support, so the arrangement was mutually beneficial. Similar possibilities existed elsewhere. Northern slaves got a good knowledge of regional geography as they often worked in the carrying trade, piloting boats or driving wagons. Some bought their freedom: small communities of free Black people existed in Chesapeake Bay and elsewhere by the middle of the seventeenth century.[44]

With the advent of eighteenth-century plantation slavery proper, conditions of relative freedom ended for Africans. Race, based on skin colour, became newly significant in defining status, all work was plantation oriented and maximum labour was wrung from slaves. While runaways often posed as self-hired labourers, most returned to their owners, a common reason for departure being the desire to reconnect with family members sold elsewhere. Permanent escape north to freedom or into southern maroon communities made for a powerful new narrative, however, and slaveowners were troubled by the hope it conveyed as much as or more than by loss of labour. The sea provided the greatest opportunities for freedom, supplying information as well as escape routes. Along with news spread by the daily voyages of slave fishermen, enslaved Caribbeans frequently crossed the Atlantic in all-Black crews, because several Caribbean towns organized deep-sea labour through slavery. In London they met with other Black people, contributing to the emergent antislavery movement.[45]

Black seafarers were of profound importance for a nascent African American consciousness because they referred back to the heyday of Atlantic Creole expertise as well as to future freedom. Seamen wrote the first six Black autobiographies published in English before 1800, and their self-presentation was strategic. They identified as Christians and Africans to fit the antislavery cause, and transmuted the varied life experience gained from seafaring into the seeds of a diasporic consciousness. Presenting themselves as citizens of the world quietly reworked the element across which the Middle Passage proceeded, making it the untamed ground of a new belonging. Olaudah Equiano (c. 1745–1797), the best-known such author, was sold into slavery and bought by an officer of the Royal Navy, seeing action in the Seven Years War before escaping again and buying his freedom in 1766. Based in England, he travelled widely for commercial purposes and became a spokesperson for the abolitionist movement. He was one of the most accomplished writers of the century, and his story, *The Interesting Narrative of the Life of Olaudah Equiano, or Gustavus Vassa, the African. Written by Himself* (1789), set the standard for the slave narrative.[46]

Recent biographical evidence found by Vincent Carretta shows that Equiano may have been born in South Carolina (though not all scholars accept this conclusion). If this was so, his account of an African upbringing and the terrifying Middle Passage would demonstrate not only the extent of his literary abilities but also a rhetorical savviness. Before 1789 most antislavery voices were white, and dramatic accounts of slavery's horrors were what Africans could most readily provide. However, Equiano defined himself primarily by movement, and his time at sea gave him the contacts and experience to represent abolitionism from a Black and cosmopolitan viewpoint. A significant aspect of the emergent eighteenth-century novel was the involvement of the reader in speculation, the very mindset under-writing slavery from a metropolis like London. This involvement made it possible for the reader's assumed relation to the world to alter. Equiano had been a slave driver in Central America and his story shows readers his own changing attitude to slavery, complicated by the fact of his having experienced it from both sides.[47] Stories like this helped pave the way for a narrative form that centralized the contradictions of modernity and invited readers to attempt to understand the related contradictions in themselves.

The rise of the reader

If the Atlantic slave trade does not directly generate the modern novel, it provides many of its conditions. It helped consolidate the nation-state as countries sought to compete in international markets, which in turn helped produce national literatures. Intensifying the 'instrumental rationality . . . market relations . . . administrative bureaucracies and modern tax systems' central to industrial modernity, slavery also increased commercial sophistication, consumerism's 'individualist sensibility', and aided the development of newspapers and early press advertising. A growing familiarity with 'action at a distance' was key. The slave trade brought together disparate worlds. Consumers of sugar, coffee, cocoa, tobacco, spices, silks, linens and dyestuffs in metropolitan European centres were joined with enslaved producers and their masters by complex chains of credit that changed consumers' lives as much as did the products. Credit was arranged by continually forming and re-forming groups of merchants who gathered and processed information relevant to particular ventures, since coordinating markets across vast distances amid slowly arriving commercial intelligence, fickle consumer tastes and the ongoing possibility or event of war carried risks.[48]

Without credit none of this would have occurred. It was credit, or belief, that, underpinning the borrowing needed to wage war in Europe and protect British trade, brought exotic products to imperial centres, enabled buying and selling in distant markets, warehousing, distributing, fitting out ships, hiring crews and transporting slaves. In 1694 the Bank of England, a private corporation, took responsibility for the government's debt, and its notes became currency as extra assets supplementing bullion on the basis of taxes yet to be received. New partnership banks, insurance offices, trading companies as well as brokers and stockjobbers invested in new kinds of securities. But the national debt crystallized anxieties around what was seen to be an entirely new way of living: on speculation and credit, or, as J.G.A. Pocock puts it, 'by men's expectations of one another's capacity for future action and performance'. For

> not only must the speculative society maintain and govern
> itself by perpetually gambling on its own wish-fulfillments
> . . . but every man was judged and governed, at every

moment, by other men's opinion of the probability that not he alone, but generations as yet unborn, would be able and willing to repay their debts at some future date which might never even arrive. Men, it seemed, were governed by opinion, and by opinion as to whether certain governing fantasies would ever become realized.[49]

The 'relationship between opinion and fantasy and business confidence' had begun to 'assume the dimensions of a social power', but this relationship was inscrutable and uncontainable, the price of getting goods from elsewhere seemingly for free (or for little more than locally produced goods cost formerly). Furthermore, as value was now assumed to precede, rather than follow, the exchange of people, goods and money involved in slave-produced commodities, and since mobile and ephemeral property was all (the strictly settled or enclosed estate enabling its increase), time and space shifted in meaning, becoming more abstract and imaginary than before. And finally, 'if the speculative society constantly gave itself credit for attaining levels of wealth, power and satisfaction which it had not yet achieved, and so sought to advance towards them, it constantly sought to transform itself by actualizing the imaginable but not predictable.'[50] Or, to put this another way, actualizing that thing whose purpose *is* its imagined unpredictability, its ability to be inhabited while its outcome remains unknown. I mean, of course, a story. For this was the age of fictions of value and of the avowable interest of everyone (the dependence of all men upon all men) in the existential possibilities of everyone else. A strange thread linked the slave working and hoping for freedom and the metropolitan English person in the eighteenth century. Their prospects rested as never before on the power attributed to the unknown in the form of individual rumour and collective belief.

Collective belief was integral to the rise of the novel, which occurred earliest and most decisively in England. Earlier generations of critics associated the novel's development with a desire for verisimilitude on the part of readers and with the establishment of a middle-class readership. But more recent studies have reminded us of the significance of the tensions Pocock describes whereby ordinary people had to credit each other with unlikely propensities tacitly as well as overtly.[51] The resultant fictionalizing tendencies can be seen in the instance of lotteries. Between 1694 and 1826 the state launched around 170 lotteries, managed by the Bank of England from 1710. Once blank tickets were introduced and the chance of winning or losing became central, uptake increased. Lotteries were one example of a craze for betting on uncertain outcomes in eighteenth-century London, from the lives of one's business partners to 'the succession of Louis XV's mistresses', the outcomes of battles or death by fire.[52]

As well as literalizing the taking of decisions on uncertain bases, lotteries enabled participants to imagine their lives taking dramatic turns, the key feature being that *anyone* could win. Replacing the earlier association of fiction with dissimulation and deceit, the mid-eighteenth-century novel not only opened the field of readerly identification to 'anyone', as we will see, but also trained readers to manage probabilities. While the physical and moral wanderings of such characters as Joseph Andrews, his sister Pamela and Moll Flanders might be excessively innocent or reckless, the reader knew better, 'entertaining various hypotheses' about narrative action, practising 'suppositional speculation' and the kind of cognitive provisionality required of many other aspects of eighteenth-century life. The mental flexibility novel-reading entailed was needed, as Catherine Gallagher points out, for assessing a potential spouse amid the new companionate marriage arrangements and in commercial contexts, including the everyday acceptance of paper money.

But the novel was arguably the only field in which the largely individual play of speculation had no particular end save enjoyment, and so could conceivably serve many purposes. It also involved no particular kind of subject, for while the proper name had been central to earlier fiction, the mid-century novel pioneered stories about 'nobody in particular', anyones whose fortunes were ever subject to change. Characters were no longer personages about whom facts could be verified or falsified but general instances of people who *could* be real but were only provisionally so.[53] In contrast to the idea that eighteenth-century English novel readers sought a sense of verisimilitude in fiction, then, it seems more likely that provisional reality fit the bill. And as we saw with the Spanish picaresque, in fiction a sense of the familiar is always a production, never a simple window on the world. In eighteenth-century England a new sense of naturalness and immediacy was conveyed in painting, oratory and acting as well as fiction by deploying a less mannered stye than formerly. This, as Jesse Molesworth claims, is to covertly fictionalize the reader or consumer, who, in sympathy with the producer, enters into the idea that they are experiencing the real, in fact a collaborative effect.[54]

The 'nonentity' of the new fictional characters, with their ordinary names, created their reality effect, whereby the reader, with limited knowledge of her or his internal workings, could actualize them.[55] Characters like Pamela or Tom Jones were subject to outrageous twists of fortune of the sort that exercised eighteenth-century readers in their newly contingent worlds. But the bridging of prior distances through produced familiarity, a complex operation, also spoke of other kinds of distant nonentity whose everyday presence, while largely masked by the exotic commodities and financial practices that brought them near, was nonetheless implied: seafarers, industrial middlemen, colony workers, slaves. I am not claiming that eighteenth-century readers thought of these distant figures when they read novels that did not feature them (although some novels did). I mean to draw attention to the similarity between the way a provisional nonentity sustains a largely unrecognized, collaborative reality effect in fiction and the many unnamed, replaceable figures that had, by their networked labours, become invisibly essential to

European life. A similarity, and a difference. These were real people who precipitated the credit mechanisms that made of the era an age of fictions to which Europeans related as to a form of expanded or qualified reality in which the credit of others may or may not come through. And other 'nobodies' populated the period in ways that connected all (as, in a way, did novel readers themselves, members of a newly emerging mass or anonymous readership): print itself, the book as commodity, the newspaper as purveyor of knowledge from afar.[56]

The latter played a significant role in the slave trade. From the 1690s buyers and sellers would come together in coffee houses, where newspapers were commonly read, to access the commodity prices, foreign exchange rates and prices for government stocks they listed, make arrangements and agree terms. By the 1730s almost all provincial printers ran papers, and by the late 1770s they were read by significant numbers of people whose tastes they served. Newspapers helped develop an informed body of public opinion throughout the century, one the government feared. They contained a substantial variety of foreign news, which they emphasized in their attempts to secure new readers. Foreign news typically featured alongside domestic news, and the 'mischances of ordinary life' would appear interspersed with accounts of more momentous events.[57] So while awareness of the distant contexts that were reshaping the conditions of eighteenth-century European life may not have been pronounced throughout the population, connections to them were available. Odysseus becomes 'no one' as he walks inland to a place so far from the sea that he cannot measure its effects on him. Eighteenth-century novel readers, whom newspapers and coffee houses and commercial credit arrangements helped *know* that there was much about their contemporary conditions that remained unknown, had fiction as a way to practise provisional unknowing about characters and situations that were distant but not impossible, connected to them by invisible, yet not entirely improbable, bonds.

And fiction was initially consumed by its non-aristocratic English readers in the same way as newspapers, that is, serially. Cheap part-books, books sold a few pages or a chapter at a time, were popular in the mid-eighteenth century, and many books were initially published in magazines with new episodes weekly or monthly. Eighteenth-century magazines contained a great variety of material, and there is evidence that authors responded to readers' views as expressed in the letter pages of publications. The reading and circulation of novels was also frequently social and public. Book clubs and subscription and circulating libraries were the main sources of books for those who could not afford to buy them, and were very social venues. Books were also read in coffee houses and aloud in other social and domestic contexts. The eighteenth-century novel's concern with physical and class mobility – witness the several novels in which journeys by coach convey key plot developments and the number of characters who fall from position or experience a rise in station – was matched by the relatively 'unfixed' nature of reading in the period and with novels' smaller size and portable form.[58]

Perhaps no novel better demonstrates the experimental possibilities of the age of increased mobilities than Laurence Sterne's *The Life and Opinions of Tristram Shandy, Gentleman* (1759–67), a famously eccentric book about displacement and unbelonging, full of characters whose ideas about the world interfere with their experience of it. It also dramatizes the role of the reader, drawing attention to the many things a novel cannot contain. Narrative progress is almost non-existent, routine wandering from a given point the norm. An opening that is about, and enacts, halted progress is indicative. One Sunday night, Tristram's mother gives Tristram's father a start in the midst of their conjugal relations by reminding him to wind up the clock, which, Tristram thinks, has given *him* a bad start in life by paternal transmission. Tristram is interested in causes and their corollaries: what makes us who we are, and whether we can know where we are going. But the novel's typically roundabout opening is vague on these matters. 'I wish either my father or my mother . . . had minded what they were about when they begot me,' the tale begins, the wish suggesting that things might have been otherwise than they turned out, but we do not learn how they did turn out or how they might otherwise have been.[59]

And thus things continue, with halts to progression and recourse to digression such that the attempt to tell the story of Tristram's life proceeds through two volumes of twenty-five and nineteen chapters respectively without Tristram yet having been born. Digression often features in mid-eighteenth-century English novels, perhaps a reaction to the incessant pace of narrative earlier in the century, as does direct readerly address, but on both counts readerly expectations are uncommonly thwarted.[60] A preface occurs between chapters Twenty and Twenty-One of volume III because, the narrator says: 'All my heroes are off my hands' and this is the first time he has had a moment to write it (III.20, p. 173). In volume IX, chapters Eighteen and Nineteen follow Chapter Twenty-Five. In Chapter Twenty of volume I, readers are enjoined to turn back and reread the previous chapter (p. 51). Formal innovations born of the age of print are exploited not only for novelty's sake but to further the paradoxical idea, in a novel, that life resists pattern and that its most significant events are not readily understood. Hence the black page in volume I, Chapter Twelve marking Parson Yorick's death and the marbled page in volume III, formerly alluded to in the form of the slab that tops the grave and now present in its meandering opaqueness, said to represent the impenetrability of the story (1.12, p. 30; III.36, p. 204).

Tristram's characters, all at a distance from themselves, are the subtlest means by which Sterne conveys the pains and compensations of modernity. References to *Don Quixote* include the theme of mistaken realities, the play with narrative genesis, the novel's general exuberance and the hobby horse. The latter, a pastime or diversion involving a fabricated horse that stands for a person's fixation or cherished idea, refers to Tristram's Uncle Toby's obsession with recreating the battle of the Siege of Namur in the Seven Years War (1756–63). But it also refers to Walter Shandy's fixation with obscure, application-less theories about names and noses and with establishing a system of education for his son that Tristram's growth outruns, and to Tristram's with the passing of time and the non-advancement of his story. An emblem of private defences against life's uncertainties,[61] the hobby horse is also a means by which Sterne complicates the expression of emotion belonging to the eighteenth-century novel of sentiment, by inserting substitutions – fake movement props – for said expression, thus conveying a lostness in the face of challenging life events in which the reader becomes involved. Sentiment, a shared sense of feeling between characters and readers, is arrived at, but in a roundabout way.[62]

While Uncle Toby and Corporal Trim both cry, for instance – the latter freely, especially when recalling the sufferings of Tristram's brother Bobby – the idea that certain gestures should accompany certain feelings is parodied, as when Corporal Trim, hearing of Bobby's death, drops his hat in the middle of an address to the servants, a hat whose 'descent . . . was as if a heavy lump of clay had been kneaded into the crown of it', expressing 'the sentiment of mortality' in its '[falling] dead' (v.7, pp. 326–7). Both the hat's nonsensical, prosaic fall – for a hat is already lifeless and is not made so by falling – and the servants' floods of tears, which contrast, emphasize a further contrast, between Bobby's sudden absence – in Trim's words, 'Are we not here now . . . and . . . gone! in a moment' (pp. 325–6) – and its excessive responses. The surprise loss or the fact of something missing is highlighted by divergent forms of overplayed presence appearing in that something's stead.

This same attachment to the concrete and prosaic is shown by Uncle Toby in his courtship by the Widow Wadman, which proceeds in tandem with the climax of the recreation of the Siege of Namur, eventually concluded by the end of the Seven Years War. While Widow Wadman wants to know where exactly in the groin

Toby received the wound that invalided him from the army, Toby, for whom all life is mediated through military obsession, imagines she must want to know where on the battlefield the wound was received. When Corporal Trim explains what is really meant, Toby's feelings on the matter are expressed by his laying his pipe 'gently upon the fender' and expressing the wish that he and Corporal Trim go to visit Toby's brother (IX.22, p. 585). Toby's studied gesture and the displacing wish convey not only his unexpressed feelings but also the distance he experiences between such feelings and himself, and, in turn, the greater distance pertaining between Toby and the Widow Wadman, as well as between Toby and the concerns of the everyday world. While on occasion Toby, Trim and Walter Shandy all express sympathetic emotion through companionable gesture or silent recognition of one another's overwroughtness, it is at moments when feeling is *not* expressed, or where completion is avoided, that the reader is called upon to supply the shortfall, in acts of companionate recognition of those whose experience is not theirs, for few readers would be as innocent of the world's ways as Toby.[63]

All *Tristram*'s central characters seek compensations, or hobby horses, for the pressures of modern life, whether the pressure to marry, to give one's children a good start or to express oneself by telling a story (as Trim and Tristram fail to do). Perhaps most modern of all is the focus on efforts thwarted by random, multi-causal circumstance, an element Alexander Welsh sees as one of the novel's Cervantine features. Fanciful versions of the world, whether chivalric or sentimental, must yield to the 'desolation' of reality. This kind of desolation, of encountering the world as it is, shorn of delusion, arguably increases as opportunities for self-improvement and self-advancement themselves increase in modernity, with their inevitable mismatch between imagined future and current circumstance or actual event.[64] For while one's lot might improve, as that of many eighteenth-century Europeans did, a collective unmooring from past conditions that, unlike those conditions, is not experienced collectively but in terms of the new focus on individual fulfilment is likely to cause challenges that are difficult to express.

Sociality is now a matter of individual feeling conveyed in company, while the conditions of such feelings are not wholly within the individual's power. Credit, as we have seen, like trade, fosters belief in individual ability but functions by means of collective delivery that is both unseen and difficult of assessment. *Tristram*'s characters' hobby horses, their private languages and world views, attach them to the world and protect them from 'death, discord, and disaster'.[65] The novel, meanwhile, presents the reader with untenable positions – by pillorying the appropriate way to deliver a sermon, for instance (II.17, pp. 106–8) – and validates instead absence, in the form, say, of Toby's unpreparedness for modern life, which makes us, as it makes Walter Shandy, feel tenderly towards him (II.12, pp. 101–2). Between the 'too much' of prescribed response, a nod to the past of mannered demonstration of one's place in the world and duty to be intelligible to others, and the 'too little' of those who substitute another world for this one in their fear of its future-oriented pace lies the novel itself. It is a form significantly lacking in meaning until the reader provides the suppositions needed to make sense of its characters' disorientation.

By way of a bridge to this chapter's final section, a word is in order about the European *Bildungsroman*, or 'novel of formation', for this is in many ways the category to which Ralph Ellison's great mid-twentieth-century novel about Black and white America, *Invisible Man* (1952), belongs. Johann Wolfgang von Goethe's Wilhelm Meister series (1795–6, 1821) is typically regarded as the instigator of the *Bildungsroman*, a term coined by the literary scholar Karl Morgenstern in 1820 and in common use around fifty years later. Although the form came to be associated with wholeness and completion, Goethe's Meister novels represent the reverse. *Wilhelm Meister's Apprenticeship* and *Wilhelm Meister's Journeyman Years* include physical travels, but even more significant is the challenge of finding a place to belong in the modern world, to fit the self to the ever-changing moment. Like Ellison's Invisible Man, Wilhelm repeatedly learns that what he thought he had learned previously is erroneous, and 'formation' is correspondingly indeterminate. Wilhelm wants to understand the self as a whole being, with its many components in harmony or clear relation, but because modernity institutes a division between self and world such that the determinants of selfhood are increasingly dispersed, this is all but impossible.[66] The *Bildungsroman*, then, shows a life continually in formation but never finally formed.

Modernity has made Wilhelm Meister's project unattainable but all the more important, for it requires the reader, too, to work out a relation to the conjectural realities of modern life.[67] Ellison's novel involves a further complication. Full selfhood, believed in by twentieth-century America, is largely denied Invisible Man. His quest for belonging, given Western modernity's dependence on racist colonialism and slavery for its emergence, brings modernity's origins directly into play. This may be why this polyphonic novel takes us back to questions that pre-date modernity and its concern with selfhood, questions now more relevant to our lives than ever. It asks what makes us human and how to live as though a form for our relating to a world in dramatic change exists when it may not yet do so. As Invisible Man discovers, given full African American citizenship is not yet on offer, when such a form does not exist we have to make it by taking apart existing ones, recalibrating the self–world relation and potentially remaking ourselves.

'Into the breaks': humanity, migration, change

From the First World War until the 1970s a 'vast … leaderless' movement occurred in the United States that we have come to term the Great Migration. Some 6 million Southern Blacks moved North in search of work and better chances: to Chicago, New York, Detroit,

Los Angeles and Philadelphia, among other places. Following the Thirteenth Amendment to the Constitution abolishing slavery in 1865 (itself following the Emancipation Proclamation of 1863), the American South instituted segregation by means of the sharecropping system. Black workers were consigned to cotton fields. A sharecropping family would be 'furnished' with a place to live and some basic necessities, the cost of which was deducted from the value of what they picked. But there was no way for the sharecropper to know, ahead of the 'settle', the annual accounting before the farm's owner, what return their family's long days' labour would amount to, and workers were almost never shown the accounts. Sometimes there was no return, and sometimes workers were told they owed their employer money. Other slavery-era abuses continued. A labourer who challenged an employer's accounting or complained about a white man's abuse of the labourer's wife could not hope to work again in the South.[68]

In the North there was work, but racism too. Chicago's Black population increased by 77 per cent in the 1940s, and when the city housing authority sought to place upwardly mobile Black families in a white neighbourhood on the city's southwest side, white squatters occupied the building, generating a riot. Similar efforts produced like white enforcements of segregation, including an incident following the acceptance of a Black family whom an admission clerk had mistaken for white.[69] Ellison's novel follows the south to north trajectory taken by so many of the protagonist's Black compatriots, and tracks the itinerant pathways racist responses force him down. Expelled from a Black college in 1933 for taking a white trustee, at his request, to a run-down part of town where Jim Trueblood, a Black man, tells the story of his unwitting act of incest with his daughter, Invisible Man heads north, not knowing that the letters he carries tell their readers, prospective employers, to raise his hopes enough to keep him on the run.

We meet the narrator in the prologue underground, where he has retreated following the Harlem riot, probably that of 1943, that occurs near the end of the novel. The story proceeds in flashback. Published two years before *Brown v. Board of Education* passed into law, ending school segregation and paving the way for the 1964 Civil Rights Act, the novel's rendition of the narrator's invisibility is linked to that of anonymous trickster figures in world literature, including Odysseus. Among several references to the *Odyssey* Book IX, the most important is the narrator's grandfather's deathbed advice to the narrator's father, described elsewhere by Ellison as a sphinx-like riddle representing, for the hero, 'the ambiguity of the past'. Invisible Man's grandfather enjoins his son to 'live with your head in the lion's mouth . . . overcome [your oppressors] with yeses, undermine 'em with grins, agree 'em to death and destruction, let 'em swoller you till they vomit or bust wide open'.[70] A clear reference to the giant Polyphemus eating Odysseus' men, the speech also alludes to the nameless slave who agrees with her or his master, operating invisibly in the belly of the beast of racist oppression. Recommending passivity and aggressivity at once, the advice troubles the narrator throughout his wanderings, its ultimate function proving to be its divergent interpretations.

'No ones' or nameless trickster figures play important roles in the creative response to racist oppression the narrator's grandfather recommends. Ellison's hero reminds us of Christian texts featuring anonymous travellers through allegorical landscapes, such as John Bunyan's *The Pilgrim's Progress* (1678), and the nameless, non-allegorical voyagers of the Middle Passage. Many slave narratives were written anonymously, as were most of the great African American spirituals, and the tradition is furthered by such texts as James Weldon Johnson's narrative of Black passing in white society, *The Autobiography of an Ex-Colored Man* (1912).[71] But it is in another Odyssean scene, when Invisible Man awakens in the hospital having endured an explosion in Liberty Paints, the factory where he has been working, to find a doctor looking at him 'out of a bright third eye that glowed from the centre of his forehead' (p. 188), that anonymous folk heroes perform their most significant roles.

The Cyclopean doctor and his colleagues ask Invisible Man questions designed to test his self-awareness, questions freighted with overtones of his people's past. He is enclosed in a glass and nickel box and receives electroshock treatment accompanied by racist slurs ('They really do have rhythm, don't they? Get hot, boy! Get hot!' (p. 193)). He is asked his name, his mother's name, and who Buckeye the Rabbit and Brer Rabbit are (pp. 196–7). Invisible Man experiences this 'fretting over identity' as a form of 'combat' (pp. 197–8) and attempts to short-circuit the electroshock machine. This is not the first instance of combative electrical short-circuiting in the novel. In the Battle Royal, a ritual the narrator has to endure before giving a speech and taking up his scholarship at the Black college, young Black men, having been made to watch a half-naked white woman dancing, are forced to fight each other blindfolded and to scramble for coins on an electrified rug (pp. 19–28). The narrator finds that if he ignores or mimics the current by laughing, he can 'contain the electricity', the only possible resistance to a process in which young Black men's ambition is pre-contained by subjection to money and the objects of white men's sexual desire.[72]

While in the Battle Royal 'heat' released in the form of intraracial violence and sexual humiliation 'maintains the constancy of white superiority',[73] in the hospital, the questions the narrator is asked produce complex emotional responses enabling something else. Asked his name, 'a tremor' shakes him, then 'swift shame' (p. 195). 'Who are you?' produces 'sluggish excitement' (p. 196). 'What is your mother's name?' elicits 'quick dislike' and recognition of context by way of the game of trading insults about one's mother known as 'the dozens'. The Buckeye and Brer Rabbit questions are key, producing 'turmoil' and 'deep, deep' laughter. 'Giddy with the delight of self-discovery and the desire to hide it' (p. 197), Invisible Man recalls childhood rhymes featuring these characters. The double quality of such figures

– whose cunning, speed and guile are masked by the innocence and seeming inconsequence of imagined animals – is transmitted to the narrator as he recognizes them and desires to hide the recognition. Such dual functions are integral to the success of these consummate escape artists, who perpetually evade dangerous situations.[74]

But there is more in play. 'An old slave', as the narrator tells us in the Epilogue, 'never had any doubts about his humanity' (p. 467), and stories and songs about Brer Fox and Brer Rabbit derive from that time. In them, animals who act like crafty humans manage a dual nature that may represent the duality slave/human. In outwitting humans they also break the continuum underwriting slavery whereby some humans were regarded as more animal-like than others. This circuit-breaking management of doubleness is recognized by the narrator, who finds an identification with Buckeye the Rabbit 'somehow too dangerous' to be borne (p. 197). Yet the recognition is enabling, and contrasts with the experience of shock treatment, in which the narrator misrecognizes his own screams, asking if what he hears is 'the *vox humana* of a hidden organ' (p. 191). This is a reference to the stops in a pipe organ typically used to 'mimic the [sound of the] human voice'. The alien sound is that of the narrator functioning as a forced mouthpiece for 1950s psychiatric normalization, a progress narrative whereby the human develops from childhood to achieve a sense of identity fitting the fearful corporatization of the Cold War world.[75]

Invisible Man's wanderings cause him repeatedly to discover a previous naivety about his prospects. Because an African American civil rights movement is not yet visible, it is hard to analyse structural discouragements (p. 411). His involvement in the Brotherhood, a left-wing organization with clear echoes of the American Communist Party, is one of the most significant of these experiences. Michael Germana observes that the novel's rendition of American attitudes to race in the first half of the century, attitudes defined by an ideology of blood purity whereby African Americans were assumed to have inferior blood, closely follows U.S. monetary policy of the period. In response to the 1929 stock market crash, the Emergency Banking Act of 1933 put the president in charge of Federal Reserve banks and authorized issuing almost $2 billion in new banknotes. In 1934 the international gold standard was suspended and gold was withdrawn from circulation, its value fixed to that of the dollar.[76]

This severing of financial circulation from an elemental bedrock of symbolic power is represented by Invisible Man's relations with the Brotherhood, where race is not considered, as it is in the South of the novel's first part, an intrinsic attribute of the blood of Black people. In the Brotherhood race is a resource that Brother Jack, one of the leaders, and the committee use to 'back' the equivalence of all citizens, as gold was used to back an arbitrary system of financial alleviation. Black members convey the Brotherhood's message that it is blind to race, hence its inclusion of Black people where others exclude them.[77] This enables the organization to jettison its Black members – including eventually the entire Harlem branch – when priorities change, having used them to increase membership and show progressive credentials.

Other ideas about circulation enable Invisible Man to make sense of his plight once the Brotherhood's cynicism becomes apparent (memorably conveyed by the popping out of Brother Jack's glass eye, another Cyclopean moment showing the Brotherhood's race blindness to be inadequate vision (pp. 380–81)). Two of these are chaos theory and cybernetics, fields that study the processes of systems that, in trying to reach their goals, work as sensitive conductors, making feedback loops that introduce changes in their conditions. Invisible Man alludes to this understanding on several occasions, including late in the novel when he vows, post-disillusionment, to escape Brotherhood control by becoming 'a supersensitive confirmer of [the members'] misperceptions' (p. 410; also pp. 210–11, 401–2, 411). The appeal of complex systems for mid-twentieth-century thinking about race and civil rights lies partly in the everyday chaotics of Black life in racist America but also, more importantly, in the eschewing of developmentalism. There is no origin story marked by blood and destiny here. Reality comes into being by chance swervings from a given path, as indicated by Michel Serres' rendition of the Presocratic philosopher Lucretius, as conveyed by Eric White:

> At uncertain times and indefinite places, the universal fall of the atoms is interrupted by what Lucretius calls the *clinamen*, 'the smallest conceivable condition for the first formation of turbulence'. The *clinamen* [is] a stochastic swerving of random fluctuation whose subsequent amplification . . . [produces] a spiralling motion that heralds the beginning of the world . . . Only because of the accidental swerving of the *clinamen* is there 'something rather than nothing . . . That which exists is improbable'.[78]

> Nature becomes "'free" and "progressive"', for

> the more complex the cosmos becomes, producing in succession physical, chemical and biological levels of organization, the more open it is . . . to further evolutionary innovation . . . there is the ever-present possibility of . . . a radical departure from the chain of causality, enabling a new beginning.[79]

The existence of enfranchised Black Americans was once improbable and was achieved incrementally but also, like the future civil rights movement, because a sufficient number of randomly located agents introduced margins of indetermination into the way things were performed, which margins made greater change possible. These margins are celebrated in the novel's understanding of music, particularly jazz, invoked by the narrator in the prologue when he describes Louis Armstrong as having made 'poetry out of being invisible' (p. 11). Invisibility provides an alternative temporality characterized by 'never quite [being] on the beat': 'Sometimes you're ahead and sometimes behind. Instead of the swift and imperceptible flowing of time, you are aware of its nodes, those points where time stands still or from which it leaps ahead. And you slip into the breaks and look around' (p. 11).

This understanding, arrived at following the chaos of the Harlem riot and formulated underground in embryo with specific reference to chaos (p. 468), speaks to the truth of the African American condition. 'Breaks' are at the heart of African American experience from the Middle Passage to segregation to mass Black male incarceration to random killings by white police. 'Slip[ping] into the breaks', punctuating a gap in time organized differently from the white mainstream, occurs in Black music as early as the slave-time field holler and work song, in which response answers call after a pause that may represent promised lands ahead or foregone, and is carried through the spirituals, the jazz tradition and into the contrapuntal rhythms of hip hop. Ellison, himself a musician, also invokes jazz as a form of participational democracy. In chaos terms it is recursive: 'acts, occasions and patterns' are replicated, but divergence is always possible. And just as participation in democracy depends on the invisibility to each citizen of every other citizen's vote as it morphs into the unpredictable outcome of the greater number, so too with Armstrong's mastery of swing, in which 'the listener's perception of unity in a group's sense of time is set askew . . . when a soloist sounds like he or she is floating above or tilting against the accompanist's time'. As Armstrong pried open 'unpredictable and . . . thrilling gaps' between his melodic phrasing, the musicians' support and the listener's expectation of hearing a tune's standard version, an 'alternative rhythmic space' between anticipation and performance was made.[80]

The requirement that the audience hold expectation in abeyance, giving it a dynamic kind of attention, was furthered by bebop. As Robert O'Brien Hokanson explains, citing jazz critic Marshall Stearns, while 'the new music's harmonies sounded like mistakes to a typical Dixieland jazz musician', many bebop numbers were 'based on chord progressions of standard jazz tunes', so that 'the piano, guitar and bass would play the accompaniment to a known tune' like 'I've Got Rhythm', and 'the soloist would improvise as usual – but nobody would play the tune', thus producing a variation on an unstated melody.[81] Invisibility is involved here. The melody, simultaneously recalled and unheard, enables observing an absence together, just as Black national organization is imaginable but still nascent in the 1950s. Often invisible to each other, members of mid-century Black communities improvise variations on the 'tunes' of American democratic organizing, with unlinked possibilities, like unseen votes, taking things forward.

The narrator's occupying of breaks increases as his belief in the Brotherhood's rigid Marxist understanding of temporal progress wanes.[82] But throughout the novel he practises his own version of slipping into breaks in the form of improvised speeches. The first, less improvised, is required after he has been ritually humiliated before drunk white men at the Battle Royal at the smoker. Later versions occur when he encounters an old Black couple being evicted and before an audience as a test of his fitness to join the Brotherhood. These later occasions become existential acts because on none of them does Invisible Man know what he is going to say, yet each time his future changes markedly and new possibilities for representing community are revealed. The most significant speech responds to the police shooting of Tod Clifton, a charismatic Harlem branch leader whom the Brotherhood has discarded and who is found by the narrator on the street selling racist paper dolls. Folded and cut dancing puppets, these pander to the idea of Black people as happy entertainers and bitterly satirize the Brotherhood, whose copycat members are likewise controlled by invisible strings.

The speech, given at Clifton's funeral, is issued in direct response to the crowd's expectation. It is also a test of the narrator's loyalty to the Brotherhood, because he is at this time in exile due to doubts about his commitment and has been told to wait for instructions, which, despite his attempts to seek them, are withheld (p. 361). The speech resonates too with the gift of a broken chain-link by Brother Tarp, a Black member of the Brotherhood who filed the link to escape a chain gang. Signifying Brother Tarp's absence from the gang and his achievement of freedom, the link, he says, represents 'yes' and 'no', but also 'a heap more', something between the two that echoes Invisible Man's grandfather's deathbed instruction (p. 313). A 'heap more' is an apt description of how the narrator feels at the funeral. Pointless, powerless and extraneous, he improvises, making an anti-speech for the anti-hero Clifton became and which he is himself becoming. As he repeats the words, 'he was standing and he fell. He fell and he kneeled. He kneeled and he bled . . . his blood . . . like any blood' (p. 367), their chain-like structure makes him a link to something important for the community, even though the importance resides in non-meaning (and may even echo the repetitive paper dolls). He has nothing to say, and the speech does not progress, enacting the situation of African Americans at mid-century. Without Brotherhood support the narrator is a lone link, yet the performative pact between himself and the crowd, conjoining around absence, is palpably charged.

The chain-like speech ('he fell and he kneeled. He kneeled and he bled . . They cut him down and he died') and mention of the ordinariness of Clifton's blood show the origins of the violent act in slavery and beliefs about devalued Black blood as well as referencing the blood-soaked work towards freedom that ended chained labour (the Underground Railroad too was a largely invisible chain). Invisible Man cannot hear any links, but the audience can. And while in his continuing to stand before the crowd uttering meaningless words and in the crowd's dogged refusal to obey his injunction to go home incomprehension does not go away, it simultaneously serves another function. In trying in all the ways he does to say that this Black man's life meant nothing, Invisible Man's speech refuses the meaning it contains. Unlike Clifton's life, and without necessarily advancing, it keeps going. Silent, the crowd says 'no'. Remaining, it says 'yes'. Between the people's mute expectation and the narrator's impotence something comes together: communal recognition of failed democracy in the form of a repeatedly broken link. The claim regarding Clifton's unimportance achieves the opposite sense, for while it is undoubtedly true that for white America Tod Clifton's death is unexceptional, this is a travesty of democracy, in which every human life should count the same.

According to the existentialist philosophy in vogue at mid-century, born of the betrayals and false allegiances of the Second World War, Clifton's death is 'absurd' because it *should* matter, having the kind of absent meaning that calls for a rebellious response. Although that is not viable at this point, or only in self-defeating terms, it is augured by the way absence of rights meets continued Black presence, in America as in this scene. As Ellison notes in a later essay, Black Americans, 'despite their social powerlessness . . . were all unwittingly endowed with the vast powers of the linguistic negative, and would now be intricately involved in the use and misuse of a specific American form of symbolic action, the terminology of democracy'.[83] The linguistic negative, like the breaks in Black music and the absent meaning of the death of Clifton, are emphasized in the novel's final pages as Invisible Man wrestles with all the possible meanings of his grandfather's advice to his father. Recognizing that his grandfather's experience of slavery enabled the complex management of his humanity *and* his chattel status without compromising the former, so that what was perceived by white America as humanity's absence was inevitably something more than white America was required to master, he determines to leave his underground haven to work once again in the world (pp. 467–8).

Interwar Black Northern workers, Joel Dinerstein claims, experienced a similar alienation to that of their enslaved forebears, in response to which the blues and jazz dance forms such as the lindy hop (jitterbug), which mimicked factory machine line movements, were survival skills embodying opposites: 'pattern and improvization', 'synthesized energy *and* control'. Ways to be somebody rather than the nobody required on the factory line, these Black art forms were also a means by which being alone amid an undifferentiated mass became being together, transforming communal unbelonging into self-expression. In its way, Ellison's novel does this too. Invisible Man is part of a vast Black American collective that as yet lacks a voice, despite moments of possible change in the system of racist oppression being introduced. Music, speeches and political organizing are occasions on which meaning is contingent and nomadic, when unforeseen outcomes become possible as a result of collective belief.[84]

The novel's final line crystallizes this chapter's exploration of the way that, when a society reaches a sufficient point of disconnection from itself, as in seventeenth-century Spain or seventeenth- or eighteenth-century England, ordinarily hapless individuals, who may be deluded but pursue their courses with uncommon dedication, come to represent the imbalances and stresses of the whole. The *Bildungsroman*, the story of one man or woman who cannot find the wholeness they seek because modernity has riven the self between past and future prospects and laid broken lives between, represents the mass of humanity that does not appear in novels. That mass experiences the contradiction of being lost amid increased opportunities, inaccessibly united by feeling alone. As if to drive a wedge into this process, *Invisible Man* closes with a question. Posing as a 'disembodied voice' across history's airwaves, the narrator admits that what frightens him most is not the idea that he may have spoken only of his own experiences, but the possibility that he speaks for everyone: 'Who knows', he asks, 'but that, on the lower frequencies, I speak for you?' (p. 469).

As Ellison elsewhere evinces, 'as a symbol of guilt and redemption, the Negro entered the deepest recesses of the American psyche and became crucially involved in its consciousness . . . and conscience.

He became keeper of the nation's sense of democratic achievement.'[85] The narrator's final question speaks to this democratic context and so it is collaborative. It is also generous while yet potentially despairing, for what hope is there for change if no one feels freer than the narrator does; if no one, no matter how privileged, feels seen? Again, it could be read as asking who will join the struggle for Black civil rights, and of course it is an invitation to acknowledge that until freedom is available to all, no human is free. The next chapter's exploration of the sorrows of exile and the testing of assumptions about belonging performed *by* sorrow should be read as a continuation of this interest in the perspectives of those who power Western modernity's changes, for they are key to understanding modernity. Its architects, unlike Odysseus, saw little value in pathways that did not yield profit for someone, irrespective of human cost. Perhaps this is why, in addition to making wanderers of so many, modernity made wanderers of many who never left home.

5

SORROW

The wanderer who speaks in the Old English poem of that name is exiled from his former war-band and afflicted with sorrow. Surviving in one manuscript, the tenth-century Exeter Book, the poem tracks a transition from lamenting this worst of situations for an Anglo-Saxon warrior to a gradual acceptance that all life is borrowed and that the only home is in heaven beyond. But the poem is also full of movement and conflict, and of the speaker's struggle to effect a relation to the complex, meandering interplay between present and past that makes up sorrow. The wanderer travels alone, 'heart-sick', 'stir[ring] the ice-cold sea with hands and oars'.[1] 'His fate is fixed' (5), and the poem's first part features much imagery of bondage and enclosure. The sound of his sorrow is 'the mute song of a muffled heart,/ Sung to no listener' (11–12), muffled because heroic convention dictates sorrow must be '[bound] with silence' and stillness, locked in a 'breast-hoard' (15–16, 23), kept from all.

The wanderer's world is timeless. He has survived many battles, and there are many descriptions of things he 'often' does in a formless manner, such as 'wait[ing] for mercy' and 'walk[ing] alone' (1–2). The conflict borne of remembering what is lost – which comforts but renews the pain of losing – is expressed in shifts between third and first person, and between expressions of despair and maximlike phrases that cut off such expression ('No man's wise till he's walked through winters', 'life is on loan' (69, 115)).[2] Inversions convey disorder, but also a grief-like process, as loss attains a kind of substance. Going 'winter-sad' over 'winding waves', seeking a new lord, the wanderer's only companion is sorrow, the loss of companions (26–7, 31–2). His reward is not 'twisted gold' but 'night-cold' (34–5). It holds him like a hearth. While 'sorrow and sleep . . . bind the mind', as expressed by alliteration, he wanders in dream, finding his lord again, then wakes alone (41–8). Yet the dream-bound self contrasts with seabirds he wakes to, whose wings are unimpeded, spread wide (50). The former hall-dwellers now 'wander his mind' (56), a freer image than locked up heart-sorrow (22), before departing. Keeping sorrow secret is a way to retain the lost lord and comrades by adhering to the lost world's code of practice.[3] But the locked-up heart transforms, through dream and reminiscence and by way of an anti-hearth – the summoning of absence – first into a hall and then into a being sent over the waves (62).

From this point, maxims increase as the speaker wonders why his mind does not 'darken', or why he is still alive (64). Statements about how wise men should act and a reference to 'the Maker of men' (71–4, 90) produce a new kind of dislocation, that between the world of the pagan Germanic warrior and Christianity, with the comforts of the latter available only to those who yield attachment to the known. Here, too, the meanderings of grief find a larger context. The world the wanderer has lost is itself passing. But gnomic statements about wisdom are also, in their way, ruined, for they appear shorn of context. Christian stoicism, indebted to Boethius' fifth-century *Consolation of Philosophy*, contrasts with the wilder vision of an entire society in ruins, the apocalypse of an undone world. As earth becomes a wasteland, 'wine-halls wander'. The verb, usually translated as 'moulder' or 'decay', shows, in its original form, that the speaker's 'self-enclosure' that has replaced the remembered hall is itself in motion, undergoing change.[4] Apocalyptic description leads to the famous *'ubi sunt'* passage in which 'the wise man' calls out: 'Where has the horse gone? Where is the rider?/ ... Where is the hall-joy?' and the answer:

Gone is the bright cup. Gone is the mailed warrior
         ... How ... time has slipped
Down under the night-helmet as if it never was. (97–102)

Manish Sharma thinks that, rather than the more familiar process of a gradual relinquishment of attachment to worldly objects, the poem instead shows an increased attachment to loss. But this is loss *as* object, whereby personal grief becomes something greater: the loss of an entire civilization and world. For 'universal transience' is still loss, even as its recognition is the precondition of hope for the eternal home with which the poem ends. As earlier, absence takes on substance, as the metonymic list of things gone provides a new basis for community in the shared pain of remembering what is no longer there. Thus, the once enclosed heart becomes 'an open ruin', the serpentine shapes on its walls testifying to earlier failed efforts to keep grief bound. As a ruin is a definition of uncontainment, so it also represents the speaker's 'twilight' realm, the time of transition between pagan and Christian worlds, where one way of experiencing the world is passing, another not fully begun.[5]

The poem has resonance with our own times. Albeit for different reasons (for civilians at least), modern individualistic cultures have tended to require us to keep grief private, and although this has changed in recent years, we know we will soon have to manage the loss of our familiar planetary environment, without knowing what will replace it. Many humans have already lost their homes and livelihoods due to global warming, and many others are practising a kind of 'forward grieving' for a world whose stability is vanishing, working out how to carry its memory with us, and whether we could eventually do otherwise and let such memory go. This poem in which a sole survivor of a tightly bound community first maintains, as a kind of memorial, that community's stoicism, before allowing the self's boundaries to be eroded by grief, and finally achieves a relation to loss as that which afflicts not only his own but all earth's people tells, paradoxically enough, our story. Between then and now, as the Industrial Revolution and scientific advances took death and loss further away for many, these positivistic moves, insufficiently balanced by negative elements representing the unknown, brought death and loss nearer for all. In the era of planet-warmed wandering, the Old English wanderer's survival *in* sorrow, whereby sorrow becomes less a personal condition than that of belonging to an unclearly changing world, and where the poet's creativity consists in allowing a lost object to become the loss we cannot avoid, will continue to have much to teach us.

Mourning is a complicated process. Contrary to popular perception, say experts, it is only once a loss is accepted that the negotiations that change the former object or relationship into something that no longer consumes the grief-stricken can begin. Modern societies emphasize personal responsibility for grief, while the larger social support networks that pertained in the past, along with explanatory frameworks like a deity or fate, are often unavailable today. This can produce guilt, or the feeling that one should be 'over' suffering by a certain time. Since the 1980s psychiatry has de-emphasized sadness in favour of depression. Bereavement is now the only cause of sorrow listed in the Diagnostic and Statistical Manual of Mental Disorders (DSM), making depression the default classification for non-bereavement-related sorrow.[6] Since U.S. medical insurance companies will only fund treatments for disorders listed in the DSM, sorrow arising from other causes such as job loss, the end of a relationship or other major life changes is either deemed non-existent or is pathologized. This is problematic because depression and sorrow are not the same. A common feature of depression is a flattening of mood and difficulty accessing nameable feelings. But an individual experiencing sorrow, as 'The Wanderer' shows, can sometimes access the conflicted, changeful affects and reflective currents that are more often submerged within the person suffering from depression.

I have in this book pushed hard at assumptions underlying beliefs about human belonging, given so many of them are based on fear of the wanderer. Lifeways achieve justifications over time, but in my view fear of something or someone is not enough to justify a way of living (unless, in certain conditions, one is living in hiding). For this reason, too, the distinction between sorrow and depression matters. Being sad can mean feeling exiled from those not undergoing a similar feeling. Sorrow is also often historically the result of exile, of being far from home because of disaster or expulsion. But the exile that is or that results in sorrow keeps loss alive and thus does something ordinary belonging does not. To feel sorrow is to experience the loss of what one only recently took for granted: peace, equanimity, satisfaction. The sorrowful are close to the non-sorrowful's experience, perhaps closest of all, given loss's keenness. And sorrow can test assumptions about belonging by bringing to the forefront their often unacknowledged bases. The sorrowful wander in their minds – and, often, in their physical being – as the back and forth between then and now, between having and losing, reminds them of the grounds of their former calmness. Those grounds are often a kind of amnesia, a forgetting that 'life is on loan' and that our evolutionary history fits us less for ease and happiness than for struggle and drama.

Sorrow also has a role to play in trauma. A traumatic event, by definition unprecedented and overwhelming, can cause protective numbing as our systems, flooded with affect, act to reduce the effect of stimuli. As a result, a traumatized person often experiences time differently. Being numb to an event may mean it is experienced belatedly or indirectly, through symptoms or in recovery.[7] Trauma is thus a paradox, because it may register in absence, destroying the linear fictions by which we manage flows of events. Those who undergo trauma often find it difficult to feel sorrow. Felt loss may belong to a later stage of recovery if it arrives at all. This makes it more, rather than less, important that markers of loss and sadness are set out, whether as memorial structures, commemorative events or accurate historical records. And although depression is a more common symptom of trauma than sorrow, sorrow's irksome liveliness can limn the often almost instantaneous self-preservation that is a more obvious response to trauma. Then, feeling shuts down, goes elsewhere, but, as with the more obvious coming and going of sorrow, it often returns, if more inaccessibly. Axioms of belonging are frequently tested by the suffering of the traumatized, for whom the worst that ideal communities exclude has happened. But they are often overtly symbolized and expressed by the sorrowful, reminding us that without testing there is no value, and that to live in sorrow can be to accurately value living.

Exile and hope: wandering Jews

The Jewish people are perhaps history's most renowned exiles, their wanderings often associated, especially by gentiles, with sorrow. The Torah relates their founding myth, that of exodus from slavery in Egypt, followed by forty years' wandering in the desert before restoration to Canaan. While there is no historical evidence for these events, the Israelites were perpetually sited between empires, first the Hittites and Egyptians, later the Assyrians, Babylonians and Egyptians, later still the Romans and the Christians. The Temple in Jerusalem was destroyed twice, first by Nebuchadnezzar in 587–586 BCE, and again in 70 CE by the Romans. Wandering became a central theme in Jewish self-understanding, while daily study that could be performed anywhere expressed the belief that the one God, Yahweh, travelled with his people and would one day deliver them from exile.[8]

Medieval Jews, too, occupied interstitial positions. Because they could not own land and faced restrictions on economic activity in both Christian and Islamic contexts, and because they had a high rate of literacy and learning due to male Jews being required to recite and debate the Torah, they were useful to rulers and others as merchants, administrators and financial advisers. Mostly, medieval Jews suffered more from popular uprisings than from persecution by established powers. In 1236 Holy Roman Emperor Frederick II called them 'the serfs of our chamber', which exempted them from local taxes, paid directly to the king.[9] The Jews' usefulness to rulers could be a double-edged sword. As the king's tax collectors they were highly visible and often targets of resentment. They traded services for royal protection. But they were not always protected. England expelled its Jews in 1290, France in 1306 and Spain in 1492.

The European Middle Ages developed the figure of Ahasuerus, the Wandering Jew, associated with Christ's sorrows because he refused Christ water on the road to Calvary and, in punishment, was condemned to eternal wandering. By the sixteenth century his image was fixed. The Wandering Jew is long-haired and barefoot, wearing threadbare clothes. He is 'wiry, gaunt, and conspicuous'. His ragged clothing represents his damaged spiritual status. A paradox, he is both a local who always answers questions in the language of address, and an alien because he is always on the move. In this way he arguably represents European Jews both in their own eyes and those of Christians: the most recognizable foreigners, the most familiar strangers. Jews were probably more visible than before when they returned to places, such as France and England, from which they had previously been expelled, and the development of printing increased circulation of the image and story of Ahasuerus. Later versions were sometimes more neutral, more overtly racist or more romantic. In the nineteenth century, Gustave Doré produced both a racist caricature for *Le Journal pour rire* (1852) and a dramatic series emphasizing the Jew's eternal sorrow and remorse over his contribution to Christ's suffering. This is a lonely figure, forever haunted by the cross, sketched in number ten of the series in the wrecked ship's masts and the more obvious vision of Christ in the clouds alongside.[10]

Yet while Christians associated Jews with sorrow, and while there are sorrowful elements in Hebrew liturgy, and while the desert wanderings are arguably the birthplace of the Jewish people, making unbelonging a perennial feature of being Jewish, it was the Jews' *success* at being strangers that proved most important to their future as humanity moved into the modern world. Yuri Slezkine identifies Jews as Mercurians, representatives of Mercury or Hermes, in contrast to Apollonians, representatives of Apollo. While Apollonians are settled natives who farm land, Mercurians are non-primary producers who deliver goods and services to them. Because Mercurian service providers belong to 'time, not land', they are seen as 'both homeless and historic, rootless and "ancient"'. This romanticization ensures the continued need for such a group. Only strangers can do things the settled are forbidden to or would rather not: collect royal taxes, lend money at interest, advise kings. Thus Mercurians must continue to be strangers. They occupy the category of the crooked, breaking rules for others. Such are the false fixities to which belonging to a permanently marginal identity can give rise.[11]

Slezkine presents many examples of Mercurians, whose god is the patron of 'rulebreakers, border crossers, and go-betweens' who live by 'wit, craft, and art', but for him the Jews are exemplary because their brand of impermanence became so strongly associated with modernity, which favours the mercurial. Whereas in premodernity the work of Hermes was typically regarded as a punishment, as the Industrial Revolution gained pace more and more Apollonians had to become 'Jewish': 'urban, mobile, literate, mentally nimble, occupationally flexible' in an anonymous market or networks of strangers. Because, in the late nineteenth and early twentieth centuries in Europe, civil service jobs were largely closed to Jews, most Jewish graduates, as well as going into familiar trades like banking, went into liberal professions: 'medicine, law, journalism, science, higher education, entertainment, and the arts'. And because modernity required intellectual restlessness and openness to invention, while the nationalist myths supporting it meant 'every people was chosen, every land promised', the Jews faced a familiar dilemma. Exemplary moderns, they became ever more visible as such. And as such, they represented modernity's perils for others: angst, loneliness, exile from land.[12]

This caused particular problems in Russia, where, at the turn of the twentieth century, most European Jews (5.2 million out of about 8.7 million) lived, about 90 per cent in the Pale of Settlement, stretching from the Baltic to the Black Sea. Attempts at assimilation began in 1804, but pogroms returned in 1881 with the assassination of Tsar Alexander II.[13] In the empire's last days, serfs were losing out to innovators who seemed to have a Jewish face. Jews had dominated the Pale's commercial life, working in tax farming, moneylending, industrial investment and (foreign) trade. Using free labour, Jewish businesses were geographically flexible, and were more inventive, and better at standardizing, specializing and differentiating themselves from others than the competition. 'Vertical integration', a common Mercurian practice whereby Jewish businesses fed other Jewish businesses within a line, was their most effective economic strategy. Other propensities, including 'superior training . . . cheap family labour', being 'accustomed to low profit margins' and the problem-solving involved in negotiating or working around legal restrictions, resulted from a long history of thriving despite constraint.[14]

While revolutionary Russia was embraced by Jews, whose experience as organizing middlemen fit them for many of its tasks, and whose literacy fit many of them for its leadership, it also left them unprotected. Lenin wanted to replace the boorish peasant with the mobile proletarian, and Bolshevism favoured 'disembodied consciousness' over peasant bulk. The Jews' imagined cunning made them seem disembodied (everywhere at once), and the most successful mobile proletarian, for some time, had been the Jew. Russia's 'uprooted Apollonians', lacking liberal protections, did not readily see the homelessness of modernization as a win. But they did know who to blame for this unnerving twist on their familiar sorrows: not the faceless state, but the moderns who had somehow leaped ahead of them. And in other countries such as Germany, where peasants became bourgeois subjects without the bourgeoisie becoming the enemy, the same applied. Jews were unmistakably talented at modernity, yet they were not interchangeable with others.[15] For the hard work involved in their success, and for succeeding despite harassment, they would pay in the coin of their difference as gentiles imagined them. They were still Jews.

Of course, many German Jews in the post-Weimar period saw themselves not as Jews but as Germans. Such was their faith in democratic nationhood that it took some time for the fact of Hitler's reception by their compatriots to sink in. Jews had been very visible in the cultural life of Weimar Germany. But it is their longer history as wanderers suited to Mercurian modernization, which modernization produces, in cycles, waves of reinvestment in the romantic idea of belonging to land, that was seized upon by the Nazis amid the strictures of the post-First World War Versailles settlement and the stock market crash of 1929. Modernity had failed Germany, and modernity was being orchestrated by Jews. Although making up less than 1 per cent of the population in 1933, to Hitler all Jews shared his obsession with Germany as victim, seeking to destroy it from within. The initial plan was to make life so uncomfortable for German Jews that they would emigrate in large numbers. Many did, although not as many as sought and failed to later.[16] While the 1935 Nuremberg Laws forbade Jews citizenship rights, the nationwide pogrom of 9–10 November 1938 known as Kristallnacht, as though all that was broken in this murderous frenzy was window glass, made it clear what Jews could expect from the state.

Most countries did not increase their immigration quotas in light of developments in Germany. Britain turned ships full of Jews away from Palestine, which it controlled. South America, East Africa and Shanghai were possible, and as many went there as possible. Eventually Jews were deported from Germany to Poland and other occupied territories, and those in places Germany conquered sent to live in ghettos, then to labour camps and finally to specialized murder camps (although significant numbers were murdered in other ways in the earlier years of the war). Jews did fight back. Those who could joined partisan resistance movements, and the famous Warsaw Ghetto Uprising of April 1943 lasted a month, a considerable feat given the starved condition of the fighters and the relative lack of outside support. Such events were of great symbolic importance, and this was not the only uprising against Nazi power.[17] As the Allied powers advanced on formerly German-held territory camps were abandoned, their inhabitants forced on hunger marches that were, despite very real threats from guards, more like wanderings. The destinations were increasingly artificial, there being few Nazi-friendly places left to go.

After the war, Jewish survivors were still wanderers, spending months and, in some cases, years, in displaced persons (DP) camps in Germany and elsewhere under the newly formed United Nations Relief and Rehabilitation Administration (UNRRA). Not yet 'Holocaust survivors', they were refugees and, at first, not separated from other prisoners who had been their tormentors. Conditions gradually improved, but while the focus for most DPs was repatriation, Jews were officially stateless. Undoubtedly, the Holocaust strengthened Zionism, the need for Jews to have a land of their own. The British passed the question to the UN, which voted to partition Palestine into Jewish and Arab states, plus an international zone around the holy places in Bethlehem and Jerusalem. Israel extended this territory by the end of the 1948 Arab–Israeli War, known by Palestinians as the Nakba (catastrophe), as again in the Six Day War of 1967. In 1950 Israel's parliament granted all Jews the right to return to Israel as citizens, and by 1956, more than 2 million had arrived.[18]

And yet, while the world largely ignored the Jews' sorrows during their time of greatest persecution, that of the Palestinians also faded from view. The Arabs rejected partition, and the Zionist leadership declared its intention to have Palestine (they would take 80 per cent by 1948, with 20 per cent remaining to Jordan). Ethnic cleansing of Palestinian villages was performed by Israeli forces in the weeks leading up to the start of the 1948 war (15 May) and continued for its duration. 'Tihur' – purifying, or cleansing – was the language used to galvanize soldiers. While the UN passed Resolution 194 in December 1948, giving refugees the option of returning to their homes and/or receiving reparations, the finances of over a million Palestinians had been invested in banks seized by Israeli powers in May. Israel ignored UN sanctions, and following its victory in the 1967 war, American peace efforts relied on the current balance of power, so Israel's proposals formed the basis of negotiations. In international deliberations the Palestinians' right of return has simply never been discussed.[19]

During the Six Day and 1973 wars, Israelis identified more strongly than previously with victims of the Holocaust. The Eichmann trial and the growing number of American book, film and televisual treatments increased consciousness of these events, and a latency period – during which trauma is being processed and can be inaccessible – had also passed (ten years or more is common). Isolation, the fate of Holocaust Jews, became an event that would go on happening, and all Jews were 'united by the hostility of the non-Jewish world'. In this understanding, Jewish chosenness becomes sacrifice, the mentality chiefly notable for its contradictions. During the 1982 Lebanon War, Ariel Sharon, then defence minister, claimed that Israel would act as the Middle East's greatest power, yet Menachem Begin as prime minister compared the threat of the Palestinian Liberation Organization to that of the Nazis.[20]

In Israel, Jews ceased to be Mercurians and became Apollonians. Many lived in kibbutzes, communities run on socialist, utopian principles and centred on agricultural labour, several later transitioning to industry. And yet, in another way, Jewish diasporic Mercurians recreated earlier worlds. Like all colonizing powers, Israel reconfigured the landscape it claimed. The Jewish National Fund made forests on the site of eradicated Palestinian villages and, in a contest over sorrows, opted for European conifers over Palestinian plants in its national parks. These trees were familiar to the Ashkenazi decision makers, whose ancestors lived in Germany, France and Eastern Europe, but they also echo the Holocaust, when Jews hid and fought and were murdered among them. In the parks, though, the predominant narrative concerns the distant past, Israel's ancient right to the land, said to be 'barren' and 'empty' before its arrival. The reconstitution of the landscape, in which Palestinian-cultivated fig and almond trees seem 'wild' and Palestinian agriculture proves 6,000 years of Jewish habitation,[21] is actually cosmopolitan in the sense that it is a fabrication, a reality melded out of materials to hand. For Jewish Mercurians, repeated strictures and persecutions required the honing of successful practices to make a tradition out of very little, albeit supported by religious usages. No longer Mercurians, Israelis have nonetheless made national traditions on relatively scant basis. And the state became a persecutor, even if this was done in part from the desperation of the longtime plight of lacking land.

Haunting and hunger: trails of tears

Forced removals of people give rise to wandering and sorrow, although they also often target those deemed wanderers, humans who do not belong. The Nazis planned to repatriate vast numbers of people, moving Polish and Soviet peasants to labour or prison camps elsewhere so Germans could farm their land, and in the 1930s Stalin deported thousands of Ukrainian peasants – 'kulaks' – to the Gulag in order to take their grain. Ukrainian grain had been requisitioned by the Bolsheviks from 1918 to 1921 during the Russian Civil War and the subsequent famine in the Volga region. The starving of Ukraine's peasants in the early 1930s (the Holodomor), the product of Stalin's 1928–33 Five-Year Plan, when about 3.3 million people died, was an entirely artificial famine. The Soviet leadership decided in the 1920s that a 'surplus' must be wrested from the peasant in order to import machinery for the growing working class. Collectivization, in which individual farmers were forced to yield land and work on state-owned farms believed to be more efficient, followed.[22]

When, in 1918, peasants were first downgraded in favour of industrial workers, it was decided that the only way to get more grain from the former was to turn them against each other. A class enemy was created: the prosperous peasant, or kulak, although even at this early point, with the 'moneylending and mortgaging' in which such peasants had engaged now illegal, kulaks were more imagined than real. Nonetheless, faced with what it considered to be a grain shortage in 1928, the Politburo vowed to seize 'kulak' grain, or peasant grain, by making kulaks into figures loathed by the peasantry. Realizing their produce could be seized, peasants initially hid it, which made the market seem unreliable, enabling Stalin to blame market spontaneity for yield shortfall. This required further requisition, as the state could not revert to a market the peasants did not trust.[23]

Those resisting grain requisition and, soon, simply possessing grain, became kulaks, who were killed or deported to the Gulag. Their leaders taken, peasants sold and slaughtered livestock, with thousands walking as far as Poland to avoid collective farms. But poor state planning, not grain hoarding, was the source of shortages. The harvest in 1930, laid down before deportation, had been uncommonly good, helped by fine weather. It was taken as standard. The first collectivized harvest in 1931 failed. The weather was poor, livestock depleted, collectivization had disrupted sowing and harvest, the best farmers had been expelled. Seed grain, from which the following year's crop is grown, was handed over by many to meet targets. By early 1932 mass starvation was in prospect, a fact of which the Soviet leadership was aware. By July, Stalin was calling the famine a Ukrainian plot designed to damage the government. Party activists brought in the crop, deportations resumed and peasants, quite unnecessarily, starved.[24]

All famine victims wander. Unlike in most famines, starving Ukrainian peasants wandered from countryside to city. They wandered, dazed, into the paths of trains, holding wasted babies up to windows in the hope someone would take them. In 1933 Stalin sealed the country's borders so peasants could not flee, and, with internal passports required to inhabit cities legally, closed cities to them. They wandered in the Gulag, too, where the policy was to feed the strong and where villagers locked their houses against them. Like those at home, they ate 'carrion . . . dogs and cats', and, in time, some killed and ate their children. While wandering peasants were sent back to villages to die, the fabrication of the kulak, as well as disincentivizing productive farming, also created a kind of peasant whose chief characteristic was to have survived. Further, kulaks had moved 'across vast distances' into unknown worlds, becoming experienced wanderers. When prison terms ended, they returned to their homelands having become the enemies of the state most initially were not, and which the government feared.[25]

Movement out of Eastern and Western Europe and Asia, on the other hand, mostly to the United States, increased dramatically in the course of the nineteenth century as a result of problems at home but primarily to support America's rapid industrializing. By the 1840s the nation welcomed hundreds of thousands of immigrants each year. Irish came to escape the famine, Germans to escape poverty, riots and revolution, Italians to improve their chances and Eastern Europeans because of economic change and political repression. Chinese labourers, escaping 'population pressures . . . natural disasters', political conflict and the fallout from the First Opium War (1839–42) worked, with dispossessed Mexicans, clearing land for agriculture, mining, breaking rocks and building railroads, often for a third of the pay of whites. While these new immigrants were considered to exhibit varying shades of whiteness and thus acceptability, Anglo-Americans were once immigrants too. Humans may have first crossed into North America at Beringia, an area of tundra and grassland 'between eastern Siberia and western Alaska', as long ago as 16,000–17,000 years before the present. But other routes are also possible. What is certain is that by the time Columbus landed in what is now the Bahamas in 1492 and Giovanni Caboto (John Cabot) on mainland North America in 1497, the Americas were long inhabited by peoples who, by the twelfth century, practised agriculture, growing 'corn, beans, squash, sunflowers' and other crops, and who engaged in long-distance trade.[26]

The story of how white people dispossessed America's native populations of their land has developed mythic lineaments. In it, Indians are wanderers and noble warriors whose unsuspecting fate is overlaid at every turn by sorrow. The reality is more complex. While Europeans did bring 'disease, slavery, starvation, and disruption' to North America's Native peoples, tribes amalgamated against them and against each other, and – as with Ukrainian kulaks – perhaps their ultimate achievement, against the acts of their oppressors, is to have survived. Five thousand years ago, coastal Native Americans probably lived in relatively mobile small villages before becoming more sedentary around 2500–2000 BCE. The Great Lakes and their surroundings are 'the confluence of a vast network of waterways' that formed the hub of life on the continent's north as far back as Paleolithic times, when Native peoples followed 'migrating waterfowl, fish, and game' along them, spreading technology and cultural expertise from the Gulf of Mexico to Lake Ontario and in return.[27]

From the twelfth to sixteenth centuries, intensive farming had largely replaced seasonal camping in this area before it declined for unknown reasons, as had the Hopewell exchange network, which produced large villages and elaborate burial mounds around 100 BCE to 500 CE. In the sixteenth and seventeenth centuries Europeans traded metal goods for beaver furs with the Iroquois, who controlled the waterways and negotiated advantageous trade deals with the French and English while fighting for dominance with their eastern neighbours. In the seventeenth century the Five Nations of the Iroquois Confederacy formed a series of agreements with the British known as the Covenant Chain, whereby all agreed to maintain peace to facilitate trade. Across America, however, almost all Native American populations were reduced by smallpox and measles epidemics originated by white settlers. And while, in the seventeenth and early eighteenth centuries, those Native peoples who survived did so by recognizing their value to European governors and working their decentralized political systems to maintain multiple connections and diplomatic ties, without access to the mechanisms controlling supply and demand, they became more dependent on Europeans for trade goods over time.[28]

Once the Seven Years War ended in 1763 it was no longer possible to play the French against the British, just as the American War of Independence (1775–83) left the Americans as the only remaining power. As Daniel Richter notes, multiplicity and movement had been key to Indian survival in the eighteenth century:

> All the groups we know by such names as 'Creek', or 'Cherokee', or 'Iroquois' were relatively new social forms produced by decades of disease, warfare, migration, and resettlement. And, nearly everywhere, people moved frequently, to the extent that 'names of communities should often be regarded as "addresses" rather than tribal designations'.[29]

The forming and reforming of alliances for survival gave the lie to the idea that nomadic 'Indians' must be taught the practices of settled agriculture to fit them for citizenship (and in any case Native

Americans had been practising agriculture centuries before), since alliance-making is key to nation-building of all kinds. But by the late eighteenth and early nineteenth centuries the idea of removal had begun to take hold. The only way to protect Native Americans from the land hunger of white settlers, the government's thinking ran, was to move them west until they had 'caught up' with their white compatriots' superior lifeways (supposedly, unstoppable land greed was not to be among the things learned).

White settlers, including, eventually, those the government had welcomed from elsewhere to build up industry, persistently encroached upon Native American lands. Their cattle destroyed cornfields, they cut Native timber, plied Natives with alcohol and committed fraud relating to land and trade. Removal became policy in 1830. Its best-known instance is that of the Cherokee, whose long trek westwards in 1838 with guns at their backs, during which 4,000 died, became known as the Trail of Tears. The Cherokee had ceded about half their land to the British by 1777, but the boundaries were not respected. Georgia ceded its western lands to the government in 1802, including what are now the states of Alabama and Mississippi, and the government agreed to extinguish Native American title as soon as feasible. By 1819, 3,000 Cherokee had relocated west of the Mississippi and 3.8 million acres of land had been ceded. In half a century the Cherokee had given up 'more than fifty eight million acres in five states' on the understanding that the remaining 10 million would be theirs. In 1820 the Cherokee Nation voted to deny citizenship to those emigrating, and informed the government that it would willingly part with no more land.[30]

If becoming 'civilized' had been going to save any Native Americans from the ravages of white land hunger, it would have saved the Cherokee (of course, by becoming civilized the government meant that Natives should give up all traditions and ancestral home-lands, becoming rootless). The tribe, its leaders literate in English and Cherokee, formed a national government. They published a newspaper, the *Cherokee Phoenix*, and, following the model of organization promising best resistance to dispossession, in 1827 authorized a constitution. When President Andrew Jackson's Indian Removal Bill dictated their removal they appealed to the Supreme Court, since they were not entitled to testify in Georgia. They won, but Jackson went ahead anyway. In Georgia remaining Cherokee land was seized and the tribe's annuity paid individually to stop them collectively defending their rights. In 1835 a breakaway fragment led by Elias Boudinot and John Ridge signed the Treaty of New Echota. The treaty surrendered all land for $5 million and promised self-government in the west – a capital crime in Cherokee law, which had outlawed ceding further land.[31]

The Cherokee left in several detachments and suffered theft, assault and rape by soldiers, and violence among themselves in holding forts when they bought alcohol with remaining annuity funds. Their own laws now illegal, they could no longer regulate drinking and gambling, which increased amid the miseries of containment. Families were separated and women forced to abandon children. The people caught measles, whooping cough and dysentery, and were mostly ill clad against rain, wind and snow. While other tribes also faced removal, many went west of their own accord (as had many Cherokee earlier), where they often found themselves on reservations with former enemies and where liquor pedlars sold to them illegally.[32] Many wandered back, preferring to die on or in search of former homelands rather than coralled in with sickness, inferior provisions and drink. But some Native peoples remained in the east, including some whose leaders had signed removal treaties. Others worked in industries created as whites took over their hunting and fishing grounds. The 1887 General Allotment Act (also known as the Dawes Act) allotted reservation Indians 65 hectares per household, with the government empowered to sell excess lands. In 1906, Indians competent to farm could be paid a fee, called a fee simple patent, to own their lands, but as no one educated them about taxes, which began immediately accruing, foreclosures followed. Eighty per cent of those who received fee patents were dispossessed.[33]

Native American rituals were banned on reservations. As with Cherokee removal, readily assimilable to the prevailing image in white consciousness of the tragic or sorrowful Indian, the most famous ritual among non-Natives is probably the Ghost Dance because of its association with the massacre at Wounded Knee Creek in 1890, in which more than 200 Lakota died. The battle was immortalized as tragedy in Dee Brown's 1970 book *Bury My Heart at Wounded Knee*, which claims, erroneously, that it marks the destruction of Native American lifeways. The Ghost Dance was one of several amalgamations of Native and Christian elements. A Paiute shaman, Wovoka, taught the ritual as a way to restore balance between Native peoples and their worlds, and tribes developed various versions. Some Lakota believed that performing it would cause the buffalo to return and white people to vanish. They wore 'Ghost Shirts' they thought were bulletproof. The movement worried the u.s. government, which banned it for the same reasons it banned other rituals: to stop Native Americans celebrating collective identity in ways uncontrollable by whites. Federal authorities feared that the great Lakota chief Sitting Bull would join the movement, arrested him at Standing Rock, and in the fallout Sitting Bull was shot dead.[34]

Afraid for his people, Spotted Elk (Big Foot) left Standing Rock with 350 followers soon after, seeking sanctuary at Pine Ridge with chief Red Cloud. Government troops intercepted them, the government having sent fully one-third of the u.s. army to South Dakota to stop Native Americans dancing in hope of a better world. While soldiers disarmed the Natives a shot was fired when a young deaf man did not understand the instruction and refused to surrender his weapon. Federal troops opened fire. But the Ghost Dance did not cease. It had pre-dated Wovoka, and became a pan-Native movement for processing loss and sorrow. It transformed ghosts, traditionally omens of death and illness for Native Americans, into those who are valued, whose return is sought. It focused on the restoration of societies despoiled by European contact, even on demographic increase.[35] Recalling the dead to life, the Ghost Dance has things in common with other lament traditions, and its fundamental tenets came to pass. Today Native traditions are being recovered, new syntheses and alliances formed, and all because, contrary to expectation, Native Americans did not disappear but survived.

In ancient Greek culture, pain – and thus sorrow – itself wanders, and there too lament practices seek to limit the extent to which mourners are exposed to it. In southern Mediterranean traditions seemingly spontaneous behaviours such as wailing, tearing the hair and scratching cheeks are in fact tightly scripted, as are sung and spoken laments. Simulating absence of control in a tightly choreographed, impersonal performance enables mourners to manage their emotions, as suffering's dangerously unmoored potential is brought within the patterned expectations of continued existence.[36] The oldest human story, the 1800 BCE Sumerian *Epic of Gilgamesh*, commemorating a king of that name who ruled Uruk – in present-day Iraq – in around 2700 BCE, also treats grief as a tensile dynamic. The movement back and forth across borders in the narrative expresses, as with the Ghost Dance, the catastrophic potential of traumatic events to disrupt ongoing life.

Gilgamesh, famed as the Builder of Walls, is felled by the death of his great friend Enkidu. Departing the city, he wanders the wilderness clad in animal skins, approaching the condition of a beast. Wandering – walking back and forth – is associated with mourning in Near Eastern traditions. Like dressing in animal skins, it is a departure from the focused drive of Gilgamesh's life. But while death is often imprisonment in this world view,[37] Gilgamesh's wandering between animal and human worlds is something else: sorrow, the expression of the distance between life untouched by loss and life lived in its presence. Gilgamesh seeks immortality but fails the test the god Utnapishtim proposes and falls asleep instead of showing heroic alertness. Sleep, symbolizing mortality, returns him to life. And in a way, despite his loss, Gilgamesh is closer to Enkidu now than when the pair shared adventures. For unlike before when he felt himself to be immortal, he now knows that every man dies, and he will in time share death with his lost friend.

A bigger problem in ancient cultures is the wandering dead, who will not rest until they are properly mourned. Several cultures, such as the Ga'anda peoples of northeast Nigeria, the Kalanga of Zimbabwe and the Merina of Madagascar, regard the journey from life to death as a process during which the spirit of the dead continues with the living, at least for a time. In ancient Greece, living and dead continually interact with each other, and the dead are known to inhabit the underworld as the living inhabit the world above. While the Greek and Mesopotamian dead are especially likely to trouble the living if expected burial practices, enabling the soul to depart the body, are not performed, they may also do so for other reasons. If they were murdered, and thus robbed of the chance of an honourable death (such as in battle), or died young or in a lonely place, they might also return, especially if a murder was unavenged. Women who died as virgins or before giving birth and who thus lacked the only kind of honour available in life could not enter the underworld and might cause trouble as they wandered between living and non-living realms. The aggrieved dead could cause illness – sleeplessness, nausea, mania, miscarriages – in the living and were sometimes dealt with by professional mediators, who may themselves have been wandering practitioners before becoming locally installed.[38]

The wandering dead can also be of use to the living. In the Central Cemetery in Bogotá, Colombia, decaying niches house *ánimas solas*, or lost souls who wander in purgatory and can thus be approached with requests. The more lost a soul is, the more they might relish the chance to perform a miraculous act and so gain entry to heaven. These nameless dead, some of whom died violently, also serve as identification points for the many displaced rural people who themselves arrived in Bogotá as a result of violence. So the wandering living seek help from and communion with fellow sufferers. A different kind of help is documented by Erik Mueggler, whose early 1990s fieldwork in southwest China sought to understand the activities of 'wild ghosts' during and after the catastrophic famine that followed the Great Leap Forward of 1958–60, during which between 30 and 40 million people died. The Yi people of Zhizuo in Yunnan province had historically managed collective responsibilities for hosting official visitors, repairing public walkways, 'burying dead outsiders' and supporting an annual cycle of rituals for 'a family of collective ancestors' through a system known as *ts'ici*, whereby public duties circulated annually among the village's wealthiest households. Essentially a way to channel the flow of wealth, energy and responsibility through a community so its members could stay in recognizable relation to their antecedents, this system, destroyed by the state, became unable to regulate relations with the dead, leading to the vengeful return of the famine dead as powerfully destructive 'wild ghosts'.[39]

The state collectivized land in the mid-1950s, and in 1957, following logic similar to that of Stalin in Ukraine, mobilized 5 million peasants to swiftly expand agriculture and industry. More than 2 million people were recruited in Yunnan to build canals and reservoirs. Agricultural production cooperatives were enlarged, their food resources recklessly consumed, while labourers worked day and night to meet targets. By 1959 some 40 to 50 per cent of the workforce was engaged in the production of steel and copper, generating an acute dearth of agricultural labour. To villagers, working day and night did not produce enough food because, according to what the party focused on, the goal was to produce not food but words, that is, correct theories about production. Whereas previously in Zhizuo a regime of rotating hospitality kept the burden commoners owed officials moving and officials largely out of community affairs, now the state had come inside the community, where, as 'an empty mouth crying out in hunger for words and grain,'[40] it drove peasants to satisfy its ever-changing requirements. It was a ravenous ghost.

The state had previously been seen as spectral because of its absent presence, making pronouncements from afar. Cadres now took the output of ancestral trust fields and replaced the 'nuanced play of reproductive metaphor', surrounding it with the logic of 'production for the sake of production', a dead end. Villagers recounted with glee how wild ghosts would undermine official efforts once rituals that had given the dead roles to play were disallowed. The *ts'ici* itself was ritually murdered at a mass meeting in 1965. The famine dead also went unrecognized. Tenth-month sacrifices, commemorating all the preceding year's dead, were abandoned in the famine years for want of animals and grain to offer, as were the night and day vigils conducting souls to the underworld with sustaining food and in which the recently dead passed gifts to the longer dead, respectively. The network of obligations among the living upheld by these rites collapsed too. Without sustaining gifts and rituals none of the famine victims entered the underworld. All of them wandered among the living, refusing exorcism. They starved in death as they had in life, and visited pain and illness on their descendants.[41]

The souls of those who died violently had always wandered, but ritual practitioners had helped preserve the living from their depredations, as the *ts'ici* system had protected them from the demands of the state. The state destroyed the boundaries maintaining these practices, entering regions where negotiations over life and death had occurred. As Mueggler discovered, the state and the people had divergent understandings of how time functioned to connect the dead and living. Official historiography saw time as a forward-moving road, but to villagers it was a spiral in which unresolved violence would change the present. The term *chènè*, or wild ghost, not only refers to a supernatural entity but describes 'states of affairs in which flows are reversed'. While these destructive beings do not help people – they are angry, insatiable and contagious – the logic of their actions provides a powerful tool for countering the narrative behind the Party's destructive acts. Telling ghost stories also enabled people to acknowledge the world so altered by loss and sorrow, as though the ghostly otherworld, its energies now unleashed, was itself the incursion of those terrible events.[42]

The artificiality of the socialist road of progress, which ignored ancestral authority, reversed once carefully managed spirals in which domains of time – ancestral, mortal, institutional – would return upon each other while incorporating new experiences. In this reversal, pieces of the past not bound by careful practice could 'infect the present'. While authoritatively controlled speech could be used to talk to ghosts, its absence spelled possession by them.[43] To figure the Maoist state as a field governed by wild ghosts also shows the state's refusal to take responsibility for the famine. But most of all, the ghosts link the famine dead to the death of the means to appease them, and thus to the function of sorrow in recalling communities to what they value through the spectre of its loss. The loss of a system for signifying catastrophe can be as great as catastrophe itself, and the relentless passage of the unavenged dead reminds the living that an artificial famine destroys reason and symbolic systems before it destroys bodies, which tools are then no longer available to assist the living with the dead. The dead plague the living, in this instance, so the living will share with them the task of keeping cultural systems for managing trauma functioning. While this is not always possible, the suffering dead remind us of its importance when they breach the life/death border. A ghost shows time can threaten the repeated patterns through which we recognize living, while rituals for expressing sorrow are a way to keep those patterns' relation to unbounded time – the time of chaos, of catastrophe, of oblivion – on track.

Seeking refuge

Humans have always fled conflicts and disasters. They also move when they can no longer improve their living conditions or when conditions are worsening. Modern Eritrea is not at war, but it operates a policy of indefinite national service with which every citizen from their mid- to late teens must comply. Conscripts are paid meagrely and often posted far from their families. To attempt escape is to risk arrest, imprisonment and torture, but many do so. Elsewhere in Africa climate change is reducing many people's ability to farm their land effectively, making for increased dependence on foreign aid and decreased opportunities to improve living standards. Protestant Huguenots fleeing Catholic France were the first to be described by the English term 'refugee', meaning someone who crosses a national border seeking sanctuary because of religious or political oppression. It was used again after the First World War's many displacements,[44] but key elements of international policy were not established until after the Second World War, when many civilians found themselves displaced from their homelands by the war, its forced removals or redrawn national borders.

The definition adopted in the 1951 Geneva Convention Relating to the Status of Refugees remains that formally used in international law. A refugee is someone outside her or his or their home country (or, in a further clause, without nationality) who cannot return as a result of 'a well-founded fear of being persecuted for reasons of race, religion, nationality, membership of a particular social group or political opinion'. This definition has been broadened in practice to include persecution carried out by others such as gangs and militias and to discriminatory employment practices. A wider definition has also been endorsed by the UN High Commissioner for Refugees (UNHCR) to cover those who are not specific targets of oppression but whose countries, such as Syria in the 2010s and onward, are unable to protect them from threats to life. Until the

2022 Russian invasion of Ukraine, the refugee movement about which Westerners heard most was that of people from the Middle East and Africa following the uprisings and conflicts set off by the 2011 Arab Spring. Reactionary responses, including the increased popularity of far-right nationalist groups and the contribution of migrant-phobia to the 2016 UK Brexit Referendum outcome and the election of President Donald Trump, are hardly new. Fears of refugee 'idleness' dictated UN policy in 1945 when displaced persons underwent vocational training in DP camps. Many countries were reluctant to offer refugees work and economic advancement.[45] Britain's distinction between those it designates 'refugees' and those it designates 'economic migrants' continues this trend.

While far-right groups characterize refugees as those seeking state-supplied economic benefits, when in fact most refugees seek the dignity of meaningful employment, the category of 'economic migrant' includes many who cannot support themselves and their families at home. In reality, rather than 'taking' jobs from those in host countries, refugees and migrants routinely perform work that locals shun, enabling locals to perform higher-skilled jobs for better pay if they choose. Refugees with higher skills increase local productivity by 'filling gaps in the labour market', enabling more to find the work they want, while refugees who start businesses, as is common, increase economic dynamism, employ locals and expand international trade and investment. The creativity that is often required to leave behind one culture and begin again in another also benefits countries of arrival, while the need to replace ageing populations with skilled workers means many of these countries – such as Germany – face ongoing shortages of labour.[46]

As to the so-called 'refugee crisis', many reject this definition. About 1.2 million people crossed the Mediterranean in 2014 and 2015, an unsurprising response to civil wars in Syria, Afghanistan and Iraq. Eighty-six per cent of the world's refugees are taken in by developing countries, while refugee flows were said to constitute a 'global refugee crisis' only once they involved Europe. The 850,000 refugees who left Turkey in 2015 constituted about 0.2 per cent of Europe's population of around 500 million, an absorbable cost, while Lebanon accommodated 'just under 1.2 million Syrian refugees' in 2015 in its population 'of roughly 4.5 million'. But people seeking to reach Europe drowned in the Mediterranean in increasing numbers from 2015 (over 3,000 that year) not because of those numbers but because of muddled political responses. Individual European governments panicked, finally agreeing in the autumn to take 120,000 migrants from the frontline states of Italy and Greece, around a ninth of the total number of arrivals. Countries erected fences, most notably Hungary, and Germany's offer to receive all refugees, including those who had been fingerprinted elsewhere, was partly reversed in response to popular opinion.[47]

The idea that refugees should be kept out of Europe rather than their numbers managed as part of the continent's global humanitarian responsibility produced fallacies such as the idea, expressed by Britain's then Home Secretary Theresa May and others in 2015, that rescuing refugees from the Mediterranean leads more of them to make the journey. When, beginning in November 2014, Operation Triton, the exercise in border protection by the European Border and Coast Guard Agency (Frontex), replaced the Italian Navy's Operation Mare Nostrum, part-funded by the EU and focused on migrant rescue, the numbers attempting the journey continued to increase. The chief difference was that 1,800 people died that year compared to 96 the previous one. Smugglers were not deterred because their customers were not deterred, and they were not deterred because when conditions become impossible in one's place of origin, almost any risk appears worth taking. To take such a risk is to formulate a plan, to have a goal to aim for. Imagining, planning and working towards escape from dire situations are ineradicably human responses, without the practice of which over centuries those of us fortunate enough to do so would not be living in relative peace and prosperity now.[48]

Nonetheless, the limbo of not being able to alter one's situation except through flight is all too often reproduced on arrival in host countries. The 1951 Refugee Convention gives refugees the right to work while waiting for their asylum claims to be processed, yet most host states restrict this right. After the end of the Cold War when the focus on Western resettlement shifted to that of enabling people to return home, providing aid to camps became the model rather than moving refugees swiftly into work and resettlement. Over half of today's refugees are in 'protracted refugee situations', with the average length of stay in a camp over two decades. The UNHCR depends on annual voluntary contributions for most of its budget, making planning difficult, and its practices have mostly developed haphazardly. In 2004 the UN Secretary-General asked the UNHCR to exceed its mandate and assist Sri Lanka and Indonesia in the wake of the Indian Ocean tsunami. It has since performed this role six times, a significant challenge for an organization whose central mandate attracts no multi-year funds.[49]

One reason appalling limbo-like conditions often pertain in camps and holding centres is because states fail to be selective about those who apply to run them. This has been the case in Germany and Italy, as Hsiao-Hung Pai's reporting found. Berlin's Templehof camp, isolated, overcrowded and the site of suicide attempts, is the result of the right to run such a centre being awarded to those without experience with migrants, solely on the basis that they can make money. Centres in Palermo that are supposed to enable integration by means of internships and training instead send migrants to work in menial jobs, taking half their wages. Money paid to shelters and camps to be spent on food, medical care, counselling and legal aid is not so spent, including in centres run by churches. Centres have an incentive to delay asylum procedures since they are paid according to numbers of migrants on their premises. And when no activities are provided, refugees are condemned to wander. This is a particular problem for child migrants. In most camps no activities, bar some occasional language learning, are organized, let alone psychological counselling or legal guidance. With nothing to do, minors, many of whom have survived traumatic circumstances, walk miles to visit other shelters, or to railway stations to meet other migrants, or wander aimlessly around towns. There they are vulnerable to those who would exploit them, but they are vulnerable in shelters as well, which are unheated in winter and where violence is not curtailed.[50]

What are the solutions to these problems? Obviously, greater selectivity over who is awarded funds and a change to the basis of awarding, since this currently depends solely on how many migrants are fingerprinted and registered, would help. Equally clearly, we need more global integration. In 2016 Turkey allowed Syrians to work once the EU pledged €3 billion to its government. Jordan also runs a programme, known as the Jordan Compact, in which, in return for U.S.$1.7 billion in investment from international donors, it offered work permits to about 200,000 Syrians in 2016. Government and businesses cooperate on Special Economic Zones, for which the EU provides trade concessions. Jordan needs manufacturing workers and to manage its security, businesses seek investment and refugees want work. It is an important experiment. Of course, it is not perfect. Work is limited to certain sectors offering only the minimum wage, is not freely chosen as international human rights law dictates and its bureaucratic procedures can be daunting. Work permits involve fees, which, when waived, fall due again. Uptake by women has been low, as they often prefer to work from home in textiles or catering, and accessing self-employment, which generates wealth and enables saving, is difficult.[51]

Uganda is another country that allows refugees to work as well as granting considerable freedom of movement. Substantial arable land means refugees in open rural settlements are given plots of it to work 'for both subsistence and commercial agriculture' and permitted market activity. Refugees in cities can start businesses. In Nakivale settlement in the country's southwest, refugees not only farm but sell crops, livestock, textiles and other goods. There is 'a Congolese cinema, a Somali transport company' running services to Kampala, and an Ethiopian restaurant all near each other as in an ordinary city. Congolese traders import *bitenge*, a brightly coloured fabric, from China and India, which is distributed along refugee-run supply lines, as is canned tuna from Thailand. While the quality of land given is not always good, the settlement nurtures skills transfer and, through autonomy, aspiration. Another camp, set up at Rwamwanja to cope with an emergency influx of refugees following renewed violence in the Democratic Republic of the Congo in 2013, quickly developed an operational economy as refugees began by selling part of their food and relief supplies to provide capital. The ability to make such decisions early in the emergency phase of a refugee scenario is clearly beneficial, enabling diversification. It also enables refugees to be something other than victims of conflict, part-shaping their destinies and acting on their own desires.[52]

Cooperation of other kinds has had worse results. Since 2004 Italy has deported failed asylum seekers to Libya and paid for the building of detention centres there to deter sub-Saharan African migrants from travelling. Human rights are routinely violated in these places, but in 2017 an agreement was signed whereby the EU funds Libya's UN-backed government to stop migrant vessels in Libyan waters and return them to Libya. There, they are supposed to be assessed by UNHCR and International Organization for Migration officials, with the asylum-eligible allowed to go on to Europe and others settled in Libya or sent home. Libya, however, is unable to perform these duties or to stop rogue agents or even ordinary citizens kidnapping and otherwise detaining migrants in camps, or collecting them from prisons for a fee, thereby becoming their 'guardians' and putting them to slave labour. In 2017 migrants were being sold for agricultural work at slave markets, an ongoing practice in various fields.[53]

If we sought to manage migration flows in sufficient numbers rather than damming them, however, it could be the case that refugees *would* wait to be legally resettled. And there are precedents. Following the Vietnam War, Western countries resettled 1.3 million refugees from Mainland Southeast Asia. Several nations, including the United States, collaborated on receiving refugees rescued at sea from frontline states, and when numbers climbed again the UNHCR worked with the Vietnamese government to screen those departing. Although not without controversy, this re-established the practice of asylum-seeking in place of illegal migration, enabling manageability. Former political prisoners were also eventually assisted to return home. Ultimately, it is strange, given the regularity with which refugee situations affect citizens, non-citizens and states, that we have not developed more effective means to deal with them. But we do not typically plan effectively for most disasters, while it is a planetary certainty that we will face more and more of them.[54]

As the Ugandan example shows, considering refugees as potential economic agents brings benefits. Similarly, as Alexander Betts and Paul Collier claim, refugees are not only or even primarily a humanitarian issue but a practical one, lying at the intersection of several policy fields: 'humanitarianism, development, migration, human rights, post-conflict reconstruction, disaster risk reduction, and state-building'. The solutions they outline to current ways of managing refugee scenarios are accordingly multilateral but also involve public–private collaborations (such as the Jordan Compact was when it began). International disaster insurance plans can also play a role, especially if the UNHCR can increase the political and economic expertise that is currently outweighed by technocratic and legal expertise owing to its historical focus on humanitarian aid delivery. There are promising moves afoot, from the refugee and host-place matching initiatives these authors document to the more interim, but equally necessary, CALM (Comme à la Maison, or Just Like Home) endeavours by which Paris citizens have, since 2015, provided beds, food and clothing to refugees awaiting asylum decisions.[55]

There is also a point to be made here about sorrow. Understandably, sorrow is something we turn away from because it is painful and because we know, on some level, that someday it will come and find us anyway. Yet as I have argued, sorrow sharpens our sense of what we value because it arises when loss is most present (as opposed to our being potentially submerged by it, as can happen with depression). In her memoir *Lost and Found* (2022), Kathryn Schulz identifies a form of the anticipatory grief I referred to earlier in the chapter, 'close to what the Portuguese call *saudade* and the Japanese . . . *mono no aware* . . . the feeling of registering, on the basis of some slight exposure, our existential condition: how lovely life is, and how fragile, and how fleeting'.[56] This is sorrow borne of attachment, as all sorrow is: what we love, we fear losing. If we are going to continue valuing places of belonging, we will increasingly have to manage the prospect of their loss, such is the progressively disaster-prone world we have created. And who better to assist with this than those who have had to depart from their home places, carrying their memories and emotional attachments with them? While traumatic situations do not always make us more effective teachers (although sometimes, they do), the sorrows of exile are undoubtedly becoming more normalized experiences. Exposure, slight or great, to the loss that shadows love, while difficult to seek, has value. And those seeking refuge have expertise we are all going to need, if not today, or tomorrow, then within our lifetimes.

6

CHANCE

High above New York City, extending 2.3 kilometres (1½ mi.) through the Meatpacking District and Chelsea on the Lower West Side, a 'park in the sky' built on a disused railway harbours wild plants, hosts art exhibitions and performances, and welcomes some 8 million visitors a year. Chance played a larger than usual role in the High Line's inception, and has been retained as a working principle of design for those who wander through its regions. Originally part of the city's rail system, the structure was abandoned in the 1980s due to a decline in traffic, and some of it demolished. At the turn of the century a group, Friends of the High Line, was formed to try and save the edifice for possible use as a recreational park; funding and permissions were secured, and the Friends continue to maintain and operate the space today. A key point of appeal for those who sought to preserve the structure was the transient-seeming beauty borne of the way nature had taken over the space since its industrial demise. Forming a kind of 'concrete carpet' with gravel mulch, which opens up the paving to random growth, has enabled more of an equal conversation between plants and built-up elements than is often seen in parks. 'Micro-environments and local situations' can flourish as they did before the location was restored.[1]

The fascination of the High Line derives not only from the way the chance-like and the planned interact in its design, but from the tension between seemingly chaotic profusion – what we think of as nature going where it will, doing its thing – and the railroad's linear progress. The park's porous surface has allowed designers to bend the paths people follow when walking areas once defined by linear tracks. The overall path is still linear, but it is as though walking it brings to mind, through the senses, the variety of aesthetic and social experiences linear pathways often exclude. As co-creator James Corner says, 'the paths are designed to force people to slow down, to stroll, to meander, so they're immersed in a certain railbed landscape of remarkable texture and colors and unusual forms.'[2] Many people come to the park to share a space with others that has street-like effects while often being more soothing and reviving, and with more of the ever-changing chaos of nature, than can be found on the everyday urban grid.

The tension between clear progression and chance-like disorder, discussed with reference to errancy and error in Chapter One, is the theme, with regard to the unpredictable and surprising, of this chapter. From holidays and the daydreaming that often precedes and follows them, to wandering online, shopping or at leisure, to managing gig work and other forms of precarious labour, we increasingly find ourselves negotiating the potential friction chance opportunities cause with previous or habitual and often necessarily more ordered ways of living. Much of this friction, welcome or not, relates to our experience of time. And while the random is in fact a patterned reality with its own distinctive laws of operation, the perception of chance as a fleeting possibility, an unrepeatable event, has a powerful hold on our imaginations.[3]

Unrepeatable – and unpredictable – events do happen in our lives and in the environments we encounter, but while we often claim to like the idea of them, we equally often attempt to preserve a steady supply of things on which we can capitalize, sometimes dressing such efforts up in the language of creative opportunity and diversification. This occurs most obviously in finance and in the behaviour of big technology companies. Less avoidably, it is a feature of living on a variety of short-term and part-time jobs without social benefits or prospects for advancement. For many living this way, the chance for a more predictable life, with less wandering and enforced chaos management, is a distant dream, and correspondingly desirable. But as this chapter will discuss, uses of time that attend to its suspensive, material dimension – for time *is* material – can show how the predictable and unpredictable relate to each other. When the latter is used against us – at least, by our fellow humans – we have historical forms of predictive organizing to turn to. We can become aware of the ways desired or useful unpredictability – a daydream, a holiday, a moment of protest – can actively reshape the future from within the now.

A version of urban pastoral or urban wilderness like the High Line, in which nature is defined by its interactions with the artificial and in which the artificial is made to seem natural, is also a temporal conversation. The lives of the (rural) poor provide a lesson for others, feeding a taste for nostalgia in those who no longer work land. This is true up to a point of the High Line, in which 'the meat lockers of the Meatpacking District, the warehouse spaces of Chelsea' and the railroad itself become markers of industrial authenticity because their heyday is gone. But an 'idealized urban wasteland' such as this can also help us see the present in a longer time frame. This may be of particular value in an era in which an openness to chance is enjoined on us in order to collapse the future into the present and devolve onto us some of the complex labour costs – relating to health, privacy and contingency planning – of corporate profits. Yet chance has a richer meaning than this. Its laws of operation still permit an opening on to the future. Allowing 'natural seeding, environmental dynamism'[4] and practising other low-interventionist ways of managing natural environments will increasingly be part of our lives as humans help the natural world recover from industry. And preserving the post-industrial as well as the industrial phases of a site by replicating nature's self-governing life may help us imagine other hybrid spaces we will need to co-create, by placing us in dialogue with what happened when we were no longer there.

Walking and dreaming

The idea of walking about in nature for its own sake is relatively recent. It becomes popular in England from the late eighteenth century once improved transport by road, rail and canal provides alternative ways for people to perform work or other task-related travel. Earlier, walking is associated not only with the relative poverty necessitating it but also often with moral error, by dint of the idea that vagrancy expresses laziness and criminality (instead of changing economic and social conditions), as we saw in Chapter Three. Although negative attitudes towards vagrancy and homelessness continue in the period, as walking loses its associations with lower-class activity and as industrialization provides the middle classes with more leisure time, increasing numbers take to rambling about in the countryside. One thing this new kind of walking was not was the 'Grand Tour', the name given to a journey through Western Europe undertaken by aristocratic young men readying themselves for public life. Mostly such young men did not walk, staying for long periods in various places before travelling by carriage on roads. And while the English middle classes did eventually travel to European cities once the preserve of the considerably better off, prompting the latter to go to other places, the novelty was that so many wandered, for pleasure, their own countryside at home.[5]

This wandering marks the beginning of modern tourism, and by the early nineteenth century we also see a travel/tourism distinction, according to which travellers take more chances on new experiences while tourists follow prescribed paths. Chance played an important role in the leisured travel that was to become tourism (or not tourism, depending on how one saw it), and its role had to do with how people were learning to see and process landscape.

Today, we think of 'the picturesque' as relating to a static, often overly domesticated or staged view of nature. But in the late eighteenth and early nineteenth centuries in Europe it was about locating a place in nature made memorable by irregularities and the 'interplay of elements' such as shadow and light and which also induced a feeling of surprise. The craze for the picturesque was influenced by popular travel guides such as those William Gilpin produced from 1782 to the Lake District. Many such guides, including Gilpin's, instructed walkers in the art of painting and how to identify a suitable view. The resulting art, while it should make a pleasing whole, should avoid straight lines and aim for a broken or variegated texture, conveying the enigmatic atmosphere variety creates.[6]

Another key element in early English tourism was the changing fashion in gardens. The 'Romantic garden', a reaction against its predecessor, the French baroque, with its ordered lines and plants cut into various shapes, favoured, like the picturesque, irregularities and surprises (we can see that the High Line's influences are not entirely new). Looking at landscape was now associated with walking or wandering through it, so that the freshness of a picturesque view approximated the start of discovery one might experience on rounding a corner and finding a small, unexpected grotto or vale of trees. Landscape walkers were expected to wander. Some influences accordingly celebrated sinuosity, such as that featured in Chinese gardens. Wandering was pleasurable because, like a good holiday, it could feel unscripted precisely to the extent that it occupied certain limits: the term of the visit, the garden, the dales. Wandering in nature also became a way to have new mental experiences. Gardens with mythic references contained subtexts that could expand the world not only in the spatially imaginative sense but temporally. Finding an unexpected allusion to the past while walking enriched because it provocatively unsettled the present moment.[7]

New moods and feelings were celebrated. A wild landscape was expected to produce passionate, inarticulate emotions. The sublime, the thrill to be had from encountering a scene with fearful, vertiginous or potentially dangerous qualities, was sought after, as were other liminal states: nostalgia, a form of not unpleasurable attachment to loss, and melancholy, which could include the enjoyment of sorrow. Surprise was especially valued by Romantic writers. As Christopher Miller notes, surprise is unusual in conveying 'both an internal feeling and an external event'. Traditionally esteemed for creating strong, vividly memorable impressions, its dual function is particularly suited to the Romantic era, when feelings are beginning to be understood as deriving from human interaction with, or even to already exist within, the larger world. While in the eighteenth-century novel strange events are increasingly brought within the realm of the possible and thus potentially homogenized in a *'spatial* taxonomy' (the outside brought in), the surprising has an important temporal dimension. A chanced-upon event causes the self to examine itself, to linger with the strange 'before and after' moment it has just encountered. What surprises can 'retain its disruptive power'.[8]

The exemplary early instance is Jean-Jacques Rousseau's 1749 experience of walking from Paris to see his friend Denis Diderot, then imprisoned at Vincennes. Idly perusing a newspaper, the *Mercure de France*, Rousseau saw that the Académie de Dijon was offering a prize for an essay on the question of whether the development of the arts and sciences had bettered or worsened human morality. Calling this, in the *Confessions* (1782), an 'instant of aberration' that changed his life entirely, Rousseau described his sudden revelation ('a fortunate chance') that humanity has not been so bettered in a letter to Malesherbes:

> If anything has ever resembled a sudden inspiration, it is the motion that was caused in me by that reading; suddenly I felt my mind dazzled by a thousand lights; crowds of lively ideas presented themselves at the same time with a strength and

confusion that threw me into an inexpressible perturbation; I feel my head seized by a dizziness similar to drunkenness. A violent palpitation oppresses me ... not being able to breathe anymore while walking, I let myself fall under one of the trees of the avenue, and I pass a half-hour there in such an agitation that when I got up again I noticed the whole front of my coat soaked with my tears without having felt that I shed them.[9]

Rousseau writes the essay – his *Discourse on the Arts and Sciences* – some of his insights having been penned on the spot, wins the competition, and strives to remain true to his discovery that naturally good humans are corrupted by their institutions.

A great walker, Rousseau seems to have idealized wandering as well as (human) nature. If our formal knowledge systems and concern with 'appearance and reputation' keep us from being happy and good, then nature might heal us. At the time, the concept was revolutionary. And while Rousseau's view of early humans 'wandering in forests ... without war and without liaisons' seems comically wishful now, the idea that wandering in nature has healing properties has endured. Claiming that walking 'animates and enlivens [his] ideas' like nothing else, Rousseau walks because nature creates in him a sense of freedom, enabling better thinking.[10] Using walks to structure writing, as he did in *Reveries of a Solitary Walker* (1782), organized into ten 'Walks' (the last unfinished), enables him to wander. The work, in which Rousseau examines himself and his views, in particular the relative values of solitude and community, lacks a clear goal or chronological arrangement. His key insight, that walking can free the mind from a focus on others so that the imagination expands, forming useful associations and allowing enjoyment of change, undoubtedly influenced later writers. The French Romantic Victor Hugo (1802–1885), for instance, associated wandering with dreamscapes in which the interplay of external stimuli and inner feeling caused sensations that were difficult to locate and that made new vistas of experience available to the walker.[11]

Freeing the mind to take advantage of chance insights or wandering thoughts is famously recommended by the English poet John Keats (1795–1821), who in an 1817 letter to his brothers describes a conversation in which he was suddenly struck by the quality enabling Shakespeare's achievements: '*Negative Capability* . . . when man is capable of being in uncertainties, Mysteries, doubts, without any irritable reaching after fact or reason'. The opposite of surprise, negative capability makes surprise possible, requiring openness to 'the complexity of experience', including an intensity of feeling. Keats's predecessor William Wordsworth (1770–1850) displays something similar in his poetry, and although startlement occurs in both poets' work, in Wordsworth the chance or sudden perception more often produces a term of reverie, of 'suspended animation'. Wordsworth's poetry often features wanderers, and his own penchant for walking seems to have helped him develop an aesthetic in which a kind of temporal suspension may illuminate the chance-like nature of human lives, often foregrounding moments of failure or difficulty in human relations.[12] The opening of such a temporal space within the machinery of industrial capitalism that puts so many on the road suggests something about the human – something admittedly difficult, and often fleeting – that capitalism cannot account for. In a world so intent on extracting value from our every whim, one whose grasp on humanity's internal landscapes first takes hold in Wordsworth's time, such reflective moments may yet be a useful resource for us.

From the late eighteenth century in England the practice of enclosing common land, begun in earnest in the early modern period, was vastly accelerated to meet the demands of towns and colonies. Farming techniques had dramatically improved and it was now cheaper to take agricultural products to urban markets. At mid-century about half of England's agricultural land was open-field;

between 1755 and 1870 almost all of it was enclosed. The lives of peasants, rural workers and small freeholding farmers became considerably harder, especially in the years to 1780, as the chance of earning a living wage and supplementing it with food grown in common areas declined. Many went on the road, and many became industrial urban workers. As 'small, squarish fields' with straight roads replaced meandering paths and cart tracks, the countryside became alien, reducing possibilities for rural movement.[13] Many roads on which people had walked for centuries were closed to them, bringing unforeseen losses. One such loss was a place to conduct courtship, when a couple dreams about and discusses the future; another was the archival functions served by wandering in a time-worn landscape in which memories of a village's or region's past are contained. It was sometimes hard, too, for walkers to know when they were trespassing. New maps omitted features relevant to villagers and spoke the language of 'private holdings and projected highways', against which middle-class recreational walking would become an effort to retain ancient paths.[14]

Wordsworth's poetry taps into the new mutability of the countryside, in which the challenge is to understand not only the changes one is seeing but 'the process of change itself': how to identify it, given inconstancy and speed are its constituents (challenges that vex us too in our digital landscapes). Wordsworth's great poem *The Prelude* (1805, 1850), which tells the story of his life's journey, uses walking to foreground the complexities of how human beings inhabit time. In the preface to *Lyrical Ballads* (1800, 1802), Wordsworth had introduced a new kind of poetry that uses ordinary language to access the feelings of ordinary – frequently rural, working – people, feelings that demonstrate their intimate knowledge of how they and their surroundings interact. Decrying the many forces – war, riots, the French Revolution – conspiring to 'blunt the [mind's] discriminatory powers' and produce a 'craving' for the extraordinary, he proposed that a poet should recollect powerful feelings in such a meditative way that, while they retain their original impact, they are tempered and subtly transformed.[15]

What was novel about these ideas was the claim that humans already possess expertise in seeing connections between themselves and the things around them, because larger forces (time, change, events in nature) leave traces in our interactions with them that we can rediscover by attending to the emotions evoked by previous encounters. As *The Prelude*, a poem ostensibly about 'the growth of a poet's mind', reveals, however, this can mean that every engagement with the remembered past undoes or dislocates itself, because nature never stops speaking to us and we never stop responding, and because the narrator who walks continually displaces himself from the present moment into a future made newly uncertain by the changing resonances of past events. And yet the recurrence of certain qualities – uncertainty, aporia, suspension – reveals something important and difficult to articulate within the period. The events of the 1790s – global war, failed harvests, recession, revolution – were hugely unsettling, and the British government responded as it did to vagrants, by refusing ambiguity altogether. Everyone was either a government loyalist or republican subversive, a patriot or a national menace.[16] The chances and hazards by which life largely proceeded for many at this time seemed not to exist officially. In Wordsworth's poetry meetings with strangers, especially vagrants, that produce a lack of resolution reinstate that ambiguity, but they also go further.

The kinds of connections between humans and the natural world posited by the preface to *Lyrical Ballads*, as by other Romantic writers and artists, were even then under threat, hence the emphasis on their importance. As industrial capitalism made rural landscapes into zones of future profits, humanity was put to work inserting things into networks of values that, their ultimate end being purchase (or that a thing be dreamed of, desired as purchase), obviated themselves as networks along with the labour essential to them. Otherwise known as commodification, this process embeds a thing in an invisible 'system of equivalences that makes all things transposable into other things, most obviously into money'. It does so by disembedding said thing from its originating context and from *that* context's contexts, so that the value of everything that not only produced a thing but gave it meaning is abstracted.[17] Things can no longer be readily connected with their contexts.

This 'thing' can also now be nature. Ann Bermingham notes that as radical historical changes in late eighteenth-century England made large sections of rural landscape unrecognizable, the countryside was offered in art and writing 'as the image of the homely, the stable', beyond history's reach. Confusion borne of the pace of change produced a desire for such comforting imagery, especially in the middle classes who were industry's new beneficiaries. The counter to this beguiling trick cannot be the countryside as it was, for that and the tangible means of recalling it are gone forever. But the speed of dramatic change can be remarked by a lost space rendered temporally. The wandering poor, the unhomely, represent the space lost to time's untrackable passage.[18] The sign that a historical process has erased the means of its recall, producing a temporal excrescence, they haunt the countryside like ghosts and disconcert observers.

In 'Salisbury Plain' (1793–4) – the plain itself a 'no-place', a physical correlative of flattening market abstraction and the ravaged countryside that supports it – a female vagrant whose husband went to war and a former soldier achieve connection in 'chance moments'. Such moments are their only home. The poem's revision, 'Adventures on Salisbury Plain', was written after the landmark high treason trials of Thomas Hardy, John Horne Tooke and John Thelwall in 1794, which criminalized debate and were intended to destroy the British radical movement for government reform. It converts the narrator from an anonymous traveller into a vagrant sailor afflicted with guilt over a criminal past. Both the sailor and the woman have now learned to persecute themselves, and the sailor's chance encounter with 'wickers' that recall druidic human sacrifices once practised on the plain drives him to sacrifice himself by taking his own life.[19] Landscape here becomes mindscape as material history crosses time to give form to the sailor's lostness. While Thelwall, author of the formally digressive work *The Peripatetic* (1793), and his co-accused were acquitted, Thelwall eventually gave up his political efforts. The government's 'assault on wandering minds' produced the kind of self-surveillance dramatized in the sailor. Dissent becomes internal, producing a self-punishing excess.[20]

The sailor has killed because he has not been paid upon discharge from impressed service. The wandering Margaret in 'The Ruined Cottage' (part of Book One of Wordsworth's *The Excursion* of 1814), whose story emerges in ghostly fashion after her death, relayed by a 'Wanderer', also demonstrates the abstractive process by which capital takes things from their larger contexts. The lost context of Margaret's life – her husband Robert, fleeing fever brought on by poor harvests, went to join the army and did not return – is given form by the repetitive walking that, as David Simpson observes, replicates that of a factory labourer, even though she walks in a bare, flat plain.[21] The poem gives us atomized individuals. The lost Robert, the helpless Margaret (and her children), the speaker who for unknown reasons is walking across the barren landscape, the Wanderer or pedlar who is oddly detached from recounted events: all seem to be missing a frame of reference.

In *The Prelude*, 'spots of time' resist the simultaneity required by commodity form. Space is not subsumed into an abstract uniformity. These 'spots' show that particular spaces, and potentially all space, contain the potential to surprise us because a part of their life is carried, submerged, within a person's experience. While the reverse seems true here, things are not so simple. The landscape is freighted with literary references, and although its bleakness is thus affirmed without resolution, an affective surplus pertains. The forces so radically altering land and people's lives at this time produce loss, grief and anomie. These aspects of this landscape's history can only

be accessed by encountering the 'surplus humanity' living on in it.²²
Margaret is not surprised by landscape (and nor is the speaker).
She concretizes its alienation, which has caused hers. While nature
is still present, here there is no community, and no chances of the
kind Robert has gone to war for. The wandering narrator records an
absence of meaning made by historical conditions, and its attendant
feeling. In emphasizing the gaps in the landscape where meaning
once was, the poem counters commodification. Registering the
affective results of missing meaning, making visible the invisible
networks ravaging human lives – these are things we still need to
do in the pressing workscapes we post-Romantics have inherited.

Rogue moments

In the nineteenth century a figure emerged that would symbolize the
contradictions of urban capitalist modernity. In his essay 'The Painter
of Modern Life' (1863) Charles Baudelaire describes a 'Monsieur G.',
an artist and 'passionate spectator' of Parisian streets, whom he likens
to the impressionable observer of another, the crowd-dependent
man of Edgar Allan Poe's famous story (1840). Although Baudelaire
asserts that Monsieur G.'s aim is 'loftier than that of a mere *flâneur*',
he also associates him with this figure, and it is the *flâneur* who has
proven so paradoxically durable as the representative, or at least the
consumer, of 'the ephemeral, the fugitive, the contingent', all key features, for Baudelaire, of modern urban life. 'For the perfect *flaneur*',
writes Baudelaire, 'it is an immense joy to set up house in the heart
of the multitude, amid the ebb and flow of movement.' But the 'perfect *flâneur*' who strolls about, observing his fellow human beings
and roaming the Paris arcades designed to lure potential shoppers, is
certainly a man. In the nineteenth century and for a long time after,
a loitering woman gazing about at others is likely to be taken for a
prostitute, as shown by the fact that an adjective describing the act
of walking the streets remains a synonym for female prostitution.²³

The urban wanderer Walter Benjamin is the most well-known writer on *flânerie*, a term the origins of which are uncertain. For Benjamin, the *flâneur* appears when the early nineteenth-century city has become large and disorienting enough to be exotic to its residents, a kind of wilderness full of people and things one will never know. Benjamin's long, unfinished work *The Arcades Project* (1927–40) is itself *flâneur*-like, revealing the author's fascination with the hybrid environments of nineteenth-century Paris built to showcase the products of industry and trade to wealthy shoppers. The arcades had 'streets' made of marble and mosaic, and their roofs, made of glass and steel, let in daylight. Like them, the *flâneur* is a mixture, representing the artist who is interested in but sufficiently detached from his surroundings to process and represent them. As modernity gains pace, the *flâneur*'s detachment signifies the alienation and distraction of the modern city dweller, less the one who sets up house in the street than the one who cannot escape consumerist pressures.[24]

For Benjamin, *flânerie*'s artist-like conversion of experiences into passing enjoyment aligns it with capitalism, which also invisibly converts things, disavowing intimate knowledge. Scholars debate whether the *flâneur* is critical of capitalism or merely confirms how it works. Industrial capitalism presents us with the prospect of many more things than we can have, and the *flâneur*'s ethos to 'look, but [not] touch' confirms this. His visual consumption of the forms of others, meanwhile – for shoppers and workers are products as well as producers in capitalist systems – echoes the interchangeability of people and things. The *flâneur*'s impressions derive from the juxtaposition of many unlike objects (as well as unlike people), from the phantasmagoric feelings industrial processes create as they make such objects appear to lack history until combined with others in an evocative dreamscape. The later Situationists, who founded the Situationist International in 1957, drew on *flânerie* as part of their practices of resistance. This later stage of capitalism, they argued, alienated people not only from the goods they made and consumed 'but also from their own experiences, emotions, creativity, and desires'.[25]

The opening of Guy Debord's foundational work *The Society of the Spectacle* (1967), which describes modern life as 'an immense accumulation of *spectacles*', provides an often unnoticed clue to the Situationist ethos, according to Frances Stracey. In English the book's second sentence, 'all that was once directly lived has become mere representation', translates the French *s'éloigner* as 'has become'. This verb (more accurately rendered by Ken Knabb's online version, 'has receded into a representation') 'has the sense of "to go away from" ... "to digress", "to deviate", "to differ", "to be estranged"'. This emphasis on capital's diversion of experience from source plays a role in the Situationist response to it. The Situationists were heirs to the Dada and Surrealist movements, one of whose techniques was to showcase capitalism's invisible displacements by defamiliarizing objects: placing them in new, unexpected contexts so both became prominent.[26] The most famous example is probably Marcel Duchamp's submission of *Fountain*, a urinal, to an exhibition in 1917, following which it was photographed by Alfred Stieglitz with a backdrop suggesting leaves and trees.

Détournement (misappropriation, diversion), the Situationists' rendering, was similarly used to emphasize the invisible estrangement from images and things experienced under capitalism. 'Constructed situations' in which 'a moment of life' is created out of impressions gathered while wandering were designed to disable a passive relation to one's surroundings. The *dérive* (drift) was a mode of moving rapidly through places, noting their psychogeographical effects: how they influence mood and affect behaviour. Chance was de-emphasized because it was thought that city environments preclude it.[27] Allowing oneself to be drawn to a place and walking through it, noticing those things that create an impression in the walker, rather than following directives built into cities' designs for how citizens are to behave, was understood as a gamble and a source of future data on alternative ways of processing urban experience (although in fact very little of that survives or was recorded).

Although their activities had relatively little effect, the Situationists inspired later practitioners and chroniclers of disruptive or experimental walking, including writers such as Peter Ackroyd, Iain Sinclair and Will Self. The latter is a vigorous apologist for the right to walk freely in urban environments often set up to exclude pedestrians, as when he records the difficulty of walking to Heathrow airport from his home in London or from JFK airport to downtown New York. And the Situationists' focus on momentariness is still useful. The *flâneur* 'wastes' or fritters away his time, but as Stracey notes, avant-garde movements of all kinds 'aim to disclose the revolutionary present', the hidden potential of each moment for unforeseen social change. The Situationists saw history in terms of 'the momentary correspondences that appear between different moments', such as the unregarded connections that exist between different avant-garde practices, focused as each is upon the future and the 'now'.[28] Given their insight that our societies alienate us not only from the things around us but from ourselves, using renditions of ourselves claiming to represent our affective and imaginative responses to the world to do so, a method heightening otherwise untrackable correspondences is worth attention. A re-evaluation of our experience of time, which often passes by unnoticed, could show ways to challenge capitalism's commodification of the present moment.

Historically, we have an example of the celebration not only of an alternative way of moving around – between cities as much as within them – but of an alternative relation to consumer culture in the form of the American hobo. Coming to prominence not long after the *flâneur* appears, in the years following the end of the American Civil War (1861–5) when returning veterans, the 1873 Wall Street crisis and related events created unemployment as a visible category (earlier, people suffered temporary joblessness), the hobo, as he came to be known, represented not only American anxieties about urban industrial life but a particular form of response to them. From the 1870s to the early decades of the twentieth century, large numbers of mostly male, mostly white migrant labourers, initially known as 'tramps' and by the 1890s as 'hobos', crossed America on foot or by jumping (illegally riding) trains to find seasonal work in factories, 'mines, forests, lakes, harvest fields, [and] construction sites'. As their numbers grew, so did a subculture – called 'hobohemia' by the Chicago School sociologist Nels Anderson after a story by Sinclair Lewis – which signalled not only their relative rootlessness but their 'transitional' status between the established working class and the new, contested forms that would replace it.[29]

Hobos were readily aligned in the minds of many who did not need to move in search of work with the mythos of the lazy, crime-prone figure of the vagrant. Yet in some ways they, or at least the larger migrant workforce they were part of, resemble many of today's gig workers, who pick up jobs from online platforms on a casual, if at times relentlessly serial, basis to piece together a living or survive an unforeseen event. By the 1870s America's rapid industrialization and an explosion in its commercial activity, with accompanying booms and busts, meant that formerly self-employed northerners now worked in factories or for others, having to buy on the market goods they had formerly grown or made themselves. Largely without resources during seasonal layoffs, these skilled workers, most of whom were young, went on the road, like today's necessarily mobile college-educated gig workers. Between 1900 and 1920, when many marginal farms failed, young men from such families became temporary migrant workers.[30] Homelessness or vagrancy at this time, as often today, tended to mean living by casual labour, wage labour when available, and when not then begging, scavenging or selling illegally gotten objects, because economic changes forced so many to live routinely at the edge of viability.

And what was the primary driver of this mass unsettlement? The railroad, which created the modern corporate world, reorganized industry, transporting raw materials to factories, commodities to markets and carrying the 'increasingly footloose working class' and those beyond it who sourced the materials, picked the crops, made the goods and went as passengers or illegal riders. Railroads also represented corporate greed, promising workers freedom when 'favourable political environments' and public money made their owners rich while exacerbating the displacement and marginality of the workers who built and used them. Finance capitalism, the extension of credit to a small number of men in service of the hope invested in the new technology's expansion, caused enormous tension within the wage labour market, for 'corporate dominance' was a new kind of power, hard to analyse, while the 1865–95 generation was, in the words of the contemporary historian and journalist Henry Adams, 'already mortgaged' to it. In a further parallel with our own times, namely the explosion in credit-related financial products key to the 2008 crash and subsequent global recession, railroad owners often failed to understand how the technology in which they were investing worked, increasing the difficulty of mapping its impact on working lives and workers' futures.[31]

The railroad, and the accompanying telegraph, also fundamentally altered citizens' relation to time. The telegraph enabled news to travel between cities almost instantaneously, assisting control of deliveries and centralization of prices for commodities and financial products, which increased investment. Time became more uniform. But the hobo jumping a train 'interrupts rhetorics of progress', perhaps most graphically in the form of men 'riding the rods', clinging to the underside of boxcars mere inches above the tracks.[32] Here the unregulated body pits itself against the machine it must work with in an agonistic relation. As death may interrupt life at any instant, each instant is met with full attention.

The hobo's necessarily active, subversive engagement with the railroad instantiates the commitment to the momentary that characterized hobohemia, which largely positioned itself against the consumerist mainstream's subsumption of time to work and the save-and-spend cycle. In a celebration of white masculinity reminiscent of the frontier – such female hobos as existed typically passed as men, and African American, Mexican and Asian men were excluded from the confraternity – hobos formed communities on the 'main stem' or central part of a town near running water and railway division points, which were known as 'jungles'. Here they met, cooked meals, did laundry, socialized, spent money and shared or borrowed resources as necessary.[33]

This turning inside out of the domestic ideal of the citizen extended to non-accumulation. Many hobos would work sporadically for a few weeks at a time, by choice, as a matter of pride and to keep work available to others, specifically to avoid the way working for longer locked one in to certain kinds of consumption. People with steady jobs and savings wanted furniture, pictures, theatre outings; they were maintaining 'artificial desire' by working. In hobohemia, the 'labour and market regulations' that made households run were made obvious by opposition because hobos paid for domestic needs with money, inverting the principle whereby one worked to maintain a home as a haven away from working. If one could choose the moment when one took and left a job by means of hard work, minimalist and often convivial living, one could suture rather than support the severing of the work–life relation and do without the idea of an expensive haven. Without 'a social position to protect', hobos gave new meaning to time, which became again largely theirs as they refused its reduction to the service of capital accumulation.[34]

Chances for the people

Ironically, the relative freedom offered by hobo life and its interven-tion in the logic of consumerism is also promised by the technology companies that, today, provide platforms (hardware and software) enabling workers to pick up jobs at times of their choosing, when in fact these companies reduce everyone to the status of consumers. Workers in the gig or 'sharing' economy who use these platforms to book jobs are rebranded as entrepreneurs who manage risk and take chances. Risk, however, is a now largely unavoidable part of workplaces. Worker protections began to decrease in the 1980s in service of 'labour market flexibility'. It was made easier to hire and fire workers and to change job structures or shift employees about within a company in search of short-term profits. More tasks were outsourced to cheaper markets, forcing increased competition and less job security. Health and pension plans once provided by em-ployers now typically require more up-front worker contributions, so that the risk of health problems or bad investments falls to workers. These developments make gig work, in which workers are under-stood to be independent contractors without employee benefits, appear less the freedom-enhancing opportunity frequently sold to them (as a 2015 Uber advertisement put it: 'Drive with Uber. No shifts, no boss, no limits') than a dressing up of business-as-usual in the era of needs-must individualist impetus and lost protections.[35]

Ironically as well, in a link with hobohemia, the gig economy has its roots in an ideal and practice of sharing that arose in the wake of the recession following the 2008 financial crisis. The gig economy is sometimes called the 'sharing economy' because at this time people sought to make money from, and sometimes to share with little or no remuneration, under-used assets like rooms in their houses (Airbnb), a couch to sleep on (Couchsurfing), tools (Neighborrow, Snapgoods), short-term hire cars (Zipcar), or leftover food (ShareSomeSugar, and more recently Olio). The sharing component, however, like the freedom of gig work itself, has since come to function less as an operative element than a gloss on what actually occurs. Airbnb charges users, who charge renters, like a hotel, but staying in a hotel is not sharing. TaskRabbit, which puts those needing tasks doing like cleaning or delivery or furniture assembly in touch with those looking for work, bills itself as a variant on the old-school concept of neighbours helping neighbours, but actually involves workers performing mostly menial tasks for money. Although TaskRabbit, like other platforms, sees itself as offering a service to consumers, its role, like theirs, is more akin to that of a broker.[36]

As to the nature of gig work for workers, most such platforms emphasize freedom of choice and convenience (TaskRabbit: 'Find jobs you love. At rates you choose. Make a schedule that fits your life'). The reality is somewhat different, but context also matters. Those who graduated during the recession, typically millennials (born 1980–2000), were significantly affected by it. In the USA 'young people ages sixteen to twenty-four had an unemployment rate of 15.5 percent in 2013 and 14.2 in early 2014', compared to 5.4 per cent for those aged 25 and over in 2014. This left many of the younger age group 'unable to rent apartments and purchase or furnish homes' without parental subsidies. Millennials also experienced substantial wage loss 'even fifteen years after college graduation'.[37] In these conditions, many young people have used platforms like TaskRabbit to avoid the uncertainty of unemployment, wandering from job to precarious job in a downturn, or risking homelessness if they lack parents who can subsidize a mortgage or rent.

'Mak[ing] a schedule that fits your life' can also be problematic. Gig workers report working conditions structurally at odds with the freewheeling or bohemian ambience a platform often portrays. While some are able to make a good living and enjoy their work, and platform companies have certainly made some things easier for consumers, a repeated concern is change to payment structures and work organization without warning or consulting workers.

A TaskRabbit change in 2014 from an open bidding system whereby Taskers could bid for jobs by pitching themselves to clients to one where workers provide availability in four-hour blocks of time and are shown to prospective employers via an algorithm took away much of the promised flexibility. Workers must respond to prospective employers within thirty minutes or lose the task, including if engaged in another task or travelling with limited mobile phone coverage on the subway. A non-response can mean the worker's profile is deactivated, and workers must accept 80 per cent of work offered. Taking oneself off the platform for a time reduces one's appearance in search results. The system change disabled workers from choosing particular jobs, instead informing them they were needed in a given category. These changes, supported by the fact that creative jobs involving video making or photography also disappeared at this time, have led some to claim that TaskRabbit is essentially now managing indentured servitude.[38]

A TaskRabbit service price increase, in a move common in platform companies, was sold to workers as a chance to increase entrepreneurship, since the charge was halved for repeat clients. But repeat client work is hard to get, and early TaskRabbit workers who were using the platform entrepreneurially before the service changes, for instance to start a small translation business outsourcing work to others, could no longer do so once they were introduced (there was also a 'crackdown on outsourcing'). 'Entrepreneur' clearly means hustling harder for repeat clients, the opposite of the expansiveness and intrepid risk the term implies. Uber drivers, too, have to accept 85 per cent of work offered, and while called 'driver-partners', a worker who drives for their luxury car service UberBLACK still has to take less lucrative jobs to avoid deactivation. Deactivation risk lends a sinister import to the idea of chance, too. Because the algorithms assigning jobs are opaque to workers, and because the system of a platform like TaskRabbit operates over set, in this case thirty-day, periods, workers who fail to accept tasks across a relatively short time frame may find their accounts paused. When this happens, even though it is algorithmic measurement that has caused the action, a worker must take a test to prove they understand the guidelines, and receives a warning.[39] This scenario of diminished or last chances is not 'mak[ing] a schedule that fits your life' so much as being schooled in obedience to the corporate machine.

And such warnings are not always forthcoming. What happened to a worker documented in Alexandrea Ravenelle's 2019 study *Hustle and Gig* not only indicates how capital can mobilize algorithmic opacity against workers but signals what is arguably the most disturbing aspect of technological platforms' interventions in how we relate to our world: wandering meaning, otherwise known as euphemism, or telling lies. Donald, a 55-year-old white male, had formerly worked in finance before redundancy led him to TaskRabbit, where he picked up cleaning and errand-running jobs. One night he received an unexpected email from the company, saying that he had been 'removed . . . from the TaskRabbit community' for 'unprofessional or unbecoming communication or behavior'. Like many gig workers, and despite asking for the earliest possible appointment, Donald was not able to speak with anyone at TaskRabbit about the reason for the action for some time. It is not uncommon for workers to wait for responses to questions from platforms for several weeks. Donald wondered if the reason for his deactivation was using a gym to take a bathroom break between jobs on a day when he had twelve deliveries, a credible guess given that TaskRabbit workers, like those on other platforms, are relentlessly electronically surveilled, and locating bathrooms while moving between jobs is one of the many challenges workers must manage.[40]

However, I want to focus on TaskRabbit's use of the word 'community' in its communication with this worker. Related to the idea of a 'sharing' economy, the company's description of itself conveys a sense of folksy togetherness. Accordingly, when used for the purpose of exclusion, the term carries a charge of ostracism and shame.

But the company does not function like a community. Like early twentieth-century factories and corporations, it provides piecework to employees and maximizes employer opportunities by policing its workers and causing them to self-police in the interests of continuing to book jobs. Algorithm-time is like factory-time, introduced by management consultant Frederick Taylor in 1911 in order to increase production by training and supervising workers in the performance of discrete tasks, without regard to the well-being of the worker.[41]

This process is taken to extremes in the instance of micro-work for platforms like Clickworker or Amazon Mechanical Turk (where work is not called work but HITs, or Human Intelligence Tasks). In this field, crowdsourced workers perform tasks like checking online ratings, tagging images or transcribing text. Some tasks last only a minute and the longest usually lasts no more than an hour. Clickwork like this clearly isolates workers, not only from each other when, working solo, they compete with global others and drive down prices, but also from any meaningful context. They must learn what needs doing and how to do it without assistance, and cannot see the labour process. Ironically, workers are isolated in the interests of collaboration, but it is capital that does the coordinating: 'a project is broken up into smaller parts for a group of workers' who do not encounter each other to complete, since this way it will get done more quickly.'[42]

Gig workers tend to 'individualize and internalize' work challenges and problems. Platform companies encourage this by calling pay cuts 'incentivizers', implying that workers are not proactive enough, and by infantilizing them for pursuing their own lives in their own time with 'retraining' tests and warnings. There are shades here of 'Adventures on Salisbury Plain', as would-be dissent becomes self-blaming. Only now, dissent does not need to be criminalized. Gig workers know that dissent can reduce their brand power in the form of the online profile that must be burnished by employer and peer approval, a diminishment in the sight and appeal of which can lead to a reduction in earnings. Structural problems being met with individual solutions is a key feature of 'flexible' working. In reality, many gig workers evince abnormal degrees of psychological flexibility and resilence on a daily basis, but these qualities are no protection against sudden changes in company policy that increase anxieties about survival (and which subtly impugn the commitment of the worker). Nor are they proof against the stress of being repeatedly faced with rank dissembling. For when moves clearly designed to increase profits are said to offer workers increased options – more flexibility, more freedom – and do not, the one who bears the frustration of this devaluing, and the untruth that is its vehicle, is the worker.[43]

Wandering meaning is rife in the platform economy. 'Sharing' is actually selling, 'partners' are really workers and 'disruption' is the addition of a layer of technological mediation to a process that remains essentially unchanged. The reason this matters is that, in order to partake of the convenience of these kinds of services – as users, that is – we are all subject to a process I would call 'symbolic capture'. Key to it is a kind of affective surcharge whereby we pay an extra price for platform corporations' lying. And we pay not only in the form of this surcharge but in the more troubling way of often failing to notice that what is happening, much of the time, is wholesale category renovation. When Uber asks forgiveness for having broken civic laws, for instance, it really means that it has the money to pay the fine for doing so rather than complying.[44] Uber exempts itself from the rules others follow (taking itself out of the normative equation) and converts its failure to comply into a *requirement* of those who uphold the regulations (who are expected to provide a surplus function). Representatives of the law are asked to give this extra, symbolic thing in recognition of the fact that Uber has banked in advance on their so doing.

I do not mean to imply that the problem lies with the surcharge's being *felt*, that is, as primary affect, although regulators and other civic authorities do experience frustration at such practices. Rather, the surcharge is 'affective' because it placeholds for affect, reaching back to another time when forgiveness acted as a control on emotion, and when its symbolic imparting or withholding could mean the difference between agreement or open war. Something of this sort is in play in the twelfth-century French peace agreements considered in Chapter One, where a settlement dispute would act as a tool of forgiveness since one of its key roles was to halt the uncontrolled increase of ill feeling.[45] Forgiveness, or 'pes', did not necessarily express feeling, but it was a way to say that feelings would justify no more actions beyond an agreed point. Uber is not the only company to engage in the above sort of cynical manouevring, and I have underlined forgiveness because its historical placeholding role in averting conflict is, in developed capitalist societies, now all but invisible. And yet, forward investment in altered meaning – the forced wandering of historical limit or control functions by stealth – causes damage to our present and future prospects.

We have inherited this function as a means to foresee and act to avert potentially spiralling conflicts. As we move into the era of increasing resource depletion, the routine advance monetizing of such functions may make their symbolic possibilities less available. Something similar happens when a worker, being fired or deactivated, is made to feel the shame of being 'removed' from a 'community'. There is risk to our civic futures when functions historically used to mobilize and manage affect are debased in the interests of corporate efficiency (disguised as care for the consumer). Shared meanings and mechanisms like ostracism and forgiveness frequently mark the outer limits of public trust in civic arrangements, including markets. They may serve when we are otherwise *in extremis*, as when bank debt was effectively forgiven to the taxpayers' cost in what came to be called the Global Financial Crisis. We saw in Chapter Three the destructive impact that unchecked transvaluations had, and have, in challenging environmental conditions in Darfur. Guns replace camels, then market opportunities guns as the privileged exchange medium between nomads and the settled. And while the guns and camels remain, the feelings that arise when humans must fight for survival can shift more rapidly and unexpectedly, provoking untrackable actions, once capital has used a dream of profit to unhook the memory of cooperation with others from one's relations to precious resources like water and land.

Fighting for survival is actually the lot of a significant number of gig workers. And scholars have begun to notice the socially damaging effect of platform corporations' investment in wandering meaning. Alex Rosenblat observes that one of the categories currently being renovated almost beyond recognition is work itself. Uber is a technology company, not a transportation company, so it does not have to pay its workers benefits, and 'technology is "connective"', enabling sharing. 'The sharing economy popularized wider changes to work culture by conflating work with altruistic contributions, bringing into question the identity of workers and devaluing work' as a category.[46] Work becomes something we do for the good of our fellow humans rather than for survival, as if we could do the former without the latter.

Rosenblat's work on Uber's supply-and-demand management sheds further light on what I mean by 'symbolic capture'. Rosenblat and Luke Stark found in 2015 that Uber displayed images of fake or phantom cabs in its consumer app, suggesting supply, while adjusting pricing to get drivers to 'roam in certain areas at certain times'. Uber claims merely to reflect the market, but its patent application suggests its algorithms are predictive, forecasting demand 'so drivers can be pre-positioned' to meet it. The predictions do not always reflect reality but are instead aimed at getting drivers to flood an area and customers not to use the competition. While drivers and customers learned to game the app (or ignore surge nudges, in the case of drivers), Uber's claim to reflect market fluctuation shows it to reflect a market it is itself creating. Not long after this research went viral, phantom cabs disappeared from Uber's passenger app screens. In 2017 a *New York Times* reporter found that Uber used phantom cabs to evade law enforcement, although this does not preclude their having other functions. Uber is capable of mimicking physical mobility and market conditions in order to make those conditions more likely.[47]

Uber does something similar with regard to altering meanings (as happens in the above instance also). It is not only that the categories on which we rely to have an agreed-upon meaning, like work, or workers, are devalued by being misrepresented as 'opportunities' or acts of communal benevolence (which means having something else called work in the background to support them). Equally problematic is what happens in the spaces between concepts, where meaning ordinarily ranges as societies in transition reconsider and revalue existing practices and how they understand them. Rosenblat notes that Uber 'treats drivers like consumers and like workers', side-stepping responsibilities by blurring categories: 'If drivers are unpaid for the work they perform, should they allege theft under labor law, or seek redress for unfair and deceptive practices under consumer protection law?' The company profits from a 'strategic ambiguity', breaking norms and laws, but it also intervenes in the production and reproduction of meaning. Where Uber's apps predict demand by gaming the mobile space between consumer demand and driver need, collapsing an imagined future into the present, its blurring of categories like consumer and worker makes the space between a category as we once understood it and a new understanding we might be moving towards less available for considered involvement. An entire society's sense of what foundational categories signify and have signified historically may be altering as a result of platform companies' mobilizing 'cultural undercurrents' to defend themselves and avoid responsibility.[48]

Nonetheless, workers are organizing. Some companies offer online worker forums, and when they do not, workers create them. Sometimes they are able to shame companies that, for instance, use interns unfairly, and there have been successful strikes by Uber and

Deliveroo workers. The most publicized success to date is the UK Supreme Court's February 2021 recognition of two Uber workers as employees and not independent contractors, charges the company had been refuting since 2016. And the nature of contemporary gig work – isolation, borderlessness, surveillance – can paradoxically unite workers because not only are their work conditions almost exactly the same as those of other workers across platforms and around the world, but precarious work conditions are now normalized across so many fields of labour.[49]

Transport companies are examples of 'lean platforms' that, as Nick Srnicek claims, work 'through a hyper-outsourced model, whereby workers are outsourced, fixed capital is outsourced, maintenance costs are outsourced, and training is outsourced. All that remains is a bare extractive minimum – control over the platform that enables a monopoly rent to be gained.'[50] This, too, however, may ultimately increase worker intent because of the pile-up of so many kinds of alienation. When nothing and no one is available for complaint or dialogue, workers are driven to share concerns with each other and to an increased consciousness of themselves as workers. When everything about a platform is made to look as though what occurs on it is 'not really work' while satisfying consumer demand, the worker becomes more aware of the physicality of what they do and may also take a perverse, resistant pride in it. In organizing together, gig workers strive to remind consumers that powering the convenience and apparent immediacy of the tools we have accepted as essential to our lives are some equally necessary truths: that bodies and lives and time are all involved, and so is working.

Offshore

Wandering meaning is a feature of financial markets, too, as we will see, and we are all arguably imperilled by capital's nomadic operations. The economist Gabriel Zucman estimates that in 2014,

8 per cent of household wealth was held in tax havens (some think the total is higher), the money-making power of which increases the gap between the world's richest and the rest. The richest 1 per cent increased its wealth from one-third to one-half of everything between 2000 and 2010, and the percentage remains much the same today (the bottom 50 per cent, meanwhile, has less than a tenth). Large firms, including platforms, park their capital elsewhere than in their home countries, avoiding taxes that governments would use to fund public services. This leaves the world's wealthiest firms, including several technology companies, with enormous sums to invest, while governments practise loose monetary policy and austerity to try and recoup the shortfall, with loose monetary policy enabling the firms to invest.[51]

While the question of where a company like Apple or Meta keeps its capital falls under the category of tax avoidance – that is, navigating tax law to one's advantage (which is not illegal) – tax evasion, the misrepresentation of the true state of one's earnings and assets to authorities, is a crime. Oliver Bullough brilliantly renders the world in which the latter is routinely practised, one characterized by mobility, anonymity and criminal intent, 'Moneyland' to convey its extraterritorial dimensions. In this world, 'Maltese passports, English libel, American privacy, Panamanian shell companies, Jersey trusts, Liechtenstein foundations, all . . . create a virtual space that is far greater than the sum of their parts'. As Bullough details, Moneylanders are quintessentially nomadic:

> If a country somewhere changes the law to restrict Moneylanders in any way, they shift themselves or their assets to obey another law that is more generous. If a country passes a generous law that offers new possibilities for enrichment, then the assets shift likewise. It is as if the very wealthiest people in countries like China, Nigeria, Ukraine, or Russia have tunnelled into this new land that lies beneath

all our nation states, where borders have vanished. They move their money, their children, their assets and themselves wherever they wish, picking and choosing which countries' laws they wish to live by. The result is that strict regulations and restrictions do not apply to them, but still constrain the rest of us.[52]

One way to become a Moneylander is to turn yourself into a corporation containing your assets and sell shares in it for money. Or you can make an anonymous shell company (another word for corporation) in a place like Delaware or the Bahamas, where disclosure laws are limited, and open a Swiss bank account in the name of the company. Then you can buy something, like consulting, from the company and send funds to its account. You'll have less tax to pay at home and can invest the money held in Switzerland. You can even spend this money via a loan from, say, an American branch of the Swiss bank for which the Swiss money acts as collateral. Shell companies can also be nested in other jurisdictions from where originally created, making prosecution difficult, and all of this has been made easier since so many of our transactions moved online. Once money is elsewhere, you can put yourself elsewhere too by buying a passport to another country (Dominica, St Lucia, Austria, Cyprus) and, at the price of an 'investment' become, as London-based 'residence and citizenship planning' firm Henley & Partners puts it, a 'global citizen'. That will make it harder for tax authorities to find you or claim jurisdiction, and if you are a wealthy white person, you could relocate to a Caribbean beach resort (in which you have invested) to which other wealthy white people have also relocated, where Caribbean people will park your car and serve you drinks.[53]

Moneyland's history is part of an older concept, 'offshore', a juridical rather than a geographical place whose origins lie in legal principles established to enable humanity's management of non-territorial spaces like the sea. These were understood according to 'principles of sovereignty' dictating the control of common regions. While this often meant resolving conflicts or 'strategic problems' between states, it also meant 'discontinuity between legal and physical boundaries'. Sovereign claims could, therefore, proceed according to theoretical elaborations about power or dominion and economics. In other words, boundaries for areas humans hold in common could be defined 'along fictional or imaginary lines, such as the upper limit of airspace', and in terms of relative claims as well as sovereign ones. Thus, countries with lightly regulated regimes can claim that 'offshore' – today, less the realm of ships and planes than mobile oligarchs and mobile money – is not under their control since they merely enable a passage through a region common to humanity.[54]

Only, of course, it isn't. Offshore is a dreamspace defined, unsurprisingly given its denizens are chiefly motivated by fear of loss of money to the state or someone else, by maximum capital expenditure producing the least imaginative, least humanly diverse results, as a glance at Henley & Partners' website or the Portuguese apartments featured in *The Economist* will show you (as will the stated long-term plans for humanity of Meta or Google). It is also a zone of euphemism or wandering meaning. Bullough notes 'fiscal friction' (tax conflicts), 'succession planning' (safeguarding wealth), 'commissions' and 'facilitation payments' (rewards for selling something or bribes). Secret clients are the '"beneficial owners" of "complex structures", otherwise known as front companies', in the jargon of the City of London's banks.[55]

Finance-related euphemism may contribute to or be part of a change to the meaning of a larger category by stealth or slippage. An instance of such a change in the field of offshore finance accompanying the increased cross-border traffic of goods, services, technology and capital known as globalization is what Stephen Gill calls 'global constitutionalism'. This is the renovating of a social order by public policy that makes the investor into an ideal citizen. Their 'property rights' become all important: the 'sovereign political subject' is 'the mobile investor'. As we saw with Uber's fudging of categories with regard to its workforce, who are simultaneously workers and consumers to the agile advantage of Uber, this category shift is dual. As Ronen Palan explains, the globalized world's 'organizing myth' constitutes itself 'in the name of [the] absent presence' of the investor-consumer. This, we might say, is offshore thinking. The 'domestic' consumers' 'freedoms' to 'consume goods and services wherever and whenever they desire' are sovereign, like those of investors to invest where they will, but also theoretical, like offshore in history. In their name, real (present) consumers pay more for state services their nomadically coded liberties are disabling.[56]

Since investors do not constitute a social class, they are politically immobile and cannot organize, so governments must represent them:

> Global constitutionalism is advanced as the new human rights of the global investor, and offshore . . . is often treated in terms of basic human rights: the right of small states to determine their own laws; the right of individuals to place their savings where they wish; the right of corporations to avoid punitive taxation and regulation.

This produces ironies. In October 2011 the City of London Police issued a 'Terrorism/Extremism update' to the business community: they 'had intelligence that the Occupy London camp [near the London Stock Exchange] contained "individuals who would fit the anti-capitalist profile" . . . "suspected activists"' who might commit terrorist acts. This is somewhat rich, given that nomadic elements of another kind, including the poor and those made homeless by the fallout from the crash three years prior, with the activist contingent who donate time and energy to protest, would not have been occupying London (or Wall Street, or Madrid, or Yerevan) had it not been for the earlier rogue actions and rampant category modification of the banks. As Nigel Wilkins, the Financial Conduct Authority worker whose dogged efforts to relay the law to his employers are detailed in Tom Burgis's *Kleptopia* (2020), noted at the time, the occupiers' demand that 'regulators be independent of the industries they regulate', though sound, was up against the misaligned priorities of the regulator. His colleagues saw their work as 'removing obstacles to the transportation and multiplication of money', or safeguarding investors' rights.[57]

'Chance discoveries' seem to have played a significant role in off-shore's development, and offshore is part of other aspects of modern capitalism in which chance is central. Palan uses Gilles Deleuze and Félix Guattari's understanding of nomadic polities (albeit theirs is a rather schematic understanding) to shed light on the work of foreign exchange markets. For Deleuze and Guattari, 'lineal' societies maintain stability through kinship, 'territorial' ones by mobilizing their subjects to 'work and innovate', and 'numerical' structures function according to numerical relationships. Deleuze and Guattari align this third type of organization with nomadic groups because everyone in a nomad band, at least in this version of things, gives space the same value as they move through it, unlike territorial societies, which privilege arrival and departure points. As Palan notes, the offshore economy is also such a space, as for the financial market trader arrival or transfer points 'are only points in the endless journey of money'. A 'real' economy's indicators, 'such as employment, trade balances, and retail sales', which involve production, are decoupled from and only matter insofar as they 'affect the market'.[58]

In this context, numbers are subjects, and money no longer mediates or stores value; its value is externally relational. As with a nomad band whose territory lies in the outcome of the present moment, many more chances can be taken. In 'nomadic offshore spaces' numbers move, but they are no longer 'a means of counting or measuring': "Currency managers . . . [look] for return on investment", and "the cues they look at first are . . . purely financial . . . interest rates, the level of the stock, bond, and futures markets . . .

the level of overall debt . . . From their point of view the economy really can be summarized by these numbers"'. The decoupling of 'real' economic measures, or even the question of buying stocks because one 'believe[s] in the underlying value of [a] company', from market operations made for some strange results by the time of the 2008 crisis, when mortgage lending, selling to customers a deal whereby they come to own a property and can realize its value – often a cherished dream for the immigrant or others who see renting as wandering – became driven by the demand for mortgage-based bonds to sell as high-returning assets to investors. A marker of the 'real' economy, housing was the nominal means of a massive expansion in speculation simply for money.[59]

To what extent were the decisions bankers (and householders or would-be householders) made in the run-up to the crisis instances of offshore thinking? Historically speaking, we probably cannot describe as offshore merely a space in the future at which, say, debts will fall due, which is largely temporal, but only places where contradictions are outsourced, such as those between integral state regimes and international markets. Certainly, conditions that were temporary, such as low 'macroeconomic volatility', a situation in which inflation is low and incomes stable, were taken to be enduring, which is simply wishful. Such conditions tend to create a situation in which increasing debts, enhanced asset prices and 'global imbalances' perpetuate those same conditions, creating the impression that they may go on forever.[60]

Yet as I will argue, there was also offshore thinking. To some degree, and perhaps rather ironically, American history in the decades before the crash involved an outsourcing of contradiction that was the legacy of the 1944 Bretton Woods decision to stop uncontrolled international money flows by pegging all currencies to the gold standard via the U.S. dollar. When this arrangement was abandoned in 1971, despite soaring inflation, interest (borrowing) rates were increased and restrictions on capital flows were lifted.

The United States ran a 'persistent account deficit' for years, supported by capital flows from the dollar reserve holdings of other countries. Expanding consumption on the basis of these reserves (which were markedly higher than ever by mid-2007) without engaging in productive investment, as happened, amounts to the determined shelving of a looming problem. But the United States also, although it was not alone in this, 'outsourced' the problem of its debts, masking its lack of investment by externalizing it *within* the banking sector and the nation's households, in the form of belief in the world-broadening powers of dispersion.[61]

As Adam Tooze observes, 'real estate is not only the largest single form of wealth' in the world, 'it is also the most important form of collateral for borrowing'. America's government-sponsored enterprises (GSEs) (Fannie Mae and, later, Freddie Mac) anchored the mortgage system after the savings and loans disaster of the late 1980s to mid-1990s by buying mortgages from commercial banks and lending at government-backed rates. Later privatized, the GSEs were the source of two developments central to the crisis: the 'originate-to-distribute' lending method and securitization. The former meant commercial banks sold the mortgages issued to customers to the GSEs and were repaid, so no longer held them on their balance sheets, enabling them to make more loans. Securitization, beginning in 1970, meant 'selling mortgages directly to investors'. Payments on the original loans supported 'interest and principal payments on the new securities', which were either mortgage-backed (MBS) or asset-backed (ABS). Credit risk was dispersed by separating those originating credit from those bearing risk, which should also mean that mortgage defaults in one part of the country need not affect others.[62]

The more capital a bank holds, the more it can raise according to its improved credit rating. But capital holdings constrain size, so in the 2000s banks created a 'shadow banking system' in which loans need not be backed by capital. Here, many new conveyances combined with established practices to provide new sources of profit from differences between pay and yield, such as when using short-term asset-backed commercial paper (ABCP) (with about ninety days' maturity) to buy long-term assets. Sponsoring banks could take profits, but debts were hidden. The thinking was rather as if a nomad band really did see space as something to be processed numerically. 'Liquidity through marketability' meant short-term liabilities could back long-term assets, given the latter could be quickly sold in liquid markets with no effect on prices. But no nomad band believes that a ratio of this sort will work at a collective level (and in this case, it didn't). All long-term assets – food, water, tools, all perpetually needed – are scaled to the capability of the moment, as is tribute, the nomad version of future expansion (since it will attract more fighters). This follows from not using a dream of home to artificially adjust the timescales at which one is living.[63]

Accompanying and rendering these developments more potentially explosive was structured finance, whereby a group of risky assets became collateralized and tranched into separate risk profiles, with high-risk lower tranches delivering the best returns. Mortgage default risks were thus diversified, although the ratings agencies issuing the designations (such as AAA for lowest risk) were inclined to cooperate with bond issuers, while their risk calculation models assumed stability, mortgage bonds being unlike those 'issued by a company facing the unpredictable force of global competition'. Investment banks hedged against fluctuating currencies and interest rates with swaps so clients could trade exposure. In the 1990s J. P. Morgan bankers inaugurated credit default swaps (CDS), a variant on the time-related trading in derivatives, where value derives from the projected future value of another asset. These, which involved banks betting on the future chances of a loan or bond defaulting, were a kind of risk-management tool and when traded meant banks could lend more because risks would be spread more broadly.[64]

But this also made risk into a type of commodity. It ultimately produced a situation in which most banks parked their supposedly low-risk, mortgage-backed debt on their books while taking on ever more risky debt, to the point where the high returns on the latter meant finding ever more potential 'homeowners' (who were likely to refinance and/or default). Ever more creative repackaging of debt enabled profits, as each layer added more leverage (ways to magnify returns, in this case), furthered the illusion that risks were being spread, and enabled the delusion that risk, which is the reason banks exist, had been erased. At the heart of all this was a relation to time and timing (again, something real nomads are adept at managing). Much of the financing of MBS came from money market cash pools (ABCP and so on), operating on short-term time frames via structured investment vehicles (SIVs) created for this purpose. The latter, with their sponsored layers of capital, earned well compared to the low rate paid for commercial paper. Repurchase agreements, or repos, were also used by banks to buy securities by selling them short term, with the price of doing so (called a haircut) the only capital needed. This worked so long as the repo agreements could be perpetually rolled over.[65] But of course they could not, and when the crisis came this reliance on short-term liquidity proved disastrous.

One of the unanswerable questions about the crisis is to what extent the semantic associations of 'home' with a wishful stability played into financial assumptions about the safety of mortgage debt, even as bad mortgage debt became the raw material for profit. It is possible 'home's associations did play such a role, given the way other categories (asset, security, collateral) were shifting meaning such that the moves being made in their name were expected to secure their meaning. But as we saw with Uber's category modification, when large profits are at stake, this is not usually the direction in which things travel. Concepts are apt to be devalued. The foreshortening of time in the interests of profit certainly relied on a kind of 'spatial' opacity, like the often intangible place occupied by 'home' in people's imaginations, in the sense that not only did most investors have no idea how banks were crafting their models, but neither did the managers of investment banks. The field was too new to have a history, so the future could not be reliably gauged. And the fantasy of diversification, like a larger region where the risk supposedly went, was misplaced because the repackaging and dodging of timescales involved in collateralized debt obligations (bundled debts), lacking a larger market, was mainly carried on between relatively few investment banks.[66] This, as we know, finally led to governments stepping in to enable cash flow, effectively nationalizing and supporting the related international claims of banks.

When their mortgages defaulted, homeless people went on the roads, became unemployed in the accompanying recession or, if young, skilled and able, left their respective countries in search of better chances. Offshore thinking and wandering meaning played significant roles in the crisis, and here Palan's description of offshore as the social space in which we are the reason for capital's operations but are simultaneously 'helpless observers' of its journey is apt. In offshore thinking, 'capital represents itself . . . as paradoxically omnipotent, unchallenged, and perhaps unchangeable, and yet strangely intangible, neurotic, and sick'.[67] In the run-up to the crisis, capital's numerical representatives were torqued on the basis of people's desire for homes and spending power both, as though the idea of home has ever been fully separable from the careful deliberations of nomads, whose ownership of resources is neither assumed nor deferred but must be fought or bartered for from within the present. The debasement of these procedures by a fantasy historically derived from computing the value of common goods like sea and air, one used to mystify their contemporary stand-in, forgotten debt, to a point of nonsensical extraction, is not the least of the costs the crisis charged to human futures.

No data

In Jennifer Egan's novel *The Candy House* (2022), 'eluders' have online proxies stand in for them as they go incognito in a world in which 'counters' seek their data. These 'typicals', as counters call them, want a chance for another life, although to counters they are deluded, for measuring things makes them no less 'mysterious'. We are familiar with big corporations wanting our data, but for most of us the ability to wander freely, relatively untracked, online – the source, in the Web's early days, of a sense of quirky coincidentality and not a little mystery – has diminished. Enormously profitable technology companies now trade in their ability to capture our attention and record our shopping and viewing choices, while the scandals of recent years show these companies' care for the privacy function, whereby we retain the ability to choose what to reveal, to be minimal. As James Williams, a former Google employee, opines:

> One of the tragic ironies about the internet is that such a decentralized structure of *information* management could enable the most centralized system of *attention* management in human history. Today, just a few people at a handful of companies . . . have the ability to shape what billions of humans think and do.[68]

As is well known, the Internet's origins lie in 1960s American military research. Its precursor, ARPANET (Advanced Research Projects Agency Network), was devised at the Department of Defense for transferring official documents, and surprised its makers when a message-sending component introduced to enable its building became 'its most attractive feature'. From that developed Usenet, whereby coded data packages were sent down telephone lines, and from which 'the anarchic, anything-goes philosophy' that came to characterize the early Internet emerged. The Internet, a 'mega-network of smaller networks with . . . dedicated servers', is a bank of information. The World Wide Web, whose inception is usually credited to Tim Berners-Lee, a computer scientist formerly employed by CERN (European Organization for Nuclear Research), was proposed in 1989 as a kind of memory storage and recovery system, an electronic version of the ones monks and other scholars ran in the European Middle Ages using trees and angels' wings as partible, yet contiguous, figures of infinity. On the Web, too, pieces of information are linked together for navigation and retrieval, in its case by the electronic information system Hypertext.[69] By 1990 the Web was in discussion and a guide to its network arrived in the form of a browser.

Microcomputers did not exist when ARPANET was planned. Back then, a central mainframe would transmit to dependent portals. Communications engineer Paul Baran, employed by RAND, the U.S. think tank dedicated to analysis for nuclear defence policy, saw that this kind of topology would be readily disrupted. His radical idea was for a distributed, not merely decentralized, network, 'in which each node (vertex) was connected to several others. This topology has a high degree of redundancy' as 'there are many possible routes from one vertex to another. Disabling even quite a high proportion of edges fails to isolate any part of the network.' When ARPANET was created, Baran's idea was used to link ARPA-funded university research sites. Computer scientist Wesley A. Clark proposed linking mainframes via a sub-network of 'smaller, interconnected computers all speaking the same language . . . dedicated simply to routing . . . information', and Baran's work helped the Internet function reliably. Beyond this point, the Internet has grown unplanned, like the self-seeding chaos of plants around the High Line's abandoned rail tracks. Within the system, packets of data travel along many different paths, finding new ones when another is blocked, before reaching their destination.[70]

Because wandering was built into the Internet's functioning, it still works. The Web is rather different. While the Internet's nodes or vertices are computers, its links the lines that run between them, the Web's vertices are electronically stored document pages, their edges the hyperlinks or Uniform Resource Locator (URL) addresses connecting them. While Web traffic follows similar transmission lines to those of the Internet, it is not 'delineated' by them: 'One transmission line can in principle connect a million . . . pages to a million others in a maze of URL links.' So, as Philip Ball suggests, we have built, in the Web, a structure the shape of which is not obvious to us, that we must navigate as though blind. But it turns out that we have created a self-organizing scale-free network (or a network with scale-free features) governed by a power law, whereby when links are increased, the number of pages with that number of links decreases by a constant factor.[71]

This may make the Web favourable to behemoths, although there are also other ways things might have gone. Berners-Lee originally envisioned 'a two-way authoring environment' in which browsers could be used as clients to read documents and as 'tools for writing new ones'. Ted Nelson, an early proponent of another version of hypertext, Xanadu, envisaged something less hierarchical, including links running both ways, than the Web became. Berners-Lee himself formed the World Wide Web Foundation in 2009 'to protect human rights across the digital landscape' and, in 2018, a platform, Solid, dedicated to decentralizing the Web, enabling user control of data and using peer-to-peer network organization rather than hubs. As to the behemoths, that they have reduced our ability to wander freely is not surprising, given making the Web's information (and other people, in the case of social media networks) more easily locatable has been their aim. Wandering around online when one needs a quick answer to a question is no fun. Today's browsers treat us as consumers, but a browser need not intrinsically do this, and among browsers some are less predatory than others. Mozilla Firefox, an open-source project about half of whose workforce consists of volunteer coders, made turning on anti-tracking features its default setting in 2019.[72]

Much has been said and written about the tendency of online life to distract us from life elsewhere, and evidence suggests that our attention spans are potentially affected by online activities. Internet portals are mostly designed to arrest 'slow' thinking, in Daniel Kahneman's formulation, whereby processes requiring 'cognitive introspection', the consulting of internal resources, or thoughtful time – what Kahneman calls 'System 2 thinking' – are not employed because 'System 1 thinking', characterized by more automatic, emotional responses, is continually provoked. David Greenfield thinks the smartphone, and the Internet more generally, is like the slot machine to which people become readily addicted because both work on a 'variable ratio reinforcement schedule'. If you go online seeking a reliable source of pleasure, you may be distracted along the way or afterwards, and often we go online simply to see what is happening in the world, or who has messaged us, or where we might next like to go on holiday. The inability to predict exactly how pleasurable (or not) our digital foray will be keeps the brain's reward centres in a state of high alertness. The chance of surprise itself can be addictive.[73]

The social media company Facebook (now Meta Platforms, Inc.) has become famous – or infamous – for engaging this precise mechanism to maximize the time users spend on its platform. During the 2016 United States presidential election it became obvious that the intentionally outrageous statements of Donald Trump and his supporters were being magnified by Facebook's algorithms because announcements would attract coverage even by neutral news outlets or those who disagreed with them. Once at the top of news feeds they would provoke more outrage or agreement, leading to more clicks, a feature that contributes to the spread of disinformation. Russian hackers used Facebook to reach would-be voters and influence them to vote for Trump, as did QAnon supporters in 2020 to encourage armed groups to shoot Black Lives Matter protesters in Kenosha, Wisconsin. 'System 1 thinking' on a global scale was practised in Myanmar in 2013 and 2014 when many Burmese citizens, most of whom are Buddhist, came online for the first time, their gateway to the Internet being Facebook. No one at the company was monitoring the rollout in Myanmar or overseeing content moderation in the country's many languages. Anti-Muslim propaganda on the platform helped fuel a violent campaign against the Rohingya minority.[74] So much for the democratic promise of connection.

Like other similar platforms, Facebook emphasizes openness and connectivity. But connections do not better the world if they are unmoderated and thoughtless, and 'openness', too, becomes rather murkier on scrutiny. It is obvious that all we see online is made possible by codework we mostly do not see, that is not open to us, and the value of sharing across networks would be better expressed by its *not* being tracked as a target for personalized advertising, the basis of which users do not see either. Facebook's tracking tools follow users off-site, and as of 2018 the data thereby gathered can be broken down into 50,000 unique categories. Google, which initially promised not to use advertising on its platform, reneged on that promise in 2000 and has, according to Shoshana Zuboff, become the inventor and pioneer of 'surveillance capitalism', an economic order 'that claims human experience as free raw material for hidden commercial practices of extraction, prediction, and sales'. As our online activities are tracked, auctioned off to advertisers and sold back to us as 'personalization' we become not surveillance capitalism's customers but the source of its 'surplus': 'Surveillance capitalism's actual customers are the enterprises that trade in its markets for future behavior.'[75]

With regard to surveillance capitalism, whose desire is to know us while remaining unknowable *by* us, we probably do not wander enough in our perceptions. When a phenomenon is unprecedented, says Zuboff, we use past paradigms to understand it, and thus innoculate ourselves to its peculiar force and power:

> This new regime's most poignant harms . . . have been difficult to grasp or theorize, blurred by extreme velocity and

camouflaged by expensive and illegible machine operations, secretive corporate practices, masterly rhetorical misdirection, and purposeful cultural appropriation. On this road, terms whose meanings we take to be positive or at least banal – 'the open internet', 'interoperability', and 'connectivity' – have been quietly harnessed to a market process in which individuals are definitively cast as means to others' market ends.

In selling predictions of our behaviour mined from search and other functions to others, a picture is built up, and if we accept future nudges, we might further its purchase.[76] And yet this picture is built out of things we do online that are related to things we do offline. We do not usually search for information on things we already know, nor do we always talk about them. The picture is always partly false, because it captures only what the machinery is seeking. What we look for, what we select from, is not everything.

A platform like Google wants us to want what it wants, according to the kind of 'enclosure' mindset we saw in Chapter Four, when sixteenth- and seventeenth-century English land enclosures caused or accompanied an annexing of imagination such that the only possibilities most people saw were to vacate land or exploit it for profit. When asked in 2008 why Google had 150 products, then CEO Eric Schmidt replied: 'You should think of Google as one product: customer satisfaction.'[77] This is a deflection, inviting the questioner's attention to wander, but also a loop, because Google wants to supply what the customer wants insofar as what the customer wants is Google's suggestions. The loop that 'personalizes' information gained from us disables our ability to wander into something new, rather than something an algorithm deems adjacent. It diminishes our chances of exposure to the unexpected.

Among several such recently developed products, Google has a Maps feature called 'Driving Mode' that suggests places to go and travel times without user selection, so if you searched for something online, even if you went offline and did other things in between, the app will assume you want to find it. Unpredictable behaviour in this context 'is the equivalent of lost revenue'. Google does not want chance. This is also the context in which *Pokémon Go*, an augmented reality game that involves hunting for cartoon characters in real locations, and which enjoyed a brief craze in 2016, is best placed. *Pokémon Go* looks like wandering, but isn't. Players are herded towards 'sponsored locations' in which companies like Starbucks or McDonald's pay Niantic Labs, the game's creator, to participate, profiting from the things *Pokémon* searchers buy while luring others as a result of crowd behaviour.[78]

Eluders exist now as well as in the near future of Egan's novel. Not many of us can live offline completely, but in addition to turning trackers off we can, funds permitting, get 'signal-blocking phone cases', 'LED privacy visors' to impede facial recognition cameras, and 'anti-neuroimaging-surveillance headgear to obstruct digital invasion of brain waves', among similar devices.[79] A 'serendipitor app' can disrupt surveillance that relies on our following predictable routines. Perhaps most important, though, is not to yield the power of negation, a much larger field than that of preference or choice because it contains whatever can be positivized within it. The phrase 'I won't read that book' includes the idea of the book, and reading, but it does not tell us what else the speaker might do, or consider, or be thinking. Not unlike the limit or control categories of ostracism and forgiveness, although larger and more useful than both, negation – and refusal, one of its subsets or applications – is a brake on the overproduction of things that are dangerous or damaging.

In 1998 employees of the TBWA\Chiat\Day advertising agency were subject to a bold new experiment in office organization. There were no cubicles or desks, and workers queued for phones and PowerBooks so, like 'wandering advertising nomads', they could be inspired working anywhere. There were sofas and tabletops in common areas, but no one knew where to go, and quiet spaces like meeting rooms hit a premium. There weren't enough phones or computers since it had been expected that staff would work at different times; workers fought for them keenly. Discouraged from leaving materials anywhere than in tiny lockers, team members could not find one another, and gradually, unable to complete work, people started keeping phones and laptops and maintaining assigned spaces.[80]

What the TBWA\Chiat\Day workers negated was not 'openness' or open space but the imposition of a particular idea of freedom. What they sought, in order to pursue the play of creativity (their work) against a background that did not change, was power over how they got and used their freedom. Although online life today seems to promise the opposite of the command to be inspired by open space, instead narrowing our options, we can, like these workers, attend to how both sets of terms – freedom or chance, and predictability – interact, moment to moment, to support an optimum way of being. Contrary to surveillance capitalism's pitch, data – the things we and others know – do not define us. The unknown and unknowable also drive us, or we would not still practise philosophy or religion, or have evolved to do either. The chance to live well comes when we find our own open space, however physically constricted, and wander about in it freely. Perhaps selling us versions of ourselves that forestall such temporal liberty will reach a saturation point, prompting us to find other ways to retain the references enabling living. Let us find those ways, and let them not preclude the human.

EPILOGUE: SANCTUARY

For over four years Rosa Sabido lived in the United Methodist Church in Mancos, Colorado. Originally from Mexico, she has lived in the United States (and until her move to the church, in the same place of residence) for over thirty years. She sought sanctuary when her routine stays of removal were denied in 2017. Like many others, Rosa had completed paperwork, waited in lines and appeared at immigration appointments for decades. But the delays grew longer, policies changed, and she lacked the legal representation to help correct earlier errors. In August 2021 a private bill was introduced into Congress on her behalf, but no action occurred before a stay of removal was to expire in April 2022, and the church ended its sanctuary offer in January before Rosa could obtain a work permit. On leaving the church, Rosa made a decision to 'become [her] own Sanctuary', staying close to those who simultaneously enabled a sense of freedom and safety. Rosa now lives in a place 5 kilometres (3 mi.) from Mancos, with beautiful scenery. Her immigration status remains unresolved.[1]

The concept of sanctuary, whereby a fugitive from the law may escape arrest, typically as a last resort, is usually traced to ancient Greece and Rome, but has likely always been practised by humans. It has been observed in primate populations as a way to manage conflicts. It exists in Middle Eastern and North African traditions and from the fourth to the seventeenth centuries was recognized in English law. In the United States, 'sanctuary cities' arose in the 1980s when some churches began offering sanctuary to Central American refugees from the wars being fought in their countries. Some city councils adopted sanctuary resolutions 'limiting the participation of local officials in the enforcement of federal immigration law'. Donald Trump made ending sanctuary cities a part of his 2016 campaign following the fatal shooting of Kathryn Steinle in San Francisco in 2015 by an undocumented migrant who had been convicted of multiple felonies. About 45 people across the United States sought sanctuary in churches after Trump increased the likelihood of undocumented migrants being deported. One effect of sanctuary cities is to challenge the power of the nation-state. A city functions like a sacred zone of exception when its authorities declare a limit to the seizing of migrants or refugees within its borders. Border controls are always local, anyway. If there is a deportation law someone has to police the relevant borders; others may redraw them. Whether sanctuary cities better or worsen things for migrants and communities is a subject of ongoing debate.[2]

This short epilogue was to have been a chapter called 'Home', which, when a conjunction was placed between it and Chapter Six, 'Chance', made it easy to remember the book's projected shape; the lines had a pleasing rhythm. But as a term 'home' is readily co-opted by banks, for whom it usually means debt (or credit), and is often figured as an achievement involving a ladder going nowhere. 'Homes' find buyers, they are static, they are investments. They are often associated, in the well-off West, with nuclear families. I have never wanted a home of this kind. I planned to unsettle the idea, but time has done this for me. As things are currently, even those of us in the most stable parts of the affluent world (even Moneylanders!) cannot expect the place we live in to necessarily survive the ravages our planet is enduring through, or beyond, our lifetimes. Floods, fires, heatwaves, volcanic eruptions, tsunamis: all volatile events once called 'extreme' are on the increase. Readiness for contingency and greater mobility must form part of everyone's thinking now.

As Linda Rabben notes, 'giving refuge to strangers is an act of reciprocal altruism.' Its history involves ceding to representatives of another power beyond this world (the divine) the question the fate an individual fleeing the law deserves. It is a space of exception reserved on the basis that even bishops and priests of God, or their equivalents in non-Christian religions, answer to a higher authority who, their traditions teach, is often harsh, always just, but also merciful. Mercy exceeds the law; a judicial representative may grant it before sentencing, but it is reserved for exceptional or unusual situations. Sanctuary is also exceptional, despite its legal recognitions. Far from erasing a border, it emphasizes it, being a place of last resort. 'Accepting strangers makes them part of the moral community,' says Rabben. 'But the ever-present tension between incorporating and rejecting strangers limits humans' willingness to bestow it.' To offer sanctuary, and, perhaps, to seek it, is to potentially alter the definition of the community one belongs to. One steps over a boundary, literal in the case of the seeker, figurative in the case of the giver. One opens oneself to an unseen order, even when seeking sanctuary is legal. The historical basis of sanctuary is exception with reference to unknown factors (often represented by the unknowable deity). We make exceptions sometimes because we cannot be certain we will never need to change category ourselves. Nor can we be certain that the law is always just, since it is we who made it.[3]

I have argued in this book that wandering is essential to who we are as humans. Not only have we wandered through most of our existence, we have relied on rogue or wandering elements to remind us of key existential variables, the forgetting of which leads to fraught situations. Socrates reminds his fellow Athenians that democracy is an experiment designed to mobilize uncertainty. We vote for what we hope will come about, but when we substantiate the relation of the individual to the whole – such that to be good is to be wealthy, or wise, or learned – we get stuck in hierarchies. Every person in a democracy has the right and the duty to seek the good, and to discover what the good is in a given situation. Socrates wanders about Athens, goading people to admit what they do not know because the good needs to be perpetually wondered about and re-established. For Socrates, the communal good would always be a question. As resources diminish and tyrants rise, fuelling the fears that fix identification, it is no less a question for us today.

In ancient Australian Aboriginal society, as we have seen, Dreaming narratives preserve this conjectural space for a nomadic people, who pass elements back and forth to each other as pieces of living landscape that the ancestors also are, combining and recombining them as land itself fractures and blends and as peoples disperse and come together. No one person owns these songs and stories, but all must preserve them. The ancestors, who pre-date us, occupy the space of the life to come and embody all the earth has taught the people. Now that we are again on the move or having to relativize settled expectations, how might those of us without such a heritage seek information from the planet to help us manage the social and geographical challenges of a more mobile future? How can we make, while wandering, adjustments to expectations and beliefs so that we do not repeat the errors, most due to positivizing findings regarding processes we introduced for convenience and projective planning, that led to the current situation?

In his book *On Time and Water* (2019) Andri Snær Magnason suggests that as we have now made nature obey human timescales we need to reconfigure how we understand nature.[4] Our not yet having done so – that is, not conceiving of nature by means of mythologies that compel us and affect our choices – leaves us simultaneously transfixed by and seemingly powerless before the changes we see around us. It is as though nature is a stranger in a way categories like the Anthropocene, the time of the domination of the humans, only further. And this is why I have invoked the idea of sanctuary.

Although we associate it with static places – temples, churches – our mobile ancestors also practised it. Given that it is a practice whereby an extrajudicial authority, or some flexibility within a community's self-understanding, is often invoked, one whose indefinable bounds might include the quality of mercy, can we renovate this practice so our finite planet becomes the wanderer, the seeker of sanctuary as place of last resort, and we the community who must alter who we are to give it?

Nature sanctuaries are themselves an established practice. But this is not what I am referring to. When we give sanctuary from within a group we put ourselves in this holding space as well, and in our context this would also mark the place of the future human. Nature becomes our intimate, our boundaries have shifted. If our planet is seeking sanctuary with us as it moves and breaks apart and we offer it, hourly, routinely, it will become part of the moral community, its future part of each decision. We need rich symbolic figures with which to rework our tendency to think only about as far as our own generation. Sanctuary is an example of a mobile carrier for the unknown. It may prove useful in reconfiguring the human as a category in the larger world we cannot enclose, as a corrective to self-centralizing resolutions. If we always had this complex, ungraspably interactive being (nature), breathing through us, at the heart of who we are, surely we would act more carefully and judiciously. At the least, we would be merciful to those fleeing its difficulties, since it is we who have produced them.

From amid sanctuary, where a people changes or acts on its beliefs, Rosa learned how to be a sanctuary herself, and to identify those offering helpful contradiction: a sense of freedom and safety together. Qualifying the United States' contradictory power to welcome and reject, a group of mostly Mexican American volunteers travels about once a month in Arizona's Sonoran Desert in search of lost or missing migrants. Mostly they find remains or corpses. Then they contact border patrol, say a prayer for the dead one's soul and plant a cross at the former location of the body. The volunteers all have jobs, so their work is limited, but people know to contact them with queries. Humane Borders also documents deaths as well as providing water stations in the desert. Alvaro Enciso, who works with the Tucson Samaritans, a faith-based non-profit in Arizona, plants crosses at Humane Borders-identified death sites. He sprays large red dots in various places in the desert, symbols out of place beyond a city, to represent the migrant, 'who belong[s] nowhere'. The dots make people wonder why they are there. They are also wounds on the body politic. Inspired by the large red dots Humane Borders uses to mark dead bodies on its maps, they also appear at the centre of the crosses Alvaro makes and paints himself. More than one such Latinx volunteer expresses the fact that when they find a corpse or a death site and perform the ritual that marks the migrant's passing from this life, it is as though it is their own life passing, as though they themselves are dying.[5]

When we perform such rituals for our fellow humans, it is so that this important moment, when our hopes, which are also transitional states, finally yielded to the body's limits *in extremis*, when the desert (or the ocean, or the fire) won out, will be remembered. But when we engage in such acts of memory and consecration we are also re-encountering nature. The desert is almost impossible alone, it is impossible injured. When we go into the desert to mark the passing of brave and desperate humans we acknowledge nature's power. We also remark a space within it that goes beyond this world, because a human who was once there is there no longer, and that human's lost hopes and drive give the desert (or the mountain, or the valley) a meaning it would not have on its own. Something new emerges in the interaction. Although in this situation intimacy with nature seems adversarial, the open-ended quality of the hope that spurred the journey is recognized in the ritual with reference to the idea of the afterlife. The unknowability of the desert is also acknowledged. The cross, or red dot, or whatever symbol is chosen, marks not only a life but, through the reference to the beyond, the fact of our adding ourselves to landscapes. We cannot but change their meaning as we encounter and adapt them; we always have. But we cannot fully control how they respond to us either. So the fact of this interchange, and our uncertainty about the outcome, are recorded.

In our future wanderings, as in our present situation, belief in the possibility of change such that we can manage the fact of, and slow, our alteration of nature will continue to be a challenge. Writing about the question of whether medieval Europeans 'believed' in the miracles their God performed through his representatives, the saints, Steven Justice notes that, according to medieval people's own evidence, and contrary to modern assumptions, 'the content of the commitment' of belief 'is cognitive – one commits oneself to the position that the propositions are true – but the mind encounters the commitment itself as something alien, peremptory, and rebarbative ... Belief concerned what was uncertain, difficult, inaccessible.' For medieval Europeans belief was a command, a discipline. It meant inhabiting a state of 'cognitive restlessness' that never ceased. Belief was met with doubt, and doubt with the will, and discussion, and dialogue. Faith was 'virtuous' only as a result of a 'complex of intellectual and voluntary practices' systematically followed 'with the goal of habituation', a form of adaptation to the fact of the world's unknowability, and our own.[6]

This is the opposite of the scenario we saw in Chapter Six where nature becomes industrially commodified. Eighteenth- and nineteenth-century industry bettered and diminished people's lives, destroying those of many through the slave trade, inaugurating the subsumption of nature within human scales of operation and human time. Romantic artists and writers too sought to remind us of the 'outside', what must remain as a resource for changes of direction even as we were bringing nature 'in' to obey us like a servant. Nature cannot renew us once we have reduced its operations to the instrumental. When Tesla and Amazon work towards incorporating other planets in our solar system into colonies in advance (which has not worked well on earth, the outcomes being part of the reason it is thought of now), they subject our cosmic contexts to this spatio-temporal foreshortening. Nothing can surprise and renew us then, though. There is nowhere left to wander. But we need not let this happen. Like the belief of medieval Europeans, impossible yet required as a marker for all we do not – and may never – know about the world's operations, and perhaps like the idea of nature needing sanctuary with us as much as our seeking sanctuary in it (for the latter idea tips, at times, into its opposite, nature as enemy in the Anthropocene), disciplines and figurations can be developed that give our transience an active role, in which we practise for our obsolescence, restructuring our place, withdrawing harms.

We have the historical resources to meet this challenge. We have extant nomadic lifeways on which to draw, records in which absent content – like probable Neolithic category-shifting and cooperation – can be inferred on the basis of signal facts, and from which we can learn what might have worked in challenging conditions. We have artistic products providing clues to questions to which earlier humans generated makeshift answers, knowing these were temporary resolutions. We have the rituals and symbolic figures suggested here, and others, to accompany the calculations we can make to rescale how we conceive of environment and agent, and an environment's larger context when its local forms are changing. We can find homes in finding shelter, on the move, as we will have to, expanding our understanding of this way of being. We can mobilize resources, including amid wars, where nomadic capital means others have unfairly gone without them. We have done a lot of these things before, and then forgotten how to. But wandering is our condition, and the task of realizing this has lately come upon us. Having foreshortened time and space to the planet's peril and that of too many of our fellow humans, the time to relearn how wandering works, to shape our lives to its tests, is no longer in the future, awaiting later generations. It is now.

REFERENCES

INTRODUCTION

1 Michael D. Frachetti, 'Multi-Regional Emergence of Mobile Pastoralism and the Growth of Non-Uniform Institutional Complexity across Eurasia', *Current Anthropology*, LIII/1 (2012), pp. 31–2.

2 Anne Porter, *Mobile Pastoralism and the Formation of Near Eastern Civilizations: Weaving Together Society* (Cambridge, 2011), pp. 2, 13, 20; Anne Porter, 'Pastoralism in the Ancient Near East', in *A Companion to the Ancient Near East*, ed. Daniel C. Snell, 2nd edn (Chichester, 2020), pp. 125–43; Mario Liverani, 'A History of the Ancient Near East', ibid., p. 13; Robert K. Englund, 'Accounting in Proto-Cuneiform', in *The Oxford Handbook of Cuneiform Culture*, ed. Karen Radner and Eleanor Robson (Oxford, 2011), pp. 32–50. See also Emanuel Marx, 'The Growth of a Conception: Nomads and Cities', in *Serendipity in Anthropological Research: The Nomadic Turn*, ed. Haim Hazan and Esther Hertzog (London, 2016).

3 Michael Stewart, *The Time of the Gypsies* (Boulder, CO, 1997), pp. 144, 160–62, 165. As Stewart's research shows, these Roms, who have little to invest, refuse or ignore the standard laws of market operations, focusing instead on the possibility of sudden change (luck), with which Romani lifeways have long historical associations, often of necessity.

1 ERRANCY

1 Dante Alighieri, *The Inferno*, trans. Courtney Langdon (Cambridge, MA, 1918), I.1, Online Library of Liberty, https://oll.libertyfund.org; *The 'Inferno' of Dante Alighieri*, trans. Ciaran Carson (London, 2002), 1.3; 1.6; OED 'error', *Grand Larousse de langue française*, 6 vols (Paris, 1972), s.v. 'erreur', cited in David W. Bates, *Enlightenment Aberrations: Error and Revolution in France* (New York, 2002), p. 20; '10.11 to move', Proto-Indo-European Etyma, Indo-European Lexicon, Linguistics Research Center, University of Texas at Austin, https://lrc.la.utexas.edu,

quoted in Kathryn Schulz, *Being Wrong: Adventures in the Margin of Error* (New York, 2010), p. 41.

2 Schulz, *Being Wrong*.

3 John 1:14: 'The word was made flesh, he lived among us', *Jerusalem Bible* (London, 1966).

4 Cristina Maria Cervone, *Poetics of the Incarnation: Middle English Writing and the Leap of Love* (Philadelphia, PA, 2012), p. 4; Nicolette Zeeman, 'Imaginative Theory', in *Middle English*, ed. Paul Strohm (Oxford, 2007), pp. 223, 226, p. 228 on errant narrators, p. 230 on composition by means of errancy; Anthony Cassell, *Inferno I* (Philadelphia, PA, 1989), pp. 17–18.

5 John M. Najemy, *A History of Florence, 1200–1575* (Malden, MA, 2006), pp. 61, 92; Marco Santagata, *Dante: The Story of His Life* (Cambridge, MA, 2016), pp. 140, 143, 163; David H. Higgins, Introduction to Dante Alighieri, *The Divine Comedy*, trans. C. H. Sisson (Oxford, 1993), p. 9; John Larner, *Italy in the Age of Dante and Petrarch, 1216–1380* (London, 1980), pp. 50–51.

6 Higgins, Commentary and Notes, *The Divine Comedy*, p. 501n; also Robert Pogue Harrison, *Forests: The Shadow of Civilization* (Chicago, IL, 1992), p. 82. Henri de Lubac, *Exégèse médiévale: Les quatres sens de l'Écriture* (Paris, 1959), vol. I, p. 119, cited in Lawrence Warner, 'The Dark Wood and the Dark Word in Dante's *Commedia*', *Comparative Literature Studies*, XXXII/4 (1995), pp. 449–78, pp. 450, 473n. See also Laura Kendrick, *Animating the Letter: The Figurative Embodiment of Writing from Late Antiquity to the Renaissance* (Columbus, OH, 1999), p. 135.

7 St Bonaventure, *Breviloquium*, Prologue, 6.5, *Doctoris Seraphici S. Bonaventurae opera omnia* (Quaracchi, 1891), cited in Warner, 'The Dark Wood', pp. 457, 475n.

8 Teodolinda Barolini, *The Undivine Comedy: Detheologizing Dante* (Princeton, NJ, 1992), p. 21.

9 Ibid., pp. 24–5; John Freccero, 'The Significance of Terza Rima', in *Dante, Petrarch, Boccaccio: Studies in the Italian Trecento in Honor of Charles S. Singleton*, ed. Aldo S. Bernardo and Anthony L. Pellegrini (New York, 1983), pp. 6, 10. For the first two phrases, *Inferno* III.26–7: Dante Alighieri, *The Divine Comedy*, trans. C. H. Sisson (Oxford, 1993); for the third, *Inferno* III.23: trans. Steven Justice, 'Chaucer's History-Effect', in *Answerable Style: The Idea of the Literary in Medieval England*, ed. Frank Grady and Andrew Galloway (Columbus, OH, 2013), p. 183. Unless otherwise stated, quotations are from the Sisson edition.

10 Justice's translation, 'Chaucer's History Effect', p. 183.

11 Aristotle, *The Physics*, I.vii, 191a (London, 1957); Ivor Leclerc, *The Nature of Physical Existence* (London, 2002), p. 115; John Magee, Introduction to Calcidius, *On Plato's 'Timaeus'*, ed. and trans. Magee (Cambridge, MA, 2016), p. xxii; Brian Stock, *Myth and Science in the Twelfth Century: A Study of Bernard Silvester* (Princeton, NJ, 1972), pp. 104, 107, 117, 231, 233.

12 Educated medieval Europeans knew of five internal senses pertaining not only to perception and cognition but also by inference to contemplation. See T. E. Hill, *'She, this in Blak': Vision, Truth and Will in Geoffrey Chaucer's 'Troilus and Criseyde'* (New York, 2006), pp. 5–6. On early Christians and their relation to forests see C. H. Lawrence, *Medieval Monasticism: Forms of Religious Life in Western Europe in the Middle Ages*, 2nd edn (London, 1989), p. 1; Corinne Saunders, *The Forest of Medieval Romance: Avernus, Broceliande, Arden* (Cambridge, 1993), pp. 10–17; Daniel Caner, *Wandering, Begging Monks: Spiritual Authority and the Promotion of Monasticism in Late Antiquity* (Berkeley, CA, 2002), pp. 20–23, 25–35. On fugitives and thieves see Jacques Le Goff, 'The Wilderness in the Medieval West', in *The Medieval Imagination* [1986], trans. Arthur Goldhammer (Chicago, IL, and London, 1988), pp. 56–7; Saunders, *The Forest of Medieval Romance*, pp. 3–4.

13 Nancy Van Deusen, 'The *Timaeus* and Cusanus', in *Mind Matters: Studies of Medieval and Early Modern Intellectual History in Honour of Marcia Colish*, ed. Cary J. Nederman, Van Deusen and E. Ann Matter (Turnhout, 2009), p. 224; Mary Carruthers, *The Book of Memory: A Study of Memory in Medieval Culture* (Cambridge, 1990), pp. 20, 33, 38; Mary Carruthers, *The Craft of Thought: Meditation, Rhetoric, and the Making of Images, 400–1200* (Cambridge, 1998), pp. 13, 77–8, 81–2, 210–12, 238–45, 273–4; Mary Carruthers and Jan M. Ziolkowski, 'General Introduction', in *The Medieval Craft of Memory: An Anthology of Texts and Pictures*, ed. Carruthers and Ziolkowski (Philadelphia, PA, 2002), pp. 2–17; 'Alan of Lille, *On the Six Wings of the Seraph*', trans. Bridget Balint, ibid., pp. 84–102; Lucy Freeman Sandler, 'John of Metz, *Tower of Wisdom*', ibid., pp. 215–25.

14 Van Deusen, 'The *Timaeus*', p. 223; Robin Kirkpatrick, *Dante's 'Inferno': Difficulty and Dead Poetry* (Cambridge, 1987), p. 12.

15 Psalm 113:3–4; Barolini, *Undivine Comedy*, pp. 226–30, 341n; Cervone, *Poetics of the Incarnation*, pp. 105–17; Peter Dronke, *Imagination in the Late Pagan and Early Christian World: The First Nine Centuries AD* (Florence, 2003), pp. 44–54.

16 *Dantis Alagherii Comedia*, ed. Federico Sanguineti (Florence, 2001), quoted in Robin Kirkpatrick, 'Afterlives Now: A Study of *Paradiso* Canto 28', in *Envisaging Heaven in the Middle Ages*, ed. Carolyn Muessig

and Ad Putter (London, 2007), p. 183, also pp. 172, 174, 178; Van Deusen, 'The *Timaeus*', p. 221.

17 J. M. Roberts, *The New Penguin History of the World*, 4th edn (London, 2004), pp. 109, 262; Ronald Hendel, 'Historical Context', in *The Book of Genesis: Composition, Reception, and Interpretation*, ed. Craig A. Evans, Joel N. Lohr and David L. Petersen (Leiden, 2012), p. 56; Dianne Bergant, *Genesis: In the Beginning* (Collegeville, MN, 2013), p. 15; Matthew J. M. Coomber, 'Reading the Old Testament in Ancient and Contemporary Contexts', in *The Pentateuch*, ed. Gale A. Yee, Hugh R. Page and Coomber (Minneapolis, MN, 2016), pp. 14–15; David McLain Carr, *An Introduction to the Old Testament: Sacred Texts and Imperial Contexts of the Hebrew Bible* (Malden, MA, 2010), p. 25; David W. Cotter, OSB, ed., *Genesis* (Collegeville, MN, 2003), pp. 7, 19.

18 Cotter, *Genesis*, pp. 10, 29, 31–2; Joel S. Kaminsky, 'The Theology of Genesis', in *The Book of Genesis*, ed. Evans et al., pp. 635–56; Edwin M. Good, *Genesis 1–11: Tales of the Earliest World* (Stanford, CA, 2011), p. 23.

19 Everett Fox, *The Five Books of Moses* (New York, 1995), p. 21, cited in Cotter, *Genesis*, p. 34. See also Fox, *In the Beginning: A New English Rendition of the Book of Genesis* (New York, 1983), pp. 12–14; *Abot de R. Natan* A, ch. 1, quoted in James L. Kugel, *Traditions of the Bible: A Guide to the Bible as it Was at the Start of the Common Era* (Cambridge, MA, 1998), pp. 102–3, quoted in Cotter, *Genesis*, p. 38.

20 On the tree of life, see Tryggve N. D. Mettinger, *The Eden Narrative: A Literary and Religio-Historical Study of Genesis 2–3* (Winona Lake, IN, 2007), p. 60; on humanity's wandering, Midrash Ha-Gadol 3:24, quoted in Avivah Gottlieb Zornberg, *The Beginning of Desire: Reflections on Genesis* (New York, 1995), p. 25.

21 Craig Wright, *The Maze and the Warrior: Symbols in Architecture, Theology, and Music* (Cambridge, MA, 2001), p. 29; Hermann Kern, *Through the Labyrinth: Designs and Meanings Over 5,000 Years*, trans. Abigail H. Clay with Sandra Burns Thomson and Kathrin A. Velder (Munich, 2000), pp. 25, 27.

22 Kern, *Through the Labyrinth*, p. 23; Vergil, *The Aeneid*, trans. Sarah Ruden (New Haven, CT, 2008), v.588–95. Unless otherwise stated, quotations are from this edition. See also Wright, *The Maze and the Warrior*, pp. 80–86.

23 On Rome as an undecidable entity and its composition, see J. D. Reed, 'Vergil's Roman', in *A Companion to Vergil's 'Aeneid' and Its Tradition*, ed. Joseph Farrell and Michael C. J. Putnam (Malden, MA, 2010), p. 78; J. D. Reed, *Virgil's Gaze: Nation and Poetry in the 'Aeneid'* (Princeton, NJ, 2007), p. 1. On Dardanus, see James E. Zetzel, 'Rome and Its Traditions',

in *The Cambridge Companion to Virgil*, ed. Charles Martindale
(Cambridge, 1997), p. 190. On the reliability of the gods, see James J.
O'Hara, *Inconsistency in Roman Epic: Studies in Catullus, Lucretius,
Vergil, Ovid and Lucan* (Cambridge, 2007), p. 79.

24 On the situation in Virgil's Rome, see David O. Ross, *Virgil's 'Aeneid':
A Reader's Guide* (Malden, MA, 2007), pp. 121–2; Lee Fratantuono,
Madness Unchained: A Reading of Virgil's 'Aeneid' (Lanham, MD, 2007),
p. xiv; Michael C. J. Putnam, 'Virgil's *Aeneid*', in *A Companion to Ancient
Epic*, ed. John Miles Foley (Malden, MA, 2005), p. 453. On Jupiter and
Octavian, see David Quint, 'Virgil's Double Cross: Chiasmus and the
Aeneid', *American Journal of Philology*, CXXXII/2 (2011), p. 275, and on
Octavian's reign, see Kate McLoughlin, *Authoring War: The Literary
Representation of War from the 'Iliad' to Iraq* (Cambridge, 2011), pp. 97–8.

25 Zetzel, 'Rome and Its Traditions', p. 189.

26 Steven H. Lonsdale, 'Simile and Ecphrasis in Homer and Virgil: The
Poet as Craftsman and Choreographer', *Vergilius*, XXXVI (1990), p. 9.

27 And later 'armies . . ./ fill the plains' and heroes 'bloomed' in 'propitious
soil' (VII.642–4). See also VII.634–6; Patricia Johnston, 'The Storm in
Aeneid VII', *Vergilius*, XXVII (1981), p. 26.

28 William Fitzgerald, 'Aeneas, Daedalus and the Labyrinth', *Arethusa*,
XVII/1 (1984), pp. 52–3.

29 Alessandro Barchiesi, 'Virgilian Narrative: Ecphrasis', in *The Cambridge
Companion to Virgil*, 2nd edn, ed. Charles Martindale and Fiachra Mac
Góráin (Cambridge, 2018), pp. 271–2; Fitzgerald, 'Aeneas', p. 53.

30 Fitzgerald, 'Aeneas', p. 57.

31 On the labyrinthine battle, see Penelope Reed Doob, *The Idea of the
Labyrinth from Classical Antiquity through the Middle Ages* (New York
and London, 1990), p. 244; Fitzgerald, 'Aeneas', pp. 60–61; also Quint,
'Virgil's Double Cross'. On the ethical quandary, Putnam, 'Virgil's
Aeneid', p. 457.

32 'Subdue the proud' is W. S. Kline's translation. Virgil, *The Aeneid*, trans.
A. S. Kline (2002), www.poetryintranslation.com; Fratantuono, *Madness
Unchained*, pp. 304–5.

33 Aaron M. Seider, *Memory in Vergil's 'Aeneid'* (Cambridge, 2013), p. 185.

34 Michael C. J. Putnam, *Virgil's Epic Designs: Ekphrasis in the 'Aeneid'*
(New Haven, CT, 1998), p. 194.

35 Sarah Spence, 'Clinching the Text: The Danaids and the End of the
Aeneid', *Vergilius*, XXXVII (1991), p. 14; Caroline K. Quenemoen, 'The
Portico of the Danaids: A New Reconstruction', *American Journal of
Archaeology*, CX/2 (2006), pp. 229–50; Putnam, *Virgil's Epic Designs*,
pp. 198–9.

36 Miranda Green, 'Who Were the Celts?', introduction to *The Celtic World*, ed. Green (London, 1995), p. 3; Simon Young, *The Celtic Revolution: How Europe was Turned Upside Down from the Early Romans to King Arthur* (London, 2016), pp. 12, 17; Richard C. Hoffmann, *An Environmental History of Medieval Europe* (Cambridge, 2014), pp. 44, 57.

37 Michael Roberts, *The Jeweled Style: Poetry and Poetics in Late Antiquity* (New York, 1989), pp. 56–8, 61.

38 Richard Tarrant, 'Aspects of Virgil's Reception in Antiquity', in *Cambridge Companion to Virgil*, ed. Martindale and Mac Góráin, pp. 47, 59; Carruthers, *Craft of Thought*, pp. 57–9; Robin Lane Fox, *Pagans and Christians* (London, 1986), p. 413; Peter Brown, *The Making of Late Antiquity* (Cambridge, MA, 1978), pp. 82–5.

39 Young, *The Celtic Revolution*, pp. 125–6; Michelle P. Brown, *The Lindisfarne Gospels: Society, Spirituality and the Scribe* (London, 2003), p. 17; Carol Farr, *The Book of Kells: Its Function and Audience* (London, 1997), p. 22; Catherine Conybeare, *Paulinus Noster: Self and Symbol in the Letters of Paulinus of Nola* (Oxford, 2000), pp. 108, 126, 128; James O'Hara, 'Virgil's Style', in *Cambridge Companion to Virgil*, ed. Martindale and Mac Góráin, pp. 248–51.

40 Kendrick, *Animating the Letter*, pp. 56–7; Brown, *The Lindisfarne Gospels*, pp. 1–2, 10.

41 Marion Archibald, Michelle Brown and Leslie Webster, 'Catalogue of the Exhibition "Heirs of Rome: The Shaping of Britain, AD 400–900"', in *The Transformation of the Roman World, AD 400–900*, ed. Webster and Brown (London, 1997), p. 240; Brown, *The Lindisfarne Gospels*, p. 76; Matthew 1:1, *Holy Bible, New International Version* (London, 1980), quoted in Brown, *The Lindisfarne Gospels*, p. 332.

42 The prayer mats which such pages recall were used in the seventh- and eighth-century Roman Church and not only in Eastern Christian churches, as they continue to be in Islam. For this point and on Eastern influences on and contexts for these pages, see Brown, *The Lindisfarne Gospels*, pp. 1–2, 8, 28–9, 272, 288, 315, 319–21; also Carruthers, *The Book of Memory*, pp. 254–5. On knotwork, see Kendrick, *Animating the Letter*, p. 87. On the unfolding of the scriptures, Origen, *Selecta in psalmos*, on Psalm 1, part 4, in *Patrologiae Cursus Completus, Series Graeca*, ed. J.-P. Migne, 161 vols in 166 parts (Paris, 1857–66), 12:1082D; Gregory the Great, *Moralia in Job*, in *Patrologiae Cursus Completus, Series Latina* (hereafter *PL*), ed. J.-P. Migne, 221 vols (Paris, 1844–55), 75:966B, both cited in Kendrick, *Animating the Letter*, p. 87. On Christ's incarnation as a knot or tangle, Gregory the Great, *Quadraginta homiliarum in evangelia* 1.20.4 (*PL* 76:1162B); Bede, *In Lucae evangelium* 1.3.16 (*PL* 92:356A); John

the Scot, *In Iohannis evangelium* I, on John 1:27 (*PL* 122:306D–307A), all cited in Kendrick, *Animating the Letter*, p. 88; see also Mildred Budny, 'Deciphering the Art of Interlace', in *From Ireland Coming: Irish Art from the Early Christian to the Late Gothic Period and Its European Context*, ed. Colum Hourihane (Princeton, NJ, 2001), pp. 183–210.

43 On the body as a tent, see Farr, *The Book of Kells*, p. 22. *Liber* also refers to 'inner bark [of a tree]', according to Carruthers, and by inference the salvific cross: *Craft of Thought*, p. 275. On the broken frame, see Joanna M. Beall, 'Interlace and Early Britain', PhD dissertation, Florida State University, Tallahassee, FL, 2010, p. 93; Hebrews 10:12–22, quoted in Brown, *The Lindisfarne Gospels*, p. 362.

44 On Eucharistic influences, see Leslie Webster, 'Encrypted Visions: Style and Sense in the Anglo-Saxon Minor Arts, AD 400–900', in *Anglo-Saxon Styles*, ed. Catherine E. Karkov and George Hardin Brown (New York, 2003), p. 18; also Michael Ryan, 'Links Between Anglo-Saxon and Early Irish Medieval Art: Some Evidence of Metalwork', in *Studies in Insular Art and Archaeology*, ed. Catherine E. Karkov and Robert T. Farrell (Oxford, OH, 1991), pp. 122–6, cited in Brown, *The Lindisfarne Gospels*, p. 326. On the 'living vine', see Farr, *The Book of Kells*, p. 46, and on temporal coexistence Meyer Schapiro, *The Language of Forms: Lectures on Insular Manuscript Art* (New York, 2005), pp. 34–6, 46, who indicates that 'differences of magnitude, intensity, frequency, rapidity, and richness and complexity of forms' are developed in this page 'in a continuous way' (p. 36). See Éamonn Ó Carragáin, 'The Ruthwell Cross and Irish High Crosses: Some Points of Comparison and Contrast', in *Ireland and Insular Art, AD 500–1200*, ed. Michael Ryan (Dublin, 1987), p. 123 for the preoccupations of the reader or viewer.

45 On Germanic elites, see Webster, 'Encrypted Visions', p. 13. On pagan cultures, see Rachel Fulton, *From Judgment to Passion: Devotion to Christ and the Virgin Mary, 800–1200* (New York, 2002), p. 41. *The Dream of the Rood*, in *The Web of Words: Structural Analyses of the Old English Poems 'Vainglory', 'The Wonder of Creation', 'The Dream of the Rood', and 'Judith', with Texts and Translations*, ed. Bernard F. Huppé (New York, 1970), pp. 22–3, 32, 35, 52–5, 87–9; Sarah Larratt Keefer, '"Either/And" as "Style" in Anglo-Saxon Christian Poetry', in *Anglo-Saxon Styles*, ed. Karkov and Brown, pp. 185, 188; M. J. Swanton, 'Ambiguity and Anticipation in "The Dream of the Rood"', *Neophilologische Mitteilungen*, LXX/3 (1969), pp. 407–25.

46 G. Ronald Murphy SJ, *The Saxon Savior: The Germanic Transformation of the Gospel in the Ninth-Century 'Heliand'* (New York, 1989), pp. 52, 76; Fulton, *From Judgment to Passion*, pp. 51–3.

47 Budny, 'Deciphering the Art of Interlace', p. 183; Beall, 'Interlace', pp. 8–11; R. Howard Bloch, *Etymologies and Genealogies: A Literary Anthropology of the French Middle Ages* (Chicago, IL, 1983), p. 98, cited in Catherine M. Jones, '"La Tresse": Interlace in the *Chanson de Geste*', *French Forum*, XV/3 (1990), p. 273n. Jones claims to have found evidence of interlace earlier, in French *chansons de geste*. Maria Luisa Donaire Fernández, '*Enfances Renier*: l'entrelacement, une technique du roman', in *Essor et fortune de la chanson de geste dans l'Europe et l'Orient latin*, Actes du IXe congrès de la Société Rencesvals 2 (Modena, 1984), pp. 490–93, cited in Jones, '"La Tresse"', p. 263.

48 Jacques Le Goff, *Time, Work and Culture in the Middle Ages* [1977], trans. Arthur Goldhammer (Chicago, IL, 1980), pp. 29–42; Eugene Vance, *Mervelous Signals: Poetics and Sign Theory in the Middle Ages* (Lincoln, NE, 1986), p. 129; Bloch, *Etymologies*, p. 171; Fredric L. Cheyette and Howell Chickering, 'Love, Anger, and Peace: Social Practice and Poetic Play in the Ending of *Yvain*', *Speculum*, LXXX/1 (2005), p. 106.

49 In this section's heading and later in the chapter I use the spelling *Amors/amors*. The Old French word for love is *amor*, and Chrétien sometimes uses *Amors* to refer to Love as a personification, an allegorical figure representing love as a living being rather than an abstract force (for instance when Laudine falls in love with Yvain and when Yvain and Gawain are about to fight). Such personification shows a Platonic influence, and by Chrétien's time the revival of European medieval interest in Greek and Roman literature may also mean that the idea of *amor* (love) as *amors* (love with associations of death or war) is in play (the words sound the same when read aloud, and *mes amors* ('my loves' or 'my feelings about love') does appear in the text). *Mors* is the Roman god of death, which Remigius of Auxerre, writing in the ninth century, says may also describe Mars, the Roman god of war, Mars' red complexion representing fire and wartime bloodshed. Remigius says this in a very popular commentary on Martianus Capella's fifth-century work *On the Marriage of Philology and Mercury*, a text often glossed in the Middle Ages and well known to the twelfth-century schools of Chartres, and thus potentially an influence on Chrétien, who may also have known Remigius's commentary. Although we know very little about Chrétien beyond what his work reveals, the associations cannot be ruled out. Remigius of Auxerre, *Commentum in Martianum Capellam*, ed. Cora E. Lutz, 2 vols (Leiden, 1962–5), cited in Jane Chance, *Medieval Mythography: From Roman Africa to the Schools of Chartres, AD 433–1177* (Tallahassee, FL, 1994), p. 578n, also pp. 242–80. On *Amors/amor*

in Chrétien, see Joseph J. Duggan, *The Romances of Chrétien de Troyes* (New Haven, CT, 2001), pp. 155–7, and on Martianus and Chrétien, see Emanuel J. Mickel, 'Mercury's Philologia and Erec's Enide', *Romance Philology*, LVI/1 (2002), pp. 1–22.

50 Eugene Vance, 'Signs of the City: Medieval Poetry as Detour', *New Literary History*, IV/3 (1973), pp. 570–71; Vance, *Mervelous Signals*, pp. 114–51; Bloch, *Etymologies*, pp. 168–74; David Crouch, *Tournament* (London, 2005), p. 12; Juliet R. V. Barker, *The Tournament in England, 1100–1400* (Woodbridge, Suffolk, 1986), pp. 13–14; R. Howard Bloch, *Medieval French Literature and Law* (Berkeley, CA, 1977), p. 258.

51 John W. Baldwin, 'Chrétien in History', in *A Companion to Chrétien de Troyes*, ed. Norris J. Lacy and Joan Tasker Grimbert (Cambridge, 2005), p. 5; Joseph Gies and Frances Gies, *Life in a Medieval City* [1969] (New York, 1981), pp. 18–19.

52 Lester K. Little, *Religious Poverty and the Profit Economy in Medieval Europe* (New York, 1978), p. 12; Gies and Gies, *Life in a Medieval City*, pp. 215–19, 221–3; Le Goff, *Time, Work and Culture*, p. 35.

53 Chrétien de Troyes, *Yvain, the Knight of the Lion* [c. 1177], trans. Burton Raffel (New Haven, CT, 1987), ll. 1001–1015. Unless otherwise stated, quotations are from this edition; Marc Shell, *The Economy of Literature* (Baltimore, MD, 1978), p. 41, cited in Vance, *Mervelous Signals*, pp. 128–9.

54 Robert S. Lopez, *The Commercial Revolution of the Middle Ages, 950–1350* [1976] (Cambridge, 1998), pp. 70–71; Bloch, *Etymologies*, pp. 164–74, and p. 156 on Abelard, Thomas of Erfurt and Peter Helias, in particular.

55 Bloch, *Etymologies*, pp. 161–4, 171–2; Georges Duby, 'In Northwestern France: The "Youth" in Twelfth-Century Aristocratic Society' [1964], in *Lordship and Community in Medieval Europe*, ed. Fredric L. Cheyette (New York, 1968), pp. 202–4; Brian Stock, *The Implications of Literacy: Written Language and Models of Interpretation in the Eleventh and Twelfth Centuries* (Princeton, NJ, 1983), pp. 480–81.

56 Vance, *Mervelous Signals*, p. 134.

57 Tony Hunt, '*Le Chevalier au Lion*: Yvain Lionheart', in *A Companion to Chrétien de Troyes*, ed. Lacy and Grimbert, p. 158; Frank Brandsma, 'Hot Pursuit? Interlace and the Suggestion of Spatial Proximity in Chrétien's *Yvain* and in the Old French Prose *Lancelot*', *Arthuriana*, XIV/1 (2004), pp. 3–14. 'The text is "silent" about geographical proximity as the young woman approaches Yvain's thread' (p. 5).

58 Cheyette and Chickering, 'Love', pp. 109–10.

59 Ibid., pp. 84–5, 87, 93–101.

2 ORIGIN

1 Filipe Duarte Santos, *Humans on Earth: From Origins to Possible Futures* (Berlin, 2012), p. 41. Consequent on our knowledge that there is no such thing as empty space nor completely stable matter, some scientists claim that our universe could be one of many that emerged accidentally as the result of the interplay of matter and gravity. See Marcelo Gleiser, *A Tear at the Edge of Creation: A Radical New Vision for Life in an Imperfect Universe* (New York, 2010), pp. 219–21; Frank Close, *The Void* (Oxford, 2007), pp. 151, 158n.

2 Gleiser, *A Tear at the Edge of Creation*, p. 64; Santos, *Humans on Earth*, p. 43.

3 Some consider weak nuclear force to be a component of electromagnetic force. See Robert Jastrow and Michael R. Rampino, *Origins of Life in the Universe* (Cambridge, 2008), pp. 15–16.

4 Gleiser, *A Tear at the Edge of Creation*, pp. 130–31.

5 Santos, *Humans on Earth*, pp. 42–3.

6 Ibid., p. 51; Jastrow and Rampino, *Origins of Life*, pp. 269, 286–93; Stefan Helmreich, *Alien Ocean: Anthropological Voyages in Microbial Seas* (Berkeley, CA, 2008), pp. 1, 6–8; Ian Tattersall, *Masters of the Planet: The Search for Our Human Origins* (New York, 2012), p. xvi.

7 Eugene Thacker, *After Life* (Chicago, IL, 2010), pp. xv, x; Richard Dawkins, *The Selfish Gene* (Oxford, 1976).

8 Timothy Earle and Clive Gamble with Hendrik Poinar, 'Migration', in *Deep History: The Architecture of Past and Present*, ed. Andrew Shryock and Daniel Lord Smail (Berkeley, CA, 2011), pp. 199, 204; J. M. Roberts, *The New Penguin History of the World*, 4th edn (London, 2004), pp. 8–9; Josephine Flood, *Archaeology of the Dreamtime: The Story of Prehistoric Australia and Its People*, revd edn (Sydney, 2005), p. 15; Peter Hiscock, *Archaeology of Ancient Australia* (Cambridge, 2008), p. 5; Tattersall, *Masters of the Planet*, p. 196.

9 Earle and Gamble with Poinar, 'Migration', pp. 207–8; Flood, *Archaeology of the Dreamtime*, p. 15; Hiscock, *Archaeology of Ancient Australia*, pp. 12, 128.

10 Josephine Flood, *The Riches of Ancient Australia* (St Lucia, QLD, 1993), p. 15; Wandjuk Marika OBE, Foreword to *Australian Dreaming: 40,000 Years of Aboriginal History*, ed. Jennifer Isaacs (Sydney, 1980), p. 5; Deborah Bird Rose, 'Dreaming Ecology: Beyond the Between', *Religion and Literature*, XL/1 (Spring 2008), p. 111; Peggy Reeves Sanday, *Aboriginal Paintings of the Wolfe Creek Crater: Track of the Rainbow Serpent* (Philadelphia, PA, 2007), p. 109; Sylvie Poirier,

A World of Relationships: Itineraries, Dreams and Events in the Australian Western Desert (Toronto, 2005), p. 61. 'There are many Aboriginal legends about giant mythical beings of the Dreamtime and some of these stories handed down from generation to generation may well enshrine memories of the now extinct megafauna (large creatures) that once roamed Australia more than fifteen thousand years ago.' Flood, *Archaeology of the Dreamtime*, p. 174.

11 Marika, Foreword to *Australian Dreaming*, p. 5; Sanday, *Aboriginal Paintings*, p. 109; C. P. Mountford, 'The Art of Arnhem Land', in *Australian Aboriginal Art*, ed. Ronald Berndt (Sydney, 1964), pp. 20–32; Flood, *Riches of Ancient Australia*, pp. 70–71; Deborah Bird Rose, *Dingo Makes Us Human: Life and Land in an Aboriginal Australian Culture* (Cambridge, 1992), p. 57.

12 Flood, *Riches of Ancient Australia*, pp. 170–71; Marika, Foreword to *Australian Dreaming*, p. 5; Isaacs, ed., *Australian Dreaming*, p. 34.

13 Flood, *Riches of Ancient Australia*, pp. 156–8; Isaacs, ed., *Australian Dreaming*, p. 35.

14 Flood, *Riches of Ancient Australia*, p. 171.

15 Robert Tonkinson, *The Mardu Aborigines: Living the Dream in Australia's Desert*, 2nd edn (Fort Worth, TX, 1991), p. 67; Rose, *Dingo Makes Us Human*, pp. 52, 55; T.G.H. Strehlow, 'The Art of Circle, Line, and Square', in *Australian Aboriginal Art*, ed. Berndt, p. 49.

16 Mussolini Harvey in Rose, 'Dreaming Ecology', p. 118; Strehlow, 'The Art of Circle, Line, and Square', p. 47.

17 H. Morphy, 'From Dull to Brilliant: The Aesthetics of Spiritual Power among the Yolngu', *Man*, n.s., XXIV/1 (March 1989), pp. 26, 29–30; Fred R. Myers, *Painting Culture: The Making of an Aboriginal High Art* (Durham, NC, 2002), p. 68.

18 Morphy, 'From Dull to Brilliant', p. 31; Strehlow, 'The Art of Circle, Line, and Square', p. 46; Nancy D. Munn, *Walbiri Iconography: Graphic Representation and Cultural Symbolism in a Central Australian Society* (New York, 1973), pp. 59, 68.

19 Munn, *Walbiri Iconography*, pp. 72–4.

20 Ibid., p. 88; Poirier, *A World of Relationships*, p. 134; Alan Rumsey, 'The Dreaming, Human Agency and Inscriptive Practice', *Oceania*, LXV/2 (1994), p. 123; Tonkinson, *The Mardu Aborigines*, pp. 79–80.

21 Poirier, *A World of Relationships*, pp. 134–6.

22 Ibid., pp. 123, 136, 138–9.

23 Flood, *Riches of Ancient Australia*, p. 73.

24 Richard D. McKirahan, 'Miletus', in *Philosophy Before Socrates: An Introduction with Texts and Commentary*, 2nd edn (Indianapolis, IN,

2010), pp. 18–19; Richard Hunter and Ian Rutherford, Introduction to *Wandering Poets in Ancient Greek Culture: Travel, Locality and Pan-Hellenism*, ed. Hunter and Rutherford (Cambridge, 2009), pp. 19–20; Roberts, *New Penguin History*, p. 172.

25 Silvia Montiglio, *Wandering in Ancient Greek Culture* (Chicago, IL, 2005), p. 154.

26 McKirahan, 'Empedocles of Acragus', in *Philosophy Before Socrates*, pp. 280, 284–5, 292; M. Laura Gemelli Marciano, 'Empedocles' Zoogony and Embryology', in *The Empedoclean Kosmos: Structure, Process and the Question of Cyclicity: Proceedings of the Symposium Philosophiae Antiquae Tertium Myconense*, ed. Apostolos L. Pierris (Patras, 2005), pp. 374–5.

27 McKirahan, 'Empedocles of Acragus', p. 269.

28 A. Martin and Oliver Primavesi, *L'Empédocle de Strasbourg (P. Strasb. gr. Inv. 1665–1666)* (Berlin, 1999); McKirahan, 'Empedocles of Acragus', pp. 290–91. Unless otherwise stated, quotations from Empedocles are from this edition.

29 McKirahan, 'Empedocles of Acragus', pp. 288–9.

30 Jean-Pierre Vernant, 'The River Ameles and the Melete Thanatou', in *Myth and Thought among the Greeks*, trans. Jeff Fort (New York, 2008), p. 148; Louis Gernet, 'Les Origines de la philosophie', *Bulletin de l'enseignement public du Maroc*, 183 (1945), p. 8, cited ibid., p. 144.

31 Marciano, 'Empedocles' Zoogony', p. 375; Vernant, 'The River Ameles', p. 140. See also Richard P. Martin, 'Read on Arrival', in *Wandering Poets*, ed. Hunter and Rutherford, pp. 101–3.

32 McKirahan, 'Pythagoras of Samos and the Pythagoreans', in McKirahan, *Philosophy Before Socrates*, p. 111; Plato, *The Republic*, trans. Desmond Lee, 2nd edn (Harmondsworth, 1987), 10.11.3, ll. 621–4; Vernant, 'The River Ameles', pp. 139–40.

33 Vernant, 'The River Ameles', pp. 149, 152.

34 Hesiod, *Theogony and Works and Days*, trans. M. L. West (Oxford, 1988), ll. 775–806, cited ibid., pp. 150–51.

35 Marciano, 'Empedocles' Zoogony', pp. 375–6, 384–7; H. Diehls and W. Kranz, *Die Fragmente der Vorsokratiker*, 6th edn (Berlin, 1951), 68 B32, quoted ibid., p. 385.; M. S. Lane, *Method and Politics in Plato's 'Statesman'* (Cambridge, 1998), p. 105.

36 Hippocrates, *De natura pueri*, 17, 1, cited in Marciano, 'Empedocles' Zoogony', p. 387; Philip van der Eijk, 'The Role of Medicine in the Formation of Early Greek Thought', in *The Oxford Handbook of Presocratic Philosophy*, ed. Patricia Curd and Daniel W. Graham (Oxford, 2008), pp. 406–7; Marciano, 'Empedocles' Zoogony', p. 380; McKirahan, 'Empedocles of Acragus', p. 270.

37 McKirahan, 'Empedocles of Acragus', pp. 287–8, 269; Marciano, 'Empedocles' Zoogony', pp. 398, 359, 391. See also Robert Parker, *Miasma: Pollution and Purification in Early Greek Religion* (Oxford, 1983), pp. 299–300.

38 Roberts, *New Penguin History*, pp. 101, 103, 196; Philip Brook Manville, *The Origins of Citizenship in Ancient Athens* (Princeton, NJ, 1990), pp. 112–17, 125, 127, 148, 150, 154–5.

39 Manville, *Origins of Citizenship*, p. 187; Parker, *Miasma*, pp. 159, 6, 186–7.

40 Daniel Graham, 'The Topology and Dynamics of Empedocles' Cycle', in *The Empedoclean Kosmos*, ed. Pierris, p. 239; Manville, *Origins of Citizenship*, pp. 189, 187, 181, 192, 193; E. R. Dodds, *Euripides' 'Bacchae'*, 2nd edn (Oxford, 1960), pp. 127–8, cited in W. Robert Connor, 'Civil Society, Dionysiac Festival, and the Athenian Democracy', in *Demokratia: A Conversation on Democracies, Ancient and Modern*, ed. Josiah Ober and Charles Hedrick (Princeton, NJ, 1996), p. 222; Parker, *Miasma*, p. 287; Montiglio, *Wandering*, pp. 73, 75.

41 Roberts, *New Penguin History*, pp. 196–7; Gregory Vlastos, 'The Historical Socrates and Athenian Democracy', *Political Theory*, XI/4 (1983), pp. 495–516; Josiah Ober, 'Living Freely as a Slave of the Law: Why Socrates Lives in Athens', in *Athenian Legacies: Essays on the Politics of Going On Together* (Princeton, NJ, 2005), pp. 158–9.

42 Michael C. Stokes, Introduction to Plato, *Apology*, trans. Stokes (Warminster, 1997), pp. 1–2, 10. Unless otherwise stated, quotations from the *Apology* are from this edition; S. C. Todd, '*Lady Chatterley's Lover* and the Attic Orators: The Social Composition of the Athenian Jury', *Journal of Hellenic Studies*, CX (1990), pp. 146–70, cited in Ober, 'Living Freely', pp. 162, 165, 167; Josiah Ober, 'How to Criticize Democracy in Late Fifth- and Fourth-Century Athens', in *Athenian Legacies*, p. 141; Plato, *Apology*, 32b; *Crito*, 51c–53c, cited in Vlastos, 'Historical Socrates', p. 499.

43 H. W. Parke and D.E.W. Wormell, *The Delphic Oracle*, 2 vols (Oxford, 1956), vol. I, pp. 402–3.

44 Ibid., pp. 1–2; Francisco J. Gonzalez, 'Caring and Conversing about Virtue Every Day: Human Piety and Goodness in Plato's *Apology*', in *Reexamining Socrates in the 'Apology'*, ed. Patricia Fagan and John Russon (Evanston, IL, 2009), p. 124; Roberts, *New Penguin History*, pp. 171–2. See also Plato, *Timaeus and Critias*, trans. Robin Waterfield (Oxford 2008), 19e.

45 Josiah Ober, 'Quasi-Rights: Participatory Citizenship and Negative Liberties', in *Athenian Legacies*, p. 105; S. R. Slings and E. De Strycker, *Plato's 'Apology' of Socrates: A Literary and Philosophical Study with a*

Running Commentary (Leiden, 1994), pp. 106, 124–6, 146, cited in Gonzalez, 'Caring and Conversing', p. 123.

46 Plato, *Euthyphro*, 9e-11b, cited in Gonzalez, 'Caring and Conversing', p. 128; see also Michael Stokes, 'Socrates' Mission', in *Socratic Questions: New Essays on the Philosophy of Socrates and Its Significance*, ed. Barry S. Gower and Stokes (New York, 1992), p. 61.

47 Xenophon, *Memorabilia* 3, 9, 10, cited in Vlastos, 'Historical Socrates', p. 502. Xenophon emphasizes the institutional knowledge required to rule, taking this position to be that of Socrates. Vlastos quotes Plato's *Euthydemus* here, showing that the parts of that text Xenophon takes to exemplify 'the royal art' – for Xenophon, statecraft – are said to be 'neither good nor evil' by Plato. Plato, *Euthydemus*, 292B4–C1, cited in Vlastos, 'Historical Socrates', p. 507, also 509.

48 Catherine H. Zuckert, 'Becoming Socrates', in *Reexamining Socrates*, ed. Fagan and Russon, p. 238; Montiglio, *Wandering*, pp. 154–5.

49 J. Peter Euben, 'Reading Democracy: "Socratic" Dialogues and the Political Education of Democratic Citizens', in *Demokratia*, ed. Ober and Hedrick, p. 346; Richard Kraut, 'Introduction to the Study of Plato', in *The Cambridge Companion to Plato*, ed. Kraut (Cambridge, 1992), pp. 2–5; S. Sara Monoson, *Plato's Democratic Entanglements: Athenian Politics and the Practice of Philosophy* (Princeton, NJ, 2000), p. 9. The discussion of the city's constitution is most likely not a reference to the *Republic*, as its action occurs on the festival of Bendis, and that of the *Timaeus* at the time of the Panathenaea. The latter festival would not normally follow two days after the former. See Gregory, Introduction to Plato, *Timaeus and Critias*, p. xiii; Kathryn A. Morgan, 'Narrative Orders in the *Timaeus* and *Critias*', in *One Book, the Whole Universe: Plato's 'Timaeus' Today*, ed. Richard D. Mohr and Barbara M. Sattler (Las Vegas, NV, 2010), p. 268; and Kraut, 'Introduction to the Study of Plato', pp. 15–16; Plato, *Timaeus and Critias*.

50 Jacob Howland, 'Partisanship and the Work of Philosophy in Plato's *Timaeus*', *Review of Politics*, LXIX/1 (2007), pp. 1–2; Gregory, Introduction to *Timaeus and Critias*, p. xxxii; Pierre Vidal-Naquet, 'A Study in Ambiguity: Artisans in the Platonic City', in *The Black Hunter: Forms of Thought and Forms of Society in the Greek World*, trans. Andrew Szegedy-Maszak (Baltimore, MD, 1986), pp. 228–9; Victor D. Hanson, 'Hoplites into Democrats: The Changing Ideology of Athenian Infantry', in *Demokratia*, ed. Ober and Hedrick, p. 293. Plato uses the term *demiourgos* to describe the legislator in the *Cratylus* and the *Laws: Cratylus* 389a; *Laws* 5.746d, cited in Vidal-Naquet, 'A Study in Ambiguity', pp. 228–9, 236, also pp. 241–2n; Vernant, 'Work and Nature

in Ancient Greece', in *Myth and Thought*, pp. 282, 285, 281. See also
Catalin Partenie, Introduction to *Plato's Myths*, ed. Partenie (Cambridge,
2009), pp. 12–13.

51 Plato, *Timaeus*, trans. Donald J. Zeyl (Indianapolis, IN, 2000). Unless
otherwise stated, further quotations from the *Timaeus* are from this
edition; Morgan, 'Narrative Orders', p. 270.

52 Morgan, 'Narrative Orders', pp. 273, 284.

53 Ibid., p. 273; John Sallis, *The Verge of Philosophy* (Chicago, IL, 2007),
p. 13; Verity Harte, *Plato on Parts and Wholes: The Metaphysics of
Structure* (Oxford, 2002), pp. 214–15.

54 Gregory, Introduction to *Timaeus and Critias*, pp. xlvii, lv–lvi; Vidal-
Naquet, 'Athens and Atlantis: Structure and Meaning of a Platonic
Myth', in *The Black Hunter*, pp. 263–84.

55 Harte, *Plato on Parts and Wholes*, p. 221.

56 Homer, *The Odyssey*, trans. Robert Fagles (London, 1996), VIII.643–4,
cited in Keimpe Algra, *Concepts of Space in Greek Thought* (Leiden, 1995),
p. 33.

57 Donald Zeyl, 'Visualizing Platonic Space', in *One Book*, ed. Mohr and
Sattler, p. 123; David Sedley, 'Two Conceptions of Vacuum', *Phronesis*,
XXVII/2 (1982), p. 175, cited in Algra, *Concepts of Space*, p. 40.

58 Gregory, *Timaeus and Critias*, p. 142n; Luc Brisson, *Le Même et l'autre
dans la structure ontologique du Timée de Platon* (Paris, 1974), pp. 35–50,
cited in Vidal-Naquet, 'A Study in Ambiguity', p. 235; Diehls and Kranz,
Die Fragmente der Vorsokratiker, B87, B33–4, cited in Apostolos Pierris,
'Nature and Function of Love and Strife in the Empedoclean System',
in *The Empedoclean Kosmos*, ed. Pierris, p. 197. In the *Timaeus* the lesser
gods use 'countless rivets' to make mortal bodies from the elements,
which they then bind into the 'ebbs and flows' of the 'immortal soul'
(43a, *Timaeus and Critias*).

59 Graham, 'Topology and Dynamics', p. 235; Josiah Ober, 'The Rules of
War in Classical Greece', in *Athenian Legacies*, pp. 58, 60; Harte, *Plato
on Parts and Wholes*, pp. 224.

60 Zeyl, Introduction to Plato, *Timaeus*, pp. xv–xx; Ober, 'Rules of War',
pp. 64, 56–7, 68; Hanson, 'Hoplites into Democrats', pp. 293, 296, 298–9.

61 Graham, 'Topology and Dynamics', p. 237; Vidal-Naquet, 'Atlantis
and Athens', pp. 268, 272; Ober, 'Rules of War', p. 69; Moses A. Finley,
Economy and Society in Ancient Greece (London, 1981), p. 94, cited in
Nicole Loraux, *The Divided City: On Memory and Forgetting in Ancient
Athens*, trans. Corinne Pache with Jeff Fort (New York, 2006), p. 24;
Plato, *Critias*, 113a–b, trans. in Vidal-Naquet, 'Athens and Atlantis',
pp. 272–3.

62 Plato, *The Statesman*, trans. J. B. Kemp, 2nd edn (Bristol, 1952), 274a2–b1, cited in Lane, *Method and Politics*, p. 108, also pp. 201–2.

3 OTHERS

1 'We are all Darfur', *The Economist*, 12 January 2019, p. 35. Western media played an obfuscating role in the conflict once the term 'genocide' began to be applied to it in 2004. The term quickly became indexed to calls for U.S. military intervention, which no one on the ground supported. While crimes against humanity were committed, the UN's Commission of Inquiry found no evidence of genocidal intent, and the American 'Save Darfur' campaign's insistent use of the term hindered rather than helped relief efforts, affixed as it was to a poor understanding of the conflict and the region. It also cemented binaries by propagating the idea that 'bad' Arabs were killing 'good' Africans, which led to needless deaths among Arabs. See Julie Flint and Alex de Waal, *Darfur: A New History of a Long War* [2005], revd edn (London, 2008), pp. 179–91; Mahmood Mamdani, *Saviors and Survivors: Darfur, Politics, and the War on Terror* (New York, 2009), pp. 5–8, 42–3, 54–69.

2 Alex de Waal, 'Who are the Darfurians? Arab and African Identities, Violence, and External Engagement', in *Darfur and the Crisis of Governance in Sudan: A Critical Reader*, ed. Salah M. Hassan and Carina E. Ray (New York, 2009), p. 125; Mamdani, *Saviors and Survivors*, pp. 110, 237; Mansour Khalid, 'Darfur: A Problem within a Wider Problem', in *Darfur*, ed. Hassan and Ray, p. 35; M. W. Daly, *Darfur's Sorrow: A History of Destruction and Genocide* (Cambridge, 2007), pp. 1–2, 117–18; Andrew S. Natsios, *Sudan, South Sudan, and Darfur: What Everyone Needs to Know* (Oxford, 2012), p. 32; Robert O. Collins, *A History of Modern Sudan* (Cambridge, 2008), pp. 6, 137, 276–7; Gabriel R. Warburg, *Historical Discord in the Nile Valley* (Evanston, IL, 1993), cited in de Waal, 'Who are the Darfurians?', p. 135; John F. McCauley, *The Logic of Ethnic and Religious Conflict in Africa* (Cambridge, 2017), pp. 142–4.

3 Mamdani, *Saviors and Survivors*, pp. 10, 237, 243; Tsega Etefa, *The Origins of Ethnic Conflict in Africa: Politics and Violence in Darfur, Oromia, and the Tana Delta* (Cham, 2019), pp. 137–8; Isam Mohamed Ibrahim, 'The Traditional Mechanisms of Conflict Resolution and Peace Building in Darfur: From an Anthropological Perspective', *International Journal of Social Sciences*, IV/9 (2013), pp. 132–40; Natsios, *Sudan*, pp. 121, 125.

4 Etefa, *Origins*, p. 127; Khalid, 'Darfur', p. 40; Alex de Waal, *The Real Politics of the Horn of Africa: Money, War and the Business of Power*

(Malden, MA, 2015), p. 45; Mamdani, *Saviors and Survivors*, p. 245; Flint and de Waal, *Darfur*, pp. 46–7.

5 J. Millard Burr and Robert Collins, *Darfur: The Long Road to Disaster* (Princeton, NJ, 2008), pp. 236–7, quoted in Etefa, *Origins*, p. 128; de Waal, *Real Politics*, p. 77; Flint and de Waal, *Darfur*, pp. 55–6.

6 Etefa, *Origins*, p. 131; de Waal, 'Who are the Darfurians?', p. 137; Mamdani, *Saviors and Survivors*, p. 246; Daly, *Darfur's Sorrow*, p. 262; Natsios, *Sudan*, pp. 148–9.

7 Mamdani, *Saviors and Survivors*, pp. 244–5; Natsios, *Sudan*, p. 141; Alex de Waal, 'Sudan Crisis: The Ruthless Mercenaries Who Run the Country for Gold', *BBC News*, www.bbc.com, 20 July 2019; Alex de Waal, 'From Camel Herder to Dictator', *Foreign Policy*, https://foreignpolicy.com, 2 July 2019; The Khartoum Process, European Union/International Centre for Migration Policy Development, 2016, www.khartoumprocess. net.

8 Brian Hughes, '"The Entire Population of this God-Forsaken Island is Terrorised by a Small Band of Gun-men": Guerrillas and Civilians During the Irish Revolution', in *Unconventional Warfare from Antiquity to the Present Day*, ed. Hughes and Fergus Robson (Cham, 2017), pp. 89–108; Alexander Hodgkins, '"A Great Company of Country Clowns": Guerrilla Warfare in the East Anglian and Western Rebellions (1549)', in *Unconventional Warfare*, ed. Hughes and Robson, pp. 180–83.

9 De Waal, *Real Politics*, p. 182.

10 Ibid., pp. 175–6, 178, 183.

11 De Waal, 'From Camel Herder to Dictator'; Mamdani, *Saviors and Survivors*, pp. 243–4.

12 Mamdani, *Saviors and Survivors*, pp. 221, 238, 242, 244–5. The Arab Gathering was a confluence of Chadian Arab groups formed to mobilize Arab cattle nomads who had fled to Darfur and were perceived as under-represented by the Chadian state. Later supported by Gaddafi, the group expanded to include camel nomads who supplied soldiers for the Janjawiid. See ibid., pp. 219–20, 231.

13 Oscar Rickett, 'Sudan Coup: Where is Hemeti?', *Middle East Eye*, www.middleeasteye.net, 29 October 2021.

14 William Honeychurch and Chunag Amartuvshin, 'Hinterlands, Urban Centers, and Mobile Settings: The "New" Old World Archaeology from the Asian Steppe', *Asian Perspectives*, XLVI/1 (2007), pp. 57–8. I have in mind here the etymological history of 'investment' – which means to clothe or cover someone or something and thereby give that person or thing power, also to lay siege to or employ something for profit – as well as the way a market like a weapons market creates second-order needs in

place of the need to manage arrangements over water and grazing for animals.

15 Michael D. Frachetti, *Pastoralist Landscapes and Social Interaction in Bronze Age Eurasia* (Berkeley, CA, 2008), p. 171, and 'Multi-Regional Emergence of Mobile Pastoralism and the Growth of Non-Uniform Institutional Complexity across Eurasia', *Current Anthropology*, LIII/1 (2012), pp. 31–2; Honeychurch and Amartuvshin, 'Hinterlands', pp. 37–8, 56–9; Anne Porter, *Mobile Pastoralism and the Formation of Near Eastern Civilizations: Weaving Together Society* (Cambridge, 2011), pp. 9–14; Thomas J. Barfield, 'Nomads and States in Comparative Perspective', in *Nomad-State Relationships in International Relations*, ed. Jamie Levin (Cham, 2020), pp. 19–43.

16 Candice Lee Goucher and Linda A. Walton, *World History: Journeys from Past to Present*, 2nd edn (Abingdon, 2013), p. 40; Jared Diamond, *Guns, Germs and Steel: A Short History of Everybody for the Last 13,000 Years* [1997] (London, 2005), pp. 99, 135–6, 140–42; Porter, *Mobile Pastoralism*, p. 1.

17 Barfield, 'Nomads and States', pp. 20–21, 26–8, 201; David Christian, *A History of Russia, Central Asia and Mongolia*, vol. I: *Inner Eurasia from Prehistory to the Mongol Empire* (Oxford, 1998), p. 189; Natalia Shishlina, 'Comment', in Frachetti, 'Multi-Regional Emergence', pp. 28–9.

18 Porter, *Mobile Pastoralism*, pp. 1, 2, 13; Anne Porter, 'Pastoralism in the Ancient Near East', in *A Companion to the Ancient Near East*, ed. Daniel C. Snell, 2nd edn (Chichester, 2020), pp. 125–43; Yang Shue, *Essays on the Debate on the Sprouts of Capitalism in China* (Beijing, 1957), p. 51, cited in Anatoly M. Khazanov, *Nomads and the Outside World*, trans. Julia Crookenden, 2nd edn (Madison, WI, 1994), p. 96; Christian, *A History of Russia*, vol. I, p. 128; Xinru Liu, *The Silk Road in World History* (Oxford, 2010), pp. 2–3. Also David Sneath, *The Headless State: Aristocratic Orders, Kinship Society, and Misrepresentations of Nomadic Inner Asia* (New York, 2007), and Daniel Fleming, *Democracy's Ancient Ancestors: Mari and Early Collective Governance* (Cambridge, 2004), pp. 7–13. I have used the term 'nomad' here to emphasize the often under-recognized value nomadic lifeways have brought to human history (for which we need a memorable catch-all term). As Porter shows, however, not all ancient Near Eastern pastoralists are nomads, although pastoralism tends to involve some movement. Porter prefers the term 'mobile pastoralism' in the context of the ancient Near East. See 'Pastoralism in the Ancient Near East', pp. 127–8.

19 Thomas T. Allsen, *Culture and Conquest in Mongol Eurasia* (Cambridge, 2001), pp. 199–202, and Michal Biran, *Chinggis Khan* (Oxford, 2007),

pp. 26, 74–5, cited in Biran, 'Introduction: Nomadic Culture', in *Nomads as Agents of Cultural Change: The Mongols and Their Eurasian Predecessors*, ed. Reuven Amitai and Biran (Honolulu, HI, 2015), p. 6; Walter Pohl, *The Avars: A Steppe Empire in Europe, 567–822*, 3rd edn (New York, 2018), p. 31; Porter, *Mobile Pastoralism*, p. 20; G. Stein, 'Structural Parameters and Sociocultural Factors in the Economic Organization of Northern Mesopotamian Urbanism in the Third Millennium BC', in *Archaeological Perspectives on Political Economies*, ed. G. Feinman and L. Nichols (Salt Lake City, UT, 2004), pp. 61–79, cited ibid., pp. 22–3. See also Fleming, *Democracy's Ancient Ancestors*, pp. 35–8.

20 On the steppe, see Shane O'Rourke, *The Cossacks* (Manchester, 2007), pp. 15–16, and Robert N. Taafe, 'The Geographic Setting', in *The Cambridge History of Early Inner Asia*, ed. Denis Sinor (Cambridge, 1990), pp. 19, 21. On the horse, see David Anthony, *The Horse, the Wheel, and Language: How Bronze-Age Riders from the Eurasian Steppes Shaped the Modern World* (Princeton, NJ, 2007), pp. 191–2, 200, 211, cited in Peter B. Golden, *Central Asia in World History* (Oxford, 2011), p. 10; Anatoly M. Khazanov, 'The Scythians and Their Neighbors', in *Nomads as Agents*, ed. Amitai and Biran, pp. 32–49, p. 34, and David Christian, 'Silk Roads or Steppe Roads? The Silk Roads in World History', *Journal of World History*, X/1 (2000), p. 10.

21 Christian, *A History of Russia*, vol. I, pp. 124–5; Anthony, *The Horse, the Wheel*, pp. 221–4, 460–62; Robert Drews, *Early Riders: The Beginnings of Mounted Warfare in Asia and Europe* (New York, 2004), pp. 1–2, 65–98, cited in Golden, *Central Asia*, pp. 11–12; Khazanov, 'Scythians', p. 34; Herodotus, *The Histories*, trans. Robin Waterfield (Oxford, 2008), IV, sections 120–36, pp. 274–80; O'Rourke, *The Cossacks*, p. 17.

22 Jack R. Harlan, 'Agricultural Origins: Centers and Non-Centers', *Science*, CLXXIV/4008 (1971), pp. 468–74; David W. Anthony, 'The Opening of the Eurasian Steppe at 2000 BCE', in *The Bronze Age and Early Iron Age Peoples of Eastern Central Asia*, ed. Victor H. Mair (Philadelphia, PA, 1998), pp. 94–113, and Elena E. Kuz'mina, *The Origin of the Indo-Iranians* (Leiden, 2007), cited in Frachetti, 'Multi-Regional Emergence', p. 3. Also Frachetti, *Pastoralist Landscapes*, pp. 7–11, 19–20, and E. N. Chernykh, *Ancient Metallurgy in the USSR: The Early Metal Age* (Cambridge, 1992), cited ibid., p. 174.

23 Anatoly M. Khazanov, 'Pastoral Nomadic Migrations and Conquests', in *The Cambridge World History*, vol. V: *Expanding Webs of Exchange and Conflict, 500 CE–1500 CE*, ed. Benjamin Z. Kedar and Merry E. Wiesner-Hanks (Cambridge, 2015), p. 360; David Christian, *A History of Russia*,

Central Asia and Mongolia, vol. II: *Inner Eurasia from the Mongol Empire to Today, 1260–2000* (Hoboken, NJ, 2008), p. 7; O'Rourke, *The Cossacks*, pp. 22–3; Dimitri Obolensky, *The Byzantine Commonwealth: Eastern Europe, 500–1453* (London, 1971), p. 56, cited in O'Rourke, *The Cossacks*, p. 23.

24 Obolensky, *The Byzantine Commonwealth*, pp. 16–17; Golden, *Central Asia*, pp. 26–7; Jos Gommans, 'The Warband in the Making of Eurasian Empires', in *Prince, Pen and Sword: Eurasian Perspectives*, ed. Maaike van Berkel and Jeroen Duindam (Leiden, 2018), pp. 302, 316, 318, 321; Peter B. Golden, 'The Stateless Nomads of Central Eurasia', in *Empires and Exchanges in Eurasian Late Antiquity: Rome, China, Iran, and the Steppe, ca. 250–750*, ed. Nicola Di Cosmo and Michael Maas (Cambridge, 2018), p. 319; Lhamsuren Munkh-Erdene, 'Where Did the Mongol Empire Come From? Medieval Mongol Ideas of People, State and Empire', *Inner Asia*, XIII/2 (2011), pp. 211–37, partly citing Rashiduddin Fazlullah's *Compendium of Chronicles*, cited in Gommans, 'The Warband', p. 319.

25 Thomas Barfield, *The Perilous Frontier: Nomadic Empires and China* (Cambridge, MA, 1989), pp. 8–16, cited in O'Rourke, *The Cossacks*, pp. 20–21; Pohl, *The Avars*, p. 22; Dimitri Obolensky, *Byzantium and the Slavs* (New York, 1994), p. 15; Joo-Yup Lee, *Qazaqliq, or Ambitious Brigandage, and the Formation of the Qazaqs* (Leiden, 2016).

26 Christian, 'Silk Roads', p. 26; Golden, *Central Asia*, p. 16; Nicholas Paul, *To Follow in Their Footsteps: The Crusades and Family Memory in the High Middle Ages* (New York, 2013), p. 4; Kathryn Hurlock and Paul Oldfield, Introduction to *Crusading and Pilgrimage in the Norman World*, ed. Hurlock and Oldfield (Woodbridge, Suffolk, 2015), p. 6; Gerhart B. Ladner, '*Homo Viator*: Medieval Ideas on Alienation and Order', *Speculum*, XLII/2 (1967), pp. 233–59; Steven Runciman, *A History of the Crusades*, vol. I: *The First Crusade* (Cambridge, 1951), p. 89. While Muslims had practised the *hajj*, or ritual journey to Mecca, since Islam's founding in the seventh century CE, the Qur'an also mentions 'vagabond saints' (*sa'ih*). These, like Christianity's Desert Fathers, seem less to have wandered physically than to have practised worldly renunciation, although some did travel. According to Houari Touati, 'the idea that roving is a condition for access to holiness was a commonplace in Muslim mysticism' of the eleventh century. See Houari Touati, *Islam and Travel in the Middle Ages* [2000], trans. Lydia G. Cochrane (Chicago, IL, 2010), pp. 158–65.

27 Peter Frankopan, *The First Crusade: The Call from the East* (Cambridge, MA, 2012), pp. 17–20, 30, 65, 71, 90–91; Runciman, *A History of the Crusades*, vol. I, p. 76.

28 Frankopan, *The First Crusade*, pp. III, 118–23; Thomas Asbridge, *The Crusades: The War for the Holy Land* (London, 2010), pp. 41, 526–30. Urban was also moving about preaching the Crusade, but his endeavours were more practically focused.

29 Janet L. Abu-Lughod, *Before European Hegemony: The World System, AD 1250–1350* (New York, 1989), pp. 12, 46–7, 141, 154. See also Richard Smith, 'Trade and Commerce Across Afro-Eurasia', in *Cambridge World History*, vol. V, ed. Kedar and Wiesner-Hanks, pp. 233–56; Peter Frankopan, *The Silk Roads: A New History of the World* (London, 2015), p. 148; Golden, *Central Asia*, pp. 83–4, 86, 90.

30 Robert Silverberg, *The Realm of Prester John* (New York, 1972), pp. 9–11, 75; Abu-Lughod, *Before European Hegemony*, p. 161; Keagan Brewer, Introduction to *Prester John: The Legend and Its Sources*, ed. and trans. Brewer (Farnham, Surrey, 2015), pp. 1, 6; Ibn al-Athir, *The Chronicle of Ibn al-Athir for the Crusading Period from al-Kamil fi'l-ta'rikh*, trans. Donald S. Richards, vol. 1 (Aldershot, 2006), pp. 359–63, cited in Brewer, *Prester John*, p. 7.

31 Brewer, *Prester John*, p. 7; Silverberg, *Realm of Prester John*, pp. 5, 8; Fulcher of Chartres, *A History of the Expedition to Jerusalem, 1095–1127*, trans. Frances Rita Ryan, ed. Harold S. Fink (Knoxville, TN, 1969), Book III, section xxxvii, p. 271.

32 Brewer, *Prester John*, pp. 4–6, 9–10; Silverberg, *Realm of Prester John*, pp. 17, 41–5; '*Epistola Presbiteri Iohannis*, The *Prester John* Letter' [*c.* 1165–70], in Brewer, *Prester John* pp. 46–91.

33 Brewer, *Prester John*, pp. 2, 10; '*Relatio de Davide (Prima Carta)*, Relation de Davide (First Version)' [1220 or early 1221], in Brewer, *Prester John*, pp. 101–13; Elizabeth Aubrey, *The Music of the Troubadours* (Bloomington, IN, 1996), p. 1.

34 On the mobility of courts, see Patrick Geary et al., 'Courtly Cultures: Western Europe, Byzantium, the Islamic World, India, China, and Japan', in *Cambridge World History*, vol. V, ed. Kedar and Wiesner-Hanks, p. 180; Ruth Harvey, 'Courtly Culture in Medieval Occitania', in *The Troubadours: An Introduction*, ed. Simon Gaunt and Sarah Kay (Cambridge, 1999), pp. 12–13. See also Fredric L. Cheyette, *Ermengard of Narbonne and the World of the Troubadours* (New York, 2001), pp. 165, 188; Gerald of Wales (Giraldus Cambrensis), *De Principis Instructione*, cited in Joan Ferrante, 'The Court in Medieval Literature: The Center of the Problem', in *The Medieval Court in Europe*, ed. Edward R. Haymes (Munich, 1986), p. 3; Walter Map, *De Nugis Curialium: Courtiers' Trifles*, ed. and trans. M. R. James, revd C.N.L. Brooke and R.A.B. Mynors (Oxford, 1983), Distinction I.1, p. 3; D I.2, p. 9; D I.10, pp. 15–16.

35 Aubrey, *Music of the Troubadours*, pp. xvi, 2, 4–6; Jeremy Yudkin, *Music in Medieval Europe* (Englewood Cliffs, NJ, 1989), p. 257; Linda M. Paterson, *Singing the Crusades: French and Occitan Lyric Responses to the Crusading Movements, 1137–1336* (Woodbridge, Suffolk, 2018); Ardis Butterfield, 'Vernacular Poetry and Music', in *The Cambridge Companion to Medieval Music*, ed. Mark Everist (Cambridge, 2011), pp. 207–8; Ardis Butterfield, *Poetry and Music in Medieval France: From Jean Renart to Guillaume de Machaut* (Cambridge, 2002), p. 25. *Trouvères* is the term for those composing in the northern dialect instead of that of the south.

36 Aubrey, *Music of the Troubadours*, pp. 82, 144–6, 244; Judith A. Peraino, *Giving Voice to Love: Song and Self-Expression from the Troubadours to Guillaume de Machaut* (Oxford, 2011), pp. 71–3; Ardis Butterfield, 'Poems Without Form? Maiden in the mor lay Revisited', in *Readings in Medieval Textuality: Essays in Honour of A. C. Spearing*, ed. Cristina Maria Cervone and D. Vance Smith (Cambridge, 2016), pp. 190–93; Bernart de Ventadorn, '*Ab Joi Mou lo Vers e.l Comens*', in *The Songs of Bernart de Ventadorn*, ed. and trans. Stephen G. Nichols Jr et al. (Chapel Hill, NC, 1962), p. 43; Guilhem de Cabestanh, '*Lo dous cossire que'm don' amors soven*', in *Proensa: An Anthology of Troubadour Poetry*, trans. Paul Blackburn, ed. George Economou (Berkeley, CA, 1978), p. 191.

37 Sarah Kay, 'Courts, Clerks, and Courtly Love', in *The Cambridge Companion to Medieval Romance*, ed. Roberta L. Krueger (Cambridge, 2000), p. 85; Peire Vidal, '*Plus que.l paubres que jatz e.l ric ostal*', in *Proensa*, ed. Economou, p. 107; Raimbaut d'Aurenga, '*Ar resplan la flors enversa*', in *Anthology of Troubadour Poetry*, ed. and trans. Alan R. Press (Edinburgh, 1971), p. 107; Peraino, *Giving Voice*, p. 63, for an extended analysis of melody see pp. 62–5 and passim; Aubrey, *Music of the Troubadours*, pp. 91–2.

38 Cheyette, *Ermengard*, p. 202, emphasis added; R. Howard Bloch, *Medieval French Literature and Law* (Berkeley, CA, 1977), p. 188.

39 Yudkin, *Music in Medieval Europe*, p. 262; Butterfield, 'Vernacular Poetry', p. 210; Bloch, *Medieval French Literature*, p. 150; Harvey, 'Courtly Culture', pp. 22–3. Counter-response was built into theological training and practice at this time. A student or master had to support either side of the *quodlibet*, or 'improvised debate', which endorsed and maintained a teacher's licence. See Bloch, *Medieval French Literature*, p. 165; Peraino, *Giving Voice*, p. 131; *Doctrina de compondre dictatz*, cited ibid., p. 100. The *Doctrina* is 'probably written by Jofre de Foixà' (ibid., p. 99).

40 Cheyette, *Ermengard*, pp. 198, 202–4. For service owed by commoners, pp. 138, 142. For service owed by nobles, pp. 194–5; Harvey, 'Courtly Culture', p. 21; Bloch, *Medieval French Literature*, pp. 187–8; Butterfield, 'Vernacular Poetry', p. 209; Joel Kaye, *A History of Balance, 1250–1375:*

The Emergence of a New Model of Equilibrium and Its Impact on Medieval Thought (Cambridge, 2014), p. 281.

41 Butterfield, *Poetry and Music*, pp. 43, 57, 131, 147, 288.

42 Carol Symes, *A Common Stage: Theater and Public Life in Medieval Arras* (New York, 2007), p. 81; John W. Baldwin, 'The Image of the Jongleur in Northern France around 1200', *Speculum*, LXXII/3 (1997), p. 639. For employment by kings: pp. 654–8, 661. For employment by churches: J.D.A. Ogilvy, '*Mimi, Scurrae, Histriones*: Entertainers of the Early Middle Ages', *Speculum*, XXXVIII/4 (1963), pp. 606, 615; Roger Loomis and Gustave Cohen, 'Were There Theatres in the Twelfth and Thirteenth Centuries?', *Speculum*, XX/1 (1945), p. 93, cited in Bryan Gillingham, 'Turtles, Helmets, Parasites and Goliards' [1994], in *Poets and Singers: On Latin and Monophonic Song*, ed. Elizabeth Aubrey (Aldershot, 2009), p. 73; Gretchen Peters, *The Musical Sounds of Medieval French Cities: Players, Patrons, and Politics* (Cambridge, 2012), pp. 170–71; Ruth E. Harvey, '*Joglars* and the Professional Status of the Early Troubadours', in *Poets and Singers*, ed. Aubrey, p. 37.

43 Peters, *Musical Sounds*, pp. 8, 12, 27, 45; Rob C. Wegman, 'The Minstrel School in the Late Middle Ages', *Historic Brass Society Journal*, XIV (2002), pp. 11–30, cited ibid., pp. 214–16; Harvey, '*Joglars*', pp. 31–2.

44 Peters, *Musical Sounds*, pp. 165–6, 221.

45 V. A. Kolve, *Telling Images: Chaucer and the Imagery of Narrative II* (Stanford, CA, 2009), pp. 224, 233, 239; Symes, *A Common Stage*, p. 81; Baldwin, 'Image of the Jongleur', p. 639.

46 Wolfgang Kemp, *The Narratives of Gothic Stained Glass* [1987], trans. Caroline Dobson Saltzwedel (Cambridge, 1997), p. 138; Joel Kaye, *Economy and Nature in the Fourteenth Century: Money, Market Exchange, and the Emergence of Scientific Thought* (Cambridge, 1998), pp. 1, 12–13; Peter the Chanter, *Verbum abbreviatum*, *Patrologia Latina*, ed. J. P. Migne (Paris, 1841–65), 205, col. 101, cited in Kemp, *Narratives*, p. 138; Symes, *A Common Stage*, pp. 69–126.

47 C. H. Lawrence, *The Friars: The Impact of the Early Mendicant Movement on Western Society* (Harlow, 1994), pp. 9–12; Lester K. Little, *Religious Poverty and the Profit Economy in Medieval Europe* (New York, 1978), p. 27; Caterina Bruschi, *The Wandering Heretics of Languedoc* (Cambridge, 2009), p. 114; Bloch, *Literature and Law*, pp. 163–6.

48 Little, *Religious Poverty*, pp. 113–28, 134; Bruschi, *Wandering Heretics*, pp. 50, 57, 62, 131.

49 Lawrence, *The Friars*, pp. 39–41, 127; Derek Pearsall, Introduction to William Langland, *Piers Plowman: A New Annotated Edition of the C-Text*, ed. Pearsall (Exeter, 2008), pp. 22–3.

50 Pearsall, Introduction to *Piers Plowman*, pp. 22, 26; Steven Justice, *Writing and Rebellion: England in 1381* (Berkeley, CA, 1994), pp. 118–21. On *Piers*-related works see Helen Barr, *Signs and Sothe: Language in the 'Piers Plowman' Tradition* (Cambridge, 1994). Wendy Scase suggests that some previously unanswered questions about the manuscript tradition may show that the poem was taught in grammar schools, which, given the work's association with rebel demands and the fact that Latin was the language of instruction, would have been daring as well as historically unprecedented. See Wendy Scase, 'Latin Composition Lessons, *Piers Plowman*, and the *Piers Plowman* Tradition', in *Answerable Style: The Idea of the Literary in Medieval England*, ed. Frank Grady and Andrew Galloway (Columbus, OH, 2013), pp. 52–3.

51 Lawrence Warner, 'William Langland: *Piers Plowman*', in *A Companion to Medieval Poetry*, ed. Corinne J. Saunders (Malden, MA, 2010), p. 401; Pearsall, Introduction to *Piers Plowman*, p. 6; Claire Marshall, *William Langland, 'Piers Plowman'* (Tavistock, 2001), p. 10. See also Mark Miller, 'Sin and Structure in *Piers Plowman*: On the Medieval Split Subject', *Modern Language Quarterly*, LXXVI/2 (2015), p. 219; Jacqueline T. Miller, 'The Writing on the Wall: Authority and Authorship in Chaucer's *House of Fame*', *Chaucer Review*, XVII/2 (1982), pp. 95–6.

52 Jill Mann, *Langland and Allegory* (Kalamazoo, MI, 1992), p. 3; Jason Crawford, *Allegory and Enchantment: An Early Modern Poetics* (Oxford, 2017), p. 82; Pearsall, Introduction to *Piers Plowman*, p. 7; Crawford, *Allegory*, p. 89. Lollardy, associated with the teachings of John Wyclif, was a form of religious dissent expressed in lay preaching and the sharing of vernacular translations of the scriptures, both forbidden. See Anne Hudson, *The Premature Reformation: Wycliffite Texts and Lollard History* (Oxford, 1988).

53 Mann, *Language and Allegory*, p. 6; William Rhodes, 'Personification, Action, and Economic Power in *Piers Plowman*', *Yearbook of Langland Studies*, XXXIV (2020), p. 133; Nicolette Zeeman, *The Arts of Disruption: Allegory and 'Piers Plowman'* (Oxford, 2020), p. 13; David Aers, *Beyond Reformation? An Essay on William Langland's 'Piers Plowman' and the End of Constantinian Christianity* (Notre Dame, IN, 2015), cited in Zeeman, *Arts of Disruption*, p. 37.

54 Zeeman, *Arts of Disruption*, pp. 99–100. Unless otherwise stated, citations and quotations are from Peter Sutton's modern English translation of the poem, the line numbers of which may differ slightly from those in the original Middle English versions. The Sutton translation is derived originally from Walter W. Skeat's amalgamation of the A, B and C versions, and amended with reference to *The Vision*

of Piers Plowman: A Critical Edition of the B-Text, ed. A.V.C. Schmidt, 2nd edn (London, 1995). *Piers Plowman: A Modern Verse Translation*, trans. Peter Sutton (Jefferson, NC, 2014), p. 4. 'Ethical adjacency' is a term for *paradiastole*. See Zeeman, *Arts of Disruption*, pp. 75–117.

55 Miller, 'Sin and Structure', p. 213; William Langland's *Piers Plowman: The C-Version*, trans. George Economou (Philadelphia, PA, 1996), Prologue, 21. References to the C version of the poem specifically, unless otherwise indicated, are to this edition.

56 Jim Knowles, 'Langland's Empty Verbs: Service, Kenosis, and Adventurous Christology in *Piers Plowman*', *Yearbook of Langland Studies*, XXVIII (2014), pp. 207, 218.

57 Robert Epstein, 'Summoning Hunger: Polanyi, *Piers Plowman*, and the Labor Market', in *Money, Commerce, and Economics in Late Medieval English Literature*, ed. C. E. Bertolet and Epstein (Cham, 2018), pp. 63, 73; Juliet Barker, *England, Arise: The People, the King and the Great Revolt of 1381* (London, 2014), p. 25; Robert Worth Frank Jr, 'The "Hungry Gap", Crop Failure, and Famine: The Fourteenth-Century Agricultural Crisis and *Piers Plowman*', *Yearbook of Langland Studies*, IV (1990), pp. 91–2, 94.

58 Frank, 'The "Hungry Gap"', p. 96; Derek Pearsall, 'Poverty and Poor People in *Piers Plowman*', in *Medieval English Studies Presented to George Kane*, ed. Edward Donald Kennedy, Ronald Waldron and Joseph S. Wittig (Wolfeboro, NH, 1988), pp. 171–2.

59 *The Statutes of the Realm*, vol. II: *1377–1504*, ed. John Raithby (1810–28), pp. 55–60; Anne Middleton, 'Acts of Vagrancy: The C Version "Autobiography" and the Statute of 1388', in *Written Work: Langland, Labor, and Authorship*, ed. Steven Justice and Kathryn Kerby-Fulton (Philadelphia, PA, 1997), pp. 217–18, 222, 229, 235, 239; Barker, *England, Arise*, pp. xiv–xvii, 36–7, 391–3.

60 Middleton, 'Acts of Vagrancy', p. 278; Matthew 4:4, 6:10; Deuteronomy 8:3. The wording of part of Matthew 4:4 is in Langland's *Piers Plowman: The C-Version*, trans. Economou, p. 230n; Matthew 13:44; Luke 15:10, discussed by Middleton, 'Acts of Vagrancy', p. 262; and Luke 10:2–11, discussed on p. 264.

61 Rhodes, 'Personification', p. 119. See Barker, *England, Arise*, pp. 156–7, on the fact that, by the 1360s, the statutes were routinely disobeyed, indicating that they did not solve labour problems for landowners.

62 Eleanor Johnson, *Staging Contemplation: Participatory Theology in Middle English Prose, Verse, and Drama* (Chicago, IL, 2018), pp. 75–107.

63 J. Thomas Kelly, *Thorns on the Tudor Rose: Monks, Rogues, Vagabonds, and Sturdy Beggars* (Jackson, MS, 1977), pp. 21, 57, 64; Linda Woodbridge, *Vagrancy, Homelessness, and English Renaissance Literature* (Urbana, IL,

2001), pp. 5, 7; Linda Woodbridge, 'The Neglected Soldier as Vagrant, Revenger, Tyrant Slayer in Early Modern England', in *Cast Out: Vagrancy and Homelessness in Global and Historical Perspective*, ed. A. L. Beier and Paul Ocobock (Athens, OH, 2008), p. 65; William Carroll, *Fat King, Lean Beggar: Representations of Poverty in the Age of Shakespeare* (New York, 1996), pp. 21–2; A. L. Beier, "A New Serfdom": Labor Law, Vagrancy Statutes, and Labor Discipline in England, 1350–1800', in *Cast Out*, ed. Beier and Ocobock, pp. 45–7; C.S.L. Davies, 'Slavery and Protector Somerset: The Vagrancy Act of 1547', *Economic History Review*, 2nd ser., XIX/3 (1966), p. 540, cited in Woodbridge, *Vagrancy*, p. 5; Carroll, *Fat King*, p. 36; Chris Fitter, "The Art of Known and Feeling Sorrows": Rethinking Capitalist Transition, and the Performance of Class Politics, in *King Lear*', *Early Modern Literary Studies*, XIX/1 (2016), n.p., https://extra.shu.ac.uk/emls/journal/index.php/emls/index; Chris Fitter, "As Full of Grief as Age": Protesting Against the Poor Law in *King Lear*', in *Shakespeare and the Politics of Commoners: Digesting the New Social History*, ed. Fitter (Oxford, 2017), p. 219.

64 Fitter, "The Art of Known and Feeling Sorrows"', pp. 7–8; Woodbridge, *Vagrancy*, pp. 1–3; Carroll, *Fat King*, pp. 36–48.

65 Examples of rogue literature include Robert Copland's *Highway to the Spital-House* [1535–6], ed. A. V. Judges (London, 2002), John Awdeley's *Fraternity of Vagabonds* [*c.* 1561], in *Rogues, Vagabonds, and Sturdy Beggars: A New Gallery of Tudor and Early Stuart Rogue Literature Exposing the Lives, Times, and Cozening Tricks of the Elizabethan Underworld*, ed. Arthur F. Kinney (Amherst, MA, 1990), pp. 99–101, and Thomas Harman's *Caveat for Common Cursitors, Vulgarly Called Vagabonds* [1566–7], ibid., pp. 115–53. See Woodbridge, *Vagrancy*, pp. 2–3, 18–19; Carroll, *Fat King*, pp. 46–7; Paul Slack, *Poverty and Policy in Tudor and Stuart England* (London, 1988), pp. 92–3, 100, cited in Woodbridge, *Vagrancy*, pp. 4, 6; 'The Neglected Soldier', pp. 65–6.

66 Robert Shaughnessy, '*King Lear*', in *The Routledge Guide to William Shakespeare* (London, 2011), p. 242; Michael Neill, "Wherefore to Dover?" Seeing Nothing in *King Lear*', *Litteraria Pragensia: Studies in Literature and Culture*, XXVI/52 (2016), p. 8; William Shakespeare, *King Lear*, ed. R. A. Foakes (London, 1997), 1.1.82–7. Unless otherwise stated, quotations are from this edition.

67 Woodbridge, *Vagrancy*, pp. 206–7, 209–10.

68 Leah Marcus, '*King Lear* and the Death of the World', in *The Oxford Handbook of Shakespearean Tragedy*, ed. Michael Neill and David Schalkwyk (Oxford, 2016), pp. 428–9; Stephen Booth, '*King Lear*', '*Macbeth*', *Indefinition and Tragedy* (New Haven, CT, 1983), pp. 47–8.

69 Fitter, '"As Full of Grief as Age"', italics original.
70 Steve Hindle, *On the Parish? The Micro-Politics of Poor Relief in Rural England, c. 1550–1750* (Oxford, 2004), pp. 381–2, cited in Fitter, '"As Full of Grief as Age"'.
71 Isabel Fonseca, *Bury Me Standing: The Gypsies and Their Journey* (London, 1995), p. 5; Yaron Matras, *I Met Lucky People: The Story of the Romani Gypsies* (London, 2014), pp. 34, 104; Angus Fraser, *The Gypsies*, 2nd edn (Oxford, 1995), pp. 1, 10, 14–19, 25–6.
72 Matras, *Lucky People*, pp. 129–30, 131–6; Fraser, *The Gypsies*, pp. 57–8; Arnold von Harff, *Die Pilgerfahrt des Ritters Arnold von Harff*, ed. E. von Groote (Cologne, 1860), pp. 67–8, quoted ibid., pp. 50–54.
73 Matras, *Lucky People*, pp. 135, 139–43, 145, 149, 163–74; Fraser, *The Gypsies*, pp. 62–3; D.M.M. Bartlett, 'Münster's *Cosmographia universalis*', *Journal of the Gypsy Lore Society*, XXXI (1952), p. 87, quoted ibid., p. 65.
74 Fraser, *The Gypsies*, p. 44; also Michael Stewart, *The Time of the Gypsies* (Boulder, CO, 1997), p. 13; Matras, *Lucky People*, p. 32; Jan Yoors, *The Gypsies* (Prospect Heights, IL, 1987), p. 5.
75 Yoors, *The Gypsies*, pp. 6–7; Jan Yoors, *Crossing: A Journal of Survival and Resistance in World War II* (London, 1972), pp. 7–16; Stewart, *Time of the Gypsies*, pp. 18–19, 59, 242; Matras, *Lucky People*, pp. 68–9, 73–4. *Gadje* Jan Yoors's story in *Crossing* of living with Roms from the age of twelve through the events of the Second World War and beyond shows the willingness with which a Romani community may welcome an outsider who wishes primarily to accompany them in their way of life.
76 Stewart, *Time of the Gypsies*, pp. 144, 160. Horse trading is typically men's work for the Roms of Harangos, near Budapest (ibid., pp. 50–57). In many Rom communities women are responsible for household work as well as being involved in trade activities. Matras, *Lucky People*, pp. 45–51, 160–62, 165.

4 STORY

1 Zachary Mason, *The Lost Books of the Odyssey* (New York, 2007), pp. 143–4.
2 Homer, *The Odyssey*, trans. Robert Fagles (New York, 1996), IX.454–5. Unless otherwise stated, quotations are from this edition.
3 Mason, *Lost Books*, p. 145.
4 Laura M. Slatkin, 'Homer's *Odyssey*', in *A Companion to Ancient Epic*, ed. John Miles Foley (Malden, MA, 2005), p. 315.
5 Stephen V. Tracy, 'The Structures of the *Odyssey*' [1997], in *Homer's 'The Odyssey*', ed. Harold Bloom (New York, 2007), p. 155. In Book XV of the *Iliad*, Zeus sends Iris to the Achaeans to command Poseidon to cease

fighting and Apollo to the Trojans to rouse Hector, while in Book XXIV Iris is sent to call Thetis so Zeus can send her to Achilles and then to Priam to tell him to ransom his son's body. Suzanne Saïd, *Homer and the 'Odyssey'* [1998], trans. Ruth Webb (Oxford, 2011), p. 97.

6 Irad Malkin, *The Returns of Odysseus: Colonization and Ethnicity* (Berkeley, CA, 1998), pp. 1–31, cited in Alex Purves, 'Unmarked Space: Odysseus and the Inland Journey', *Arethusa*, XXXIX/1 (2006), p. 2; see also p. 3. While the death that comes 'from the sea' could refer to an assassin born elsewhere, sufficient ambiguity remains to license Mason's reimagining.

7 *Odyssey* XXIII.249, Purves's translation, 'Unmarked Space', p. 5; Fagles's translation, XXIII.283–4.

8 Purves, 'Unmarked Space', pp. 9, 13.

9 Aristotle, *Poetics*, ed. Leonardo Tarán and Dimitri Gutas (Leiden, 2012), 21.1457b7, quoted in Purves, 'Unmarked Space', p. 13; see also pp. 15–16.

10 Richard P. Martin, 'Telemachus and the Last Hero Song', *Colby Quarterly*, XXIX/3 (1993), p. 240, cited in Purves, 'Unmarked Space', p. 17; Sheila Murnaghan, *Disguise and Recognition in the 'Odyssey'*, 2nd edn (Lanham, MD, 2011), pp. 16–17; Purves, 'Unmarked Space', p. 17.

11 Edwin Williamson, 'Miguel de Cervantes (1547–1616): *Don Quixote*: Romance and Picaresque', in *The Cambridge Companion to European Novelists*, ed. Michael Bell (Cambridge, 2012), p. 19; Gerhart Hoffmeister, 'Picaresque Novel', *The Literary Encyclopedia*, www.litencyc.com, 2 February 2004; Ning Ma, *The Age of Silver: The Rise of the Novel East and West* (Oxford, 2016), pp. 86, 90–91.

12 Henry Kamen, *Spain, 1469–1714: A Society of Conflict*, 2nd edn (London, 1991), pp. xiii–xv, 37–8.

13 Ibid., pp. 49, 89; B. W. Ife, 'The Historical and Social Context', in *The Cambridge Companion to Cervantes*, ed. Anthony J. Cascardi (Cambridge, 2002), p. 16; Ma, *Age of Silver*, pp. 91–2; Lisa Jardine, *Worldly Goods: A New History of the Renaissance* (New York, 1996), p. 83.

14 Kamen, *Spain*, p. 222; Jardine, *Worldly Goods*, pp. 86–8, 104; Ife, 'Historical and Social Context', p. 20; Ma, *Age of Silver*, p. 92.

15 Peter N. Dunn, *Spanish Picaresque Fiction: A New Literary History* (New York, 1993), p. 137; Elvira Vilches, *New World Gold: Cultural Anxiety and Monetary Disorder in Early Modern Spain* (Chicago, IL, 2015), p. 220; Ife, 'Historical and Social Context', pp. 24, 26–7.

16 Ife, 'Historical and Social Context', p. 28; Kamen, *Spain*, p. 229.

17 Kamen, *Spain*, pp. 108, 225, 227; Vilches, *New World Gold*, p. 220; Carroll B. Johnson, *Cervantes and the Material World* (Urbana, IL, 2000), pp. 18–19.

18 Ife, 'Historical and Social Context', p. 27.

19 Alfonso J. García Osuna, Introduction to *The Life of Lazarillo de Tormes: A Critical Edition including the Original Spanish Text*, ed. and trans. García Osuna (Jefferson, NC, 2005), pp. 9–10; Giancarlo Maiorino, *At the Margins of the Renaissance: 'Lazarillo de Tormes' and the Picaresque Art of Survival* (University Park, PN, 2003), p. 5.

20 Edward H. Friedman, 'Roads Untaken: The Spanish Picaresque Novel', in *A History of the Spanish Novel*, ed. J.A.G. Ardila (Oxford, 2015), pp. 98–9.

21 Yirmiyahu Yovel, 'The Birth of the Picaro from the Death of Shame', *Social Research*, LXX/4 (2003), p. 1303.

22 Friedman, 'Roads Untaken', p. 112.

23 Ma, *Age of Silver*, p. 91; Kamen, *Spain*, p. 229.

24 Williamson, 'Miguel de Cervantes', p. 20.

25 Miguel de Cervantes, *Don Quixote*, trans. Edith Grossman (London, 2003), I, Chapter 8, pp. 64–5. Unless otherwise stated, citations and quotations are from this edition.

26 Anthony J. Cascardi, 'Consequences of *Don Quixote*: The Unbearable Lightness of Cervantes' Influence', in *History of the Spanish Novel*, ed. Ardila, p. 130; Williamson, 'Miguel de Cervantes', p. 32.

27 Ma, *Age of Silver*, p. 93; report cited in Anne J. Cruz, *Discourses of Poverty: Social Reform and the Picaresque Novel in Early Modern Spain* (Toronto, 1999), p. 80, cited in Ma, *Age of Silver*, p. 94.

28 The phrase 'unconquerable mind' in the heading is taken from William Wordsworth, 'To Toussaint L'Ouverture', *Morning Post*, 2 February 1803:
   . . . Live, and take comfort. Thou hast left behind
   Powers that will work for thee; air, earth, and skies;
   There's not a breathing of the common wind
   That will forget thee; thou hast great allies;
   Thy friends are exultations, agonies,
   And love, and man's unconquerable mind.

29 A. L. Beier, *Masterless Men: The Vagrancy Problem in England, 1560–1640* (London, 1985), pp. 161–3; Susan Marks, *A False Tree of Liberty: Human Rights in Radical Thought* (Oxford, 2020), p. 25; M. J. Daunton, *Progress and Poverty: An Economic and Social History of Britain, 1700–1850* (Oxford, 1995), pp. 93–5. 'Overall, about 47 per cent of England was enclosed in 1600 and about 71 per cent in 1700' (ibid., p. 104). Between 1750 and 1850 all remaining open-field areas were enclosed. Pat Hudson, *The Industrial Revolution* (London, 1992), p. 73.

30 Marks, *False Tree of Liberty*, pp. 24–6; K.D.M. Snell, *Annals of the Labouring Poor: Social Change and Agrarian England, 1660–1900* (Cambridge, 1985), pp. 179–80.

31 Snell, *Annals of the Labouring Poor*, p. 194; Daunton, *Progress and Poverty*, pp. 52, 69–70; Marks, *False Tree of Liberty*, p. 26.

32 Rachel Foxley, *The Levellers: Radical Political Thought in the English Revolution* (Manchester, 2013), p. 4; Jonathan Scott, *England's Troubles: Seventeenth-Century English Political Instability in European Context* (Cambridge, 2000), p. 244. While early activists who became Levellers took down fences, this was not practised by members of the movement as it developed. On the Levellers see Noeleen McIlvenna, *A Very Mutinous People: The Struggle for North Carolina, 1660–1713* (Chapel Hill, NC, 2009), pp. 8–9.

33 Ryan Hackenbracht, *National Reckonings: The Last Judgment and Literature in Milton's England* (New York, 2019), pp. 77–8; Marks, *False Tree of Liberty*, p. 71; Thomas N. Corns, Ann Hughes and David Loewenstein, Introduction to *The Complete Works of Gerrard Winstanley*, ed. Corns, Hughes and Loewenstein (Oxford, 2009), pp. 13, 43; David Loewenstein, *Representing Revolution in Milton and His Contemporaries: Religion, Politics, and Polemics in Radical Puritanism* (Cambridge, 2001), p. 48.

34 Scott, *England's Troubles*, p. 244; Marks, *False Tree of Liberty*, p. 54.

35 Marks, *False Tree of Liberty*, p. 87; Veronika Bennholdt-Thomsen and Maria Mies, *The Subsistence Perspective: Beyond the Globalised Economy*, trans. Patrick Camiller et al. (London, 2000), and Raj Patel, *The Value of Nothing* (London, 2011), pp. 122, 129, both cited in Marks, *False Tree of Liberty*, p. 265.

36 Marcus Rediker, *Between the Devil and the Deep Blue Sea: Merchant Seamen, Pirates, and the Anglo-American Maritime World, 1700–1750* (Cambridge, 1987), pp. 77–8.

37 Ibid., p. 83; Peter Linebaugh and Marcus Rediker, *The Many-Headed Hydra: The Hidden History of the Revolutionary Atlantic* (Boston, MA, 2000), p. 150; Rediker, *Between the Devil and the Deep Blue Sea*, pp. 33, 92–4, 101–2, 104, 106.

38 Linebaugh and Rediker, *Many-Headed Hydra*, pp. 151–2, 157; Rediker, *Between the Devil and the Deep Blue Sea*, pp. 79–80, 254; Marcus Rediker, *Villains of All Nations: Atlantic Pirates in the Golden Age* (Boston, MA, 2004), p. 23.

39 Rediker, *Villains of All Nations*, p. 8; Janice E. Thomson, *Mercenaries, Pirates, and Sovereigns: State-Building and Extraterritorial Violence in Early Modern Europe* (Princeton, NJ, 1996), p. 23; Virginia West Lansford, *Piracy and Privateering in the Golden Age Netherlands* (Basingstoke, 2005), pp. 3–4.

40 Rediker, *Villains of All Nations*, pp. 9, 65–8, 71–4; Dian H. Murray,

Pirates of the South China Coast, 1790–1810 (Stanford, CA, 1987), pp. 71–3, 153.

41 Alvin O. Thompson, *Flight to Freedom: African Runaways and Maroons in the Americas* (Kingston, Jamaica, 2006), pp. 175–210; Johnhenry Gonzalez, *Maroon Nation: A History of Revolutionary Haiti* (New Haven, CT, 2019), pp. 2–9; Rediker, *Villains of All Nations*, p. 63.

42 Daniel O. Sayers, *A Desolate Place for a Defiant People: The Archaeology of Maroons, Indigenous Americans, and Enslaved Laborers in the Great Dismal Swamp* (Gainesville, FL, 2014); McIlvenna, *A Very Mutinous People*, pp. 13–27; Julius Sherrard Scott III, 'The Common Wind: Currents of Afro-American Communication in the Era of the Haitian Revolution', PhD dissertation, Duke University, Durham, NC, 1986, pp. 15, 43–5.

43 Marcus Rediker, *The Slave Ship: A Human History* (New York, 2007); David Brion Davis, *Inhuman Bondage: The Rise and Fall of Slavery in the New World* (New York, 2006); Robin Blackburn, *The Making of New World Slavery: From the Baroque to the Modern, 1492–1800* (London, 1997). For numbers, Blackburn, *The Making of New World Slavery*, p. 3; Philip D. Curtin, *The Atlantic Slave Trade: A Census* (Madison, WI, 1969), and Paul E. Lovejoy, 'The Volume of the Atlantic Slave Trade: A Synthesis', *Journal of African History*, XXIII/4 (1982), pp. 473–501, both cited in W. Jeffrey Bolster, *Black Jacks: African American Seamen in the Age of Sail* (Cambridge, MA, 1997), pp. 11, 243n; Ira Berlin, *Many Thousands Gone: The First Two Centuries of Slavery in North America* (Cambridge, MA, 1998), p. 17.

44 Berlin, *Many Thousands Gone*, pp. 23, 26, 34, 38, 52, 56–7, 64, 70.

45 Ibid., pp. 96, 106; John Hope Franklin and Loren Schweninger, 'The Quest for Freedom: Runaway Slaves and the Plantation South', in *Slavery, Resistance, Freedom*, ed. G. S. Boritt, Scott Hancock and Ira Berlin (New York, 2007), pp. 23–6; Bolster, *Black Jacks*, pp. 19–20.

46 Bolster, *Black Jacks*, pp. 4, 6, 37. Ritual and symbolic use of water was a powerful way in which enslaved Africans understood and reconstructed their situation. In several West African traditions, water was associated with the transmigration of souls, while for the Kongo people the oceanic Kalunga line divided the spirit world from the living. The dead below the sea were the real source of power, placing slave traffic in a larger context. See Robert Farris Thompson, *Flash of the Spirit: African and Afro-American Art and Philosophy* (New York, 1983), pp. 72–83, 108–42, and Gwendolyn Midlo Hall, *Africans in Colonial Louisiana: The Development of Afro-Creole Culture in the Eighteenth Century* (Baton Rouge, LA, 1992), pp. 47, 50, both cited in Bolster, *Black Jacks*, pp. 62–5;

Vincent Carretta, 'Olaudah Equiano: African British Abolitionist and Founder of the African American Slave Narrative', in *The Cambridge Companion to the African American Slave Narrative*, ed. Audrey A. Fisch (Cambridge, 2007), pp. 44–5.

47 Vincent Carretta, 'Questioning the Identity of Olaudah Equiano, or Gustavus Vassa, the African', in *The Global Eighteenth Century*, ed. Felicity Nussbaum (Baltimore, MD, 2003), pp. 226–35, cited in Carretta, 'Olaudah Equiano', p. 47; see also p. 50. At issue are baptismal and naval records indicating that Equiano was born in South Carolina. See Alexander X. Byrd, 'Eboe, Country, Nation, and Gustavus Vassa's *Interesting Narrative*', *William and Mary Quarterly*, LXIII/1 (2006), pp. 123–48, for an account that is not entirely at odds with Carretta's findings, and Paul E. Lovejoy, 'Autobiography and Memory: Gustavus Vassa, alias Olaudah Equiano, the African', *Slavery and Abolition*, XXVII/3 (2006), pp. 317–47, who suggests alternative interpretations of the documentary evidence and argues that Equiano was born in Africa. Douglas Chambers is also inclined to qualify the documentary evidence noted by Carretta and opts for an African birth for Equiano. 'Chambers on Carretta, *Equiano the African: Biography of a Self-Made Man*', *H-Atlantic*, https://networks.h-net.org.

48 Blackburn, *The Making of New World Slavery*, p. 4; Jacob M. Price, 'What Did Merchants Do? Reflections on British Overseas Trade, 1660–1760', *Journal of Economic History*, XLIX/2 (1989), pp. 267–84, cited in Patrick O'Brien, 'Inseparable Connections: Trade, Economy, Fiscal State, and the Expansion of Empire', in *The Oxford History of the British Empire*, vol. II: *The Eighteenth Century*, ed. P. J. Marshall (Oxford, 1998), p. 60.

49 O'Brien, 'Inseparable Connections', pp. 60, 64; Colin Nicholson, *Writing and the Rise of Finance: Capital Satires of the Early Eighteenth Century* (Cambridge, 1994), p. 6; P.G.M. Dickson, *The Financial Revolution in England: A Study in the Development of Public Credit, 1688–1756* (London, 1967), p. 11; J.G.A. Pocock, 'Modes of Political and Historical Time in Early Eighteenth-Century England', *Studies in Eighteenth-Century Culture*, V (1976), pp. 96–7.

50 Nicholson, *Writing and the Rise of Finance*, p. 5; Ian Baucom, *Specters of the Atlantic: Finance Capital, Slavery, and the Philosophy of History* (Durham, NC, 2005), pp. 16–17; Dickson, *Financial Revolution*, p. 40; Pocock, 'Modes of Political and Historical Time', p. 97.

51 Ian Watt, *The Rise of the Novel: Studies in Defoe, Richardson and Fielding* (London, 1957); Michael McKeon, *The Origins of the English Novel, 1600–1740* (Baltimore, MD, 1987); see also John Richetti, Introduction

to *The Cambridge Companion to the Eighteenth-Century Novel*, ed. Richetti (Cambridge, 1996), p. 2, cited in Jesse Molesworth, *Chance and the Eighteenth-Century Novel: Realism, Probability, Magic* (Cambridge, 2010), p. 1; Catherine Gallagher, 'The Rise of Fictionality', in *The Novel*, ed. Franco Moretti, 2 vols (Princeton, NJ, 2006), vol. I, pp. 340–41, 345.

52 Lorraine Daston, *Classical Probability in the Enlightenment* (Princeton, NJ, 1988), pp. 163–82, cited in Marieke de Goede, *Virtue, Fortune, and Faith: A Genealogy of Finance* (Minneapolis, MN, 2005), pp. 51–2.

53 Molesworth, *Chance and the Eighteenth-Century Novel*, p. 32; Gallagher, 'The Rise of Fictionality', pp. 341–2, 346–7.

54 Molesworth, *Chance and the Eighteenth-Century Novel*, pp. 29–31.

55 D. A. Miller, *The Novel and the Police* (Berkeley, CA, 1988), pp. 200–220, cited in Gallagher, 'The Rise of Fictionality', p. 357.

56 Catherine Gallagher, *Nobody's Story: The Vanishing Acts of Women Writers in the Marketplace, 1670–1820* (Oxford, 1994), pp. xiii, xvi, xviii. See also Deidre Shauna Lynch, 'Novels in the World of Moving Goods', in *A Concise Companion to the Restoration and Eighteenth Century*, ed. Cynthia Wall (Malden, MA, 2005), pp. 122–3, 138, and Gordon S. Wood, 'Conspiracy and the Paranoid Style: Causality and Deceit in the Eighteenth Century', *William and Mary Quarterly*, XXXIX/3 (1982), pp. 410–11. Novels about moving objects (a banknote, a hackney coach, a coin) were common in the period, indicating the value created by circulation and the idea that increased opportunities for middlemen increased the prosperity of the state. Lynch, 'Novels in the World of Moving Goods', pp. 139–40.

57 Markman Ellis, *The Coffee-House: A Cultural History* (London, 2004), pp. 173–4; John Brewer, *The Pleasures of the Imagination: English Culture in the Eighteenth Century* (London, 2013), p. 116; Hannah Barker, *Newspapers, Politics, and Public Opinion in Late Eighteenth-Century England* (Oxford, 1998), p. 2; Adrian Randall, *Riotous Assemblies: Popular Protest in Hanoverian England* (Oxford, 2006), pp. 11–13; Jeremy Black, *The English Press in the Eighteenth Century* (Abingdon, 1987), pp. 140, 143.

58 On part-books and serial production, see Brewer, *Pleasures of the Imagination*, pp. 116, 122, 148, 153, and Brian Maidment, 'Periodicals and Serial Publications, 1780–1830', in *The Cambridge History of the Book in Britain*, vol. V: *1695–1830*, ed. Michael F. Suarez and Michael L. Turner (Cambridge, 2009), p. 498. On magazines, see Marilyn B. Butler, 'Culture's Medium: The Role of the Review', in *The Cambridge Companion to British Romanticism*, ed. Stuart Curran (Cambridge, 1993), p. 122, cited in Maidment, 'Periodicals and Serial Publications',

p. 503. On places where books were read, see Christopher Flint, 'The Eighteenth-Century Novel and Print Culture: A Proposed Modesty', in *A Companion to the Eighteenth-Century English Novel and Culture*, ed. Paula R. Backscheider and Catherine Ingrassia (Malden, MA, 2005), pp. 350–51; Lynch, 'Novels in the World of Moving Goods', p. 123.

59 Christopher Ricks, 'Introductory Essay' [1967], in Laurence Sterne, *The Life and Opinions of Tristram Shandy, Gentleman* [1759–67], ed. Melvyn New and Joan New (London, 1997), p. xvii; Laurence Sterne, *Tristram Shandy*, vol. I, Chapter One, p. 6: unless otherwise stated, citations and quotations are from this edition; Patricia Meyer Spacks, *Novel Beginnings: Experiments in Eighteenth-Century Fiction* (New Haven, CT, 2006), p. 255.

60 Joseph Drury, *Novel Machines: Technology and Narrative Form in Enlightenment Britain* (Oxford, 2017), pp. 116–17; Helen Ostovich, 'Reader as Hobby-Horse in *Tristram Shandy*', *Philological Quarterly*, LXVIII/3 (1989), pp. 325–42.

61 Frances M. Bothwell del Toro, 'The Quixotic and the Shandean: A Study of the Influence of Cervantes' *Don Quixote* on Laurence Sterne's *Tristram Shandy*', PhD dissertation, Florida State University, Tallahassee, FL, 1981, p. 227; Alexander Welsh, 'The Influence of Cervantes', in *Cambridge Companion to Cervantes*, ed. Cascardi, pp. 81–5; David H. Richter, *Reading the Eighteenth-Century Novel* (Hoboken, NJ, 2017), p. 105.

62 John Mullan, *Sentiment and Sociability: The Language of Feeling in the Eighteenth Century* (Oxford, 1988), pp. 148–99. The 'novel of sentiment' or sensibility is a type of novel, prominent in the eighteenth century, that appeals to the reader's emotions. It explores the display and effects of feeling or affect in characters and aims to provoke the emotions of readers.

63 Ibid., p. 188.

64 The term 'desolation' is from José Ortega y Gasset, *Meditations on Quixote* [1914], trans. Evelyn Rugg and Diego Marin (New York, 1961), pp. 144–5, quoted in Welsh, 'Influence of Cervantes', p. 84; on consumerism and self-improvement, see Celia Lury, *Consumer Culture* (New Brunswick, NJ, 1997), p. 10, cited in Matt Erlin, *Necessary Luxuries: Books, Literature, and the Culture of Consumption in Germany, 1770–1815* (New York, 2014), pp. 85–6.

65 Mullan, *Sentiment and Sociability*, p. 168.

66 Martin Swales, 'Johann Wolfgang von Goethe (1749–1832): The German *Bildungsroman*', in *Cambridge Companion to European Novelists*, ed. Bell, pp. 132, 137; Liisa Steinby, 'Temporality, Subjectivity, and the Representation of Characters in the Eighteenth-Century Novel from

Defoe's *Moll Flanders* to Goethe's *Wilhelm Meisters Lehrjahre*', in
Narrative Concepts in the Study of Eighteenth-Century Literature, ed.
Steinby and Aino Mäkikalli (Amsterdam, 2017), pp. 155–6; Don Slater,
Consumer Culture and Modernity (Oxford, 1997), p. 20, cited in Erlin,
Necessary Luxuries, pp. 85–6.

67 Swales, 'Johann Wolfgang von Goethe', p. 138.

68 Isabel Wilkerson, *The Warmth of Other Suns: The Epic Story of America's
Great Migration* (New York, 2010), pp. 8–9; Nicholas Lemann, *The
Promised Land: The Great Black Migration and How It Changed America*
(New York, 1991), pp. 6, 18–20.

69 Lemann, *The Promised Land*, pp. 71, 73–4.

70 Patrice D. Rankine, *Ulysses in Black: Ralph Ellison, Classicism, and
African American Literature* (Madison, WI, 2006), pp. 121–44; Ralph
Ellison, 'Change the Joke and Slip the Yoke', in *The Collected Essays of
Ralph Ellison*, ed. John F. Callahan (New York, 1995), p. 110; Ralph
Ellison, *Invisible Man* [1952] (London, 1965), p. 17. Unless otherwise
stated, citations and quotations are from this edition.

71 Eric J. Sundquist, Introduction to *Cultural Contexts for Ralph Ellison's
'Invisible Man': A Bedford Documentary Companion*, ed. Sundquist
(Boston, MA, 1995), p. 4.

72 Johnnie Wilcox, 'Black Power: Minstrelsy and Electricity in Ralph
Ellison's *Invisible Man*', *Callaloo: A Journal of African Diaspora Arts
and Letters*, XXX/4 (2007), p. 995.

73 Herman Beavers, 'Documenting Turbulence: The Dialectics of Chaos
in *Invisible Man*', in *Ralph Ellison and the Raft of Hope: A Political
Companion to 'Invisible Man'*, ed. Lucas E. Morel (Lexington, KY, 2004),
p. 206.

74 B. A. Botkin, ed., *A Treasure of American Folklore: Stories, Ballads, and
Traditions of the People* (New York, 1944), p. 408.

75 *Vox humana*: Wilcox, 'Black Power', p. 1002. On 1950s normalization,
see William H. Whyte, *The Organization Man* (London, 1957), an
in-depth exposé of the ideology of corporate belonging and Cold War
American masculinity.

76 Michael Germana, *Standards of Value: Money, Race, and Literature
in America* (Iowa City, IA, 2009), p. 130.

77 Ibid., p. 121.

78 Michel Serres, *La Naissance de la physique dans le texte de Lucrèce:
Fleuves et turbulence* (Paris, 1977), pp. 13, 33, quoted in Eric Charles
White, 'Negentropy, Noise, and Emancipatory Thought', in *Chaos and
Order: Complex Dynamics in Literature and Science*, ed. N. Katherine
Hayles (Chicago, IL, 1991), pp. 264–5.

79 White, 'Negentropy', p. 264.

80 Gordon Slethaug, *Beautiful Chaos: Chaos Theory and Metachaotics in Recent American Fiction* (New York, 2000), p. 81, quoted in Beavers, 'Documenting Turbulence', p. 208; Martin Williams, *The Jazz Tradition*, 2nd revd edn (New York, 1993), p. 56, quoted in Paul Allen Anderson, 'Ralph Ellison's Music Lessons', in *The Cambridge Companion to Ralph Ellison*, ed. Ross Posnock (Cambridge, 2005), p. 86.

81 Marshall W. Stearns, *The Story of Jazz* [1956] (New York, 1972), p. 229, cited in Robert O'Brien Hokanson, 'Jazzing It Up: The Be-Bop Modernism of Langston Hughes', *Mosaic*, XXXI/4 (1998), pp. 65–6.

82 Anderson, 'Ralph Ellison's Music Lessons', p. 88.

83 Albert Camus, *The Myth of Sisyphus* [1942], trans. Justin O'Brien (London, 1955); Ralph Ellison, 'Perspective of Literature', in *The Collected Essays*, p. 778.

84 Joel Dinerstein, *Swinging the Machine: Modernity, Technology, and African American Culture between the World Wars* (Amherst, MA, 2003), p. 16, quoted in Wilcox, 'Black Power', p. 998; Fred Moten, *In the Break: The Aesthetics of the Black Radical Tradition* (Minneapolis, MN, 2003), pp. 11–25, cited in Andrew Radford, 'Ralph Ellison and Improvised History', *Midwest Quarterly*, LII/2 (2011), p. 115.

85 Ellison, 'Perspective of Literature', p. 778.

5 SORROW

1 Christine Fell, 'Perceptions of Transience', in *The Cambridge Companion to Old English Literature*, ed. Malcolm Godden and Michael Lapidge, 2nd edn (Cambridge, 2013), p. 181; 'The Wanderer', in *The Complete Old English Poems*, ed. and trans. Craig Williamson (Philadelphia, PA, 2017), pp. 1, 3–4. Unless otherwise stated, quotations are from this edition.

2 William Alfred, 'The Drama of *The Wanderer*', in *The Wisdom of Poetry: Essays in Early English Literature in Honor of Morton W. Bloomfield*, ed. Larry D. Benson and Siegfried Wenzel (Kalamazoo, MI, 1982), p. 36.

3 S. L. Clark and Julian S. Wasserman, 'The Imagery of *The Wanderer*', *Neophilologus*, LXIII/2 (1979), p. 293; Manish Sharma, 'Heroic Subject and Cultural Substance in *The Wanderer*', *Neophilologus*, XCVI/4 (2012), p. 614.

4 Sharma, 'Heroic Subject', p. 622; Patrick Cook, '*Woriað þa Winsalo*: The Bonds of Exile in "The Wanderer"', *Neophilologus*, LXXX/1 (1996), p. 129.

5 Sharma, 'Heroic Subject', p. 623; Alfred, 'The Drama of *The Wanderer*', p. 44; Clark and Wasserman, 'The Imagery of *The Wanderer*', pp. 291, 295; Margrét Gunnarsdóttir Champion, 'From Plaint to Praise: Language as Cure in "The Wanderer"', in *Old English Literature: Critical Essays*, ed. R. M. Liuzza (New Haven, CT, 2002), p. 338.

6 Vamik D. Volkan and Elizabeth Zintl, *Life after Loss: The Lessons of Grief* (London, 2018), p. 13; Allan V. Horvitz and Jerome C. Wakefield, *The Loss of Sadness: How Psychiatry Transformed Normal Sorrow into Depressive Disorder* (Oxford, 2007), pp. 51, 33.

7 Cathy Caruth, Introduction to *Trauma: Explorations in Memory*, ed. Caruth (Baltimore, MD, 1995), p. 6; David J. Morris, *The Evil Hours: A Biography of Post-Traumatic Stress Disorder* (Boston, MA, 2015), pp. 45–6.

8 Raymond P. Scheindlin, *A Short History of the Jewish People from Legendary Times to Modern Statehood* (Oxford, 1998), p. 29; Michael Brenner, *A Short History of the Jews* [2008], trans. Jeremiah Riemer (Princeton, NJ, 2010), p. 11; Melvin Konner, *Unsettled: An Anthropology of the Jews* (New York, 2003), pp. xvii, 9, 18.

9 Konner, *Unsettled*, p. 142; Benjamin Ginsberg, *The Fatal Embrace: Jews and the State* (Chicago, IL, 1993), p. 9; David Biale, *Power and Powerlessness in Jewish History* (New York, 1986), p. 66.

10 George K. Anderson, *The Legend of the Wandering Jew* [1965] (Providence, RI, 1970), pp. 5, 47, 49; Richard I. Cohen, 'The "Wandering Jew" from Medieval Legend to Modern Metaphor', in *The Art of Being Jewish in Modern Times*, ed. Barbara Kirshenblatt-Gimblett and Jonathan Karp (Philadelphia, PA, 2008), pp. 147, 149, 158.

11 Jean-Christophe Attias and Esther Benbassa, *Israel, the Impossible Land* [1998], trans. Susan Emanuel (Stanford, CA, 2003), p. 152; Yuri Slezkine, *The Jewish Century* (Princeton, NJ, 2004), pp. 7, 9.

12 Slezkine, *The Jewish Century*, pp. 8, 22, 41, 43–4, 50, 75.

13 Ibid., p. 195; Chaim Potok, *Wanderings: Chaim Potok's History of the Jews* (London, 1978), pp. 374–6.

14 Slezkine, *The Jewish Century*, pp. 118–23.

15 Leonard Schapiro, 'The Role of the Jews in the Russian Revolutionary Movement', *Slavonic and East European Review*, XL (1961), p. 153, and Erich Haberer, *Jews and Revolution in Nineteenth-Century Russia* (Cambridge, 1995), pp. 270–71, both cited in Slezkine, *The Jewish Century*, p. 154; also pp. 159–60, 163, 193.

16 The Treaty of Versailles, signed in 1919, required Germany to disarm, concede territory and pay substantial reparations to the countries that constituted the Entente powers. On population and emigration see Timothy Snyder, *Bloodlands: Europe Between Hitler and Stalin* (New York, 2010), pp. ix, 111, and Brenner, *A Short History*, pp. 322–3, 327, 331.

17 Brenner, *A Short History*, pp. 331, 333–7, 344; Snyder, *Bloodlands*, pp. 185–9, 192; Konner, *Unsettled*, pp. 272–3.

18 Ben Shephard, *The Long Road Home: The Aftermath of the Second World War* (London, 2010), p. 5; Gerard Daniel Cohen, *In War's Wake:*

Europe's Displaced Persons in the Postwar Order (Oxford, 2012), p. 134; Alan Dowty, *Israel/Palestine* [2005], 3rd edn (Cambridge, 2012), p. 86; Brenner, *A Short History*, pp. 353–4; Ilan Pappe, *The Ethnic Cleansing of Palestine* (Oxford, 2006), p. 31.

19 Pappe, *Ethnic Cleansing*, pp. 41–3, 47–9, 82, 89–119, 131, 133–7, 146–7, 150–69, 171, 181–7, 188, 212, 237–8, 242, 244; Dowty, *Israel/Palestine*, p. 96. More recently, as memories of Arab–Israeli conflicts fade, Palestinian problems have become submerged by more immediate Arab concerns. Yemenite Jews have been settled in the United Arab Emirates, and other Arab countries, including Saudi Arabia, have also welcomed Jews. See 'Welcome Back: Jews in the Arab World', *The Economist*, 22–28 January 2022, in which Kamal Alam claims that Arabs 'begrudgingly look at Israel and Jews as models for running a successful country that feeds itself without oil' (p. 39).

20 Biale, *Power and Powerlessness*, pp. 158, 160–61; Emil Fackenheim, *God's Presence in History* (New York, 1970), and Zeev Schiff and Ehud Yaari, *Israel's Lebanon War*, trans. Ina Friedman (New York 1985), both cited ibid., p. 163.

21 Pappe, *Ethnic Cleansing*, pp. 227–9, 233.

22 Snyder, *Bloodlands*, pp. 13–14, 19–20, 24–8, 35; Anne Applebaum, *Red Famine: Stalin's War on Ukraine* (London, 2017), p. 133; Robert Conquest, *Harvest of Sorrow: Soviet Collectivization and the Terror-Famine* (London, 1986), p. 35.

23 Conquest, *Harvest of Sorrow*, pp. 45–6, 89, 91, 93; Snyder, *Bloodlands*, p. 14.

24 Snyder, *Bloodlands*, pp. 26–7, 29–30, 33, 34, 37, 39–40.

25 Ibid., pp. 22–3, 45, 48, 50, 78–9.

26 Matthew Frye Jacobson, *Whiteness of a Different Color: European Immigrants and the Alchemy of Race* (Cambridge, MA, 1999), pp. 41, 43–4, 47; May M. Ngai, 'Race, Nation, and Citizenship in Late Nineteenth-Century America, 1878–1900', in *Race and Ethnicity in America: A Concise History*, ed. Ronald H. Bayor (New York, 1999), pp. 113, 115, 119–20; Michael Leroy Oberg, *Native America: A History*, 2nd edn (Hoboken, NJ, 2018), pp. 14, 21; Fen Montaigne, 'The Fertile Shore', *Smithsonian*, www.smithsonianmag.com, January 2020; David Treuer, *The Heartbeat of Wounded Knee: Native America from 1890 to the Present* (New York, 2019), p. 27; John E. Kicza, 'First Contacts', in *A Companion to American Indian History*, ed. Philip J. Deloria and Neal Salisbury (Malden, MA, 2004), pp. 32–3.

27 Treuer, *Heartbeat*, pp. 30–32, 35, 43.

28 Ibid., pp. 43–6; Oberg, *Native America*, pp. 47–8; Daniel K. Richter,

Facing East from Indian Country: A Native History of Early America (Cambridge, MA, 2001), pp. 164, 170–71, 174–5, 178.

29 Richter, *Facing East*, pp. 187–8; Treuer, *Heartbeat*, p. 51; Colin G. Galloway, *The American Revolution in Indian Country: Crisis and Diversity in Native American Communities* (Cambridge, 1995), p. xvi, quoted in Richter, *Facing East*, p. 180; also Oberg, *Native America*, p. 4.

30 Oberg, *Native America*, pp. 159–60, 164; Theda Perdue and Michael D. Green, *The Cherokee Nation and the Trail of Tears* (New York, 2007), pp. 17–18.

31 Oberg, *Native America*, pp. 160–62, 164; Perdue and Green, *Cherokee Nation*, pp. 93–4, 97–100.

32 Perdue and Green, *Cherokee Nation*, pp. 120, 122–3, 137; Tim Alan Garrison, 'On the Trail of Tears: Daniel Butrick's Record of the Removal of the Cherokees', in *Removing Peoples: Forced Removal in the Modern World*, ed. Richard Bessel and Claudia B. Haake (Oxford, 2009), pp. 46, 54; Journal of Daniel Butrick, 1 July 1838, cited ibid., p. 61; Oberg, *Native America*, p. 165.

33 Oberg, *Native America*, pp. 182, 189, 212–13, 217, 219; Treuer, *Heartbeat*, p. 149.

34 Treuer, *Heartbeat*, pp. 5, 153–8; Oberg, *Native America*, p. 215.

35 Oberg, *Native America*, p. 215; Gregory E. Smoak, *Ghost Dances and Identity: Prophetic Religion and American Indian Ethnogenesis in the Nineteenth Century* (Berkeley, CA, 2005), p. 115; Russell Thornton, *We Shall Live Again: The 1870 and 1890 Ghost Dance Movements as Demographic Revitalization* (Cambridge, 1986).

36 Aeschylus, *Prometheus Bound*, ed. and trans. Alan H. Sommerstein (Cambridge, MA, 2014), pp. 275–6, cited in Silvia Montiglio, *Wandering in Ancient Greek Culture* (Chicago, IL, 2005), p. 65; Margaret Alexiou, *The Ritual Lament in Greek Tradition* [1974], 2nd edn, revd Dimitrios Yatromanolakis and Panagiotis Roilos (Lanham, MD, 2002), p. 6; Ernesto De Martino, *Morte e pianto rituale: Dal lamento funebre antico al pianto di Maria* (Turin, 1975), pp. 95, 125, cited in Robert Pogue Harrison, *The Dominion of the Dead* (Chicago, IL, 2003), pp. 55–9.

37 Michael J. Clarke, *Achilles Beside Gilgamesh: Mortality and Wisdom in Early Epic Poetry* (Cambridge, 2019), pp. 91, 100.

38 H. Aschwanden, *Symbols of Death: An Analysis of the Consciousness of the Karanga* (Gweru, 1987), p. 212; Maurice Bloch, 'Death and the Concept of Person', in *On the Meaning of Death: Essays on Mortuary Rituals and Eschatological Beliefs*, ed. Sven Cederroth, Claes Corlin and Jan Lindstrom (Uppsala, 1988), p. 13, and Marla C. Burns, 'Ga'anda Scarification', in *Marks of Civilization*, ed. Arnold Rubin (Los Angeles,

CA, 1988), pp. 71–2, all cited in Karina Croucher, *Death and Dying in the Neolithic Near East* (Oxford, 2012), p. 11; Alexiou, *Ritual Lament*, p. 5; Sarah Iles Johnston, *Restless Dead: Encounters Between the Living and the Dead in Ancient Greece* (Berkeley, CA, 1999), pp. 36, 52, 80, 86, 88, 109–10, 152; Markham Geller, *Forerunners to Udug-hul: Sumerian Exorcistic Incantations* (Wiesbaden, 1985), p. 39, cited in Jerrold S. Cooper, 'Wind and Smoke: Giving Up the Ghost of Enkidu, Comprehending Enkidu's Ghosts', in *Rethinking Ghosts in World Religions*, ed. Muzhou Pu (Leiden, 2009), p. 27; Homer, *The Odyssey*, trans. Robert Fagles (New York, 1996), XI.13–41, XX.61–82, cited in Johnston, *Restless Dead*, pp. 152–3.

39 Christien Klaufus, 'Superstar-Saints and Wandering Souls: The Cemetery as a Cultural Hotspot in Latin American Cities', in *Death Across Cultures: Death and Dying in Non-Western Cultures*, ed. Helaine Selin and Robert M. Rakoff (Cham, 2019), pp. 288–9; Jasper Becker, *Hungry Ghosts: China's Secret Famine* (London, 1996), pp. 270–73; Erik Mueggler, *The Age of Wild Ghosts: Memory, Violence, and Place in Southwest China* (Berkeley, CA, 2001), pp. 7, 96, 266.

40 *Dangdai Zhongguo de Yunnan* (Contemporary China's Yunnan) (Beijing, 1991), vol. I, p. 136, cited in Mueggler, *Age of Wild Ghosts*, p. 176; also pp. 177–9, 182, 184, 187, 197.

41 Mueggler, *Age of Wild Ghosts*, pp. 5–7, 161, 166, 168–71, 192–4.

42 Ibid., pp. 97, 197, 204, 252; Veena Das, 'Language and Body: Transactions in the Construction of Pain', in *Social Suffering*, ed. Arthur Kleinman, Das and Margaret Lock (Berkeley, CA, 1997), p. 67, cited ibid., p. 253.

43 Mueggler, *Age of Wild Ghosts*, pp. 265–6.

44 Patrick Kingsley, *The New Odyssey: The Story of Europe's Refugee Crisis* (London, 2016), pp. 42–50; Alexander Betts and Paul Collier, *Refuge: Transforming a Broken Refugee System* (London, 2017), p. 28; Alexander Betts, *Survival Migration: Failed Governance and the Crisis of Displacement* (New York, 2013), pp. 16–17; David Miller and Christine Straehle, Introduction to *The Political Philosophy of Refuge*, ed. Miller and Straehle (Cambridge, 2020), p. 3; Peter Gatrell, *The Making of the Modern Refugee* (Oxford, 2013), pp. 44–56.

45 UNHCR, *Convention and Protocol Relating to the Status of Refugees* (Geneva, 1996), Article 1 (A); Miller and Straehle, Introduction to *The Political Philosophy of Refuge*, pp. 3–4; UNHCR, *UNHCR Resettlement Handbook* (Geneva, 2011), p. 19, cited ibid., p. 4; Tara Zahra, *The Great Departure: Mass Migration from Eastern Europe and the Making of the Free World* (New York, 2016), pp. 187–90, 192–3.

46 Hsiao-Hung Pai, *Bordered Lives: How Europe Fails Refugees and Migrants* (Oxford, 2018), pp. 9, 203; Kingsley, *New Odyssey*, p. 262;

Philippe Legrain, 'Refugees Work: A Humanitarian Investment that Yields Economic Dividends', *Tent Partnership for Refugees*, www.tent.org, May 2016; Alexander Betts, Louise Bloom, Josiah Kaplan and Naohiko Omata, *Refugee Economies: Rethinking Popular Assumptions*, Refugee Studies Centre, University of Oxford, 2014, pp. 18–20, www.rsc.ox.ac.uk; Kieran Oberman, 'Border Rescue', in Miller and Straehle, *The Political Philosophy of Refuge*, p. 92.

47 Pai, *Bordered Lives*, p. 222; Kingsley, *New Odyssey*, pp. 4–7; Betts and Collier, *Refuge*, pp. 2, 9, 91; UNHCR, *UNHCR Refugees/Migrants Emergency Response – Mediterranean*, https://data2.unhcr.org and *Lebanon, Populations 2015*, https://reporting.unhcr.org, both cited in Kingsley, *New Odyssey*, pp. 6–7. Germany's offer to receive refugees fingerprinted elsewhere is a waiver response to the Dublin Regulation, which requires that the European country in which an asylum seeker first arrives should either provide for them or send them back whence they came.

48 Kingsley, *New Odyssey*, pp. 125–7; Oberman, 'Border Rescue', pp. 81–2.

49 Betts and Collier, *Refuge*, pp. 7–8, 49, 53–4, 59, 156.

50 Pai, *Bordered Lives*, pp. 58, 61, 63, 92–7, 99, 101, 126, 170–71.

51 Ibid., p. 120; Kingsley, *New Odyssey*, p. 292; Betts and Collier, *Refuge*, pp. 168–75; Amanda Gray Meral, 'Assessing the Jordan Compact One Year On: An Opportunity or a Barrier to Better Achieving Refugees' Right to Work', *Journal of Refugee Studies*, XXXIII/1 (2020), pp. 52–3, 55–6.

52 Betts and Collier, *Refuge*, pp. 160, 162–4, 166.

53 Pai, *Bordered Lives*, pp. 166–7; Ian Urbina, 'The Invisible Wall: Inside the Secretive Libyan Prisons that Keep Migrants Out of Europe', *New Yorker*, 6 December 2021, pp. 36–47; Aryn Baker, '"It Was As If We Weren't Human": Inside the Modern Slave Trade Trapping African Migrants', *Time*, www.time.com, 14 March 2019.

54 Kingsley, *New Odyssey*, p. 294; Mark Cutts, ed., 'The State of the World's Refugees 2000: Fifty Years of Humanitarian Action – Chapter 4: Flight from Indochina', *UNHCR News*, www.unhcr.org, cited ibid.; Betts and Collier, *Refuge*, p. 221; Daniel J. Clarke and Stefan Dercon, *Dull Disasters? How Planning Ahead Will Make a Difference* (Oxford, 2016).

55 Betts and Collier, *Refuge*, pp. 217–21; Clarke and Dercon, *Dull Disasters?*; Pai, *Bordered Lives*, p. 226.

56 Kathryn Schulz, *Lost and Found: A Memoir* (New York, 2022), p. 223.

6 CHANCE

1 See www.thehighline.org/history; Joshua David and Robert Hammond, *High Line: The Inside Story of New York City's Park in the Sky* (New

York, 2011), pp. 3–122; James Corner in Jared Keller, 'First Drafts: James Corner's High Line Park', *The Atlantic*, www.theatlantic.com, 6 July 2011.

2 Keller, 'First Drafts'; Tom Baker, 'The Garden on the Machine', in *Deconstructing the High Line: Postindustrial Urbanism and the Rise of the Elevated Park*, ed. Christoph Lindner and Brian Rosa (New Brunswick, NJ, 2017), pp. 113–14.

3 Francesca Merlin, 'Chance and Randomness', in *Encyclopedia of Astrobiology*, ed. Muriel Gargaud et al. (Heidelberg, 2015), pp. 283–4.

4 Baker, 'The Garden on the Machine', p. 113; William Empson, *Some Versions of Pastoral* (London, 1935), cited ibid., p. 111; see also pp. 113–14, 118–20.

5 Anne D. Wallace, *Walking, Literature, and English Culture: The Origins and Uses of Peripatetic in the Nineteenth Century* (Oxford, 1993), pp. 51, 61–2; Robin Jarvis, *Romantic Writing and Pedestrian Travel* (Basingstoke, 1997), pp. 9, 14, 17.

6 James Buzard, *The Beaten Track: European Tourism, Literature and the Ways to Culture, 1800–1918* (Oxford, 1993), pp. 6, 94; Fred Inglis, *The Delicious History of the Holiday* (London, 2000), p. 18; Orvar Löfgren, *On Holiday: A History of Vacationing* (Berkeley, CA, 1999), pp. 24–5; Jarvis, *Romantic Writing*, pp. 55–7.

7 Löfgren, *On Holiday*, pp. 24–5; Rebecca Solnit, *Wanderlust: A History of Walking* (New York, 2000), pp. 89–90; Baker, 'The Garden on the Machine', p. 113; Jarvis, *Romantic Writing*, p. 56.

8 Edmund Burke, *A Philosophical Inquiry into the Origin of Our Ideas of the Sublime and Beautiful*, ed. Adam Phillips (Oxford, 1990), pp. 36, 53, cited in Robin Jarvis, *The Romantic Period: The Intellectual and Cultural Context of English Literature, 1789–1830* (Harlow, 2004), pp. 180–81; Christopher R. Miller, *Surprise: The Poetics of the Unexpected from Milton to Austen* (New York, 2015), p. 5; David Vallins, *Coleridge and the Psychology of Romanticism: Feeling and Thought* (Basingstoke, 2010), pp. 2, 15; Jane Kneller, 'Early German Romanticism: The Challenge of Philosophizing', in *The Routledge Companion to Nineteenth-Century Philosophy*, ed. Dean Moyar (Hoboken, NJ, 2010); Inglis, *The Delicious History*, p. 31; Michael McKeon, *The Origins of the English Novel, 1600–1740* (Baltimore, MD, 1987), cited in Miller, *Surprise*, p. 9.

9 Jean-Jacques Rousseau, *The Collected Writings of Rousseau*, vol. V: *The Confessions and Correspondence, Including the Letters to Malesherbes*, ed. Christopher Kelly, Roger D. Masters and Peter G. Stillman, trans. Kelly (Hanover, NJ, 1995), VIII, p. 295; Letter to M. de Malesherbes, 12 January 1762, Appendix I, p. 575.

10 Charles E. Butterworth, 'Interpretative Essay', in Jean-Jacques Rousseau, *The Reveries of a Solitary Walker* [1782], trans. Butterworth (New York,

1979), pp. 152–3; Solnit, *Wanderlust*, p. 17; Jean-Jacques Rousseau, 'Second Discourse' [1755], in *The First and Second Discourses*, ed. Roger D. Masters, trans. Masters and Judith R. Masters (New York, 1964), p. 137, quoted ibid., p. 18; Rousseau, *Confessions*, IV, p. 136.

11 Solnit, *Wanderlust*, p. 21; C. W. Thompson, *Walking and the French Romantics: Rousseau to Sand and Hugo* (Bern, 2003), p. 27; Victor Hugo, *Voyages: France et Belgique (1834–7)*, ed. Claude Gély (Grenoble, 1974), pp. 280–83, cited ibid., pp. 114–15.

12 John Keats, Letter to George and Tom Keats, 21, 27(?) December 1817, in *Selected Letters of John Keats, based on the text of Hyder Edward Rollins*, revd edn, ed. Grant F. Scott (Cambridge, MA, 2002), p. 60; Li Ou, *Keats and Negative Capability* (New York, 2009), p. 2; Geoffrey H. Hartman, *Wordsworth's Poetry, 1787–1814* (New Haven, CT, 1977), p. 12, cited in Miller, *Surprise*, p. 173; David Simpson, *Wordsworth, Commodification and Social Concern: The Poetics of Modernity* (Cambridge, 2009), pp. 28, 122, 138. See also Jarvis, *Romantic Writing*, pp. 119–20.

13 Ann Bermingham, *Landscape and Ideology: The English Rustic Tradition, 1740–1860* (Berkeley, CA, 1986), p. 9, Carl J. Dahlman, *The Open-Field System and Beyond* (Cambridge, 1980), pp. 167–8, and W. G. Hoskins, *The Making of the English Landscape* (Harmondsworth, 1955), p. 179, all cited in Wallace, *Walking, Literature, and English Culture*, pp. 69–71; Jarvis, *Romantic Writing*, p. 184.

14 Jarvis, *Romantic Writing*, p. 184; Kim Taplin, *The English Path* (Woodbridge, Suffolk, 1979), pp. 65–84, and John Barrell, *The Idea of Landscape and the Sense of Place, 1730–1840* (Cambridge, 1972), pp. 94–6, both cited in Wallace, *Walking, Literature, and English Culture*, pp. 114–15; also pp. 167–8.

15 The term 'mutability' is used by John Ruskin in the nineteenth century to describe a change in aesthetic sensibility brought on by the Industrial era, according to which people must 'expect the utmost satisfaction . . . from what is impossible to arrest, and difficult to comprehend'. *Modern Painters*, vol. III (Chicago, n.d.), p. 272, quoted in Wallace, *Walking, Literature, and English Culture*, p. 72. On change see Wordsworth's letters to the *Morning Post*, 9 December 1844 and undated, in the Appendix to his *Guide to the Lakes*, ed. Ernest de Selincourt (Oxford, 1970), pp. 152, 163–4, quoted ibid., p. 73; Prefaces of 1800 and 1802 to Samuel Taylor Coleridge and William Wordsworth, *Lyrical Ballads*, ed. R. L. Brett and A. R. Jones (London, 2005), 1800: pp. 291, 294–6, 307; 1802: p. 301.

16 The phrase 'the growth of a poet's mind' formed part of the original title of *The Prelude*. On the remembered past see for example William

Wordsworth, *The Prelude*, in *The Poems of William Wordsworth: Collected Reading Texts from the Cornell Wordsworth Series*, ed. Jared Curtis (Penrith, 2011), vol. II, V.389–413, XI.316–43, 368–89. See also Celeste Langan, *Romantic Vagrancy: Wordsworth and the Simulation of Freedom* (Cambridge, 1995), pp. 142–3, and Toby R. Benis, *Romanticism on the Road: The Marginal Gains of Wordsworth's Homeless* (Basingstoke, 2000), pp. 4, 57–9.

17 Henri Lefebvre, *The Production of Space* [1974], trans. Donald Nicholson-Smith (Oxford, 1991), pp. 306, 340, 402, cited in Simpson, *Wordsworth, Commodification and Social Concern*, p. 6; Karl Polanyi, *The Great Transformation: The Political and Economic Origins of Our Time* [1944] (Boston, MA, 2001), pp. 75–6, quoted in Robert Epstein, 'Summoning Hunger: Polanyi, *Piers Plowman*, and the Labor Market', in *Money, Commerce, and Economics in Late Medieval English Literature*, ed. Craig E. Bertolet and Epstein (Cham, 2018), p. 61.

18 Bermingham, *Landscape and Ideology*, p. 9, quoted in Gary Harrison, *Wordsworth's Vagrant Muse: Poetry, Poverty and Power* (Detroit, MI, 1994), p. 41. Spectrality is emphasized in Wordsworth's poetic renditions of the countryside by Simpson, *Wordsworth, Commodification and Social Concern*.

19 Hartman, *Wordsworth's Poetry*, pp. 120–23, cited in Benis, *Romanticism on the Road*, p. 64, also pp. 67, 80; William Wordsworth, *Adventures on Salisbury Plain* (1795–c. 1799), in *The Salisbury Plain Poems*, ed. Stephen Gill (New York, 1975), pp. 154–62.

20 Quentin Bailey, *Wordsworth's Vagrants: Police, Prisons, and Poetry in the 1790s* (Aldershot, 2011), p. 61; Judith Thompson, Introduction to John Thelwall, *The Peripatetic*, ed. Thompson (Detroit, MI, 2001), p. 16; Benis, *Romanticism on the Road*, p. 60. As Bailey notes, the soldier's psychological trajectory also mimics the passage from solitary confinement to confession to punishment then being recommended by the government's revised penal code. *Wordsworth's Vagrants*, pp. 72–83.

21 William Wordsworth, *The Excursion*, in *The Poems of William Wordsworth*, vol. II, I.919–22; Simpson, *Wordsworth, Commodification and Social Concern*, p. 47.

22 Wordsworth, *The Prelude*, XI.258–79, 319–43, 383–9. See also Simpson, *Wordsworth, Commodification and Social Concern*, pp. 40–41, 138. The phrase 'surplus humanity' is from Mike Davis, *Planet of Slums* (London, 2006), p. 174, cited in Phil Jones, *Work Without the Worker: Labour in the Age of Platform Capitalism* (London, 2021), p. 9. On the absence of meaning to which the poet is attuned see Wordsworth, Preface to *Lyrical Ballads* 1802, p. 300.

23 Charles Baudelaire, 'The Painter of Modern Life' [1863], in *The Painter of Modern Life and Other Essays*, trans. and ed. Jonathan Mayne (London, 1964), pp. 7, 9, 12–13; Edgar Allan Poe, 'The Man of the Crowd' [1840], in *The Selected Writings of Edgar Allan Poe*, ed. G. R. Thompson (New York, 2004), pp. 232–9; Deborah Epstein Nord, 'The Urban Peripatetic: Spectator, Streetwalker, Woman Writer', *Nineteenth-Century Literature*, XLVI/3 (1991), pp. 351–75.

24 Walter Benjamin, *Charles Baudelaire, a Lyric Poet in the Era of High Capitalism*, trans. Harry Zohn (Cambridge, 1972); Solnit, *Wanderlust*, pp. 198–200; Priscilla Parkhurst Ferguson, 'The *Flâneur* On and Off the Streets of Paris', in *The Flâneur*, ed. Keith Tester (London, 1994), pp. 23, 31, 33.

25 Walter Benjamin, *Gesammelte Schriften*, ed. Rolf Tiedemann and Hermann Schweppenhäuser (Frankfurt, 1972–89), vol. V, pp. 540, 546, 562, 968, cited in Susan Buck-Morss, 'The Flaneur, the Sandwichman and the Whore: The Politics of Loitering', *New German Critique*, XXXIX/1 (1986), pp. 105–6. Also Martina Lauster, 'Walter Benjamin's Myth of the *Flâneur*', *Modern Language Review*, CII/1 (2007), pp. 141–3; Esther Leslie, *Walter Benjamin: Overpowering Conformism* (Sterling, VA, 2000), p. 185; Sadie Plant, *The Most Radical Gesture: The Situationist International in a Postmodern Age* (London, 1992), p. 1.

26 Guy Debord, *The Society of the Spectacle* [1967], trans. Donald Nicholson-Smith (New York, 1994), p. 12; Guy Debord, *The Society of the Spectacle* [1967], trans. Ken Knabb, Bureau of Public Affairs, 2014, p. 2, https://files.libcom.org/files/The%20Society%20of%20the%20 Spectacle%20Annotated%20Edition.pdf; Frances Stracey, *Constructed Situations: A New History of the Situationist International* (London, 2014), p. 7; Michael Gardiner, *Critiques of Everyday Life* (London, 2000), pp. 24, 30–37.

27 Guy Debord, 'Définitions', *Internationale Situationniste*, I (June 1958), p. 13, cited in Stracey, *Constructed Situations*, p. 8; Guy Debord, 'Theory of the Dérive', *Les Lèvres nues*, IX (November 1956), reprinted in *Internationale Situationniste*, II (December 1958), trans. Ken Knabb, www.cddc.vt.edu/sionline/si/theory.html.

28 Will Self, *Psychogeography* (London, 2007), pp. 15, 47–62; Stracey, *Constructed Situations*, pp. 54–5.

29 Todd DePastino, *Citizen Hobo: How a Century of Homelessness Shaped America* (Chicago, IL, 2003), pp. 3–5, 9, 61; John Lennon, *Boxcar Politics: The Hobo in U.S. Culture and Literature, 1869–1956* (Amherst, MA, 2014), p. 13; Sinclair Lewis, 'Hobohemia', *Saturday Evening Post*, CLXXXIX, 7 April 1919, pp. 3–6, 121, and Nels Anderson, *The Hobo: The Sociology*

of the Homeless Man [1923] (Chicago, IL, 1965), p. 3, both cited in
DePastino, *Citizen Hobo*, p. 281n.

30 DePastino, *Citizen Hobo*, pp. 9–10; Frank Tobias Higbie, *Indispensable
Outcasts: Hobo Workers and Community in the American Midwest,
1880–1930* (Urbana, IL, 2003), p. 207.

31 Carlos A. Schwantes and James P. Ronda, *The West the Railroads
Made* (Seattle, WA, 2008), and Richard White, *Railroaded: The
Transcontinentals and the Making of Modern America* (New York, 2011),
both cited in Lennon, *Boxcar Politics*, p. 30; also pp. 8, 15, 182–3; Charles
Francis Adams Jr, Henry Adams and Francis Amasa Walker, *Chapters
of Erie and Other Essays* (Boston, MA, 1871), p. 98, and Henry Adams,
The Education of Henry Adams: An Autobiography (New York, 1918),
p. 240, also Daniel Headrick, *Tools of Empire: Technology and European
Imperialism in the Nineteenth Century* (Oxford, 1981), p. 187, all cited in
Lennon, *Boxcar Politics*, p. 33.

32 Lennon, *Boxcar Politics*, pp. 35, 43.

33 DePastino, *Citizen Hobo*, pp. 70, 76, 79–81; Lennon, *Boxcar Politics*,
pp. 25–6.

34 DePastino, *Citizen Hobo*, pp. 68–9, 91; *Industrial Worker*, 1 May 1912, cited
ibid, p. 185; also p. 138; hobo quoted in DePastino, *Citizen Hobo*, p. 81.

35 Alex Rosenblat, *Uberland: How Algorithms are Rewriting the Rules
of Work* (Berkeley, CA, 2018), pp. 4, 22, 207–8; Guy Standing, *The
Precariat: The New Dangerous Class* (London, 2011), pp. 9–10; Nick
Srnicek, *Platform Capitalism* (Cambridge, 2016), p. 14; Jacob S. Hacker,
The Great Risk Shift (New York, 2006), cited in Alexandrea J. Ravenelle,
Hustle and Gig: Struggling and Surviving in the Sharing Economy
(Berkeley, CA, 2019), pp. 36–7, 51.

36 Ravenelle, *Hustle and Gig*, pp. 26, 55; Julia Ticona, *Left to Our Own
Devices: Coping with Insecure Work in a Digital Age* (New York, 2022),
p. 5.

37 Ravenelle, *Hustle and Gig*, p. 25; Lisa B. Kahn, 'The Long-Term Labor
Market Consequences of Graduating from College in a Bad Economy',
Labour Economics, XVII/2 (2010), pp. 303–16, cited ibid., p. 10.

38 See the 'success' stories in Ravenelle, *Hustle and Gig*; also Jamie
Woodcock, *The Fight Against Platform Capitalism: An Inquiry into the
Global Struggles of the Gig Economy* (London, 2021), p. 35, and on worker
difficulties pp. 4, 47, 63; Ravenelle, *Hustle and Gig*, pp. 1–2, 55, 72–3;
Caleb Garling, 'Hunting Task Wabbits', *Medium*, 2 December 2014,
cited ibid., p. 55; also p. 152.

39 Nathaniel Popper, 'How a Gig Worker Revolt Begins', *New York
Times*, www.nytimes.com, 19 November 2019, cited in Woodcock,

The Fight Against Platform Capitalism, p. 63; Ravenelle, *Hustle and Gig*, p. 80; Juliet Schor, 'The Sharing Economy: Reports from Stage One', unpublished paper, 2015, cited ibid., p. 56; also pp. 78–9; Rosenblat, *Uberland*, pp. 101–2.

40 Ravenelle, *Hustle and Gig*, pp. 15, 61–3, 83; Phoebe V. Moore, 'E(a)ffective Precarity, Control and Resistance in the Digital Workplace', in *Digital Objects, Digital Subjects: Interdisciplinary Perspectives on Capitalism, Labour and Politics in the Age of Big Data*, ed. David Chandler and Christian Fuchs (London, 2019), pp. 133, 135.

41 Juliet Webster, 'Microworkers of the Gig Economy', *New Labor Forum*, xxv/3 (2016), p. 59; Frederick Taylor, *The Principles of Scientific Management* [1911] (New York, 1967).

42 Woodcock, *The Fight Against Platform Capitalism*, pp. 55, 58; Webster, 'Microworkers', pp. 57, 60; Jones, *Work Without the Worker*, p. 9. As Webster notes, 'Microwork is notoriously low paid. Ninety per cent of tasks on Amazon Mechanical Turk . . . pay less than $0.10 per task' (p. 58). See Lilly Irani, 'The Cultural Work of Microwork', *New Media and Society*, xvii/5 (2015), pp. 720–39, cited in Woodcock, *The Fight Against Platform Capitalism*, p. 61.

43 Webster, 'Microworkers', p. 61; Ticona, *Left to Our Own Devices*, pp. 23–7, 29–31. Relatedly, Ravenelle found that gig workers, in common with other temporary workers, were disinclined to report sexual harassment, in part because the emphasis on 'trust' on a platform like TaskRabbit meant they sometimes failed to recognize or acknowledge it for what it was (pp. 120–24). On brand anxiety see Ravenelle, *Hustle and Gig*, p. 85; Ticona, *Left to Our Own Devices*, pp. 23–7, 36, and on flexibility see ibid., pp. 29–34, 40; Webster, 'Microworkers', p. 61; Moore, 'E(a)ffective Precarity', p. 128.

44 Rosenblat, *Uberland*, p. 203; Ravenelle, *Hustle and Gig*, pp. 30, 151.

45 Fredric L. Cheyette and Howell Chickering, 'Love, Anger, and Peace: Social Practice and Poetic Play in the Ending of *Yvain*', *Speculum*, lxxx/1 (2005), pp. 84–5, 87, 93–101.

46 See the 'strugglers' in Ravenelle, *Hustle and Gig*; Rosenblat, *Uberland*, pp. 203, 206.

47 Alex Rosenblat, 'Uber's Phantom Cabs', *Vice*, www.vice.com, 28 July 2015; Tim Hwang and Madeleine Clare Elish, 'The Mirage of the Marketplace: The Disingenuous Ways Uber Hides Behind Its Algorithm', *Slate*, https://slate.com, 17 July 2015, cited in Srnicek, *Platform Capitalism*, p. 26; Rosenblat, *Uberland*, pp. 98–100; Alex Hern, 'Have Uber's "Phantom Cars" Disappeared?', *The Guardian*, www.theguardian.com, 7 August 2015; Mike Isaac, 'How Uber Deceives the Authorities

Worldwide', *New York Times*, 3 March 2017, cited in Rosenblat, *Uberland*, p. 100.

48 Rosenblat, *Uberland*, pp. 30, 206, 208. See also Harry Arthurs, 'The False Promise of the Sharing Economy', in *Law and the 'Sharing Economy': Regulating Online Market Platforms*, ed. Derek McKee, Finn Makela and Teresa Scassa (Ottawa, 2018).

49 Webster, 'Microworkers', p. 61; Woodcock, *The Fight Against Platform Capitalism*, pp. 4, 28, 41–4, 48; Jack Linchuan Qiu, 'Network Labour and Non-elite Knowledge Workers in China', *Work Organization, Labour and Globalization*, IV/2 (2010), pp. 80–95, cited in Webster, 'Microworkers', p. 62; Harry Campbell, 'What Regulators Could Gain by Listening to Rideshare Drivers', in *Beyond the Algorithm: Qualitative Insights for Gig Work Regulation*, ed. Deepa das Acevedo (Cambridge, 2021), p. 210; Greig de Puiter, 'The Work of the "Creative Workers Organize"' project, and Regis Pradal, 'The Work of InternsGoPro', both presentations to the Dynamics of Virtual Work conference, Peniche, Portugal, June 2015, both cited in Webster, 'Microworkers', p. 62. See also Popper, 'How a Gig Worker Revolt Begins', cited in Woodcock, *The Fight Against Platform Capitalism*, pp. 63–5; Mary-Ann Russon, 'Uber Drivers Are Workers Not Self-Employed', *BBC News*, www.bbc.co.uk/news, 19 February 2021; Webster, 'Microworkers', p. 62. Conditions being normalized across fields was also the basis on which the Industrial Workers of the World (IWW) was formed in 1905, a general workers' union briefly taken over, in 1908, by hobos. See DePastino, *Citizen Hobo*, pp. 95–6.

50 Srnicek, *Platform Capitalism*, p. 76, quoted in Woodcock, *The Fight Against Platform Capitalism*, p. 29.

51 Gabriel Zucman, *The Hidden Wealth of Nations: The Scourge of Tax Havens*, trans. Teresa Lavender Fagan (Chicago, IL, 2015), pp. 3–4; James S. Henry, 'The Price of Offshore Revisited: New Estimates for "Missing" Global Private Wealth, Income, Inequality, and Lost Taxes', *Tax Justice Network*, www.taxjustice.net, July 2012, cited in Oliver Bullough, *Moneyland: Why Thieves and Crooks Now Rule the World and How to Take It Back* (London, 2018), p. 47, see also p. 15; 'Global Inequality' (2021), *Inequality.org*, https://inequality.org, accessed 31 May 2022; Tom Burgis, *Kleptopia: How Dirty Money is Conquering the World* (London, 2020), p. 27; Srnicek, *Platform Capitalism*, pp. 18–19; Ronen Palan, *The Offshore World: Sovereign Markets, Virtual Places, and Nomad Millionaires* (New York, 2003), p. 30.

52 Bullough, *Moneyland*, p. 21.

53 Burgis, *Kleptopia*, p. 12; Michael Findley, Daniel Nielson and Jason Sharman, 'Global Shell Games: Testing Money Launderers' and Terrorist

Financiers' Access to Shell Companies', working paper, Centre for
Governance and Public Policy, Griffith University, Queensland, 2012,
cited in Zucman, *The Hidden Wealth of Nations*, p. 10, and see 'Tax
Fraud 101', pp. 10–11, from which my version is adapted; also Bullough,
Moneyland, pp. 88, 136–8, 149–53, 155.

54 Palan, *The Offshore World*, pp. 2, 23–5; Myres McDougal and William
T. Burke, *The Public Order of the Oceans: A Contemporary International
Law of the Sea* (New Haven, CT, 1962), p. 597, cited ibid., p. 25.

55 Bullough, *Moneyland*, pp. 46, 52, 136; Burgis, *Kleptopia*, p. 217, also
p. 231; Michael Lewis, *The Big Short: Inside the Doomsday Machine*
(New York, 2010), pp. 126–8.

56 Stephen Gill, 'New Constitutionalism, Democratization and Global
Political Economy', *Pacifica Review*, X/1 (1998), p. 25, cited in Palan, *The
Offshore World*, p. 13; Regis Debray, *Critique of Political Reason* (London,
1981), cited ibid., p. 14.

57 Palan, *The Offshore World*, p. 14; 'Terrorism/Extremism Update' from
City of London Police to the City of London Business Community,
2 December 2011; Shiv Malik, 'Occupy London's Anger Over Police
"Terrorism" Document', *The Guardian*, 5 December 2011, cited in Burgis,
Kleptopia, p. 136, also p. 137.

58 Palan, *The Offshore World*, pp. 182–3; Gilles Deleuze and Félix Guattari,
A Thousand Plateaus: Capitalism and Schizophrenia [1980], trans. Brian
Massumi (Minneapolis, MN, 1987), pp. 351–423, 478, cited ibid., pp. 166,
168–71; Joel Kurtzman, *The Death of Money: How the Electronic Economy
Has Destabilized the World's Economy and Created Financial Chaos*
(Boston, MA, 1993), pp. 65, quoted in Palan, *The Offshore World*, p. 171.

59 Palan, *The Offshore World*, p. 171; Kurtzman, *The Death of Money*, pp.
39, 65, quoted ibid., pp. 171–2, and Éric Alliez, *Capital Times: Tales from
the Conquest of Time*, trans. Georges Van Den Abbeele (Minneapolis,
MN, 1996), p. 10, cited ibid.; Gillian Tett, *Fool's Gold: The Inside Story of
J. P. Morgan and How Wall Street Greed Corrupted Its Bold Dream and
Created a Financial Catastrophe* (New York, 2009), pp. 95–6.

60 Palan, *The Offshore World*, p. 109; Andrew Farlow, *Crash and Beyond:
Causes and Consequences of the Global Financial Crisis* (Oxford, 2013),
pp. 5–6.

61 Bullough, *Moneyland*, pp. 27–8; Alasdair Roberts, *The Logic of
Discipline: Global Capitalism and the Architecture of Government*
(Oxford, 2010), pp. 26–8; Adam Tooze, *Crashed: How a Decade of
Financial Crises Changed the World* (London, 2018), pp. 11; Farlow,
Crash and Beyond, pp. 6–8, 23, and on the UK see pp. 35–6.

62 Tooze, *Crashed*, pp. 43, 45–8; Farlow, *Crash and Beyond*, p. 63.

63 Farlow, *Crash and Beyond*, pp. 58–60; Tett, *Fool's Gold*, p. 162.

64 Tett, *Fool's Gold*, pp. 52–3; Tooze, *Crashed*, pp. 49–50; Neil Fligstein and Adam Goldstein, 'The Anatomy of the Mortgage Securitization Crisis', in *Markets on Trial: The Economic Sociology of the U.S. Financial Crisis*, ed. Michael Lounsbury and Paul M. Hirsch (Bingley, West Yorkshire, 2010), pp. 29–70, cited ibid., p. 50; on credit default swaps see Tett, *Fool's Gold*, pp. 9–11, 21, 44–8.

65 Tett, *Fool's Gold*, pp. 95–7; Tooze, *Crashed*, pp. 60–61, 64; Tobias Adrian and Hyun Song Shin, 'Financial Intermediaries and Monetary Economics', *Federal Reserve Bank of New York Staff Reports*, CCCXCVIII (revised May 2010), cited ibid., p. 61.

66 Tett, *Fool's Gold*, pp. 99, 133; see also Farlow, *Crash and Beyond*, pp. 65, 71.

67 Palan, *The Offshore World*, p. 189.

68 Jennifer Egan, *The Candy House* (London, 2022), p. 82; James Williams, *Stand Out of Our Light: Freedom and Resistance in the Attention Economy* (Cambridge, 2018), p. 36.

69 Philip Ball, *Critical Mass: How One Thing Leads to Another* (London, 2004), pp. 472–3; Tim Berners-Lee, 'Information Managment: A Proposal', CERN Internal Report, May 1990, p. 9, www.w3.org, cited ibid., p. 473.

70 Ball, *Critical Mass*, pp. 474–7.

71 Ibid., p. 478; Albert-László Barabási, Réka Albert and Hawoong Jeong, 'Scale-Free Characteristics of Random Networks: The Topology of the World-Wide Web', *Physica A: Statistical Mechanics and Its Applications*, CCLXXXI/1 (2000), pp. 69–77, cited ibid., pp. 479–82, see also p. 289.

72 Alex Wright, *Glut: Mastering Information Through the Ages* (Washington, DC, 2007), p. 228; Ted Nelson, 'I Don't Buy In', http://ted.hyperland.com/buyin.txt, cited ibid., pp. 226–7; Katrina Brooker, '"I Was Devastated": Tim Berners-Lee, the Man Who Created the World Wide Web, Has Some Regrets', *Vanity Fair*, 1 July 2018; 'Schumpeter: Firefox and Friends', *The Economist*, 20 July 2019.

73 Nicholas Carr, *The Shallows: What the Internet is Doing to Our Brains* (New York, 2010); Jia Fu et al., 'Impaired Orienting in Youth with Internet Addiction: Evidence from the Attention Network Task (ANT)', *Psychiatry Research*, CCLXIV (2018), pp. 54–7, cited in David N. Greenfield, 'Digital Distraction: What Makes the Internet and Smartphone So Addictive?', in *Human Capacity in the Attention Economy*, ed. Sean M. Lane and Paul Atchley (Washington, DC, 2021), pp. 32, 37; Daniel Kahneman, *Thinking, Fast and Slow* (New York, 2011), cited in Paul Atchley, Sean M. Lane and Kacie Mennie, 'A Central Framework for Understanding the Impact of Information Technology

on Human Experience', in *Human Capacity in the Attention Economy*, ed. Lane and Atchley, p. 18; Greenfield, 'Digital Distraction', pp. 32–3.

74 Sheera Frenkel and Cecilia Kang, *An Ugly Truth: Inside Facebook's Battle for Domination* (London, 2021), pp. 105–37, 182; Ryan Mac and Craig Silverman, 'How Facebook Failed Kenosha', *BuzzFeed News*, 3 September 2020, cited ibid., pp. 279–80, also pp. 169–80.

75 Ryan Mac, Charlie Warzel and Alex Kantrowitz, 'Growth at Any Cost: Top Facebook Executive Defended Data Collection in 2016 Memo – and Warned that Facebook Could Get People Killed', *BuzzFeed News*, 29 March 2018, cited in Frenkel and Kang, *An Ugly Truth*, pp. 84–5; Sheryl Sandberg, 'Facebook Names Sheryl Sandberg to its Board of Directors', press release, 25 June 2012, cited in Frenkel and Kang, *An Ugly Truth*, p. 86; Shoshana Zuboff, 'You Are Now Remotely Controlled', *New York Times*, 24 January 2020, cited in Frenkel and Kang, *An Ugly Truth*, p. 61; Julia Angwin and Terry Parris Jr, 'Facebook Lets Advertisers Exclude Users by Race', *ProPublica*, 28 October 2016, cited in Frenkel and Kang, *An Ugly Truth*, p. 163; Steven Levy, *In the Plex: How Google Thinks, Works, and Shapes Our Lives* (New York, 2011), pp. 83–5, cited in Shoshana Zuboff, *The Age of Surveillance Capitalism: The Fight for a Human Future at the New Frontier of Power* (New York, 2019), pp. 74–83, 'The Definition', n.p., p. 10.

76 Zuboff, *The Age of Surveillance Capitalism*, pp. 53–4, 74–89; Levy, *In the Plex*, pp. 45–9.

77 Zuboff, *The Age of Surveillance Capitalism*, p. 129.

78 Alastair Barr, 'Google Maps Guesses Where You're Headed Now', *Wall Street Journal* blog, 13 January 2016, cited ibid., p. 154, also pp. 144–7, 316.

79 S. A. Rogers, 'How to Be Invisible: 15 Anti-Surveillance Gadgets and Wearables', *WebUrbanist*, 28 November 2016, cited in Zuboff, *The Age of Surveillance Capitalism*, pp. 489–90; Dan Howarth, 'Headgear to Thwart Mind-Reading Surveillance Cameras by Fabrica Researchers', *Dezeen*, www.dezeen.com, 12 December 2013.

80 Warren Berger, 'Lost in Space', *Wired*, www.wired.com, 1 February 1999.

EPILOGUE: SANCTUARY

1 'Private Bill for Rosa Introduced in U.S. Congress', https://rosabelongshere.org, 23 August 2021; Housing update, www.facebook.com/RosaBelongsHere, 3 June 2022.

2 Linda Rabben, *Give Refuge to the Stranger: The Past, Present and Future of Sanctuary* (Walnut Creek, CA, 2011), pp. 43–5, 50–52; Karl Shoemaker, *Sanctuary and Crime in the Middle Ages, 400–1500* (New

York, 2011); Loren Collingwood and Benjamin Gonzalez O'Brien, *Sanctuary Cities: The Politics of Refuge* (New York, 2019), p. 16; David Kelly, 'Shelter in Place? She's Been Doing That Inside a Colorado Church for More than Three Years', *LA Times*, www.latimes.com, 3 September 2020; Harald Bauder and Jonathan Darling, Introduction to *Sanctuary Cities and Urban Struggles: Rescaling Migration, Citizenship, and Rights*, ed. Bauder and Darling (Baltimore, MD, 2020), pp. 4–5; Jennifer J. Bagelman, *Sanctuary City: A Suspended State* (New York, 2016).

3 Rabben, *Give Refuge to the Stranger*, pp. 47, 53.

4 Andri Snær Magnason, *On Time and Water*, trans. Lytton Smith (London, 2020).

5 Alexandra King, '"No Olividado": These Americans Find and Bury Missing Migrants', *CNN*, https://edition.cnn.com, 19 December 2019; Barbara Sostaita, 'Making Crosses, Crossing Borders: The Performance of Mourning, the Power of Ghosts, and the Politics of Countermemory in the U.S.–Mexico Borderlands', Mediation, in *Conversations: An Online Journal of the Center for the Study of Material and Visual Cultures of Religion*, 2016, https://mavcor.yale.edu.

6 Thomas Aquinas, *Quaestiones disputatae de veritate*, ed. A. Dondaine (Rome, 1972–6), vol. II, q. 14 a. 1 co., and Tommaso d'Aquino (Thomas Aquinas), *Commento alle Sentenze di Pietro Lombardo*, trans. R. Coggi (Bologna, 2000), lib. 3 d. 23 q. 2 a. 2 qc. 3 ad 2. 52, both cited in Steven Justice, 'Did the Middle Ages Believe in Their Miracles?', *Representations*, CIII/1 (2008), pp. 12–14.

BIBLIOGRAPHY

Abu-Lughod, Janet L., *Before European Hegemony: The World System,
   AD 1250–1350* (New York, 1989)
Alighieri, Dante, *The Divine Comedy*, trans. C. H. Sisson (Oxford, 1993)
Anderson, George K., *The Legend of the Wandering Jew* [1965]
   (Providence, RI, 1970)
Aubrey, Elizabeth, *The Music of the Troubadours* (Bloomington, IN, 1996)
Baldwin, John W., 'The Image of the Jongleur in Northern France around
   1200', *Speculum*, LXXII/3 (1997), pp. 635–63
Ball, Philip, *Critical Mass: How One Thing Leads to Another* (London, 2004)
Barfield, Thomas J., *The Perilous Frontier: Nomadic Empires and China*
   (Cambridge, MA, 1989)
—, 'Nomads and States in Comparative Perspective', in *Nomad-State
   Relationships in International Relations*, ed. Jamie Levin (Cham, 2020),
   pp. 19–43
Baudelaire, Charles, 'The Painter of Modern Life' [1863], in *The Painter of
   Modern Life and Other Essays*, ed. and trans. Jonathan Mayne
   (London, 1964), pp. 1–40
Beall, Joanna M., 'Interlace and Early Britain', PhD dissertation, Florida State
   University, Tallahassee, FL, 2010
Beier, A. L., *Masterless Men: The Vagrancy Problem in England, 1560–1640*
   (London, 1985)
—, '"A New Serfdom": Labor Law, Vagrancy Statutes, and Labor Discipline
   in England, 1350–1800', in *Cast Out: Vagrancy and Homelessness in
   Global and Historical Perspective*, ed. Beier and Paul Ocobock
   (Athens, OH, 2008), pp. 35–63
Benis, Toby R., *Romanticism on the Road: The Marginal Gains of
   Wordsworth's Homeless* (Basingstoke, 2000)
Berlin, Ira, *Many Thousands Gone: The First Two Centuries of Slavery in North
   America* (Cambridge, MA, 1998)

Betts, Alexander, and Paul Collier, *Refuge: Transforming a Broken Refugee System* (London, 2017)

Blackburn, Robin, *The Making of New World Slavery: From the Baroque to the Modern, 1492–1800* (London, 1997)

Bloch, R. Howard, *Medieval French Literature and Law* (Berkeley, CA, 1977)

—, *Etymologies and Genealogies: A Literary Anthropology of the French Middle Ages* (Chicago, IL, 1983)

Bolster, W. Jeffrey, *Black Jacks: African American Seamen in the Age of Sail* (Cambridge, MA, 1997)

Brewer, Keagan, ed. and trans., *Prester John: The Legend and its Sources* (Farnham, Surrey, 2015)

Brown, Michelle P., *The Lindisfarne Gospels: Society, Spirituality and the Scribe* (London, 2003)

Bullough, Oliver, *Moneyland: Why Thieves and Crooks Now Rule the World and How to Take it Back* (London, 2018)

Burgis, Tom, *Kleptopia: How Dirty Money is Conquering the World* (London, 2020)

Butterfield, Ardis, *Poetry and Music in Medieval France: From Jean Renart to Guillaume de Machaut* (Cambridge, 2002)

Carruthers, Mary, *The Book of Memory: A Study of Memory in Medieval Culture* (Cambridge, 1990)

—, *The Craft of Thought: Meditation, Rhetoric, and the Making of Images, 400–1200* (Cambridge, 1998)

Cervantes, Miguel de, *Don Quixote*, trans. Edith Grossman (London, 2003)

Cheyette, Fredric L., *Ermengard of Narbonne and the World of the Troubadours* (New York, 2001)

—, and Howell Chickering, 'Love, Anger, and Peace: Social Practice and Poetic Play in the Ending of *Yvain*', *Speculum*, LXXX/1 (2005), pp. 75–117

Chrétien de Troyes, *Yvain, the Knight of the Lion* [*c.* 1177], trans. Burton Raffel (New Haven, CT, 1987)

Christian, David, *A History of Russia, Central Asia and Mongolia*, vol. I: *Inner Eurasia from Prehistory to the Mongol Empire* (Oxford, 1998)

—, *A History of Russia, Central Asia and Mongolia*, vol. II: *Inner Eurasia from the Mongol Empire to Today, 1260–2000* (Hoboken, NJ, 2008)

Conquest, Robert, *Harvest of Sorrow: Soviet Collectivization and the Terror-Famine* (London, 1986)

Cotter, David W., OSB, ed., *Genesis* (Collegeville, MN, 2003)

Daly, M. W., *Darfur's Sorrow: A History of Destruction and Genocide* (Cambridge, 2007)

David, Joshua, and Robert Hammond, *High Line: The Inside Story of New York City's Park in the Sky* (New York, 2011) de Waal, Alex, *The Real Politics of the Horn of Africa: Money, War and the Business of Power* (Malden, MA, 2015)

DePastino, Todd, *Citizen Hobo: How a Century of Homelessness Shaped America* (Chicago, IL, 2003)

Doob, Penelope Reed, *The Idea of the Labyrinth from Classical Antiquity through the Middle Ages* (New York and London, 1990)

Earle, Timothy, and Clive Gamble with Hendrik Poinar, 'Migration', in *Deep History: The Architecture of Past and Present*, ed. Andrew Shryock and Daniel Lord Smail (Berkeley, CA, 2011), pp. 159–79

Ellison, Ralph, *Invisible Man* [1952] (London, 1965)

Empedocles of Acragus, 'Fragments', in Richard McKirahan, *Philosophy before Socrates: An Introduction with Texts and Commentary*, 2nd edn (Indianapolis, IN, 2010), pp. 230–92

Etefa, Tsega, *The Origins of Ethnic Conflict in Africa: Politics and Violence in Darfur, Oromia, and the Tana Delta* (Cham, 2019)

Farlow, Andrew, *Crash and Beyond: Causes and Consequences of the Global Financial Crisis* (Oxford, 2013)

Ferrante, Joan, 'The Court in Medieval Literature: The Center of the Problem', in *The Medieval Court in Europe*, ed. Edward R. Haymes (Munich, 1986), pp. 1–25

Fitter, Chris, '"The Art of Known and Feeling Sorrows": Rethinking Capitalist Transition, and the Performance of Class Politics', in *King Lear*', *Early Modern Literary Studies*, XIX/1 (2016), https://extra.shu.ac.uk

——, '"As Full of Grief as Age": Protesting Against the Poor Law in *King Lear*', in *Shakespeare and the Politics of Commoners: Digesting the New Social History*, ed. Fitter (Oxford, 2017), pp. 217–37

Fitzgerald, William, 'Aeneas, Daedalus and the Labyrinth', *Arethusa*, XVII/1 (1984), pp. 51–65

Flint, Julie, and Alex de Waal, *Darfur: A New History of a Long War*, revd edn (London, 2008)

Flood, Josephine, *Archaeology of the Dreamtime: The Story of Prehistoric Australia and Its People*, revd edn (Sydney, 2005)

Frachetti, Michael D., *Pastoralist Landscapes and Social Interaction in Bronze Age Eurasia* (Berkeley, CA, 2008)

——, 'Multi-Regional Emergence of Mobile Pastoralism and the Growth of Non-Uniform Institutional Complexity across Eurasia', *Current Anthropology*, LIII/1 (2012), pp. 2–38

Frankopan, Peter, *The First Crusade: The Call from the East* (Cambridge, MA, 2012)

Fraser, Angus, *The Gypsies*, 2nd edn (Oxford, 1995)

Fratantuono, Lee, *Madness Unchained: A Reading of Virgil's 'Aeneid'* (Lanham, MD, 2007)

Frenkel, Sheera, and Cecilia Kang, *An Ugly Truth: Inside Facebook's Battle for Domination* (London, 2021)

Gallagher, Catherine, 'The Rise of Fictionality', in *The Novel*, ed. Franco Moretti (Princeton, NJ, 2006), vol. I, pp. 336–63

Gatrell, Peter, *The Making of the Modern Refugee* (Oxford, 2013)

Golden, Peter B., 'The Stateless Nomads of Central Eurasia', in *Empires and Exchanges in Eurasian Late Antiquity: Rome, China, Iran, and the Steppe, ca. 250–750*, ed. Nicola Di Cosmo and Michael Maas (Cambridge, 2018), pp. 317–32

Gommans, Jos, 'The Warband in the Making of Eurasian Empires', in *Prince, Pen and Sword: Eurasian Perspectives*, ed. Maaike van Berkel and Jeroen Duindam (Leiden, 2018), pp. 297–383

Harrison, Robert Pogue, *The Dominion of the Dead* (Chicago, IL, 2003)

Harte, Verity, *Plato on Parts and Wholes: The Metaphysics of Structure* (Oxford, 2002)

Harvey, Ruth, 'Courtly Culture in Medieval Occitania', in *The Troubadours: An Introduction*, ed. Simon Gaunt and Sarah Kay (Cambridge, 1999), pp. 8–27

Herodotus, *The Histories*, trans. Robin Waterfield (Oxford, 2008)

Homer, *The Odyssey*, trans. Robert Fagles (New York, 1996)

Honeychurch, William, and Chunag Amartuvshin, 'Hinterlands, Urban Centers, and Mobile Settings: The "New" Old World Archaeology from the Asian Steppe', *Asian Perspectives*, XLVI/I (2007), pp. 36–64

Jarvis, Robin, *Romantic Writing and Pedestrian Travel* (Basingstoke, 1997)

Johnston, Sarah Iles, *Restless Dead: Encounters Between the Living and the Dead in Ancient Greece* (Berkeley, CA, 1999)

Kamen, Henry, *Spain, 1469–1714: A Society of Conflict*, 2nd edn (London, 1991)

Kendrick, Laura, *Animating the Letter: The Figurative Embodiment of Writing from Late Antiquity to the Renaissance* (Columbus, OH, 1999)

Kern, Hermann, *Through the Labyrinth: Designs and Meanings Over 5,000 Years*, trans. Abigail H. Clay with Sandra Burns Thomson and Kathrin A. Velder (Munich, 2000)

Khazanov, Anatoly M., 'The Scythians and Their Neighbors', in *Nomads as Agents of Cultural Change: The Mongols and Their Eurasian Predecessors*, ed. Reuven Amitai and Michal Biran (Honolulu, HI, 2015), pp. 32–49

Kingsley, Patrick, *The New Odyssey: The Story of Europe's Refugee Crisis* (London, 2016)

Konner, Melvin, *Unsettled: An Anthropology of the Jews* (New York, 2003)

Langland, William, *Piers Plowman: A New Annotated Edition of the C-Text*,
 ed. Derek Pearsall (Exeter, 2008)
——, *Piers Plowman: A Modern Verse Translation*, trans. Peter Sutton
 (Jefferson, NC, 2014)
Lennon, John, *Boxcar Politics: The Hobo in U.S. Culture and Literature,
 1869–1956* (Amherst, MA, 2014)
*The Life of Lazarillo de Tormes: A Critical Edition including the Original
 Spanish Text*, ed. and trans. García Osuna (Jefferson, NC, 2005)
Linebaugh, Peter, and Marcus Rediker, *The Many-Headed Hydra: The Hidden
 History of the Revolutionary Atlantic* (Boston, MA, 2000)
Löfgren, Orvar, *On Holiday: A History of Vacationing* (Berkeley, CA, 1999)
Ma, Ning, *The Age of Silver: The Rise of the Novel East and West* (Oxford, 2016)
Mamdani, Mahmood, *Saviors and Survivors: Darfur, Politics, and the War on
 Terror* (New York, 2009)
Marciano, M. Laura Gemelli, 'Empedocles' Zoogony and Embryology', in
 *The Empedoclean Kosmos: Structure, Process and the Question of Cyclicity,
 Proceedings of the Symposium Philosophiae Antiquae Tertium Myconense*,
 ed. Apostolos L. Pierris (Patras, 2005), pp. 373–404
Marks, Susan, *A False Tree of Liberty: Human Rights in Radical Thought*
 (Oxford, 2020)
Mason, Zachary, *The Lost Books of the Odyssey* (New York, 2007)
Matras, Yaron, *I Met Lucky People: The Story of the Romani Gypsies*
 (London, 2014)
Middleton, Anne, 'Acts of Vagrancy: The C Version "Autobiography" and
 the Statute of 1388', in *Written Work: Langland, Labor, and Authorship*,
 ed. Steven Justice and Kathryn Kerby-Fulton (Philadelphia, PA, 1997),
 pp. 208–318
Miller, Mark, 'Sin and Structure in *Piers Plowman*: On the Medieval Split
 Subject', *Modern Language Quarterly*, LXXVI/2 (2015), pp. 201–24
Molesworth, Jesse, *Chance and the Eighteenth-Century Novel: Realism,
 Probability, Magic* (Cambridge, 2010)
Montiglio, Silvia, *Wandering in Ancient Greek Culture* (Chicago, IL, 2005)
Mueggler, Erik, *The Age of Wild Ghosts: Memory, Violence, and Place in
 Southwest China* (Berkeley, CA, 2001)
Munn, Nancy D., *Walbiri Iconography: Graphic Representation and Cultural
 Symbolism in a Central Australian Society* (New York, 1973)
Ober, Josiah, 'Living Freely as a Slave of the Law: Why Socrates Lives in
 Athens', in *Athenian Legacies: Essays on the Politics of Going On Together*
 (Princeton, NJ, 2005), pp. 157–70
Oberg, Michael Leroy, *Native America: A History*, 2nd edn
 (Hoboken, NJ, 2018)

O'Rourke, Shane, *The Cossacks* (Manchester, 2007)

Pai, Hsiao-Hung, *Bordered Lives: How Europe Fails Refugees and Migrants* (Oxford, 2018)

Palan, Ronen, *The Offshore World: Sovereign Markets, Virtual Places, and Nomad Millionaires* (New York, 2003)

Perdue, Theda, and Michael D. Green, *The Cherokee Nation and the Trail of Tears* (New York, 2007)

Peters, Gretchen, *The Musical Sounds of Medieval French Cities: Players, Patrons, and Politics* (Cambridge, 2012)

Plato, *Apology*, trans. Michael C. Stokes (Warminster, 1997)

—, *Timaeus and Critias*, trans. Robin Waterfield (Oxford 2008)

Pocock, J.G.A., 'Modes of Political and Historical Time in Early Eighteenth-Century England', *Studies in Eighteenth-Century Culture*, v (1976), pp. 87–102

Poirier, Sylvie, *A World of Relationships: Itineraries, Dreams and Events in the Australian Western Desert* (Toronto, 2005)

Porter, Anne, *Mobile Pastoralism and the Formation of Near Eastern Civilizations: Weaving Together Society* (Cambridge, 2011)

—, 'Pastoralism in the Ancient Near East', in *A Companion to the Ancient Near East*, ed. Daniel C. Snell, 2nd edn (Chichester, 2020), pp. 125–43

Purves, Alex, 'Unmarked Space: Odysseus and the Inland Journey', *Arethusa*, XXXIX/1 (2006), pp. 1–20

Ravenelle, Alexandrea J., *Hustle and Gig: Struggling and Surviving in the Sharing Economy* (Berkeley, CA, 2019)

Rediker, Marcus, *Between the Devil and the Deep Blue Sea: Merchant Seamen, Pirates, and the Anglo-American Maritime World, 1700–1750* (Cambridge, 1987)

—, *Villains of All Nations: Atlantic Pirates in the Golden Age* (Boston, MA, 2004)

Rose, Deborah Bird, *Dingo Makes Us Human: Life and Land in an Aboriginal Australian Culture* (Cambridge, 1992)

Rosenblat, Alex, *Uberland: How Algorithms are Rewriting the Rules of Work* (Berkeley, CA, 2018)

Schapiro, Meyer, *The Language of Forms: Lectures on Insular Manuscript Art* (New York, 2005)

Shakespeare, William, *King Lear*, ed. R. A. Foakes (London, 1997)

Sharma, Manish, 'Heroic Subject and Cultural Substance in *The Wanderer*', *Neophilologus*, XCVI/4 (2012), pp. 611–29

Sherrard Scott, Julius III, 'The Common Wind: Currents of Afro-American Communication in the Era of the Haitian Revolution', PhD dissertation, Duke University, Durham, NC, 1986

Silverberg, Robert, *The Realm of Prester John* (New York, 1972)
Simpson, David, *Wordsworth, Commodification and Social Concern:*
     The Poetics of Modernity (Cambridge, 2009)
Slezkine, Yuri, *The Jewish Century* (Princeton, NJ, 2004)
Snyder, Timothy, *Bloodlands: Europe Between Hitler and Stalin*
     (New York, 2010)
Solnit, Rebecca, *Wanderlust: A History of Walking* (New York, 2000)
Sterne, Laurence, *The Life and Opinions of Tristram Shandy, Gentleman*
     [1759–67], ed. Melvyn New and Joan New (London, 1997)
Stewart, Michael, *The Time of the Gypsies* (Boulder, CO, 1997)
Stracey, Frances, *Constructed Situations: A New History of the Situationist*
     International (London, 2014)
Symes, Carol, *A Common Stage: Theater and Public Life in Medieval Arras*
     (New York, 2007)
Tett, Gillian, *Fool's Gold: The Inside Story of J. P. Morgan and How Wall Street*
     Greed Corrupted its Bold Dream and Created a Financial Catastrophe
     (New York, 2009)
Thompson, Alvin O., *Flight to Freedom: African Runaways and Maroons*
     in the Americas (Kingston, Jamaica, 2006)
Tooze, Adam, *Crashed: How a Decade of Financial Crises Changed the World*
     (London, 2018)
Treuer, David, *The Heartbeat of Wounded Knee: Native America from 1890*
     to the Present (New York, 2019)
Vance, Eugene, *Mervelous Signals: Poetics and Sign Theory in the Middle Ages*
     (Lincoln, NE, 1986)
Vergil, *The Aeneid*, trans. Sarah Ruden (New Haven, CT, 2008)
Vlastos, Gregory, 'The Historical Socrates and Athenian Democracy',
     Political Theory, XI/4 (1983), pp. 495–516
Wallace, Anne D., *Walking, Literature, and English Culture: The Origins*
     and Uses of Peripatetic in the Nineteenth Century (Oxford, 1993)
'The Wanderer', in *The Complete Old English Poems*, ed. and trans. Craig
     Williamson (Philadelphia, PA, 2017), pp. 453–8
Warner, Lawrence, 'The Dark Wood and the Dark Word in Dante's
     Commedia', *Comparative Literature Studies*, XXXII/4 (1995), pp. 449–78
Webster, Juliet, 'Microworkers of the Gig Economy', *New Labor Forum*,
     XXV/3 (2016), pp. 56–64
Wilcox, Johnnie, 'Black Power: Minstrelsy and Electricity in Ralph Ellison's
     Invisible Man', *Callaloo: A Journal of African Diaspora Arts and Letters*,
     XXX/4 (2007), pp. 987–1009
Wilkerson, Isabel, *The Warmth of Other Suns: The Epic Story of America's*
     Great Migration (New York, 2010)

Woodbridge, Linda, *Vagrancy, Homelessness, and English Renaissance Literature* (Urbana, IL, 2001)

Woodcock, Jamie, *The Fight Against Platform Capitalism: An Inquiry into the Global Struggles of the Gig Economy* (London, 2021)

Wordsworth, William, Prefaces of 1800 and 1802, in Samuel Taylor Coleridge and William Wordsworth, *Lyrical Ballads*, ed. R. L. Brett and A. R. Jones (London, 2005), pp. 287–314

——, *The Prelude*, in *The Poems of William Wordsworth: Collected Reading Texts from the Cornell Wordsworth Series*, vol. II, ed. Jared Curtis (Penrith, 2011)

Wright, Craig, *The Maze and the Warrior: Symbols in Architecture, Theology, and Music* (Cambridge, MA, 2001)

Zuboff, Shoshana, *The Age of Surveillance Capitalism: The Fight for a Human Future at the New Frontier of Power* (New York, 2019)

ACKNOWLEDGEMENTS

This book has been long in the making and I have naturally accrued many debts. It is a pleasure to thank all who helped. The project was initially made possible by funds from the University of Auckland and was begun in earnest while I was a research fellow at the Birkbeck Institute for the Humanities at the University of London. Thanks to Costas Douzinas and his staff for welcoming and supporting me, and to Warwick Gould, then director of the Institute of English Studies at the School of Advanced Study, University of London, where I was a research fellow at a later point. I was working on another project by then, but happily some of the two fields' material overlapped. Steve Connor was an early enthusiast of the book, and Erin Soros arranged an audience at the University of East Anglia which produced useful questions at an early stage of the work. I also benefited from sharing ideas in progress at the European Society for the Study of English conference in London on a Literature and Medicine panel organized by Nieves Pascual and Ulrika Maude. Later, Becky Davis and Shannon Gayk gave me spots at the 48th International Congress on Medieval Studies at Kalamazoo, Michigan, and the International Piers Plowman Society conference at the University of Washington in Seattle, respectively, where I was able to learn from many brilliant scholars. In Auckland and elsewhere, people who inspired me with related work of their own, answered questions or who simply declared their ongoing interest in the book include Tracy Adams, Arka Basu, Tom Bishop, Brian Boyd, Jan Cronin, Pansy Duncan, Selina Ershadi, Jonathan Gill, Paul Gough, Rina Kim, Leah James-Lynch, Bryonny Muir, Zhang Qian (Spring), Daniel Satele, Lyndsey Stonebridge and Joanne Wilkes. Thanks also to Anna Klein for a lunchtime conversation about *The Canterbury Tales* and the materials of the second chapter. Many of my students on 'The Modern Novel' over the years contributed too, even if they did not know it. It was a joyful thing to discuss *Invisible Man* and other works featuring searchers and wanderers in such depth together. Thanks are also due to the staff of the University of Auckland Library, the British Library, the University of London Library at

Senate House and the Library at the Warburg Institute, where it is a pleasure to wander in the stacks. Thanks to Arka, Bryonny, Daniel, Jan, Spring and Pam Bossward for friendship and discussion of wandering-related matters, to Neha Arora and Alexa Wilson for the same plus advice on Berlin, to Ramiro Silva for the wonderful apartments in which I've lived and worked in London over the years, and to my teachers in advanced contemporary at City Academy and the London Russian Ballet School. Gustavo Restivo has assisted my life and work in a great many ways for which I'm immensely thankful, as have Valda Mehrtens and Possum, soulmate and friend of long-standing and sometimes, bless him, last resort. I thank my editors at Reaktion Books, Vivian Constantinopoulos and Amy Salter, for all their help and encouragement, and Simon McFadden for the impressive cover. Lastly, I'd like to thank the late Dolores Thomas, who spotted me in competition many years ago and offered to teach me a gypsy dance, for which I was required to choose from two descriptions without hearing the music. The piece I chose embedded in my teenaged soul a love of all things Rom – or, as some competition judges thought, reawakened such a love – and I never felt so alive and connected to our human past as when I danced it. For that honour, and your expertise, *mil gracias*, Dolores.

INDEX